JOHN F. KENNEDY
IN QUOTATIONS

ALSO COMPILED BY
DAVID B. FROST

Ronald Reagan in Quotations:
A Topical Dictionary, with Sources,
of the Presidential Years (McFarland, 2012)

John F. Kennedy in Quotations

A Topical Dictionary, with Sources

Compiled by David B. Frost

McFarland & Company, Inc., Publishers
Jefferson, North Carolina, and London

LIBRARY OF CONGRESS CATALOGUING-IN-PUBLICATION DATA

Kennedy, John F. (John Fitzgerald), 1917–1963.
John F. Kennedy in quotations :
a topical dictionary, with sources /
compiled by David B. Frost.
p.   cm.
Includes bibliographical references and index.

ISBN 978-0-7864-7492-9
softcover : acid free paper ∞

1. Kennedy, John F. (John Fitzgerald), 1917–1963 —
Quotations — Dictionaries.   2. United States — Politics and
government —1961–1963 — Quotations, maxims, etc. —
Dictionaries.   3. United States — Politics and government —
1953–1961— Quotations, maxims, etc. — Dictionaries.
4. Quotations, American — Dictionaries.
I. Frost, David B., 1945–   II. Title.
E838.5.K42 2013   081.03 — dc23   2013001098

BRITISH LIBRARY CATALOGUING DATA ARE AVAILABLE

© 2013 David B. Frost. All rights reserved

*No part of this book may be reproduced or transmitted in any form
or by any means, electronic or mechanical, including photocopying
or recording, or by any information storage and retrieval system,
without permission in writing from the publisher.*

On the cover: President John F. Kennedy, 1961 (Library of Congress)

Manufactured in the United States of America

*McFarland & Company, Inc., Publishers
Box 611, Jefferson, North Carolina 28640
www.mcfarlandpub.com*

For my children

Table of Contents

INTRODUCTION 1

Agriculture 3

American Leadership 7
General 7; Image Abroad 13; Importance of Domestic Strength 15

American Spirit 18

Arts and Humanities 22

Berlin 24

Budgetary and Fiscal Policies 26
Deficits 26; Monetary Policy 27; Spending 28; Taxation 29

Business 31

Civic Duty 33

Communism and the Cold War . . . 36
General 36; U.S.–Soviet Negotiations 44

Cuba 45
General 45; Cuban Missile Crisis 47

Democracy 48

Domestic Social Issues 49
General 49; Automation and Its Effects 53; Housing 54; Juvenile Delinquency 54; Minimum Wage 55; Unemployment 55

Economic Policies 57
General 57; Economic Growth 58; Government's Role 59

Education 61

Energy Policy 67

Environment 68

Equal Opportunity and Civil Rights 72
General 72; African American Leadership 78; Civil Rights Protests 79; Federal Intervention 80; Voting Rights 80

Foreign Assistance 81

Foreign Policy 86
General 86; Europe 92; Israel and the Middle East 93; Latin America 94; Southeast Asia 97

Founding Fathers 98

Free Enterprise System 99

Freedom and Liberty 100

God and Country 108

Government 110
General 110; Building for the Future 113; Checks and Balances 115; Modern-Day Complexities 116; Working Together 117

Healthcare 121

Human Rights 122

International Relations 123

International Trade 129

Table of Contents

Kennedy on Kennedy 132
  His Age 132; Family 132; Irish Heritage 133; Optimism and Aspirations 133; Political Philosophy 138; Religious Faith 139

Labor Unions 141
  General 141; Collective Bargaining 143

National Security 144
  General 144; Armed Forces 147; Military Strength 148

NATO (North Atlantic Treaty Organization) 151

New Frontier 153

News Media 155

Nuclear Weapons 157
  General 157; Arms Control 159; Nuclear Test Bans 161

Peace 163

Peace Corps 166

Physical Fitness 168

Political Leadership 169

Politics 174
  General 174; Political Parties 176 (General 176; Democrats 179; Republicans 183); Richard M. Nixon 184

Presidency 186

Public Service 192

Science and Technology 194

Senior Citizens 195

Soviet Union 197

Space Exploration 197

United Nations 201

Voluntarism 202

Washington, D.C. 203

INDEX 205

Introduction

John F. Kennedy's term as president was a tragically short one, spanning fewer than three years. Even so, and despite the judgment of many historians that his accomplishments while in the White House were relatively modest, scholars nonetheless rank John F. Kennedy among the nation's most important and influential presidents. Among the American public at large, Kennedy's standing is even higher. Indeed, there are few Americans old enough to remember Kennedy's presidency who do not recall where they were the day he was assassinated.

As limited as Kennedy's accomplishments may have been, his legacy in American politics is not. In 1960, many Americans believed that the nation's important economic, social, and cultural battles had already been fought and won during the 1930s and 40s. There was no American frontier remaining to be explored. To John F. Kennedy, however, America was standing at the edge of a New Frontier—a frontier beyond which lay vast areas still to be charted and settled. Whether it was regaining America's leadership in space, moving against racial segregation in the south, or simply building an America that left no one behind, Kennedy believed that the 1960s was no time for America to be "resting on its oars." His call to Americans to "ask not what your country can do for you; ask what you can do for your country," was a call to arms: a call to his fellow countrymen to take on the challenges of that New Frontier.

The Kennedy years were marked by more than the domestic challenges of the New Frontier, however. By the time John F. Kennedy took office in January 1961, the Cold War between the United States and the Soviet Union had rolled into its second decade. Although the military tension between the two superpowers never escalated into direct military conflict—despite coming dangerously close in Berlin in 1961 and later during the Cuban missile crisis in 1962—the goal of containing, if not reversing, the spread of communism become even more central to America's foreign policy during the Kennedy presidency.

Despite the high hopes that many Americans held when John F. Kennedy took office, his record was a mixed one, falling short of its full promise in a number of domestic and foreign policy areas. His inability to achieve much of the New Frontier's legislative agenda, the failed Bay of Pigs invasion he sanctioned, and the further enmeshing of the United States in Vietnam are not the marks of a great or even near-great presidency. On the other side of the ledger, however, Kennedy's commitment to "put Americans on the moon and bring them back again" within the decade, his establishing of the Peace Corps, and his negotiation of the first nuclear test ban treaty with the Soviet Union are all significant and enduring accomplishments.

No true accounting of John F. Kennedy's presidency, however, can ignore the piv-

Introduction

otal role he played in rekindling in millions of Americans a renewed sense of national confidence, purpose, and optimism — a rekindling of the belief that America's possibilities are unbounded — a belief that America's "brightest days are ahead." It is that inspirational role which perhaps explains so much about why John Fitzgerald Kennedy remains such an important figure in our nation's history and imagination.

John F. Kennedy in Quotations is a compilation of more than 2,000 quotations selected from the speeches and other public addresses that Kennedy delivered to an audience, either in person or in a radio or television broadcast, while president, and earlier, between Kennedy's January 2, 1960, announcement of his intention to seek the Democratic Party's nomination for president and the November 8 general election.

Presidential statements, proclamations, and executive orders that were released by the Office of the Press Secretary but which were not actually delivered by President Kennedy have not been used as a source, nor have the position papers or other written statements that were issued by then–Senator Kennedy's campaign organization.

The quotations are organized topically into more than forty primary subject areas, many with subsections, thereby providing ready access to Kennedy's views across a range of policy issues. The title and date of the speech from which each quotation was taken, as well as, where appropriate, the speech's venue and audience, are also provided.

President Kennedy's speeches and addresses are contained in the *Public Papers of the President: John F. Kennedy*, and together with the campaign speeches that were delivered following the Democratic National Convention (July 15, 1960), were taken from the *American Presidency Project*, an online reference site established by John T. Wooley and Gerhard Peters at the University of California at Santa Barbara. The speeches that were delivered between Kennedy's January 2 announcement of his candidacy and the July 15 nominating convention were taken from the *Selected Speeches of John F. Kennedy* archive, maintained online by the John F. Kennedy Presidential Library and Museum. Many of the post-convention speeches are available at both sites.

AGRICULTURE

1. "[A question our nation faces is] whether our food surpluses can help us build a more stable peace abroad and feed our own hungry here at home instead of wasting in warehouses at the taxpayers' expense." Indiana Primary Announcement of Senator John F. Kennedy, Indianapolis, Indiana (February 4, 1960).

2. "We have no wish to become a nation of giant commercial corporation farms and absentee landlords. Our whole vitality as a nation depends on a contrary course. So let us beware of programs that aid most those who need it least.... Our job is to look out for the family farmer — and we can count on the family farmer to look out for the future of our soil — and the future of our country." Remarks of Senator John F. Kennedy, Stutusman County Democratic Committee Dinner, Jamestown, North Dakota (February 6, 1960).

3. "[F]arm program[s] should be run for farmers by farmers ... [and] on the local level should be in the hands of farmer committees elected by farmers themselves. No bureaucrat, no economist or scientist, knows the needs and trends and variations of the local farm picture as well as local farmers." Remarks of Senator John F. Kennedy, Stutusman County Democratic Committee Dinner, Jamestown, North Dakota (February 6, 1960).

4. "If we can get men in government who understand the farmer's problems — who recognize his need for inexpensive credit — who know he's a good credit risk — who treat him as a first class citizen, not a pauper looking for a hand-out, then our farm economy can grow and flourish. And the whole country will grow and flourish with it." Remarks of Senator John F. Kennedy, Stevens Point, Wisconsin (March 10, 1960).

5. "[A] healthy agricultural economy is vital to our economic well being.... [W]e cannot have prosperity in the city without prosperity on the farm." Remarks of Senator John F. Kennedy, Farm Forum, Alexandria, Indiana (April 7, 1960).

6. "In our relatively short life as a nation, the development of our agriculture has been one of the wonders of the world. Our farmers make up less than one percent of the world's population but produce 40 percent of the world's corn and 20 percent of the world's meat. Why, then, should serious economic troubles face our farmers?" Remarks of Senator John F. Kennedy, Farm Forum, Alexandria, Indiana (April 7, 1960).

7. "The growth and greatness of our Nation is rooted deep in its soil. Our farms have provided us with the abundance and the resources we have needed to support our rise to our present position of world leadership." Remarks of Senator John F. Kennedy, Easton, Maryland (May 14, 1960).

8. "[W]hen the farmer suffers, everyone suffers." Remarks of Senator John F. Kennedy, Quentin Burdick Birthday Dinner, Fargo, North Dakota (June 19, 1960).

9. "[We must] gear national production to international need — to grow food for stomachs and not for storage...." Remarks of Senator John F. Kennedy, Quentin Burdick Birthday Dinner, Fargo, North Dakota (June 19, 1960).

10. "[The] theory that uncontrolled production can solve our agricultural problems is impractical and unworkable. It has been tried and it has failed. Whenever he is faced with the declining unit prices the farmer is forced to increase production, bringing more surpluses and still lower prices. It is a losing battle — a battle which the farmer cannot win.... [W]e must provide for adjustment between supply and demand." Remarks of Senator John F. Kennedy, Iowa (June 26, 1960).

11. "No domestic issue in this election [1960] is more important than the farm issue. No part of the American way of life is more important — or in more trouble — than the family farm." Remarks of Senator John F. Kennedy, Midwest Farm Conference, Des Moines, Iowa (August 21, 1960).

12. "A revolution of abundance is better than one of scarcity. But people are being driven out of agriculture at a fantastic rate. The young people leave the farm and never come back. The families hit by failure, merger, or foreclosure move to the city, regardless of whether the city has jobs or homes.... We must harness these revolutions. We must ride these waves of change. We must learn to manage our abundance — to bring the great productive capacity of American agriculture into balance with total needs at home and abroad...." Remarks of Senator John F. Kennedy, Midwest Farm Conference, Des Moines, Iowa (August 21, 1960).

13. "We believe ... in an agricultural program that lifts the farmer up, that does not liquidate him, that does not catch him in a cost-price squeeze that liquidates his profits and drives him into the urban centers of the United States." Remarks of Senator John F. Kennedy, Eastern Carolina Stadium, Greenville, North Carolina (September 17, 1960).

14. "[A]n [effective] agricultural program [must strike a balance between] ... how much we can usefully consume here in the United States, how much we need for our surplus foods to take care of our own people, and how much we can usefully distribute in the cause of peace around the world. And then we should put a limit on the production ... if we are going to have security for the American farmer." Remarks of Senator John F. Kennedy, State Fair, Nashville, Tennessee (September 21, 1960).

15. "We challenge now ... problems which dwarf in complexity every week the kind of problems which those men [of a 100 years ago] dealt with in their lifetimes. [D]ealing with the problem of agriculture, how we are going to harness our capacity, how we are going to harness our abundance and make our abundance fruitful for ourselves and for people all around the world is a problem far more vast, far more complicated, than any which faced any 19th century statesman." Remarks of Senator John F. Kennedy, Corn Palace, Mitchell, South Dakota (September 22, 1960).

16. "The farmer of the United States does not need new speeches.... They need a new program ... for today American agriculture ... is gripped in a technological revolution which has been a source of strength and vitality to the United States, though it has cost, in many cases, the American farmer greatly." Speech by Senator John F. Kennedy, National Plowing Contest, Sioux Falls, South Dakota (September 22, 1960).

17. "[T]he American farmer [is] the most efficient in our history, and if there is one area of competition where we are now ahead of the Soviet Union, it is in the area of agricultural production." Speech by Senator John F. Kennedy, National Plowing Contest, Sioux Falls, South Dakota (September 22, 1960).

18. "[R]ising productivity [in agriculture] is a source of national power and strength, [but] it can be a disaster to the individual farmer, for when production rises and it exceeds demand, then farm prices fall disastrously.... Other areas of our economy are better able to deal with excess production.... But the individual farmer, and there are hundreds of thousands of them, cannot do this on his own. He lacks bargaining power in the market. He needs help and support of the Federal Government." Speech by Senator John F. Kennedy, National Plowing Contest, Sioux Falls, South Dakota (September 22, 1960).

19. "[T]he farmer is the only man in our economy who buys everything he buys at retail, sells everything he sells at wholesale, and pays the freight both ways." Speech by Senator John F. Kennedy, National Plowing Contest, Sioux Falls, South Dakota (September 22, 1960).

20. "[S]urpluses which are unconsumed by our own people and by people around the world, break the price. The balance between supply and demand, useful supply, supply to our own people, and the hungry people around the world.... [B]ring that kind of supply into balance with that kind of demand [and that] can bring us a successful farm program." Remarks of Senator John F. Kennedy, Airport Rally, Fort Dodge, Iowa (September 22, 1960).

21. "I would like to see the next President ... take 100 acres of farmland and say, 'This percentage can be grown for distribution of a decent price in the marketplace for our people here at home. This percentage can be sold in the marketplaces of the world for a decent price. This percentage of that 100 acres will be for our own people, for schoolchildren, for surplus food, for our older people who get surplus food packages; that percentage will be used for the American people. This percentage will be used and not called a surplus, but will be used as an asset in the great struggle of the sixties to decide whether the underdeveloped world, where people starves by the millions, will come with us or with the Communists.'" Remarks of Senator John F. Kennedy, Airport Rally, Fort Dodge, Iowa (September 22, 1960).

22. "[I]f Mr. Khrushchev had the choice between 50 scientists and 50 American farmers, he would take the farmers and be right, because the secret of growing food with only a small percentage of the population is the great asset which we have in the sixties, and an asset greater than sputnik and more meaningful in the long run than any other asset that this country has...." Remarks of Senator John F. Kennedy, Airport Rally, Fort Dodge, Iowa (September 22, 1960).

23. "Farmers are the No.1 market for the auto industry, and the auto industry is the No.1 market for the steel industry. Sooner or later if farming comes to decline, the economy of the rest of the country declines.... [I] believe that on the front of the desk of the next President ... is going to have to be the problems of American agriculture." Remarks of Senator John F. Kennedy, Farmers Union Gta [Grain Terminal Association] Convention, St. Paul, Minnesota (October 2, 1960).

24. "[Our national] farm program [should] raise farm income to full parity levels as soon as it is feasible to do so [and] [b]y parity income, I mean an income which will give average farm producers a return on their farming investment, their labor, and their managerial effort equal to the returns that are earned by comparable resources in other industries. Parity income should be the yardstick of equity for the farmers. After all, it is income that has real meaning in terms of farmers' needs, and no fair-minded American who seeks the same for themselves can possible object to this goal as part of our national policy." Remarks of Senator John F. Kennedy, Farmers Union Gta [Grain Terminal Association] Convention, St. Paul, Minnesota (October 2, 1960).

25. "The Lord has been good to us and I think we can repay his generosity by devising programs that feed our people well. And also feed those who look to us, whose assistance we need, whose good feeling we welcome, whose identification of interest is necessary if this country is going to maintain its position." Remarks of Senator John F. Kennedy, Farmers Union Gta [Grain Terminal Association] Convention, St. Paul, Minnesota (October 2, 1960).

26. "I shook hands coming over here tonight with some farmers, and how can you tell that they are farmers? It is because their hands are twice as big. I don't know what they do with it all day but it is twice as big because they work longer and harder than anybody with the possible exception of candidates for the Presidency." Remarks of Senator John F. Kennedy, Truman Shopping Center, Grand View, Missouri (October 22, 1960).

27. "I understand nearby there was a farmer who planted some corn. He said to his neighbor, 'I hope I break even this year. I really need the money.'" Remarks of Senator John F. Kennedy, Truman Shopping Center, Grand View, Missouri (October 22, 1960).

28. "We want to make sure that the great abundance that American farmers have brought to us is used as a blessing around the world. This is a blessing from the Lord. He has been generous to us and we have to make sure that we use all that we have." Speech by Senator John F. Kennedy, Faneuil Hall, Boston, Massachusetts (November 7, 1960).

29. "[A]merican agriculture is of concern to us all, whether we live on the farm or in the city, and of concern to hundreds of millions of people around the world who look to this tremendous capacity which we have ... to produce food for ourselves and a good portion of the world. This is really a most outstanding accomplishment of our civilization in this century." Remarks Upon Signing the Agricultural Act of 1961 (August 8, 1961).

30. "As the Pilgrims gave thanks more than three centuries ago for a bountiful harvest, so we give thanks in 1961 for the blessing of our agriculture and the continued opportunity that the

great productivity of our farms gives us in sharing our food with the world's hungry." Remarks in Connection with the United Nations Freedom from Hunger Campaign (November 22, 1961).

31. "It [American agricultural production] is a great asset, not only for ourselves but for people all over the world; and I think that instead of using the term 'surpluses,' and regarding it, in a sense, as a failure, we should regard it as one of the great evidences of our country's capacity, and also as a great resource, in order to demonstrate our concern for our fellow men." Remarks in Connection with the United Nations Freedom from Hunger Campaign (November 22, 1961).

32. "A strong America ... depends on its farms and natural resources." Annual Message to the Congress on the State of the Union (January 11, 1962).

33. "Th[e] tremendous increase in productivity in American farms ... is really the most astonishing phenomenon in the free world...." Remarks to Representatives of State Agricultural Stabilization and Conservation Committees (April 4, 1962).

34. "The farmers ... who work long and hard ... must be assured, for their labor, of an adequate return.... [W]e have to attempt within our governmental policies [of price support] to provide an adequate balance between supply and demand. If the Government should withdraw its efforts ... then there would be a collapse of farm prices ... and disaster would follow from the farms to the cities." Remarks to Representatives of State Agricultural Stabilization and Conservation Committees (April 4, 1962).

35. "Agriculture is one of our best dollar earners. The balance of trade in our favor in agriculture [is] ... a tremendous source of dollars — and therefore gold — to this country at a very important time." Remarks to Groups Interested in Improving Sales of Agricultural Products Abroad (May 12, 1962).

36. "Our agricultural problems and opportunities are different from those of much of the world. We have a tremendous capacity to produce.... In other countries their problem has been different: an inadequacy of supply. So how we shall maintain our production ... improve our consumption ... maintain the income of our farmers ... take care of those who no longer are needed to produce our food ... [all] in a way which serves the very basic needs of the people of the world...?" Remarks to Participants in the World Food Forum (May 17, 1962).

37. "There is no problem more complicated and more important than that of solving the tremendous problem of distributing our food production in an equitable way, with reasonable prices, and [e]nsuring our farmers of a better life." Remarks by Telephone to a Democratic Rally at St. Cloud, Minnesota (October 7, 1962).

38. "[T]he people who live on our farms ... make it possible for this country to progress as it has...." Remarks to Members of the National Conference on Cooperatives and the Future (April 30, 1963).

39. "[T]he important principle which ... this country has learned ... is that agriculture cannot be controlled successfully or dominated by the national government. It requires very dedicated work by the individual on the farm and it requires extensive cooperative and community work." Remarks to a Group of Agricultural Leaders from Latin America (October 8, 1963).

AMERICAN LEADERSHIP

General

40. "[F]riendly words, and good-will trips, and public relations programs are not enough to protect the free world from communist domination ... only a strong America can hope to be a peacemaking America." Remarks of Senator John F. Kennedy, Jefferson-Jackson Dinner, Minneapolis, Minnesota (June 4, 1960).

41. "There are new problems, new dangers, new horizons — and we have rested long enough. The world is changing — the perils are deepening — the irresistible march of history moves forward. We must now take the leadership in that great march — or be forever left behind." Speech by Senator John F. Kennedy, Memorial Program, 25th Anniversary of Signing Social Security Act, Hyde Park, New York. (August 14, 1960).

42. "We cannot possibly fail in the United States ... because if we fail here we betray not only ourselves but we betray all those who look to us with confidence and hope." Remarks of Senator John F. Kennedy, Airport Rally, Presque Isle, Maine (September 2, 1960).

43. "I want it said in 1970 that we are first, scientifically and militarily, educationally, economically. We should be first because we represent the greatest system of government ever devised.... [W]e are the greatest country on earth." Remarks of Senator John F. Kennedy, Picnic, Muskegon, Michigan (September 5, 1960).

44. "I think it is up to us to demonstrate that this is a great country, representing the greatest form of government ... that freedom and strength go hand in hand, and are not contradictory." Speech by Senator John F. Kennedy, High School Auditorium, Pocatello, Idaho (September 6, 1960).

45. "[W]e have a responsibility not only to ourselves but we have a responsibility toward all those [around the world] who look to us for leadership...." Rear Platform Remarks of Senator John F. Kennedy, Chico, California (September 8, 1960).

46. "During the American Revolution Thomas Paine said, 'The cause of America is the cause of all mankind.' I believe [that with] the great world revolutions that are sweeping us now, that the cause of all mankind is the cause of America." Remarks of Senator John F. Kennedy, Airport, Bakersfield, California (September 9, 1960).

47. "[T]here are no second chances in this life; there are no chances that we can turn to other powers to defend our interests.... We stand as the last thin line between the spread of communism and a free world. If we fail here, if we don't fulfill our potential ... then we fail not only ourselves but we fail the cause of freedom." Remarks of Senator John F. Kennedy, York County Fair, York, Pennsylvania (September 16, 1960).

48. "[O]nly an America which is applying its full resources of imagination and thought and strength to the resolution of the world's great problems — only such an America will be able to maintain its position as the champion of peace and the protector of freedom everywhere." Speech by Senator John F. Kennedy, Coliseum, Raleigh, North Carolina (September 17, 1960).

49. "It would be easier, perhaps, if we were Switzerland or Norway or Denmark or Sweden, a small country out of the course of world events. But world events and our own power and our own desire to be free have made us the leader of the free world. If we fail, the whole cause of freedom fails. If we succeed, the cause of freedom succeeds." Remarks of Senator John F. Kennedy, Corn Palace, Mitchell, South Dakota (September 22, 1960).

50. "The reason Franklin Roosevelt and Woodrow Wilson were world leaders was not because they forced their solutions, but because they stood for great moral principles in good times and bad, against friend and foe, and ... if the United States is going to lead the world again, ... we [must] associate ourselves with great causes once again...." Remarks of Senator John F. Kennedy, Corn Palace, Mitchell, South Dakota (September 22, 1960).

51. "[W]hile there are a great many clouds on the horizon, and there are a great many uncertainties ... I think that we represent the way to the future. If we associate with it, if we are identified with it ... if we associate with it, if we become part of it, then our security is assured and our leadership is assured." Remarks of Senator John F. Kennedy, Hotel Utah, Salt Lake City, Utah (September 23, 1960).

52. "I believe that the responsibility of our generation of Americans is to build a society here in this country so vital, so vigorous, so effective, that it serves as an example to the world, that it serves as an example to those who wish to decide which road they shall take." Remarks of Senator John F. Kennedy, State Capitol, Albany, New York (September 29, 1960).

53. "What we want for ourselves, we want for others." Remarks of Senator John F. Kennedy, Lake Meadow Shopping Center, Chicago, Illinois (October 1, 1960).

54. "We cannot afford to stand still. If ... we rest on our oars ... who is going to defend the United States when trouble comes? Who is going to speak for us? Who is going to come to our rescue? We depend upon ourselves. We depend upon our own strength. We depend upon our own right arms, and ... the world of freedom depending upon the United States, cannot afford to stand still, cannot afford to look back, cannot afford to rest on its oars, cannot afford to stand still...." Remarks of Senator John F. Kennedy, Hibbing, Minnesota (October 2, 1960).

55. "[T]he opportunity before United States is bright. In many ways, our time is like the time Dickens described at the beginning of his book: 'It was the best of times and the worst of times.' It is the worst of times because we face the most severe challenge that we have ever faced, and because in many ways the future will be somber. But it is the best of times because we have a chance to strike a blow, not only for our own security, but for the freedom of those who look to us for assistance and succor, who look to us for an example of what freedom can do." Remarks of Senator John F. Kennedy, St. Paul Hotel, St. Paul, Minnesota (October 2, 1960).

56. "I do not say that the future is easy. I do not say that time and events have not placed a heavy burden upon us all. It would be nice to turn those burdens over to some other country and some other people, but we have had them placed on us, and I do not regret it." Remarks of Senator John F. Kennedy, Belleville, Illinois (October 3, 1960).

57. "There are many domestic matters that disturb us ... but they are all wrapped up in the one subject: How can the United States maintain its position, how can the United States build a stronger country here and help the cause of freedom throughout the world. I don't make any mistake about it, that the 1960s are going to be the most difficult and dangerous time in the life of our country. Anyone who says that the future is easy is wholly wrong. I think the future is going to be a difficult one...." Remarks of Senator John F. Kennedy, Belleville, Illinois (October 3, 1960).

58. "If the United States is on the move, the cause of freedom is strong. If we stand still, freedom loses." Remarks of Senator John F. Kennedy, Main Intersection, East St. Louis, Illinois (October 3, 1960).

59. "[T]his country cannot be satisfied with being second best.... This country cannot settle for being first, if; first, but; first, when; first, maybe. We want to be first on the far side of the moon and here in this country...." Remarks of Senator John F. Kennedy, Courthouse Steps, Dayton, Ohio (October 17, 1960).

60. "I think the future belongs to freedom. I think the future belongs to those who want to be free, and that includes the great majority of the population of the world. But we have to give them leadership. We have to show that freedom can be strong." Remarks of Senator John F. Kennedy, Keyworth Stadium, Hamtramck, Michigan (October 26, 1960).

61. "Now the trumpet summons us again — not as a call to bear arms, though arms we need — not as a call to battle, though embattled we are — but a call to bear the burden of a long twilight struggle, year in and year out, 'rejoicing in hope, patient in tribulation' — a struggle against the common enemies of man: tyranny, poverty, disease and war itself." Inaugural Address (January 20, 1961).

62. "[N]o group of people in any generation since democracy was first developed by the ancient Greeks nearly twenty-four or -five hundred years ago, have ever borne a responsibility as great as ours. And I welcome it — and I welcome it tonight." Address in Chicago at a Dinner of the Democratic Party of Cook County (April 28, 1961).

63. "Now our great responsibility is to be the chief defender of freedom, in this time of maximum danger. Only the United States has the power and the resources and the determination. We have committed ourselves to the defense of dozens of countries stretched around the globe who look to us for independence, who look to us for the defense of their freedom." Address in Chicago at a Dinner of the Democratic Party of Cook County (April 28, 1961).

64. "[W]e are a city on a hill and ... one of our great responsibilities during these days is to make sure that we ... set an example to the world not only of helping and assisting them to fulfill their own destiny, but also demonstrating what a free people can do." Remarks at a Dinner of the Big Brothers of America (June 7, 1961).

65. "We are a prosperous country and people, who are very content with our own country. We do not desire anything but peace and to be let alone. And yet the American people ... have assumed broad burdens stretching around the world, which we are glad to assume because we believe it is in a most important cause." Toasts of the President and President Kekkonen [of Finland] (October 16, 1961).

66. "[T]here is no source of strength greater in the free world ... there is no source of strength greater than the people of the United States: courageous, persevering, long-sighted." Remarks at a Political Rally in Trenton, New Jersey (November 2, 1961).

67. "It is our task to maintain our country as a strong example of what a free society can be...." Remarks at a Political Rally in Trenton, New Jersey (November 2, 1961).

68. "[W]e are neither 'warmongers' nor 'appeasers,' neither 'hard' nor 'soft.' We are Americans, determined to defend the frontiers of freedom, by an honorable peace if peace is possible, but by arms if arms are used against us." Address in Seattle at the University of Washington's 100th Anniversary Program (November 16, 1961).

69. "I know that many Americans are often unhappy and concerned about all the problems that the United States faces abroad, but [we] ... should take pride and satisfaction in realizing that only the United States, and [its] ... power and strength and commitment, permits dozens of countries scattered all over the world to maintain their freedom...." Remarks in Phoenix at the 50th Anniversary Dinner Honoring Senator Hayden (November 17, 1961).

70. "Other countries look to their own interests. Only the United States has obligations which stretch ten thousand miles across the Pacific, and three or four thousand miles across the Atlantic, and thousands of miles to the south. Only the United States — and we are only 6 percent of the world's population — bears this kind of burden." Remarks in Phoenix at the 50th Anniversary Dinner Honoring Senator Hayden (November 17, 1961).

71. "The hour of decision has arrived. We cannot afford to 'wait and see what happens,' while the tide of events sweeps over and beyond us. We must use time as a tool, not as a couch. We must carve out our own destiny. This is what Americans have always done — and this, I have every confidence, is what we will continue to do in each new trial and opportunity that lies ahead." Address in New York City to the National Association of Manufacturers (December 6, 1961).

72. "[O]ur nation is commissioned by history to be either an observer of freedom's failure or the cause of its success. Our overriding obligation ... is to fulfill the world's hopes by fulfilling our own faith." Annual Message to the Congress on the State of the Union (January 11, 1962).

73. "The United States did not rise to greatness by waiting for others to lead." Annual Message to the Congress on the State of the Union (January 11, 1962).

74. "[I]t is the fate of this generation ... to live with a struggle we did not start, in a world we did not make. But the pressures of life are not always distributed by choice. And while no nation has ever faced such a challenge, no nation has ever been so ready to seize the burden and the glory of freedom. And in this high endeavor, may God watch over the United States of America." Annual Message to the Congress on the State of the Union (January 11, 1962).

75. "[F]ew generations, in all history, ha[ve] been granted the role of being the great defender of freedom in its hour of maximum danger. This is our good fortune; and I welcome it...." Annual Message to the Congress on the State of the Union (January 11, 1962).

76. "We bear great responsibilities and great burdens not only to ourselves ... but to so many around the world whose future hangs in the balance and depends so much on us. We may not feel that our efforts are always appreciated ... but we want to make sure that our efforts are effective, and that this generation — which faces the greatest challenges that any country, any free people, have ever faced ... that we shall meet our responsibility ... to our country, [and] ... in a larger sense ... to all those who desire to live a life of freedom and a life which permits them to participate with their neighbors and with God in the way they choose." Remarks at the 10th Annual Presidential Prayer Breakfast (March 1, 1962).

77. "We carry the major share of the responsibility and the burdens for the defense of Europe — in Berlin itself ... in ... southeast Asia ... in our own hemisphere ... in Africa itself — in the Middle East — in India and Pakistan.... This is a tremendous burden which falls upon the United States.... We are only 6 percent of the world's population and yet we carry this struggle in all parts of the globe. So no American citizen should feel ... this country is not making a major effort to maintain the cause of freedom around the globe." Remarks at the White House to Members of the American Legion (March 1, 1962).

78. "[No] ... citizen of this country ... wishes to relax that burden [to maintain the cause of freedom around the world] [or] ... feels that we have carried it long enough, [or] ... feels that now others should pick it up. We want others to bear their proportionate share of the burden but we do not suggest that we in the United States should fail or flinch or become fatigued." Remarks at the White House to Members of the American Legion (March 1, 1962).

79. "We live in a difficult time, and our problems are difficult, and I know many Americans get discouraged, and also are concerned with whether we are doing enough in many areas of the world. My strong feeling is that the people of this country are not fully aware of what a tremendous burden we really carry, and really how pleased we should be and proud of the tremendous effort which we make to sustain freedom in so many places." Remarks at the 18th Annual Washington Conference of the Advertising Council (March 7, 1962).

80. "The United States ... is the source of strength of the entire free world. We are criticized and denounced regularly ... in every section of the free world. But the fact of the matter is that ... the United States is the sentinel at the gate. [I] do not think that any of us should regret this role — and I do not." Address at Miami Beach at a Fundraising Dinner in Honor of Senator Smathers (March 10, 1962).

81. "[T]his country of ours [is] ... a model for the world." Remarks to Members of the White House Conference on National Economic Issues (March 21, 1962).

82. "This is a difficult time in the life of the United States, because the United States bears such heavy burdens. I know that many of us, in fact on occasions all of us, wish for those days when the United States lived an isolated existence. But today the United States carries the major burden in so many areas...." Address in Milwaukee at the Jefferson-Jackson Dinner (May 12, 1962).

83. "I do not regard the great interests of this country in a narrow sense. Our interests are really the free world's interests. And I am constantly impressed ... with the fact that this rather small country in the relative sense ... that we are carrying the burden for the defense of freedom in nearly every part of the globe." Remarks of Welcome to Participants in the Summer Intern Program for College Students (June 20, 1962).

84. "[T]his Nation — conceived in revolution, nurtured in liberty, maturing in independence — has no intention of abdicating its leadership in that worldwide movement for independence to any nation or society committed to systematic human oppression." Address at Independence Hall, Philadelphia (July 4, 1962).

85. "[T]his Nation has special responsibilities as one of the leaders of the free world, as its richest and most powerful nation, as possessor of its most important currency, and as the chief banker for international trade. We did not seek all of these burdens, but we do not shrink from them." Remarks to the Board of Governors of the World Bank and the International Monetary Fund (September 20, 1962).

86. "It is odd that this country, which was wholly founded in a long neutral tradition, and isolationist tradition, should, in 1962, as it has been since 1945, be the great and almost solitary hope for the maintenance of freedom around the world." Remarks at the State Fairgrounds in Louisville, Kentucky (October 13, 1962).

87. "[W]e ... should realize that the hope of the free world, the hope of the enslaved world ... rests upon ... all of us ... who've held back the Communist advance ... and who, today, stand watch and ward for freedom in 40 or 50 different countries. That is a proud role which we did not seek, but from which we do not flinch." Remarks at the Municipal Airport, Niagara Falls, New York (October 14, 1962).

88. "The United States, which has a great faculty for self-criticism ... and quite rightly values it as one of our essential freedoms, I think fails to take into account what an ... extraordinary job this country has done over the last 17 years [since the end of World War II] in the defense of freedom. All around the world there are hundreds and millions of people, and dozens of countries who would not be free if it were not for the will and the courage and the power of the people of the United States of America...." Remarks at the High School Football Stadium, Los Alamos, New Mexico (December 7, 1962).

89. "If at times our actions seem to make life difficult for others, it is only because history has made life difficult for us all." Annual Message to the Congress on the State of the Union (January 14, 1963).

90. "America was to be the great experiment, a testing ground for political liberty, a model for democratic government, and although the first task was to mold a nation on these principles here on this continent, we would also lead the fight against tyranny on all continents." Remarks at the 50th Annual Meeting of the Anti-Defamation League of B'nai B'rith (January 31, 1963).

91. "[A]ll of us, whether we are doing one thing or the other ... wherever we may be, all of us are committed to a great objective, and that is to see the United States of America, of which we are proud, not only meet its responsibilities here at home ... but also continue to be ... the keystone of the arch of freedom all around the world." Remarks at Redstone Arsenal, Huntsville, Alabama (May 18, 1963).

92. "Without the United States there are literally dozens of countries that would not now be free, and with the United States, and with our determination, and with our strong look forward, not only shall they be free, but also the people who come after them." Remarks at Redstone Arsenal, Huntsville, Alabama (May 18, 1963).

93. "[N]ever in history has so much depended upon one people, and I think never in history has one people been so willing to assume that responsibility." Remarks Upon Arrival at the Missile Range, White Sands, New Mexico (June 5, 1963).

94. "[T]he United States, by the force of events, history, and by our own choice — and I want to emphasize 'by our own choice'— ha[s] been propelled into the world where we are the key, the archstone, the basic element in the strength of the entire free world." Remarks to the American Embassy Staff at Bad Godesberg [Germany] (June 23, 1963).

95. "I am proud of the fact that in the years since 1945 the United States, after 150 years of withdrawal, of isolation, has found it possible to play a significant part in the great fight for freedom all around the globe. I can tell you that the people of the United States do not regard this effort as a burden. They regard it as a privilege to play their part in these great days." Remarks at the City Hall in Bonn (June 23, 1963).

96. "The ... United States, as a major nuclear power, does have a special responsibility in the world. It is ... a threefold responsibility — a responsibility to our own citizens; a responsibility to the people of the whole world who are affected by our decisions; and to the next generation of humanity." Address Before the 18th General Assembly of the United Nations (September 20, 1963).

97. "There have been some disappointments and some defeats. But it seems to me, all in all, as we look at the world, however imperfect it may be, however frustrating it may be, however limited our authority may be on occasions, however impossible we may find it to have our writ accepted, nevertheless, the United States is secure, it is at peace, and a good many dozens of countries are secure because of us." Address in Duluth [Minnesota] to Delegates to the Northern Great Lakes Region Land and People Conference (September 24, 1963).

98. "I do not share with those who feel that this responsibility should be passed on to others. The fact ... is that there are no others who can combine our geographic position, our natural wealth, and the determination of our people. And, therefore, until such a people someday arrives, I think the United States should stand guard at the gate." Remarks at the High School Memorial Stadium, Great Falls, Montana (September 26, 1963).

99. "From the beginning of this country ... [we] lived an isolated existence. [W]e were an unaligned country.... We were by statute as well as by desire. We had believed that we could live behind our two oceans in safety and prosperity.... The end of isolation consequently meant a wrench with the very lifeblood, the very spine, of the Nation. Yet, as time passed, we came to see that the end of isolation was not such a terrible error.... We came to see that it was the inevitable result of growth, the economic growth, the military growth, and the cultural growth of the United States. No nation so powerful and so dynamic and as rich as our own could hope to live in isolation from other nations...." Address in Salt Lake City at the Mormon Tabernacle (September 26, 1963).

100. "Each one of us has moments of longing for the past, but two world wars have clearly shown us ... that we cannot turn our back on the world outside. If we do, we jeopardize our economic well-being, we jeopardize our political stability, we jeopardize our physical safety. To turn away now is to abandon the world to those whose ambition is to destroy a free society. To yield these burdens up ... is to surrender the freedom of our country inevitably, for without the United States, the chances of freedom surviving, let alone prevailing around the globe, are nonexistent." Address in Salt Lake City at the Mormon Tabernacle (September 26, 1963).

101. "The world is full of contradiction and confusion, and our policy seems to have lost the black and white clarity of simpler times.... It is little wonder ... [that] we look back to the old days with nostalgia ... that there is a desire in the country to go back to the time when our Nation lived alone ... that we increasingly want an end to entangling alliances, an end to all help to foreign countries, a cessation of diplomatic relations with countries or states whose principles we dislike, that we get ... the United States out of the United Nations, and that we ... take refuge behind a wall of force. This is an understandable effort to recover an old feeling of simplicity, yet in world affairs, as in all other aspects of our lives, the days of the quiet past are gone forever." Address in Salt Lake City at the Mormon Tabernacle (September 26, 1963).

102. "No country in history has had so large a proportion of its citizenry serving its country in the cause of peace outside of its own borders. They have had them for war, they have had them for conquest; but we seek a world of diversity, a world of freedom.... And to do that, with all of its complexities and all of its difficulties, we have done it ... almost singlehanded." Remarks at the Convention Center in Las Vegas, Nevada (September 28, 1963).

103. "Some say that they are tiring of this task [defending freedom against Communism], or tired of world problems and their complexities, or tired of hearing those who receive our aid disagree with us. But are we tired of living in a free world? ... Are we going to stop now merely because we have not produced complete success? I do not believe our adversaries are tired and I cannot believe that the United States of America in 1963 is fatigued." Remarks at the Dinner of the Protestant Council of the City of New York (November 8, 1963).

104. "[T]he struggle is by no means over ... it is essential that we not only maintain our effort, but that we persevere; that we not only endure ... but also prevail. It is essential, in short, that the word go forth from the United States to all who are concerned about the future of the Family of Man; that we are not weary in well-doing. And we shall, I am confident, if we maintain the pace, we shall in due season reap the kind of world we deserve and deserve the kind of world we will have." Remarks at the Dinner of the Protestant Council of the City of New York (November 8, 1963).

105. "However disappointing life may be around the world, the forces of freedom are still in the majority, and they are in the majority after 18 years because the United States has been willing to bear the burden." Remarks in New York City at the AFL-CIO Convention (November 15, 1963).

Image Abroad

106. "It is not enough to restate our claim to the Declaration of Independence. It is not enough to deplore violence in other lands. It is up to us to prove that our way — the way of peaceful change and democratic processes — can fulfill those goals better than any other system under the sun. It is up to us to rebuild our image abroad by rebuilding our image here at home." Remarks of Senator John F. Kennedy, NAACP Rally, Los Angeles, California (July 10, 1960).

107. "The United States looks tired. It looks like our brightest days have been in the past. It looks like the Communists are reaching for the future, and we sit back and talk about the ideals of the American Revolution. The way to put the ideals of the American Revolution into significance is to act on them, not to talk about them." Remarks of Senator John F. Kennedy, San Francisco International Airport, Francisco, California (September 3, 1960).

108. "I am not content to see the vision of the United States as a strong and vital country dimmed around the world. I am not satisfied to see people in Latin America, Africa, and Asia, who used to look to President Roosevelt, Woodrow Wilson, and Truman, now wonder what has happened to us, why we are on the decline, and look to Khrushchev and Peiping." Remarks of Senator John F. Kennedy, Oakland Park, Pontiac, Michigan (September 5, 1960).

109. "Americans wonder why it was that Africans who some years ago quoted Thomas Jefferson and Lincoln and Franklin Roosevelt now quote Karl Marx in the Congo. They wonder why the nations of South America who once were engaged in a great enterprise called the good neighbor policy should now stone the Vice President of the United States. They wonder why America, which was once regarded ... with so much friendship on the island of Cuba should now be reviled and attacked by the erratic leader of that island only 90 miles from our shore. It seems to me ... that we are all [in] danger of losing the respect of the people of the world, because we are in danger of losing those very qualities which once caused them to respect us." Speech by Senator John F. Kennedy, Civic Auditorium, Portland, Oregon (September 7, 1960).

110. "[T]he people of the world respect strength. In former years they were grateful to the United States for the military protection that we guaranteed them. But now they are no longer certain that America's lead will continue in the future when they see the missile gap widen, and once our atomic monopoly begins to cease, and they are uneasy about a military strategy that relies so heavily upon massive retaliation, because they are not interested in seeing their house preserved, only to see it blown up." Speech by Senator John F. Kennedy, Civic Auditorium, Portland, Oregon (September 7, 1960).

111. "[T]he people of the world respect achievement. For most of the 20th century they admired American science and American education, which was second to none. But now they are not at all certain about which way the future lies. The first vehicle in outer space was called sputnik, not Vanguard. The first country to place its national emblem on the moon was the Soviet Union, not the United States. The first canine passengers to outer space who safely returned were named Strelka and Belka, not Rover or Fido, or even Checkers." Speech by Senator John F. Kennedy, Civic Auditorium, Portland, Oregon (September 7, 1960).

112. "Today in many cases those leaders [in Africa] look east to Peking and Moscow. They have lost their confidence in us. They don't see the United States as a great revolutionary country which is on the move. They see us as a country which has had its high noon, which is now in a plateau, which belongs to the past, not the future." Rear Platform Remarks of Senator John F. Kennedy, Tulare, California (September 9, 1960).

113. "I believe a strong America is one that leads the free world, not just because we are the richest or the strongest or the most powerful, but because we exert that leadership for the cause of freedom around the globe. Because we act as well as react, because we propose as well as oppose, and because we have earned the respect of our friends as well as the respect of our enemies, and because we are moving on the road to peace." Remarks of Senator John F. Kennedy, Memorial Auditorium, Dallas, Texas (September 13, 1960).

114. "What is our image around the world? What are we identified with? The status quo? The past? The special few in the interests in a few countries? Those on their way out? Or are we identified with the fight against poverty and hunger and the aspiration of the people? What would we stand for in this country? Do we stand for a better chance for all our people? Do we practice what we preach? [W]hat we preach is difficult to practice, but we do preach it and we must practice it.... [W]e preach the best doctrine ever known, the equality of man, the Government gets consent from the governed, and that everyone is entitled to life, liberty, and the pursuit of happiness, and we will maintain that position." Speech by Senator John F. Kennedy, Syria Mosque, Pittsburgh, Pennsylvania (October 10, 1960).

115. "[T]he issue [is not] whether they love us. The question is whether people around the world want to follow the same system of freedom that has so benefited us. That is the great issue, not whether we are loved." Remarks of Senator John F. Kennedy, Roosevelt Raceway, Mineola, New York (October 12, 1960).

116. "Many Americans sometimes point out to those who criticize us from abroad that this is a great country, that we have a free system, that we are moving steadily forward in the implementation of our ideals, and then they are disappointed that they are not more impressed abroad. I think the reason is that we have set an extremely high standard for ourselves. We have set a higher standard than any other country, really, than any other system." Speech by Senator John F. Kennedy, Wittenburg College Stadium, Springfield, Ohio (October 17, 1960).

117. "Our prestige abroad is not what we say it is, but what it is. It is not the esteem of good men for good words; it is the esteem of good men for good action." Speech of Senator John F. Kennedy, Auditorium, Kansas City, Missouri (October 22, 1960).

118. "[O]ur failure to be first in outer space ... cost us more heavily in prestige, and I do not define prestige as popularity. I define prestige as influence, as an ability to persuade people to accept your point of view. That probably cost us more in the fifties than any other failure or any other decision or any other action. It persuaded people who lived in the underdeveloped countries that the Soviet Union, which was once so far behind, was now the equal and the superior in some degree of the United States." Remarks of Senator John F. Kennedy, Shaunee Mission East High School, Kansas City, Kansas (October 22, 1960).

119. "[P]restige is not popularity. Prestige is the image which you give of a vital society which persuades other people to follow our leadership." Remarks of Senator John F. Kennedy, Street Rally, Elgin, Illinois (October 25, 1960).

120. "Prestige means power and influence, and our ability to persuade [other] people...." Remarks of Senator John F. Kennedy, Liberty Mall, Cook Memorial Library, Libertyville, Illinois (October 25, 1960).

121. "[T]he position of the United States in the world [can be] summed up in the word 'prestige.' By prestige I do not mean popularity. I do not think it makes so much difference whether we are loved personally or beloved around the world. What does make a difference, however, is that the people of the world who desire to be free ... to look at the United States, not only as a powerful leading nation, but also a nation which personifies the ideal of what freedom can accomplish." Remarks of Senator John F. Kennedy, Lawrence Park Shopping Center, Philadelphia, Pennsylvania (October 29, 1960).

122. "No policeman is universally popular — particularly when he uses his stick to restore law and order on his beat." Annual Message to the Congress on the State of the Union (January 11, 1962).

123. "The image of America which is seen from abroad is in many ways inaccurate. Our problems in some ways are more serious, our riches are less, our hopes are greater than may be imagined from far away." Remarks to a Group of Foreign Students (May 8, 1963).

124. "Our willingness to undertake the hard tasks of leadership, to station our soldiers and sailors and airmen far away from home ... to assume the burdens of preventing another war, all this which we in America sometimes take for granted and which we think other people take for granted have earned the American people a high reputation and brought us steadfast good will." Radio and Television Message to the American People After Returning from Europe (July 5, 1963).

Importance of Domestic Strength

125. "You cannot be successful abroad unless you are successful at home because every problem ... here in the United States has its implications abroad.... Every time we waste our food in a hungry world here in this country, that affects the foreign policy and the security of the United States Every time we deny to one of our citizens the right of equality of opportunity before the law, the right to send their children to schools on the basis of equality, so much weaker are we in Africa, Asia, and Latin America, where we are a white minority in a colored world." Speech by Senator John F. Kennedy, Portland Stadium, Portland, Maine (September 2, 1960).

126. "[I]f the security of the United States is going to be protected, if our position as a leader of the free world is going to be maintained, [then] we [must] recognize the close relationships between the vitality of our own domestic economy and our position around the world. If we stand still here at home, we stand still around the world. The reason that Woodrow Wilson and Franklin Roosevelt and Harry Truman were so successful in their foreign policy was because they were so successful in their domestic policy." Rear Platform Remark of Senator John F. Kennedy, Red Bluff, California (September 8, 1960).

127. "If we succeed here, if we are strong in this country, if we are carrying out policies of assistance to our people, if we hold out the hand of friendship abroad, if we present an image of vitality and strength, then the people around the world will determine that the future belongs to freedom. But if we stand still, if we look back, if we mark time while the Communists move ahead, then people in Latin America, Africa, and Asia, will determine that the future belongs to the East and not to the West." Remarks of Senator John F. Kennedy, the Alamo, San Antonio, Texas (September 12, 1960).

128. "It is a country that is moving at home that moves abroad.... I don't think you can be successful abroad unless you are successful in the United States. Unless you are a liberal here, you can't be a liberal abroad." Remarks of Senator John F. Kennedy, Senior Citizens Rally, City Center, New York, New York (September 14, 1960).

129. "The people of the world want to know that freedom can bring the good life, that if they follow the road that we have marked, that their life will be productive, their people will be working, they will be solving their problems at home.... Unless we are progressive and liberal and forward looking here at home, we cannot possibly be progressive and forward looking and liberal abroad. The two are tied together." Statewide TV Speech by Senator John F. Kennedy, Zembo Mosque Temple, Harrisburg, Pennsylvania (September 15, 1960).

130. "[W]e are defending not only ourselves, but we also defend the case of freedom. If we build a strong and vital country here, we affect not only our own independence and those directly allied with us; we also affect the security of all those who wish to follow in the same road that we take. Therefore, I think this generation of Americans has special responsibilities and special obligations.... I think our obligation is to concern ourselves with our country here, and then hold out the hand of friendship to all those who wish to follow on our road." Remarks of Senator John F. Kennedy, Troy, New York (September 29, 1960).

131. "[W]e can best [contribute to the cause of freedom] by maintaining ... a strong ... economy, by meeting our problems here at home, by building a stronger industry ... [and] by providing the [world's] best educational system...." Remarks of Senator John F. Kennedy, Town Square, Alton, Illinois (October 3, 1960).

132. "This country will not maintain its freedom, this country will not maintain its commitments around the world, unless we have a strong and vigorous economy, able to maintain our commitments, able to build, able to move." Remarks of Senator John F. Kennedy, National Stockyards, East St. Louis, Illinois (October 3, 1960).

133. "The United States must be true to itself; if must meet its own responsibilities. It must build greater strength in this country because it alone defends freedom all around the globe." Speech by Senator John F. Kennedy, Little White House, Warm Springs, Georgia (October 10, 1960).

134. "I believe it our function to so build our society here, to so reinvigorate it, to so move it, that people around the globe ought to wonder how they can follow our role...." Speech by Senator John F. Kennedy, Little White House, Warm Springs, Georgia (October 10, 1960).

135. "[W]e have to prove what they hear we are talking about, what we are preaching about, what the Declaration of Independence says, what the Constitution says. We have to prove that we mean it, not last year, not 10 years ago ... but today.... If we are going to live by these high words we are going to have to live it every day. We can't turn it on and off." Remarks of Senator John F. Kennedy, Hotel Theresa, New York, New York (October 12, 1960).

136. "What we are speaks louder than our words, and if we are building a better society here, if we are treating our people fairly, regardless of their race or their religion, then everyone who comes to our country will see what we are and go away impressed." Remarks of Senator John F. Kennedy, Hotel Theresa, New York, New York (October 12, 1960).

137. "[T]he United States ... is going to have to build a society with sufficient vigor, develop its resources with sufficient energy, provide a better life for our people with fair opportunity, with a sufficient sense of justice, if the United States is going to be in fact the leader of the free world.... All of the Voice of America, all of the radio broadcasts, all of the books we send abroad, pale in significance to the kind of society that we are building here in the United States." Remarks of Senator John F. Kennedy, Railroad Station, Ann Arbor, Michigan (October 14, 1960).

138. "The place to build our prestige in the world is here in the United States. The place to build strength for freedom is here in the United States. If we are on the upward move, if the wave of our vitality and energy as a nation is coming in ... then the United States is strong, and when the United States is strong, the world is strong, the chance of freedom is strong, the U.S. influence is strong, our prestige is greater." Remarks of Senator John F. Kennedy, Capitol Steps, Lansing, Michigan (October 14, 1960).

139. "[I]f [the future] is going to belong to us, if people around the world are going to decide to follow our leadership, we must lead, we must set an example, we must meet our own problems, we must hold out a helping hand to them. That is our opportunity." Remarks of Senator John F. Kennedy, New Castle County Airport, Wilmington, Delaware (October 16, 1960).

140. "The kind of society we build here, the kind of country we develop here, that is the test of our ability to lead around the world. What we are speaks far louder than what we say." Remarks of Senator John F. Kennedy, University of Illinois Campus, Champaign-Urbana, Illinois (October 24, 1960).

141. "There are no domestic issues and foreign issues. There are issues which are tied together, tied together to bring a stronger America, and if this country is strong then we are strong around the world. All of the speeches, all of the statements, all of the propaganda that we send around the world means nothing next to our own record." Remarks of Senator John F. Kennedy, University of Illinois Campus, Champaign-Urbana, Illinois (October 24, 1960).

142. "[T]he cause of all mankind is the cause of America. We serve not only ourselves; we serve others, those who wish to follow our example. And in order to serve them, in order to be faithful to our trust, in order to hold out the lamp of hope to all those now subjugated who hope someday to be free, we have to build a strong society here. We have to demonstrate that in any contest with the Communist system, that we are going to win." Remarks of Senator John F. Kennedy, Keyworth Stadium, Hamtramck, Michigan (October 26, 1960).

143. "[T]he United States cannot possibly afford at a time when we are the chief defender of freedom and when freedom is under attack all over the globe — we cannot afford to be second in education, in space, in housing, in industrial production, in the kind of society and opportunity we present." Remarks of Senator John F. Kennedy, Trade Union Council of Liberal Party, New York, New York (October 27, 1960).

144. "Our hope for freedom, our hope for peace, depends upon our leading a free world coalition, a coalition that is put together voluntarily. How long will they listen to the sound of our trumpet if they believe it blows a faltering note, if they believe that we represent the way of the past; that the Communists represent the way of the future? To lead the free world, to defend freedom, to roll back the Communist advance requires a powerful, committed, dedicated and moving America...." Remarks of Senator John F. Kennedy, Johnston Hall, Moravian College, Bethlehem, Pennsylvania (October 27, 1960).

145. "[O]ur chance for peace, our chance for freedom, our chance to meet our commitments to freedom around the globe, depend on one factor, a strong, progressive, forward-looking America. If we fail, freedom fails. If we succeed, freedom succeeds" Remarks of Senator John F. Kennedy, Wilkes-Barre, Pennsylvania (October 28, 1960).

146. "[Our] own vision of a shining America [must be one] which meets its opportunities and its responsibilities, which stands once again as the unchallenged leader of freedom, a country and a leadership which identifies itself in this country with the needs of people and identifies itself around the world with the needs of the people; ... not ... as pawns in the cold war, but as people who want to be free. And we will associate with them not merely in the struggle against communism, but in the struggle against the disease and ignorance and illiteracy and lack of hope." Remarks of Senator John F. Kennedy, Reyburn Plaza, Philadelphia, Pennsylvania (October 31, 1960).

147. "If we are going to be strong abroad if we are going to win the peace, if we are going to maintain our prestige, it will be not only by speeches and debates and good will missions; it will be by building in this country a strong and vital and progressive society, committed to finishing the unfinished business, building here the kind of country which will serve as an example to freedom all around the globe." Remarks of Senator John F. Kennedy, City Park, Lewiston, Maine (November 6, 1960).

148. "[I]f we cannot fulfill our own ideals here, we cannot expect others to accept them." Annual Message to the Congress on the State of the Union (January 11, 1962).

149. "[W]hen the youngest child alive today has grown to the cares of manhood, our position in the world will be determined first of all by what provisions we make today — for his education, his health, and his opportunities for a good home and a good job and a good life." Annual Message to the Congress on the State of the Union (January 11, 1962).

150. "[A] nation which is dedicated to progress, which does not try to freeze history in its tracks, which is determined to serve the people and their welfare, and their freedom, which is committed to progress — this is the nation which is most likely to unite the people of the world against aggression and for peace." Remarks by Telephone to a Dinner Meeting of the Ohio State Democratic Convention in Columbus (September 21, 1962).

151. "This country is as strong abroad only as it's strong at home. It is the great productive power of the United States of America, combined with the will and determination of the people of this country, that makes it possible for us to fulfill our role in space [and in defending freedom] around the world." Remarks at the Hippodrome Arena in St. Paul, Minnesota (October 6, 1962).

152. "[A] strong and vital America is essential to the freedom of the world...." Remarks in Baltimore at the Fifth Regiment Armory (October 10, 1962).

153. "America's rise to world leadership in the century since the Civil War has reflected more than anything else our unprecedented economic growth." Address and Question and Answer Period at the Economic Club of New York (December 14, 1962).

154. "[A] leading nation, a nation upon which all depend not only in this country but around the world, cannot afford to be satisfied, to look back or to pause. On our strength and growth depend the strength of others, the spread of free world trade and unity, and continued confidence in our leadership and our currency." Address and Question and Answer Period at the Economic Club of New York (December 14, 1962).

155. "[U]pon our achievement of greater [economic] vitality and strength here at home hang our fate and future in the world: our ability to sustain and supply the security of free men and nations, our ability to command their respect for our leadership, our ability to expand our trade without threat to our balance of payments, and our ability to adjust to the changing demands of cold war competition and challenge." Annual Message to the Congress on the State of the Union (January 14, 1963).

156. "We shall be judged more by what we do at home than by what we preach abroad. Nothing we could do to help the developing countries would help them half as much as a booming U.S. economy. And nothing our opponents could do to encourage their own ambitions would encourage them half as much as a chronic lagging U.S. economy." Annual Message to the Congress on the State of the Union (January 14, 1963).

157. "The [military] force that we have ... permit[s] us to develop ourselves, our resources, improve the life of our people and make it possible for what Thomas Jefferson called the disease of liberty to be catching all around the globe." Remarks in San Diego at the Marine Corps Recruit Depot (June 6, 1963).

158. "This is a difficult time in the life of the United States, and people look all around the world and wonder whether we are moving forward or backward. Whether the world is more dangerous or easier, I don't think anyone can say. But I think they can say that there is every reason to hope, and there is every reason for us to concentrate our energy in making those decisions here in the United States which will maintain the strength of the United States so that we can in turn meet our responsibilities around the globe." Remarks at the Cheney Stadium in Tacoma, Washington (September 27, 1963).

159. "Whatever we are able to do in this country, whatever success we are able to make of ourselves, whatever leadership we are able to give, whatever demonstration we can make that a free society can function and move ahead and provide a better life for its people — all those things that we do here have their effect all around the globe." Remarks in New York City at the National Convention of the Catholic Youth Organization (November 15, 1963).

160. "It is our responsibility not merely to denounce our enemies and those who make themselves our enemies but to make this system work, to demonstrate what freedom can do, what those who are committed to freedom and the future can do." Remarks in New York City at the National Convention of the Catholic Youth Organization (November 15, 1963).

AMERICAN SPIRIT

161. "[W]e know that our country has surmounted great crises in the past, not because of our wealth, not because of our rhetoric, not because we had longer cars and white iceboxes and bigger television screens than anyone else, but because our ideas were more compelling and more penetrating and more wise and enduring." Remarks of Senator John F. Kennedy, Roosevelt Birthday Ball, Salt Lake City, Utah (January 30, 1960).

162. "[W]e must be strong — we must summon all our resources — both the resources of mind and spirit — and the resources which lie beneath the earth and in our mountains, and in our great rivers — those resources on which we have built a great nation — those resources on which our continued greatness depends." Remarks of Senator John F. Kennedy, Reception, Madison, Wisconsin (February 24, 1960).

163. "[W]e have in this country all the strength and all the vision and all the will we need — if we will only use them." Remarks of Senator John F. Kennedy, Testimonial Dinner, Nashua, New Hampshire (March 5, 1960).

164. "We celebrate the past to awaken the future." Speech by Senator John F. Kennedy, Memorial Program, 25th Anniversary of Signing Social Security Act, Hyde Park, New York (August 14, 1960).

165. "To meet these urgent responsibilities [that lie ahead] will take determination, and dedication, and hard work. But I believe that America is ready to move from self-indulgence to self-denial. It will take will and effort. But I believe that America is ready to work. It will take vision and boldness. But I believe that America is still bold." Speech by Senator John F. Kennedy, Memorial Program, 25th Anniversary of Signing of Social Security Act, Hyde Park, New York (August 14, 1960).

166. "The untapped energies of the American people ... are more powerful than the atom itself [and] must once again be committed to great national objectives." Speech by Senator John F. Kennedy, The Edgewater, Anchorage, Alaska (September 3, 1960).

167. "In the year 1789, in the city of Hartford, Conn., the skies at noon turned from blue to gray and by mid-afternoon the city had darkened over so densely that in that religious age men fell on their knees, and begged a final blessing before the end came. The Connecticut House of Representatives was in session, and many of the members clamored for immediate adjournment. The speaker of the house, one Colonel Davenport, came to his feet and he silenced the din with these words, 'The day of judgment is either approaching or it is not. If it is not, there is no cause for adjournment. If it is, I choose to be found doing my duty. I wish, therefore, that candles may be brought.' I hope in a difficult and dangerous time in the life of our country that all of us may bring candles to help illuminate our country's way." Remarks of Senator John F. Kennedy, Michigan State Fair, Detroit, Michigan (September 5, 1960).

168. "[T]hose who are afraid to ask the American people for a greater effort and a greater sacrifice and a greater national contribution ... are, in reality, selling America short. It is they who have lost their faith in America and in the American capacity to do great things." Remarks of Senator John F. Kennedy, Civic Center, Denver, Colorado (September 23, 1960).

169. "In almost every area of competition — military, diplomatic, economic, scientific, and educational — the Communists are now capable of competing with the United States on nearly equal terms. But in one area the Communists can never overcome us — unless we fall back to their level — and that is the area of spiritual values — moral strength — the strength of our will and our purpose — the qualities and traditions that make this Nation a shining example to all who yearn to be free." Speech by John F. Kennedy, Mormon Tabernacle, Salt Lake City, Utah (September 23, 1960).

170. "[H]owever good this country may be, it can be better. This country has been made by people who were not satisfied." Remarks of Senator John F. Kennedy, North Tonawanda, New York (September 28, 1960).

171. "The United States was a great revolutionary country. As long as we maintain that spirit, we are going to hold the imagination of the world." Remarks of Senator John F. Kennedy, Marion County Court House, Marion, Illinois (October 3, 1960).

172. "[W]hen the American people are given leadership, when [it has been] pointed out [to them] the unfinished business of our society ... they can accomplish anything." Speech by Senator John F. Kennedy, Fair Grounds, Saginaw, Michigan (October 14, 1960).

173. "All things are possible ... [in] this country if once we determine where we want to go and what we must do in order to get there. Lincoln said 100 years ago, 'The times are new and the perils are new. We must disentangle ourselves from the past.' And I believe we must in 1960. The problems are entirely new and the solutions must be as new. But I believe the same spirit which in other days and in other years and in other times served this country so well, [will] motivate this country [again]." Speech by Senator John F. Kennedy, Fair Grounds, Saginaw, Michigan (October 14, 1960).

174. "We are Americans. That is a proud boast. That is a great privilege, to be a citizen of the United States, and we must meet our responsibilities." Remarks of Senator John F. Kennedy, Truman Shopping Center, Grand View, Missouri (October 22, 1960).

175. "[It has been said that] 'Ideals are like stars. You will not succeed in touching them with your hands, but the seafaring man who follows the waters follows the stars, and if you choose them as your guides, you can reach your destiny.' Our stars and our ideal is the welfare of our country and the welfare of freedom." Speech by Senator John F. Kennedy, Milwaukee, Wisconsin (October 23, 1960).

176. "I don't think any American wants historians to write that these [the next 10 years] were the years when the tide began to run out for the United States. I believe Americans want to say again that we believe in this country, that our ability to meet our assignments is unlimited, that our brightest days are still ahead, and that we are going to go to work again." Remarks of Senator John F. Kennedy, Courthouse Rally, Peoria, Illinois (October 24, 1960).

177. "I believe the people of this country are strong enough and tough enough and courageous enough to know the truth...." Remarks of Senator John F. Kennedy, City Square, Mount Clemens, Michigan (October 26, 1960).

178. "[W]e ... have no greater asset than the willingness of a free and determined people, through its elected officials, to face all problems frankly and meet all dangers free from panic or fear." Annual Message to the Congress on the State of the Union (January 30, 1961).

179. "[W]e love our country, not for what it was, though it has always been great — not for what it is, though of this we are deeply proud — but for what it some day can and, through the efforts of us all, some day will be." Address at a Luncheon Meeting of the National Industrial Conference Board (February 13, 1961).

180. "This country from its earliest inception has been divided between those who prophesied doom and gloom for the future and those who recognized that their brightest hopes for this country would be more than fulfilled.... Those who bet on the United States, in the long run have proved to be correct. Those who have been bold about this country have seen their great predictions and estimations come true." Remarks in Seattle at the Silver Anniversary Dinner Honoring Senator Magnuson (November 16, 1961).

181. "[T]here have always been those on the fringes of our society who have sought to escape their own responsibility by finding a simple solution, an appealing slogan or a convenient scapegoat.... At times these fanatics have achieved a temporary success among those who lack the will or the wisdom to face unpleasant facts or unsolved problems. But in time the basic good sense and stability of the great American consensus has always prevailed." Address in Los Angeles at a Dinner of the Democratic Party of California (November 18, 1961).

182. "[The] concept of the moving ahead of a great country on a great errand is what I think can give this country its leadership in the future as it has in the past." Remarks in Pueblo, Colorado Following Approval of the Fryingpan-Arkansas Project (August 17, 1962).

183. "The great strength of this country is unlimited if this country makes up its mind that as a country it's going to move forward. Not the President, not the Senators, not the Congressmen, not the governors, not the commissioners, not the mayors, but 180 million Americans can advance this country into a bright future." Remarks at the Air Terminal in Fresno, California, After Inspecting Western Conservation Projects (August 18, 1962).

184. "[T]his country has performed its great function because ... its people have had brains, and we have appreciated the cult of excellence, and we have developed that talent in a way which has served our country and served mankind." Remarks at the High School Football Stadium, Los Alamos, New Mexico (December 7, 1962).

185. "The quality of American life must keep pace with the quantity of American goods. This country cannot afford to be materially rich and spiritually poor." Annual Message to the Congress on the State of the Union (January 14, 1963).

186. "[America] has been made by people ... who came here within a short space of 200 years. We are a combination of all of the streams which have passed through all of the countries of the world, and the people who came here were, I think, among the most adventuresome." Remarks to Delegates Attending the World Youth Forum (March 7, 1963).

187. "We are a very self-critical society. It is one of the factors of freedom which we value the most." Remarks at a White House Musical Program for Youth (April 22, 1963).

188. "We are, even though we hesitate to admit it, a cultured people and ... [w]hen we use that word, we use it in the sense — really in the Greek sense — of the full man and woman living in a full system of freedom who develops his own resources and talents and in so doing serves the greater good of all of our people." Remarks at a White House Musical Program for Youth (April 22, 1963).

189. "America is a complicated country ... which has made itself one out of many ... when a flood of immigrants came to this country — Italian, Irish, German, Scandinavian, French — and built a society which has very strong roots in Europe but which is in a sense unique." Remarks of Welcome to a Group from Valdagno, Italy (May 17, 1963).

190. "[N]ow and in the years to come, those who oppose us, those who wish us ill must contend with the strong determination of Americans to not only endure and survive but also to prevail." Remarks in San Diego at the Marine Corps Recruit Depot (June 6, 1963).

191. "Americans ... represent the best hope on earth, [and] are a proud, progressive people, who are determined to maintain their freedom and their liberty, and to maintain the freedom and liberty of those associated with us." Remarks Upon Arrival at Honolulu International Airport (June 8, 1963).

192. "There are strong commitments that ... all Americans feel about self-determination, about individual liberty, about national independence, and about progress for all people. This is what the United States stands for in the best sense. We are short of our goals, but it is where we are going...." Toasts of the President and President Nyerere of Tanganyika (July 16, 1963).

193. "[T]he United States stands for freedom, ... the promises in the Constitution and the Declaration of Independence [and] while they may not be fully achieved we are attempting to move to the best of our ability in that direction...." Remarks to Delegates to the 18th Annual American Legion "Boys Nation" (July 24, 1963).

194. "This country has become rich because nature was good to us, and because the people who came from Europe, predominantly, also were among the most vigorous. The basic resources were used skillfully and economically...." Address at the University of Wyoming (September 25, 1963).

195. "[T]he qualities that we seek in America, the qualities which we like to feel this country has, [are] courage, patience, faith, self-reliance, perseverance, and, above all, an unflagging determination to see the right prevail." Address in Salt Lake City at the Mormon Tabernacle (September 26, 1963).

196. "We cannot fulfill our vision and our commitment and our interest in a free and diverse future without unceasing vigilance, devotion, and, most of all, perseverance, a willingness to stay with it, a willingness to do with fatigue, a willingness not to accept easy answers, but instead, to maintain the burden ... until finally we live in a peaceful world." Address in Salt Lake City at the Mormon Tabernacle (September 26, 1963).

197. "Robert Frost, the late poet, once remarked, 'What makes a nation in the beginning is a good piece of geography.' Our greatness today rests in part on this good piece of geography that is the United States, but what is important is what the people of America do with it." Remarks at the Convention Center in Las Vegas, Nevada (September 28, 1963).

198. "Our national strength matters, but the spirit which informs and controls our strength matters just as much." Remarks at Amherst College Upon Receiving an Honorary Degree (October 26, 1963).

199. "A nation reveals itself not only by the men it produces but also by the men it honors, the men it remembers." Remarks at Amherst College Upon Receiving an Honorary Degree (October 26, 1963).

200. "The men who create power make an indispensable contribution to the Nation's greatness, but the men who question power make a contribution just as dispensable, especially when that questioning is disinterested, for they determine whether we use power or power uses us." Remarks at Amherst College Upon Receiving an Honorary Degree (October 26, 1963).

ARTS AND HUMANITIES

201. "I think it is most important not that we regard artistic achievement and action as a part of our armor in these difficult days, but rather as an integral part of our free society. We believe that an artist, in order to be true to himself and his work, must be a free man or woman...." Remarks of Welcome at the White House Concert by Pablo Casals (November 13, 1961).

202. "This [the creation of a national cultural center in Washington, D.C.] is a most important national responsibility, and I can assure you that if you will be willing to help, that this administration will give it every possible support." Remarks to the Trustees and Advisory Committee of the National Cultural Center (November 14, 1961).

203. "One of our great assets in this country are the talented boys and girls who devote their early lives to music, to appreciation of music, to an understanding of it. This is a great and I think vital force in American life. It is a part of American life which I think is somewhat unheralded around the world." Remarks at a White House Musical Program for Youth (April 16, 1962).

204. "[O]ne of the great myths of American life is that nothing is pleasanter or easier than lying around all day and painting a picture or writing a book and leading a rather easy life. In my opinion, the ultimate in self-discipline is a creative work. Those of us who work in an office every day are actually the real gentle livers of American society." Toasts of the President and Andre Malraux, French Minister for Cultural Affairs (May 11, 1962).

205. "We do not manage our cultural life in this country, nor does any free society, but it is an important part. It is one of the great purposes." Toasts of the President and Andre Malraux, French Minister for Cultural Affairs (May 11, 1962).

206. "I know that there is some feeling by Americans that the arts are developed in solitude, that they are developed by inspiration and by sudden fits of genius. But the fact of the matter is that success comes in music or in the arts like success comes in every other form of human endeavor by hard work, by discipline, over a long period of time." Remarks at the White House Concert by the National High School Symphony Orchestra (August 6, 1962).

207. "[M]ore Americans went to symphonies [in 1961] than went to baseball games. This may be viewed as an alarming statistic, but I think that both baseball and the country will endure and the country will be better off, perhaps, for it." Remarks at the White House Concert by the National High School Symphony Orchestra (August 6, 1962).

208. "[W]hen the National Cultural Center is finally built, it'll be possible for us to organize, I think, contests of groups from all parts of the country who can come to Washington, and then the winner can be selected and sent abroad with the support of the people of the United States through the United States Government." Remarks to the Members of the Schola Cantorum of the University of Arkansas (September 4, 1962).

209. "I think that too often we are, in a sense, as General de Gaulle has said, the daughter of Europe, and our view on these [artistic and cultural] matters which affect the life of the spirit really, looks more to Europe.... But I think in music, architecture, art, writing, all the rest, we've had a good deal of life and vitality in this country in recent years...." Remarks to Members of the First Inter-American Symposium (November 19, 1962).

210. "We don't want to see the artistic and intellectual life used as a weapon in a cold war struggle, but we do feel that it's an essential part of the whole democratic spirit." Remarks to Members of the First Inter-American Symposium (November 19, 1962).

211. "[O]ur culture and art do not speak to America alone. To the extent that artists struggle to express beauty in form and color and sound, to the extent that they write about man's struggle with nature or society, or himself, to that extent they strike a responsive chord in all humanity." Remarks at a Closed Circuit Television Broadcast on Behalf of the National Cultural Center (November 29, 1962).

212. "Genius can speak at any time, and the entire world will hear it and listen. Behind the storm of daily conflict and crisis ... the poet, the artist, the musician, continues the quiet work of centuries, building bridges of experience between peoples, reminding man of the universality of his feelings and desires and despairs, and reminding him that the forces that unite are deeper than those that divide." Remarks at a Closed Circuit Television Broadcast on Behalf of the National Cultural Center (November 29, 1962).

213. "[A]s a great democratic society, we have a special responsibility to the arts, for art is the great democrat calling forth creative genius from every sector of society, disregarding race or religion or wealth or color." Remarks at a Closed Circuit Television Broadcast on Behalf of the National Cultural Center (November 29, 1962).

214. "[I] am certain that after the dust of centuries has passed over our cities, we, too, will be remembered not for victories or defeats in battle or in politics, but for our contribution to the human spirit." Remarks at a Closed Circuit Television Broadcast on Behalf of the National Cultural Center (November 29, 1962).

215. "[W]e will continue to press ahead with the effort to develop an independent artistic force and power of our own." Remarks at the National Gallery of Art Upon Opening the Mona Lisa Exhibition (January 8, 1963).

216. "[I]t essential that this [National] Cultural Center be finished. Every major capital in the world, and a good many capitals of States ... ha[ve] a center which demonstrates the performing arts, serves as the place for exhibiting the finest in the Nation's cultural life. Washington does not have one and I think this country suffers not only in the minds of our own people, but I think in the general impression of this society of ours as being one that is [not] interested in many forms of human activity. I think if we can build this Center it will be a very good thing for this country." Remarks Upon Signing Bill to Amend the National Cultural Center Act (August 19, 1963).

217. "When power leads man towards arrogance, poetry reminds him of his limitations. When power narrows the areas of man's concern, poetry reminds him of the richness and diversity of his existence. When power corrupts, poetry cleanses. For art establishes the basic human truth which must serve as the touchstone of our judgment." Remarks at Amherst College Upon Receiving an Honorary Degree (October 26, 1963).

218. "The artist, however faithful to his personal vision of reality, becomes the last champion of the individual mind and sensibility against an intrusive society and an officious state. The great artist is thus a solitary figure.... In pursuing his perceptions of reality, he must often sail against the currents of his time. This is not a popular role." Remarks at Amherst College Upon Receiving an Honorary Degree (October 26, 1963).

219. "If sometimes our great artists have been the most critical of our society, it is because their sensitivity and their concern for justice, which must motivate any true artist, makes him aware that our Nation fa[lls] short of its highest potential. I see little of more importance to the future of our country and our civilization than full recognition of the place of the artist." Remarks at Amherst College Upon Receiving an Honorary Degree (October 26, 1963).

220. "If art is to nourish the roots of our culture, society must set the artist free to follow his vision wherever it takes him. We must never forget that art is not a form of propaganda; it is a form of truth.... In free society art is not a weapon and it does not belong to the sphere of polemics and ideology. Artists are not engineers of the soul. It may be different elsewhere. But [in a] democratic society ... the highest duty of the writer, the composer, the artist is to remain true to himself and to let the chips fall where they may." Remarks at Amherst College Upon Receiving an Honorary Degree (October 26, 1963).

221. "I look forward to an America which will not be afraid of grace and beauty.... I look forward to an America which will reward achievement in the arts as we reward achievement in business or statecraft. I look forward to an America which will steadily raise the standards of artistic accomplishment and which will steadily enlarge cultural opportunities for all of our citizens." Remarks at Amherst College Upon Receiving an Honorary Degree (October 26, 1963).

222. "[In a] democratic society — in it, the highest duty of the writer, the composer, the artist is to remain true to himself.... In serving his vision of the truth, the artist best serves his nation. And the nation which disdains the mission of art invites the fate of Robert Frost's hired man, the fate of having 'nothing to look backward to with pride, and nothing to look forward to with hope.'" Remarks at Amherst College Upon Receiving an Honorary Degree (October 26, 1963).

BERLIN

223. "Berlin is a small island of free men in the midst of communist territory. A hundred manned and fortified miles separate it from the western frontier.... Its only protection against aggression is a small garrison of NATO troops constantly menaced by vast Russian land forces. It has been the object of vicious threats — of hostile moves.... But despite all dangers and hardships, Berlin has sustained its freedom and rebuilt its economy. Its assets have been the courage and vitality of its people, reinforced by our own determination that Berlin shall — and must — remain free." Remarks of Senator John F. Kennedy, University of Wisconsin, Milwaukee, Wisconsin (March 24, 1960).

224. "[B]erlin is more than a symbol of personal liberty. It is a living contradiction of the Soviet dogma that only a communist society can bring material prosperity. [T]he people of East Berlin ... and all of Eastern Europe, can look up from their bare, drab, toilsome existence and see in their midst the buoyant, vital, expanding economy of West Berlin ... the new surge of energy which has rebuilt a war-torn city and restored prosperity to its people. Probably no other city in the world represents a greater challenge to Russian dogma. And the Russians know it." Remarks of Senator John F. Kennedy, University of Wisconsin, Milwaukee, Wisconsin (March 24, 1960).

225. "[B]erlin is important as a symbol — as perhaps the chief symbol of the free world's determination not to yield to Russian threats and Russian pressure. Thomas Paine wrote that 'every man must finally see the necessity of protecting the rights of others as the most effectual security of his own.' The protection of the freedom of Berlin is the surest protection of our own freedom." Remarks of Senator John F. Kennedy, University of Wisconsin, Milwaukee, Wisconsin (March 24, 1960).

226. "[A] solution to the problems of that beleaguered city [Berlin] is only possible in the context of a solution of the problems of Germany and, indeed, the problems of all Europe. We must look forward to a free Berlin, in a United Germany in a Europe where tensions and armaments have been reduced...." Remarks of Senator John F. Kennedy, U.S. Senate (June 14, 1960).

227. "[T]he security of Western Europe and therefore our own security are deeply involved in our presence and our access rights to West Berlin

... [that] are based on law and not on sufferance.... [W]e are determined to maintain those rights at any risk, and thus meet our obligation to the people of West Berlin, and their right to choose their own future." Radio and Television Report to the American People on Returning from Europe (June 6, 1961).

228. "We are there [in West Berlin] as a result of our victory over Nazi Germany — and our basic rights to be there, deriving from that victory, include both our presence in West Berlin and the enjoyment of access across East Germany.... [O]ur presence in West Berlin, and our access thereto, cannot be ended by any act of the Soviet government. The NATO shield was long ago extended to cover West Berlin — and we have given our word that an attack upon that city will be regarded as an attack upon us all." Radio and Television Report to the American People on the Berlin Crisis (July 25, 1961).

229. "West Berlin is ... the great testing place of Western courage...." Radio and Television Report to the American People on the Berlin Crisis (July 25, 1961).

230. "[T]he freedom of [West Berlin] is not negotiable. We cannot negotiate with those who say 'What's mine is mine and what's yours is negotiable.'" Radio and Television Report to the American People on the Berlin Crisis (July 25, 1961).

231. "We do not want to fight — but we have fought before. [O]thers in earlier times have made the same dangerous mistake of assuming that the West was too selfish and too soft and too divided to resist invasions of freedom in other lands. Those who threaten to unleash the forces of war on a dispute over West Berlin should recall the words of the ancient philosopher: 'A man who causes fear cannot be free from fear.'" Radio and Television Report to the American People on the Berlin Crisis (July 25, 1961).

232. "[T]he choice of peace or war is largely theirs, not ours. It is the Soviets who have stirred up this crisis. It is they who are trying to force a change. It is they who have opposed free elections.... And as Americans know from our history on our own old frontier, gun battles are caused by outlaws, and not by officers of the peace. In short, while we are ready to defend our interests, we shall also be ready to search for peace.... We do not want military considerations to dominate the thinking of either East or West." Radio and Television Report to the American People on the Berlin Crisis (July 25, 1961).

233. "I hear it said that West Berlin is militarily untenable. And so was Bastogne. And so, in fact, was Stalingrad. Any dangerous spot is tenable if men — brave men — will make it so." Radio and Television Report to the American People on the Berlin Crisis (July 25, 1961).

234. "To sum it all up: we seek peace — but we shall not surrender. That is the central meaning of this [Berlin] crisis, and the meaning of your government's policy." Radio and Television Report to the American People on the Berlin Crisis (July 25, 1961).

235. "[O]ur presence in Berlin ... and the freedom of two million West Berliners [are] not [to] be surrendered either to force or through appeasement — and to maintain those rights and obligations, we [the United States and its NATO allies] are prepared to talk, when appropriate, and to fight, if necessary." Annual Message to the Congress on the State of the Union (January 11, 1962).

236. "The wall in Berlin, to lock people in, I believe is the obvious manifestation, which can be demonstrated all over the world, of the superiority of our system." Address at Miami Beach at a Fundraising Dinner in Honor of Senator Smathers (March 10, 1962).

237. "So long as our [military] presence [in West Germany] is desired and required, our forces and commitments will remain. For your safety is our safety, your liberty is our liberty, and any attack on your soil is an attack upon our own. Out of necessity, as well as sentiment, in our approach to peace as well as war, our fortunes are one." Remarks Upon Arrival in Germany (June 23, 1963).

238. "Europe can never be complete until everywhere in Europe, and that includes Germany, men can choose, in peace and freedom, how their countries shall be governed, and choose — without threat to any neighbor — reunification with their countrymen." Address in the Assembly Hall at the Paulskirche in Frankfurt [Germany] (June 25, 1963).

239. "The shield of the military commitment with which we, in association with two other great powers, guard the freedom of West Berlin will not be lowered or put aside so long as its presence is needed." Address at the Free University of Berlin [Germany] (June 26, 1963).

240. "What will count in the long run are the realities of Western strength, the realities of Western commitment, the realities of Germany as a nation and a people, without regard to artificial boundaries of barbed wire. Those are the realities upon which we rely and on which history will move...." Address at the Free University of Berlin [Germany] (June 26, 1963).

BUDGETARY AND FISCAL POLICIES

Deficits

241. "What nation's budget is balanced if its forests go to ruin, if its water becomes contaminated, if its mines lie idle, if its rich soil blows away as dust, if its older people and its native Indians suffer indefensible privation, if its homeowners and small businessmen are caught in the frustrating squeeze of a high-interest and tight-money economy? This is bad business and bad budgeting and bad for the country." Remarks of Senator John F. Kennedy, Phoenix, Arizona (April 9, 1960).

242. "[T]he budget should normally be balanced. The exception apart from a serious or extraordinary threat to the national security is serious unemployment. In boom times we should run a surplus and retire the debt. When men ... are unemployed in serious numbers, the opposite policies are in order. We should seek a balanced budget over the course of the business cycle with surpluses during good times more than offsetting the deficits which may be incurred during slumps." Speech by Senator John F. Kennedy at the Associated Business Publications Conference, Biltmore Hotel, New York, New York (October 12, 1960).

243. "A long-term deficit requires long-term solutions, and we must not be panicked by setbacks of a short-run nature." Address in New York City to the National Association of Manufacturers (December 6, 1961).

244. "The myth persists that Federal deficits create inflation and budget surpluses prevent it.... Obviously deficits are sometimes dangerous — and so are surpluses. But honest assessment plainly requires a more sophisticated view than the old and automatic cliché that deficits automatically bring inflation." Commencement Address at Yale University (June 11, 1962).

245. "[In the area of] fiscal policy ... the myths are legion and the truth hard to find. [A] prime example [is] the problem of the Federal budget. We persist in measuring our federal fiscal integrity today by the conventional or administrative budget — with results which would be regarded as absurd in any business firm ... or in any careful assessment of the reality of our national finances. The administrative budget has sound administrative uses. But for wider purposes it is less helpful.... [It] ... is not simply irrelevant; it can be actively misleading." Commencement Address at Yale University (June 11, 1962).

246. "There are myths also about our public debt. It is widely supposed that this debt is growing at a dangerously rapid rate ... [but] debts, public and private, are neither good nor bad, in and of themselves. Borrowing can lead to over-extension and collapse — but it can also lead to expansion and strength. There is no single, simple slogan ... that we can trust." Commencement Address at Yale University (June 11, 1962).

247. "A transitional Federal deficit ... as a result of a tax cut, reflects a prudent investment in this Nation's future growth, but [a] chronic [deficit] produced by a lagging economy ... would surely increase the real burden of any debt and set back ... future growth." Remarks and Question and Answer Period at the American Bankers Association Symposium on Economic Growth (February 25, 1963).

248. "[A] debt, prudently undertaken, for gainful purposes, by one whose income is capable of carrying it, can greatly strengthen the debtor." Remarks and Question and Answer Period at the American Bankers Association Symposium on Economic Growth (February 25, 1963).

249. "[W]hen private demands are insufficient ... we can enlarge our Federal spending or we can reduce taxes in order to enlarge private spending. If a Federal deficit results ... or if an existing deficit is increased by it, that deficit is not some new additional factor; it is simply the reflection, although not the purpose, of our revenue and expenditure policies." Address and Question and Answer Period at the 20th Anniversary Meeting of the Committee for Economic Development (May 9, 1963).

250. "The popular fear of deficits arises from the fact that what is sound policy at one time can be unsound policy at another.... [B]ecause a government can be fiscally irresponsible by running a deficit under one set of conditions does not make it fiscally responsible to avoid all deficits under wholly different conditions." Address and Question and Answer Period at the 20th Anniversary Meeting of the Committee for Economic Development (May 9, 1963).

251. "Prosperity is the real way to balance our budget." Radio and Television Address to the Nation on the Test Ban Treaty and the Tax Reduction Bill (September 18, 1963).

252. "A full employment economy is the only way to balance the budget. A recession-ridden economy ... on the other hand, is a guarantee of chronic, higher deficits and continually deeper debt." Address and Question and Answer Period in Tampa Before the Florida Chamber of Commerce (November 18, 1963).

Monetary Policy

253. "[T]ight money is a real disaster. It is the worst possible policy for our financial resources. They are harder to find. They are more expensive to use. The large corporation has plenty of its own capital ... [b]ut the small businessman or homeowner or farmer — the man who has to borrow before he can expand, and already finds every cost is at a record high — is caught in the squeeze: dollars are harder and more expensive to get, and go a lot less further once you get them." Remarks of Senator John F. Kennedy, Phoenix, Arizona (April 9, 1960).

254. "I would never want us in the position of being forced to tinker with the dollar in order to maintain our competitive position in the world export market." Speech by Senator John F. Kennedy at the Associated Business Publications Conference, Biltmore Hotel, New York, New York (October 12, 1960).

255. "[W]e must have a flexible, balanced and, above all, coordinated monetary and fiscal policy. I do not, let me make clear, advocate any changes in the constitution of the Federal Reserve System. It is important to keep the day-to-day operations of the Federal Reserve removed from political pressures. The President's responsibility — if he is to lead — includes longer range coordination an a direction of economic policies, subject to our system of checks and balances. And I believe the Federal Reserve Board ... would also cooperate with future strong and well considered Presidential leadership which expresses the responsible will of Congress and the people." Speech by Senator John F. Kennedy at the Associated Business Publications Conference, Biltmore Hotel, New York, New York (October 12, 1960).

256. "[W]e Democrats do not intend to devalue the dollar from its present rate. We will defend its value and its soundness. [W]e will seek a balanced budget over the years ... seeking a budget surplus in good years as a brake on inflation [and] ... we will place less reliance on a high interest rate policy which discourages investment...." Remarks of Senator John F. Kennedy, Airport Rally, Roanoke, Virginia (November 4, 1960).

257. "[O]ne of the contributions to maintaining the stability of the dollar [is] ... a budget which is in balance...." Remarks at the Conference Opening the 1962 Savings Bond Campaign (January 19, 1961).

258. "[W]hatever is required will be done to ... make certain that, in the future as in the past, the dollar is as 'sound as a dollar.'" Annual Message to the Congress on the State of the Union (January 30, 1961).

259. "This Administration will not distort the value of the dollar in any fashion. And this is a commitment." Annual Message to the Congress on the State of the Union (January 30, 1961).

260. "[T]he problems of fiscal and monetary policies ... demand subtle challenges for which technical answers, not political answers, must be provided." Commencement Address at Yale University (June 11, 1962).

261. "We in the United States feel no need to be self-conscious in discussing the dollar. It is not only our national currency; it is an international currency. It plays a key role in the day-to-day functioning of the free world's financial framework. It is the most effective substitute for gold in the international payments system. If the dollar did not exist as a reserve currency, it would have to be invented...." Remarks to the Board of Governors of the World Bank and the International Monetary Fund (September 20, 1962).

262. "Indeed there is no field in which the wider interest of all more clearly outweighs the narrow interest of one [than in monetary policy]. We have lived by that principle, as bankers to freedom, for a generation. Now that other nations ... have found new economic strength, it is time for common efforts here, too. The great free nations of the world must take control of our monetary problems if those problems are not to take control of us." Address in the Assembly Hall at the Paulskirche in Frankfurt [Germany] (June 25, 1963).

263. "We are determined to do whatever must be done in the interest of this country and, indeed, in the interest of all, to protect the dollar as a convertible currency at its present fixed rate." Address at the Meeting of the International Monetary Fund (September 30, 1963).

264. "The fiscal and monetary policies which we have followed ... were [not] taken for the benefit of business alone. They were taken to benefit the country. Some of them were labeled pro-business, some of them were labeled anti-business, some of them were labeled both by opposing groups. But that kind of label is meaningless. This administration is 'pro' the public interest." Address and Question and Answer Period in Tampa Before the Florida Chamber of Commerce (November 18, 1963).

Spending

265. "[M]istakes have been made ... money has been wasted.... It is difficult to spend the people's money in an effective way, always wisely ... and we find errors ... in many sections of governmental spending in the past.... It's done every day in the military establishment, in the White House, in the Congress. There is waste.... What we've got to do is to try to make sure that there is as little waste as possible...." Remarks at the Eighth National Conference on International Economic and Social Development (June 16, 1961).

266. "The government must not be demanding more from the savings of the country, nor draining more from the available supplies of credit, when the national interest demands a priority for productive, creative investment...." Address in New York City to the National Association of Manufacturers (December 6, 1961).

267. "[E]ach sector ... of activity must be approached on its own merits and in terms of specific national needs. Generalities in regard to federal expenditures, therefore, can be misleading—each case, science, urban renewal, education, agriculture, natural resources, each case must be determined on its merits if we are to profit from our unrivaled ability to combine the strength of public and private purpose." Commencement Address at Yale University (June 11, 1962).

268. "If Government is to retain the confidence of the people, it must not spend more than can be justified on grounds of national need or spent with maximum efficiency." Address and Question and Answer Period at the Economic Club of New York (December 14, 1962).

Taxation

269. "I don't know any other society which attempts what this country attempts to do [administer an essentially voluntary tax collection system], which requires really the good will and support of the citizens of the United States in contributing a large share of their income to the maintenance of the American society." Remarks to the Joint Conference of Regional Commissioners and District Directors of the Internal Revenue Service (May 1, 1961).

270. "I hope that ... we will continue to work so that the burdens of the tax system become as fairly distributed as possible, so that they are distributed in a way which stimulates our economy and stimulates our growth to the extent that is possible, and not retards it." Remarks to the Joint Conference of Regional Commissioners and District Directors of the Internal Revenue Service (May 1, 1961).

271. "We need ... presidential standby authority, subject to congressional veto, to adjust personal income tax rates downward within a specified range and time, to slow down an economic decline before it has dragged us all down...." Annual Message to the Congress on the State of the Union (January 11, 1962).

272. "The single most important fiscal weapon available to strengthen the national economy is the federal tax policy. The right kind of tax cut at the right time is the most effective measure that this Government could take to spur our economy forward." Radio and Television Report to the American People on the State of the National Economy (August 13, 1962).

273. "Every dollar released from taxation that is spent or invested will help create a new job and a new salary. And these new jobs and new salaries can create other jobs and other salaries and more customers and more growth for an expanding American economy." Radio and Television Report to the American People on the State of the National Economy (August 13, 1962).

274. "[L]ightening tax burdens as the [European] Common Market countries have done so successfully ... will improve the competitive position of American business, encourage investment at home instead of abroad, and improve our balance of payments and will help make us all — individuals and as a nation — help us make the most of our economic resources." Radio and Television Report to the American People on the State of the National Economy (August 13, 1962).

275. "[T]his administration intends to cut taxes in order to build the fundamental strength of our economy [in order] ... to prevent the even greater budget deficit that a lagging economy would otherwise surely produce. The worst deficit comes from a recession...." Radio and Television Report to the American People on the State of the National Economy (August 13, 1962).

276. "[T]he present patchwork of special [tax] provisions and preferences lightens the tax load of some only at the cost of placing a heavier burden on others. It distorts economic judgments and channels an undue amount of energy into efforts to avoid tax liabilities. It makes certain types of less productive activity more profitable than other more valuable undertakings. All this inhibits our growth and efficiency...." Address and Question and Answer Period at the Economic Club of New York (December 14, 1962).

277. "There are a number of ways by which the Federal Government can meet its responsibilities to aid economic growth.... But the most direct and significant kind of Federal action aiding economic growth ... is to reduce the burden on private income and the deterrents to private initiative which are imposed by our present tax system...." Address and Question and Answer Period at the Economic Club of New York (December 14, 1962).

278. "[I]t is a paradoxical truth that tax rates are too high today and tax revenues are too low and the soundest way to raise the revenues in the long run is to cut the rates now.... [O]nly full employment can balance the budget, and tax reduction can pave the way to that employment. The purpose of cutting taxes now is not to incur a budget deficit, but to achieve the more prosperous, expanding economy which can bring a budget surplus." Address and Question and Answer Period at the Economic Club of New York (December 14, 1962).

279. "[O]ur practical choice is not between a tax-cut deficit and a budgetary surplus. It is between two kinds of deficits: a chronic deficit of inertia, as the unwanted result of inadequate revenues and a restricted economy; or a temporary deficit of transition, resulting from a tax cut designed to boost the economy, increase tax revenues, and achieve — and I believe this can be done — a budget surplus. The first type of deficit is a sign of waste and weakness; the second reflects an investment in the future." Address and Question and Answer Period at the Economic Club of New York (December 14, 1962).

280. "It is increasingly clear that ... so long as our national security needs keep rising, an economy hampered by restrictive tax rates will never produce enough revenue to balance our budget just as it will never produce enough jobs or enough profits." Address and Question and Answer Period at the Economic Club of New York (December 14, 1962).

281. "[I]t is increasingly clear — to those ... who are responsible for our economy's success — that our obsolete tax system exerts too heavy a drag on private purchasing power, profits, and employment. Designed to check inflation in earlier years, it now checks growth instead. It discourages extra effort and risk. It distorts the use of resources. It invites recurrent recessions, depresses our Federal revenues, and causes chronic budget deficits.... [N]ow is the time to act. We cannot afford to be timid or slow." Annual Message to the Congress on the State of the Union (January 14, 1963).

282. "[A] temporary tax cut could provide a spur to our economy — but a long run problem compels a long-run solution." Annual Message to the Congress on the State of the Union (January 14, 1963).

283. "Tax reduction[s] [can] not be passed if each group continues to treat growth as a crop to be divided, or if each group examines what is available through the wrong end of the telescope. [I]f the low-income man looks at the dollar amounts of the cut, he will decide the rich are getting all the breaks, and if the high income looks at the percentage cuts, he will decide the opposite. Meanwhile, those in the middle, hearing all this, will be convinced that they will get less than either the rich or the poor." Remarks and Question and Answer Period at the American Bankers Association Symposium on Economic Growth (February 25, 1963).

284. "[T]he businessman's greatest need is new market demand, and the wage earner's greatest need is expanding business activity. The Nation's greatest need is a tax bill that [by lowering taxes] will help fulfill both of these objectives." Remarks and Question and Answer Period at the American Bankers Association Symposium on Economic Growth (February 25, 1963).

285. "We are attempting to do something new, and that is to talk about a tax cut at a time when we have a deficit ... [and] ... we are trying to do [it] because it is important [to economic growth.]" Address Before the 19th Washington Conference of the Advertising Council (March 13, 1963).

286. "We all praise tax reduction because it 'releases' money into the private sector — but so do Federal expenditures.... To cut a dollar of expenditures for every dollar of taxes cut would be to remove with one hand the stimulus we give with the other." Remarks and Question and Answer Period Before the American Society of Newspaper Editors (April 19, 1963).

287. "The tax policy of the Federal Government can either stimulate or retard the economy...." Remarks to the National Advisory Council of the Small Business Administration (May 16, 1963).

288. "[A] [t]ax reduction is essential to ... increasing our productivity and our competitive ability, [to] increasing the attractiveness of investing at home instead of abroad, [and to] help[ing] us improve our balance of payments. By expanding consumption and investment it will help us create more jobs. By removing a restrictive brake on national growth and income, it will work against the recurrent forces of recession. And by reducing the costly drain of unemployment and recession, while expanding our national income and tax revenues, it will, combined with an ever stricter control of expenditures, reduce and eventually end the pattern of chronic budgetary deficits." Remarks at the National Conference of the Business Committee for Tax Reduction in 1963 (September 10, 1963).

289. "[W]ithout a quick and assured tax cut this country can look forward to more unemployment, to more lags in income, to larger budget deficits, and to more waste and weakness in economy, and that, in my opinion, is real fiscal irresponsibility." Remarks at the National Conference of the Business Committee for Tax Reduction in 1963 (September 10, 1963).

290. "[H]igh [tax] rates do not leave enough money in private hands to keep this country's economy growing and healthy. They have helped to cause recessions in previous years ... and unless they are reduced, they can cause recessions again." Radio and Television Address to the Nation on the Test Ban Treaty and the Tax Reduction Bill (September 18, 1963).

291. "[A] tax cut means ... a balanced Federal budget [because] as the national income grows, the Federal Government will ultimately end up with more revenues." Radio and Television Address to the Nation on the Test Ban Treaty and the Tax Reduction Bill (September 18, 1963).

292. "A tax cut can help us balance our international accounts and end the outflow of gold by helping make the American economy more efficient and more productive and more competitive, by enabling our goods to compete with those who are developing foreign factories, and by making investment in America more attractive than investment abroad." Radio and Television Address to the Nation on the Test Ban Treaty and the Tax Reduction Bill (September 18, 1963).

293. "This Nation needs a tax cut now, not a tax cut if and when, but a tax cut now, and for the future. This Nation needs a tax cut now that will benefit every family, every business, in every part of the Nation." Radio and Television Address to the Nation on the Test Ban Treaty and the Tax Reduction Bill (September 18, 1963).

294. "Recessions are not inevitable ... and I believe that some day in this country we can wipe them out. We already have the ability to reduce their frequency, their importance, and their duration, and this tax cut is the single most important weapon that we can now add." Radio and Television Address to the Nation on the Test Ban Treaty and the Tax Reduction Bill (September 18, 1963).

295. "[O]ur tax reduction and reform program ... can ... improve our long-range position ... help attract capital investment, improve our ability to sell goods and services in world markets, stimulate the growth of our economy and the employment of our people, give greater freedom to monetary policy, and play a vital supporting role in our determination to achieve equal rights and opportunities for all of our citizens." Address at the Meeting of the International Monetary Fund (September 30, 1963).

296. "If jobs are the most important domestic issue that this country faces, then clearly no single step can now be more important in sustaining the economy of the United States than the passage of our tax bill. [I]t ... will help consumer markets and build investment demand and build business incentives and, therefore, provide jobs ... to the economy of the United States...." Remarks in New York City at the AFL-CIO Convention (November 15, 1963).

BUSINESS

297. "[W]e must enforce our nation's anti-trust laws with more vigor. Small business is constantly threatened by the tendency toward concentration and merger now visible in every area of our economy. Only by forceful and dynamic anti-trust action will we be able to preserve the American tradition of free competition." Remarks of Senator John F. Kennedy, Chamber of Commerce Luncheon, North Clackamas, Oregon (April 22, 1960).

298. "One of the great challenges of the sixties will be to ... strengthen the small independent businessman against the large business units which threaten to crowd him from the American economic scene — and to ... [protect] this historic cornerstone of our free enterprise system." Remarks of Senator John F. Kennedy, Weirton, West Virginia (May 1, 1960).

299. "It is true that much defense work can only be done by large, well-equipped plants. But ... much of the production and services now supplied by giant firms could easily be handled by the nation's independent businessmen. Our government spending should — and must — be directed toward preserving individual enterprise — not toward strengthening large firms at the expense of all others." Remarks of Senator John F. Kennedy, Weirton, West Virginia (May 1, 1960).

300. "Small business is constantly threatened by the tendency toward concentration and merger.... Only by forceful and dynamic anti-trust action will we be able to preserve the American tradition of free competition which the anti-trust laws were intended to preserve." Remarks of Senator John F. Kennedy, Weirton, West Virginia (May 1, 1960).

301. "[T]he real spirit of American business is not represented by those involved in price-fixing, conflict-of-interest, or collusion. The real spirit is in [businesses'] recognition of [its] public responsibilities, [its] pursuit of the truth, [its] desire for better industrial relations, better technological progress, and better price stability and economic growth." Address at a Luncheon Meeting of the National Industrial Conference Board (February 13, 1961).

302. "The complaint has often been made ... that the Federal Government is a 'silent partner' in every corporation — taking roughly half of all of [a business's] ... net earnings without risk to itself. But it should be also realized that this makes business a not always 'silent partner' of the Federal Government — that our revenues and thus our success are dependent upon [business] ... profits and ... success — and that, far from being natural enemies, Government and business are necessary allies." Address at a Luncheon Meeting of the National Industrial Conference Board (February 13, 1961).

303. "[T]here is no inevitable clash between the public and the private sectors — or between investment and consumption — nor ... between Government and business. All elements in our national economic growth are interdependent. Each must play its proper role...." Address at a Luncheon Meeting of the National Industrial Conference Board (February 13, 1961).

304. "When business does well in this country, we have full employment, and this country is moving ahead, then it strengthens our image as a prosperous and vital country in this great fight in which we are engaged. When [business] ... do[es] well, the United States does well, and our policies abroad do well. And when [business] ... do[es] badly, all suffer." Address in New York City to the National Association of Manufacturers (December 6, 1961).

305. "[America cannot] maintain the kind of high employment which we must maintain, unless you [American businesses] are making profits, and reinvesting, and producing; and therefore as we are committed to the goal ... of trying to make sure that everyone who wants a job will find it, then quite obviously we must make the system work, and the business community must prosper." Address in New York City to the National Association of Manufacturers (December 6, 1961).

306. "Our domestic programs call for substantial increases in employment, but it is business, not Government, who must actually perform these jobs.... [W]e ... recognize that beneath all the laws and guidelines and tax policies and stimulants we can provide, these matters all come down, quite properly in the last analysis, to private decision by private individuals." Address Before the United States Chamber of Commerce on Its 50th Anniversary (April 30, 1962).

307. "It is easy to charge an administration is anti-business, but it is more difficult to show how an administration, composed we hope of rational men, can possibly feel they can survive without business, or how the Nation can survive unless the Government and business and all other groups in our country are exerting their best efforts in an atmosphere of understanding — and I hope cooperation." Address Before the United States Chamber of Commerce on Its 50th Anniversary (April 30, 1962).

308. "Corporate plans are not based on a political confidence in party leaders, but on an economic confidence in the Nation's ability to invest and produce and consume." Commencement Address at Yale University (June 11, 1962).

309. "I would like to see this country's small businessmen improve and expand and not have the control over economic life in either the hands of the Government or a few larger groups." Remarks to the National Advisory Council of the Small Business Administration (May 16, 1963).

310. "Many businessmen, who are prospering as never before during this administration, are convinced nevertheless that we must be anti-business ... that a Democratic administration is out to soak the rich, increase controls for the sake of controls, and extend at all costs the scope of the Federal bureaucracy. The hard facts contradict these doubts. This administration is interested in the healthy expansion of the entire economy ... [a] program, in my opinion, in which American business has the largest stake." Address and Question and Answer Period in Tampa Before the Florida Chamber of Commerce (November 18, 1963).

CIVIC DUTY

311. "We want from you [high school students] not the sneers of the cynics or the despair of the faint-hearted. We ask of you enlightenment, vision, illumination." Remarks of Senator John F. Kennedy, Convocation of Marshall County Junior and Senior High School, Plymouth, Indiana (April 8, 1960).

312. "All of us value our country, all of us wish to serve it, all of us wish to preserve it." Remarks of Senator John F. Kennedy, Steer Roast, Euclid Beach Park, Cleveland, Ohio (September 25, 1960).

313. "I believe that the unfinished business of this society is to begin this country on the upward go, for every citizen to be willing to devote his time and his energy to the service of this country." Speech by Senator John F. Kennedy, Southern Illinois University Stadium, Carbondale, Illinois (October 3, 1960).

314. "All of us [veterans] who are here today ... must also recognize that our obligations and our service to our country were not passed by military service in time of war. We also must serve our country in time of peace." Remarks of Senator John F. Kennedy, Veteran's Hospital, Marion, Illinois (October 3, 1960).

315. "During the war between the Spartans and the Persians, and after 300 Spartans were wiped out at Thermopylae, they carved a sign in the rock which said, 'Passerby, tell Sparta we fell faithful to her service.' Now, in 1960, and in the sixties, we are asked to live in the service of this country. We are asked to contribute to it. We are asked to build a stronger and better society...." Remarks of Senator John F. Kennedy, Evansville, Indiana (October 4, 1960).

316. "We want students and graduates to recognize that ... [America's] college[s] ... have not been built up, have not been developed, merely to advance the private economic interest of its graduates. They have a greater purpose in mind. No college graduate can go out from any college today without being a man of his Nation and a man of his time, without pursuing in his own life, not only his private interest, but the welfare of his country." Remarks of Senator John F. Kennedy, University of Kentucky, Lexington, Kentucky (October 8, 1960).

317. "I believe all of us recognize now in a free society that we are all politicians, in a sense we are all officeholders, in a sense we all bear part of the burden of maintaining free government." Remarks of Senator John F. Kennedy, Albion, Michigan (October 14, 1960).

318. "All of us are involved in the discipline of self-government. All of us in this country, in a sense, are officeholders. All of us make an important decision as to what this country must be and how it must move and what its function shall be, and what its image shall be, and whether it shall stand still ... or whether it shall once again move forward." Speech by Senator John F. Kennedy, Wittenburg College Stadium, Springfield, Ohio (October 17, 1960).

319. "[When I am talking to students] I am confident I am talking to the future rulers of America in the sense that all educated citizens participate in government...." Speech of Senator John F. Kennedy, Wittenburg College Stadium, Springfield, Ohio (October 17, 1960).

320. "Political action is the highest responsibility of a citizen. I hold the view that any American in these times should be willing to accept the discipline of political action." Remarks of Senator John F. Kennedy, Pat Clancy Dinner, Astor Hotel, New York, New York (October 20, 1960).

321. "[I] hold the view that we wish to serve our country, that it deserves the best from us...." Remarks of Senator John F. Kennedy, Courthouse Rally, Peoria, Illinois (October 24, 1960).

322. "[T]he most sober function of a citizen of a free country ... is the selection of a President of the United States." Remarks of Senator John F. Kennedy, Upper Darby, Pennsylvania (October 29, 1960).

323. "[Expressing] your judgment as responsible citizens about where our country is now, where it must be, what it must do, what your vision is of its future ... is the most solemn and sober responsibility that a citizen of this great Republic has, and you must exercise it." Speech by Senator John F. Kennedy, Convention Hall, Philadelphia, Pennsylvania (October 31, 1960).

324. "If we are not willing to look life in the eye, if we are not willing to measure our needs against our performance, then of course we will follow the fate which other free people have followed in the last 2,000 years when they come face to face with hard tests. I want to be sure that we meet that test. [I] want to be sure that we meet it by recognizing it, by being willing to meet our responsibilities as citizens of this country." Speech by Senator John F. Kennedy, Commack Arena, Commack, Long Island, New York (November 6, 1960).

325. "And so, my fellow Americans: ask not what your country can do for you — ask what you can do for your country." Inaugural Address (January 20, 1961).

326. "[I] can assure you that we love our country, not for what it was, though it has always been great — not for what it is, though of this we are deeply proud — but for what it some day can and, through the efforts of us all, some day will be." Address at a Luncheon Meeting of the National Industrial Conference Board (February 13, 1961).

327. "Was John Milton to conjugate Greek verbs in his library when the liberty of Englishmen was imperiled? No, quite obviously, the duty of the educated man or woman, the duty of the scholar, is to give his objective sense, his sense of liberty to the maintenance of our society at a critical time." Remarks at George Washington University Upon Receiving an Honorary Degree (May 3, 1961).

328. "[T]he history of this nation is a tribute to the ability of an informed citizenry to make the right choices in response to danger...." Address at the 39th Annual Convention of the National Association of Broadcasters (May 8, 1961).

329. "[E]ach citizen should be concerned not with what his country can do for him, but what he can do for his country." Remarks at Annapolis to the Graduating Class of the United States Naval Academy (June 7, 1961).

330. "[P]rivate citizens, regardless of their committed points of view, can, and sometimes do, dedicate themselves to work in the public interest." Remarks to the Members of the Commission on Money and Credit (June 19, 1961).

331. "All of us, I know, love our country, and we shall all do our best to serve it." Radio and Television Report to the American People on the Berlin Crisis (July 25, 1961).

332. "This is a free society and a free economy, and we do believe that freedom and ... progress is best served by permitting people to advance their private interests.... But I don't think that there's any American who would ... feel that the public interest is served alone by serving one's private interest. I think all of us have a public obligation, all of us owe some of our lives and some of our effort to the advancement of the interests of our society...." Remarks at the 18th Annual Washington Conference of the Advertising Council (March 7, 1962).

333. "Two thousand years ago the proudest boast was to say, 'I am a citizen of Rome.' Today, I believe, in 1962 the proudest boast is to say, 'I am a citizen of the United States.' And it is not enough to merely say it; we must live it." Remarks in New Orleans at a Civic Reception (May 4, 1962).

334. "There is nothing more unfortunate than someone who says he is a citizen of the United States, the greatest democracy in the world, and can't take the trouble to register [to vote]. There are people in this country who've been shot because they've tried to register. We want every citizen of this State to register and we want them to come and vote." Remarks at the Municipal Mall in Flint, Michigan (October 6, 1962).

335. "This is a great inheritance. It is a proud privilege to be a citizen of the Great Republic, to hear its songs sung, to realize that we are the descendants of 40 million people who left other countries, other familiar scenes, to come here to the United States to build a new life, to make a new opportunity for themselves and their children." Remarks at the 50th Annual Meeting of the Anti-Defamation League of B'nai B'rith (January 31, 1963).

336. "[E]very American, in addition to pursuing his own private interests, owes an obligation to maintain this free country of ours." Remarks to Participants in the Senate Youth Program (February 1, 1963).

337. "I hope that you will decide to give some of your life to public service, that some of you will run for office, that others of you will work in the Peace Corps, that others of you will work in your own home towns and decide that every American, in addition to pursuing his own private interests, owes an obligation to maintain this free country of ours. This is a free society. You can do it whether you want to or not, but I hope you decide to serve the United States in its great years." Remarks to Participants in the Senate Youth Program (February 1, 1963).

338. "[O]ur private schools [must] prepare young men and women for service to the community and to the Nation. The inheritance of wealth creates responsibilities; so does privilege in education." Recorded Message to the Alumni of the Choate School, Wallingford, Connecticut (May 4, 1963).

339. "Our voting turnout is much too low, much less than other democracies in Western Europe, and we want to try to find out how we can simplify the laws to encourage voting and also why there is [so much] apathy.... In a country with our educational system and our great tradition, we have to do much better...." Remarks to Members of the President's Commission on Registration and Voting Participation (May 8, 1963).

340. "[T]his Nation was not founded solely on the principle of citizens' rights. Equally important, though too often not discussed, is the citizen's responsibility. For our privileges can be no greater than our obligations. The protection of our rights can endure no longer than the performance of our responsibilities. Each can be neglected only at the peril of the other." Remarks in Nashville at the 90th Anniversary Convocation of Vanderbilt University (May 18, 1963).

341. "[Our] ... responsibilities [as Americans] ... are many in number and different in nature. They do not rest with equal weight upon the shoulders of all. Equality of opportunity does not mean equality of responsibility. All Americans must be responsible citizens, but some must be more responsible than others, by virtue of their public or their private position, their role in the family or community, their prospects for the future, or their legacy from the past. Increased responsibility goes with increased ability, for 'of those to whom much is given, much is required.'" Remarks in Nashville at the 90th Anniversary Convocation of Vanderbilt University (May 18, 1963).

342. "[A] special burden rests on the educated men and women of our country to reject the temptations of prejudice and violence, and to reaffirm the values of freedom and law on which our free society depends." Remarks in Nashville at the 90th Anniversary Convocation of Vanderbilt University (May 18, 1963).

343. "[E]very generation of Americans must be expected in their time to do their part to maintain freedom for their country and freedom for those associated with it; ... there is no final victory but rather all Americans must be always prepared to play their proper part in a difficult and dangerous world." Remarks in New York City at the Dedication of the East Coast Memorial to the Missing at Sea (May 23, 1963).

344. "The problems of the Western world are, in many ways, different than they were 2000 years ago, but our obligations as citizens remain the same — to defend our common heritage from those who would divide and destroy it; to develop and enrich that heritage so that it is passed on to those who come after us." Remarks at the Rathaus in Cologne [Germany] After Signing the Golden Book (June 23, 1963).

345. "The scholar, the teacher, the intellectual, have a higher duty than any of the others, for society has trained [them] to think as well as do." Address at the Free University of Berlin [Germany] (June 26, 1963).

346. "This is a great country and requires a good deal of all of us, so I can imagine nothing more important than ... to continue to work in public affairs and be interested in them, not only to bring up a family, but also give part of your time to your community, your State, and your country." Remarks to the Delegates of Girls Nation (August 2, 1963).

347. "To make this very difficult, sensitive, and complicated system [democracy], which demands so much of us in the qualities of self-restraint and self-discipline, to make it possible for us to live together in harmony, to carry out those policies which provide domestic tranquility here at home, and security for us abroad, requires the best of all of us." Remarks to Student Participants in the White House Seminar in Government (August 27, 1963).

348. "[I] think it is up to all of us, not only to look to our private interest, but also look to our obligations to the United States. All of us feel that love of country, but I think we must put it to practical use." Remarks at the Cheney Stadium in Tacoma, Washington (September 27, 1963).

349. "There is inherited wealth in this country and also inherited poverty. And ... [those] who are given a running start in life — unless they are willing to put back into our society those talents, the broad sympathy, the understanding, the compassion — unless they are willing to put those qualities back into the service of the Great Republic, then obviously the presuppositions upon which our democracy are based are bound to be fallible." Remarks at Amherst College Upon Receiving an Honorary Degree (October 26, 1963).

COMMUNISM AND THE COLD WAR

General

350. "[I]t is our job to prove that we can devote as much energy, intelligence, idealism and sacrifice to the survival and triumph of the open society as the Russian despots can extort by compulsion in defense of their closed system of tyranny." Remarks of Senator John F. Kennedy, University of New Hampshire, Durham, New Hampshire (March 7, 1960).

351. "[A]s as long as Mr. Khrushchev is convinced that the balance of world power is shifting his way — as long as he is convinced that time and the course of history is on his side — then no amount of good will trips or kitchen debates can compel him to substitute fruitful negotiations for force." Speech by Senator John F. Kennedy, Alexandra, Virginia (August 24, 1960).

352. "[A] great worldwide battle [goes on] as to whether the Communist or the free world is ultimately going to prevail. [I]f we can demonstrate to a watching world that we are on the march, that we have not passed our peak but our peak is still ahead of us, that our best days are yet to come, that the Communist system is old and tired, that the Communist system is on its way down, and that here in the United States we are still experiencing high noon, then we shall be successful. But, if the Communist system is able ... to demonstrate that it is on the advance, that we are standing still ... then all those people around the world who stand today poised on the razor edge of decision will make a determination that perhaps the future belongs not to us but to our adversaries. Therefore, our response must be clear. We must be willing to devote our national energies to demonstrating ... that we are first and will continue to be first regardless of what challenges may be hurled against us." Text of Telephone Address by Senator John F. Kennedy, Amvet Convention, Miami Beach, Florida (August 26, 1960).

353. "We believe in securing the best for our country because nothing but the best will do, because we believe this is the best country, and because we realize that isn't the President ... it is the country that is in trouble and it is we who are in trouble. The reason we are in trouble is because we are faced by a dedicated and determined adversary [the Soviet Union] who recognizes that we live in a revolutionary world and who is reaching toward the future." Speech by Senator John F. Kennedy, Fair Grounds, Bangor Maine (September 2, 1960).

354. "The great issue which the United States faces in this campaign [of 1960] is our relation with the Sino-Soviet bloc, how we can live in the same world with them, possessing, as we both do, a hydrogen capacity which could destroy mankind as well as our society, and also maintain our security and the security of the free world. That is the basic issue which is before us as Americans, and as believers in freedom...." Speech by Senator John F. Kennedy, High School Auditorium, Pocatello, Idaho (September 6, 1960).

355. "[W]e have to ... to make sure that the people of the world feel that this system of ours has endless vitality, that we are moving ahead, that we are solving our problems, that they can look to us for leadership in the future, that the balance of power is shifting to us, not to the Communists. That, I think, is the basic issue of this [1960] campaign." Speech by Senator John F. Kennedy, High School Auditorium, Pocatello, Idaho (September 6, 1960).

356. "The hard, tough question for the next decade ... is whether we or the Communist world can best demonstrate the vitality of our system. Which system, the Communist system or the system of freedom is going to be able to convince the watching millions ... as to which direction the world is moving. I think it should move with us. I think ours is the best system." Remarks of Senator John F. Kennedy, State Fairgrounds, Salem, Oregon (September 7, 1960).

357. "I do not agree with Mr. Khrushchev when he says he is going to bury us. I think ... that our high noon is in the future, that our best days are ahead that our system is in keeping with the basic aspirations of the human people, all over the globe, and the Communist system is doomed to fail." Remarks of Senator John F. Kennedy, State Fairgrounds, Salem, Oregon (September 7, 1960).

358. "Some say it will be arguments, arguments in the kitchen, debates in the United Nations ... that will impress Mr. Khrushchev. [But] [h]e has engaged in his life in many arguments. He has engaged as a member of the Communist Party in many debates. He has exchanged threats and insults with the best of them and the worst of them.... [A]rguments are not enough and propaganda is not enough.... The only thing that will deter Mr. Khrushchev from loosing his hounds on us will be a strong America." Remarks of Senator John F. Kennedy, Memorial Auditorium Dallas, Texas (September 13, 1960).

359. "We are a great revolutionary power ... which believes in the most progressive concepts which any country has ever been able to develop.

Why should we look pallid and tired, while the Soviet Union, whose system of government is hostile to all the aspirations of human personality should look progressive...? ... It is our fault that we are missing our chance in this great watershed of history. I can assure you that if we are successful [in the 1960 election], we are going to begin to move again ... and our position will be known around the world." Speech by Senator John F. Kennedy, Democratic Women's Luncheon, Commodore Hotel, New York, New York (September 14, 1960).

360. "Across the face of the globe freedom and communism are locked in a deadly embrace. At this moment and during the past few months and years, the Communist expansion has been on the move.... It is up to our generation of Americans to check this advance." Statewide TV Speech by Senator John F. Kennedy, Zembo Mosque Temple, Harrisburg, Pennsylvania (September 15, 1960).

361. "Mr. Khrushchev is not a fool and we ought to realize that.... He is shrewd, he is vigorous, he is informed, and he is competent. He is not putting on an act when he talks about the inevitable triumph of the Communist system, for this is what he believes, and this is what he is determined to achieve...." Speech by Senator John F. Kennedy, Pikesville Armory, Pikesville, Maryland (September 16, 1960).

362. "Mr. Khrushchev [claims] 'that the old and the rotten will always fight with the newly emerged, but it is a law of history that the new will always win.' But it is freedom that is new, and despotism and tyranny that is as old as civilization is — and it is freedom that will win — not because of any law of history — but because we will have the strength and the determination that will bring the victory." Speech by Senator John F. Kennedy, Coliseum, Raleigh, North Carolina (September 17, 1960).

363. "This [Communism] is no ordinary enemy and this is no ordinary struggle. Extraordinary efforts are called for by every American who knows the value of freedom and who believes that this country still has its greatest contributions to make to that cause." Speech by Senator John F. Kennedy, Sheraton Park Hotel, Washington, D.C. (September 20, 1960).

364. "The enemy is lean and hungry and the United States is the only strong sentinel at the gate." Speech by Senator John F. Kennedy, Sheraton Park Hotel, Washington, D.C. (September 20, 1960).

365. "Mr. Khrushchev is not impressed by words, nor is Mr. Castro, nor are the satellite leaders. They are not impressed by speeches. They are not impressed by debates. They are impressed by power. They are impressed by strength. They are impressed by the determination of the American people. They are impressed by our vitality as a free society." Remarks of Senator John F. Kennedy, Tri-Cities Airport, Bristol, Virginia, Tennessee (September 21, 1960).

366. "When the Communists ... are able to mobilize all of the resources to serve the state, when they operate a garrison state, when they are fully mobilized for the cold war, whether we can pursue a free society and pursue our own lives, and yet have sufficient public purpose to maintain our freedom, I think that is the big question that is before the United States, which transcends party differences." Remarks of Senator John F. Kennedy, Sioux City, Iowa (September 22, 1960).

367. "[Mr. Khrushchev] ... represents the same Communist system — still dedicated to achieving world domination. He maintains the same objectives, the same views and essentially the same tactics. It is we who have changed our tactics. We tried arguing with Mr. Khrushchev in the kitchen.... But ... Mr. Khrushchev is not the enemy. He may personify it. His antics may dramatize it. But the real enemy is the Communist system itself, unyielding, uncompromising, and unchanging in its drive for world dominion." Speech by Senator John F. Kennedy, Democratic Fund-Raising Dinner, Syracuse, New York (September 29, 1960).

368. "If we were using our ... [resources] to the fullest ... then the economy of this country would move and no one could catch the United States. But if we drift, if we use our people and our resources at slow speed, then at a time when the world is in turmoil and in revolution, people to the South of us, people in Africa, people in Asia are going to determine that the way of the future belongs to the Communists." Remarks of Senator John F. Kennedy, Courthouse, Terre Haute, Indiana (October 5, 1960).

369. "Our high noon is yet to come. The Communist system is as old as Egypt, and if we do our job, if we demonstrate vigor and vitality here, we can radiate it around the world until finally all those who wish to be free will finally come with us. That is the opportunity. That is our chance." Remarks of Senator John F. Kennedy, Government Square, Cincinnati, Ohio (October 6, 1960).

370. "Mr. Khrushchev does not stay in New York because he enjoys New York. He stays there because he is carrying out his consistent campaign to destroy us." Remarks of Senator John F. Kennedy, Public Square, Youngstown, Ohio (October 9, 1960).

371. "Mr. Khrushchev ... want[s] to impress on every country there that he is on the march, that he is confident of the future, that he is determined it shall be Communist, and that any country and any people and any system that stands in his way will be crushed." Remarks of Senator John F. Kennedy, Grand Rapids, Michigan (October 14, 1960).

372. "[The Communists] believe that the United States lacks the nerve, the will, and the determination for a long, long hard fight. It is one thing to stand up to a military invasion, it is one thing to go to war and defeat the Japanese and Hitler. It is quite another thing, year after year, decade after decade, to be engaged in struggles all around the world, in countries which we did not know anything about 10 years ago, but where we and the Communists are now locked in deadly embrace." Speech by Senator John F. Kennedy, American Legion Convention, Miami Beach, Florida (October 18, 1960).

373. "[I] want Mr. Khrushchev and Mr. Castro to know that after this [1960] election a new generation of Americans has assumed responsibility of leadership, men who fought in Europe and in the Pacific in order to maintain this country's freedom, and they are not going to preside over its liquidation, here, in Latin America, in Africa, Asia, or any place in the world." Speech by Senator John F. Kennedy, Hillsborough County Courthouse, Tampa, Florida (October 18, 1960).

374. "[T]his globe around us is going to move in the direction of freedom or going to move in the direction of slavery. The Communist system is militant, hopeful, confident, optimistic, and it has been able to identify itself all too successfully with the desire of these people in the underdeveloped world to live a better life. We have not done so." Remarks of Senator John F. Kennedy, University of Illinois Campus, Champaign-Urbana, Illinois (October 24, 1960).

375. "As long as we build our strength, as long as we are on the move, as long as we are a progressive society, then the future belongs to us and not to Mr. Khrushchev." Remarks of Senator John F. Kennedy, Keyworth Stadium, Hamtramck, Michigan (October 26, 1960).

376. "Words are not substitutes for strength. Mr. Khrushchev has listened to words all his life. What he respects is the power of a free society...." Remarks of Senator John F. Kennedy, Pottsville, Pennsylvania (October 28, 1960).

377. "I do not believe that there is any doubt that we can maintain our freedom, but I think it is going to be a hard, close struggle to maintain the balance of freedom in the world today. Every advantage is not on our side. We are faced by dedicated adversaries who are confident of their ultimate success, who are able to mobilize their resources in order to serve their cause, and who are now on the offensive all around the globe." Remarks of John F. Kennedy, Cheltenham Shopping Center, Philadelphia, Pennsylvania (October 29, 1960).

378. "[W]hen the great question before us ... [is] our ability to maintain a national and international competition, with a monolithic power which is able to mobilize all of the resources of the state, both human and material, for the service of the state—we cannot possibly afford to drift or lie at anchor, or rest." Remarks of Senator John F. Kennedy, Street Rally, New Haven, Connecticut (November 6, 1960).

379. "The Communist system gets its power not from Mr. Khrushchev. All the speeches and debates and arguments and finger waving to Mr. Khrushchev ... — this whole struggle is far more serious than that. Who can be so ill informed that he thinks the tensions of the power struggle disappear by good will missions, by debates, and by arguments. They will disappear or they will be overcome only by what we do here." Speech by Senator John F. Kennedy, Boston Garden, Boston, Massachusetts (November 7, 1960).

380. "We cannot sit still. We cannot look back. We cannot just stay as we are. We have to recognize that we are face to face with a dangerous adversary that is determined to destroy us and freedom, and unless we are prepared to move, unless we are prepared to lead, unless we are prepared to build a strong and vital country here in the United States, then our hopes for freedom in our generation will begin to fade.... That is the issue of our times. Can we demonstrate that a free society can move ahead, that it can speak with power...? These are the things that we must do...." Remarks of Senator John F. Kennedy, Street Rally, Phoenix, Arizona (November 3, 1960).

381. "What gives the Communist system its power and force is the productive strength of the Soviet Union. What gives freedom its power and force are not merely words and speeches but the productive power of the United States put to great purposes." Remarks of Senator John F. Kennedy, City Hall, Providence, Rhode Island (November 7, 1960).

382. "We must never be lulled into believing that either power [the Soviet Union or Communist China] has yielded its ambitions for world domination.... On the contrary, our task is to convince them that aggression and subversion will not be profitable routes to pursue these ends. Open and peaceful competition — for prestige, for markets, for scientific achievement, even for men's minds — is something else again. For if Freedom and Communism were to compete for man's allegiance in a world at peace, I would look to the future with ever increasing confidence." Annual Message to the Congress on the State of the Union (January 30, 1961).

383. "I do not regard religion as a weapon in the cold war. I regard it as the essence of the differences which separate those on the other side of the Iron Curtain and ourselves." Remarks at the Dedication Breakfast of International Christian Leadership, Inc. (February 9, 1961).

384. "The whole basis of the struggle [with the Communists] is ... our strong belief in religious freedom, our strong conviction ... that the blessings which come to us come not from the generosity of the state but from the hand of God — and this alternate concept that the state is the master and the people the servants." Remarks at the Dedication Breakfast of International Christian Leadership, Inc. (February 9, 1961).

385. "[I]t is clear that the forces of communism are not to be underestimated.... The advantages of a police state — its use of mass terror and arrests to prevent the spread of free dissent — cannot be overlooked by those who expect the fall of every fanatic tyrant. If the self-discipline of the free cannot match the iron discipline of the mailed fist — in economic, political, scientific and all the other kinds of struggles as well as the military — then the peril to freedom will continue to rise." Address Before the American Society of Newspaper Editors (April 20, 1961).

386. "[W]e are opposed around the world by a monolithic and ruthless conspiracy that relies primarily on covert means for expanding its sphere of influence — on infiltration instead of invasion, on subversion instead of elections, on intimidation instead of free choice, on guerrillas by night instead of armies by day. It is a system which has conscripted vast human and material resources into the building of a tightly knit, highly efficient machine.... Its preparations are concealed, not published. Its mistakes are buried, not headlined. Its dissenters are silenced, not praised. No expenditure is questioned, no rumor is printed, no secret is revealed. It conducts the Cold War ... with a war-time discipline no democracy would ever hope or wish to match." Address "The President and the Press" Before the American Newspaper Publishers Association, New York City, New York (April 27, 1961).

387. "The Communists [are] ... disciplined, organized, subject to an international discipline, promising under their system that all will be well, knowing that if they can win just once, then the iron grip of the totalitarian state goes upon the population — those who resist become refugees, or are shot — and they manage to control the population." Address in Chicago at a Dinner of the Democratic Party of Cook County (April 28, 1961).

388. "Our great ally is ... that people do desire to be free, that people will sacrifice everything in their desire to maintain their independence. And as the true nature of the Communist conspiracy becomes better known around the globe, when people come to realize ... that the Communist advance does not represent a means of liberation but represents a final enslavement, then ... they will rally to the cause to which we have given our support and our commitment." Address in Chicago at a Dinner of the Democratic Party of Cook County (April 28, 1961).

389. "[T]he ability of a totalitarian state to mobilize all of its resources for the service of the state, whatever the human cost, has great attraction for those who live on the marginal edge of existence, fired with a strong feeling of ancient wrongs and grievances.... Once a state succumbs ... to this attraction, to the lure of communism, to the lure of totalitarianism — even for a moment — resistance is then crushed, opposition is destroyed, and despotic power is maintained even when finally the people may realize they have been cruelly misled." Address at the 39th Annual Convention of the National Association of Broadcasters (May 8, 1961).

390. "[W]e [cannot] mistake the nature of the struggle [with the Communists] . It is not for concessions or territory. It is not simply between different systems. It is an age old battle for the survival of liberty itself. And our great advantage — and we must never forget it — is that the irresistible tide that began ... in ancient Greece is for freedom, and against tyranny. And that is the wave of the future — and the iron hand of totalitarianism can ultimately neither seize it nor turn it back." Address Before the Canadian Parliament in Ottawa (May 17, 1961).

391. "[I] believe just as strongly that time will prove it [Communist theory] wrong, that liberty and independence and self-determination — not communism — is the future of man, and that free men have the will and the resources to win the struggle for freedom." Radio and Television Report to the American People on Returning from Europe (June 6, 1961).

392. "The immediate threat to free men is in West Berlin. But that isolated outpost is not an isolated problem. The threat is worldwide. Our effort must be equally wide and strong, and not be obsessed by any single manufactured crisis." Radio and Television Report to the American People on the Berlin Crisis (July 25, 1961).

393. "[T]here is no ignoring the fact that the tide of self-determination has not reached the Communist empire where a population ... lives under governments installed by foreign troops instead of free institutions — under a system which knows only one party and one belief— which suppresses free debate, and free elections, and free elections, and free newspapers, and free books and free trade unions — and which builds a wall to keep truth a stranger and its own citizens prisoners." Address in New York City Before the General Assembly of the United Nations (September 25, 1961).

394. "Terror is not a new weapon. Throughout history it has been used by those who could not prevail, either by persuasion or example. But inevitably they fail, either because men are not afraid to die for a life worth living, or because the terrorists themselves came to realize that free men cannot be frightened by threats, and that aggression would meet its own response." Address in New York City Before the General Assembly of the United Nations (September 25, 1961).

395. "I believe in time those forces that we so strongly believe in, which are in every individual's breast, whether he lives here or any other part of the world, will eventually provide the final answer to the challenge of communism." Remarks at a Political Rally in Trenton, New Jersey (November 2, 1961).

396. "I've never felt that we should attempt to use the great impulse towards God and towards religion, which all people feel, as an element in a cold war struggle. Rather, it's not an arm, it is the essence of the issue — not the organization of economy so much, but as the supremacy of moral law, and therefore the right of the individual, his rights to be protected by the state and not be at the mercy of the state." Remarks to the Trustees of the Union of American Hebrew Congregations (November 13, 1961).

397. "We cannot, as a free nation, compete with our adversaries in tactics of terror, assassination, false promises, counterfeit mobs and crises. We cannot, under the scrutiny of a free press and public, tell different stories to different audiences, foreign and domestic, friendly and hostile. We cannot abandon the slow processes of consulting with our allies to match the swift expediencies of those who merely dictate to their satellites." Address in Seattle at the University of Washington's 100th Anniversary Program (November 16, 1961).

398. "[A] global civil war has divided and tormented mankind [since the end of World War II]. But it is not our military might, or our higher standard of living, that has most distinguished us from our adversaries. It is our belief that the state is the servant of the citizen and not his master." Annual Message to the Congress on the State of the Union (January 11, 1962).

399. "[O]ur basic goal remains the same: a peaceful world community of free and independent states.... Some may choose forms and ways that we would not choose for ourselves — but it is not for us that they are choosing. We can welcome diversity — the Communists cannot. [W]e offer a world of choice — they offer the world of coercion. And the way of the past shows clearly that freedom, not coercion, is the wave of the future." Annual Message to the Congress on the State of the Union (January 11, 1962).

400. "[T]he basis of the issue which separates us [the United States] from those who make themselves our adversary [the Soviet Union] [which is] at the heart of the matter ... is the position of the individual — his importance, his sanctity, his relationship to his fellow men, his relationship to his country and his state. This is in essence the struggle...." Remarks at the 10th Annual Presidential Prayer Breakfast (March 1, 1962).

401. "[T]he Communists rest everything on the idea of a monolithic world — a world where all knowledge has a single pattern, all societies move toward a single model, and all problems and roads have a single solution and a single destination. The pursuit of knowledge ... rests everything on the opposite idea — on the idea of a world based on diversity, self-determination, freedom. And that is the kind of world to which we Americans, as a nation, are committed by the principles upon which the great Republic was founded." Address in Berkeley at the University of California (March 23, 1962).

402. "As men conduct the pursuit of knowledge, they create a world which freely unites national diversity and international partnership. This emerging world is incompatible with the Communist world order. It will irresistibly burst the bonds of the Communist organization and the Communist ideology. And diversity and independence, far from being opposed to the American conception of world order, represent the very essence of our view of the future of the world." Address in Berkeley at the University of California (March 23, 1962).

403. "No one who examines the modern world can doubt that the great currents of history are carrying the world away from the monolithic idea towards the pluralistic idea — away from communism and towards national independence and freedom. No one can doubt that the wave of the future is not the conquest of the world by a single dogmatic creed but the liberation of the diverse energies of free nations and free men." Address in Berkeley at the University of California (March 23, 1962).

404. "Too often our hands are tied by rigid statutory perspectives of the Communist world. Everything is seen in terms of black and white. Either nations are for us or against us; either completely under Soviet domination or completely free. But this is not the case. There are varying shades even within the Communist world. We must be able to seize the initiative when the opportunity arises ... behind the Iron Curtain. We must be ready to gradually, carefully, and peacefully work for closer relations by nourishing the seeds of liberty." Remarks at the Pulaski Day Parade, Buffalo, New York (October 14, 1962).

405. "[A]s the older colonialism recedes, and the neocolonialism of the Communist powers stands out more starkly than ever, they [the developing and nonaligned countries] realize more clearly that the issue in the world struggle is not communism versus capitalism, but coercion versus free choice." Annual Message to the Congress on the State of the Union (January 14, 1963).

406. "[T]he Soviet-Chinese disagreement is over means, not ends. A dispute over how best to bury the free world is no grounds for Western rejoicing." Annual Message to the Congress on the State of the Union (January 14, 1963).

407. "[I]t is the closed Communist societies, not the free and open societies which carry within themselves the seeds of internal disintegration." Annual Message to the Congress on the State of the Union (January 14, 1963).

408. "The disarray of the Communist empire has been heightened by two ... formidable forces. One is the historical force of nationalism — and the yearning of all men to be free. The other is the gross inefficiency of their economies. For a closed society is not open to ideas of progress — and a police state finds that it cannot command the grain to grow." Annual Message to the Congress on the State of the Union (January 14, 1963).

409. "The combination of economic development plus political freedom ... all of which are extremely difficult to sustain, all of which are under attack, all these rather radical revolutionary doctrines ... are under attack [by the Communists]." Remarks to a Group of Economics Students from Abroad (April 10, 1963).

410. "[I]n the cold war ... our two countries [the United States and the Soviet Union] bear the heaviest burdens. For we are both devoting massive sums of money to weapons that could be better devoted to combating ignorance, poverty, and disease. We are both caught up in a vicious and dangerous cycle in which suspicion on one side breeds suspicion on the other, and new weapons beget counter-weapons." Commencement Address at American University in Washington (June 10, 1963).

411. "The Communist drive to impose their political and economic system on others is the primary cause of world tension today. For there can be no doubt that, if all nations could refrain from interfering in the self-determination of others, the peace would be much more assured." Commencement Address at American University in Washington (June 10, 1963).

412. "However repugnant the Communist system is to all of us, it nevertheless has been able to enlist the devotion of a good many people all around the globe." Remarks in Bonn at the Signing of a Charter Establishing the German Peace Corps (June 24, 1963).

413. "While the wall is the most obvious and vivid demonstration of the failures of the Communist system, for all the world to see, we take no satisfaction in it, for it is ... an offense not only against history but an offense against humanity, separating families, dividing husbands and wives and brothers and sisters, and dividing a people who wish to be joined together." Remarks in the Rudolph Wilde Platz, Berlin [Germany] (June 26, 1963).

414. "[T]he very nature of the modern technological society requires human initiative and the diversity of free minds. So history, itself, runs against the Marxist dogma, not towards it." Address at the Free University of Berlin [Germany] (June 26, 1963).

415. "While progress remains to be made [in free countries] in all of the areas of social progress, the fact remains that no totalitarian system offers any promise of solution." Remarks at a Dinner Given in His Honor by President Segni [of Italy] (July 1, 1963).

416. "[T]hose who sell their souls to the Communist system under the mistaken belief that the Communist system offers a quick and sure road to economic prosperity, have been proven wholly wrong. Berlin is an obvious example. Eastern and Western Europe are obvious contrasts.... [T]he last decade has conclusively proven that communism is a system which has outlived its time, that the true road to prosperity, the true road to progress, is by democratic means." Remarks at a Dinner Given in His Honor by President Segni [of Italy] (July 1, 1963).

417. "Communism has sometimes succeeded as a scavenger but never as a leader. It has never come to power in any country that was not disrupted by war, internal repression or both. [T]he Communists cannot reconcile their ambitions for domination with other men's ambition for freedom. They cannot look with confidence on a world of diversity and free choice.... The increasing strains appearing within this once monolithic bloc ... make it increasingly clear that this system, with all its repression of men and nations, is outmoded and doomed to failure." Remarks in Naples [Italy] at NATO Headquarters (July 2, 1963).

418. "[Peaceful cooperation] will require a new approach to the cold war — a desire not to 'bury' one's adversary, but to compete in a host of peaceful arenas, in ideas, in production, and ultimately in service to all mankind. The contest will continue ... but it should be a contest in leadership and responsibility instead of destruction, a contest in achievement instead of intimidation." Address Before the 18th General Assembly of the United Nations (September 20, 1963).

419. "We know that the struggle between the Communist system and ourselves will go on. We know it will go on in economics, in productivity, in ideology.... But what we hope to do is lessen the chance of a military collision between these two great nuclear powers which together have the power to kill 300 million people in the short space of a day. That is what we are seeking to avoid." Remarks at the Yellowstone County Fairgrounds, Billings, Montana (September 25, 1963).

420. "[T]he whole theory of historical inevitability, the belief that all roads must lead to communism, sooner or later, has been shattered by the determination of those who believe that men and nations will pursue a variety of roads, that each nation will evolve according to its own traditions and its own aspirations, and that the world of the future will have room for a diversity of economic systems, political creeds, religious faiths, united by the respect for others, and loyalty to a world order." Address in Salt Lake City at the Mormon Tabernacle (September 26, 1963).

421. "The United States and the Soviet Union still have wholly different concepts of the world, its freedom, its future. We still have wholly different views on the so-called wars of liberation and the use of subversion. And so long as these basic differences continue, they cannot and should not be concealed. They set limits to the possibilities of agreements, and they will give rise to further crises, large and small, in the months and years ahead...." Address at the University of Maine (October 19, 1963).

422. "[A]merican policy ... towards the Soviet Union [is] directed at a single, comprehensive goal — namely, convincing the Soviet leaders that it is dangerous for them to engage in direct or indirect aggression, futile for them to attempt to impose their will and their system on other unwilling people, and beneficial to them, as well as to the world, to join in the achievement of a genuine and enforceable peace." Address at the University of Maine (October 19, 1963).

423. "[A] pause in the cold war is not a lasting peace — and a detente does not equal disarmament." Address at the University of Maine (October 19, 1963).

U.S.–Soviet Negotiations

424. "[C]ivility is not a sign of weakness, and sincerity is always subject to proof. Let us never negotiate out of fear. But let us never fear to negotiate." Inaugural Address (January 20, 1961).

425. "[W]e shall always be prepared to discuss international problems with any and all nations that are willing to talk — and listen — with reason. If they have proposals — not demands — we shall hear them. If they seek genuine understanding — not concessions of our rights — we shall meet with them." Radio and Television Report to the American People on the Berlin Crisis (July 25, 1961).

426. "[A]s long as we know what comprises our vital interests and our long-range goals, we have nothing to fear from negotiations at the appropriate time, and nothing to gain by refusing to take part in them. [W]hen a single clash could escalate overnight into a holocaust of mushroom clouds, a great power does not prove its firmness by leaving the task of exploring the other's intentions to sentries or those without full responsibility. Nor can ultimate weapons rightfully be employed, or the ultimate sacrifice rightfully demanded of our citizens, until every reasonable solution has been explored." Address in Seattle at the University of Washington's 100th Anniversary Program (November 16, 1961).

427. "No one should be under the illusion that negotiations for the sake of negotiations always advance the cause of peace. If for lack of preparation they break up in bitterness, the prospects of peace have been endangered. If they are made a forum for propaganda or a cover for aggression, the processes of peace have been abused." Address in Seattle at the University of Washington's 100th Anniversary Program (November 16, 1961).

428. "[I]t is a test of our national maturity to accept the fact that negotiations are not a contest spelling victory or defeat. They may succeed — they may fail. They are likely to be successful only if both sides reach an agreement which both regard as preferable to the status quo — make an agreement in which each side can consider its own situation to be improved. And this is most difficult to obtain." Address in Seattle at the University of Washington's 100th Anniversary Program (November 16, 1961).

429. "[W]hile we shall negotiate freely, we shall not negotiate freedom. Our answer to the classic question of Patrick Henry is still no — life is not so dear, and peace is not so precious, 'as to be purchased at the price of chains and slavery.' And that is our answer even though, for the first time since the ancient battles between Greek city-states, war entails the threat of total annihilation, of everything we know, of society itself. For to save mankind's future freedom, we must face up to any risk that is necessary. We will always seek peace — but we will never surrender." Address in Seattle at the University of Washington's 100th Anniversary Program (November 16, 1961).

430. "Experience has taught us that an agreement [with the Soviets] to negotiate does not always mean a negotiated agreement." Address in Berkeley at the University of California (March 23, 1962).

431. "[W]e [do not] mistake honorable negotiation for appeasement. While we shall never weary in the defense of freedom, neither shall we ever abandon the pursuit of peace." Annual Message to the Congress on the State of the Union (January 14, 1963).

432. "The purpose of our military strength is peace.... We do not believe that war is unavoidable or that negotiations are inherently undesirable. We do believe that an end to the arms race is in the interest of all and that we can move toward that end with injury to none.... [A]s we arm to parley, we will not reject any path or refuse any proposal without examining its possibilities for peace." Remarks in Naples [Italy] at NATO Headquarters (July 2, 1963).

433. "[T]he United States and the Soviet Union have frequently communicated suspicion and warnings to each other, but very rarely hope.... [T]oo often these meetings have produced only darkness, discord, or disillusion." Radio and Television Address to the American People on the Nuclear Test Ban Treaty (July 26, 1963).

434. "[W]hile maintaining our readiness for war, let us exhaust every avenue for peace. Let us always make clear our willingness to talk, if talk will help, and our readiness to fight, if fight we must. Let us resolve to be the masters, not the victims, of our history, controlling our own destiny without giving way to blind suspicion and emotion. Let us distinguish between our hopes and our illusions, always hoping for steady progress toward less critically dangerous relations with the Soviets, but never laboring under any illusions about Communist methods or Communist goals." Address at the University of Maine (October 19, 1963).

CUBA

General

435. "There is no doubt of the Communist orientation of the Castro government. They are our enemy and will do anything to contribute to our downfall. Not only as a satellite of the Soviet Union in the future but they also attempt to spread their revolution through all of Latin America." Telephone Address of Senator John F. Kennedy, Amvet Convention, Miami Beach, Florida (August 26, 1960).

436. "[The Soviet military presence in Cuba is] the most glaring failure of American foreign policy today ... a disaster that threatens the security of the whole Western Hemisphere ... a Communist menace that has been permitted to arise under our very noses, only 90 miles from our shores." Speech by Senator John F. Kennedy, Democratic Dinner, Cincinnati, Ohio (October 6, 1960).

437. "The slogans, the manifestos, and the broadcasts of this revolution reflected the deepest aspirations of the Cuban people. They promised individual liberty and free elections ... an end to harsh police-state tactics ... [and] a better life for a people long oppressed by both economic and political tyranny. But in the 2 years since that revolution swept Fidel Castro into power, those promises have all been broken. There have been no free election — and [a]ll political parties — with the exception of the Communist Party — have been destroyed. All political dissenters have been executed, imprisoned, or exiled. All academic freedom has been eliminated. All major newspapers and radio stations have been seized. And all of Cuba is in the iron grip of a Communist-oriented police state. Castro and his gang have betrayed the ideals of the Cuban revolution and the hopes of the Cuban people." Speech by Senator John F. Kennedy, Democratic Dinner, Cincinnati, Ohio (October 6, 1960).

438. "The story of the transformation of Cuba from a friendly ally to a Communist base is — in large measure — the story of a government in Washington which lacked the imagination and compassion to understand the needs of the Cuban people — which lacked the leadership and vigor to move forward to meet those needs — and which lacked the foresight and vision to see the inevitable results of its own failures ... a new Soviet satellite ... in the making." Speech by Senator John F. Kennedy, Democratic Dinner, Cincinnati, Ohio (October 6, 1960).

439. "[W]e will defend our naval base at Guantanamo under all circumstances — and continue to seek reparation for his [Castro's] seizures of American property." Speech by Senator John F. Kennedy, Democratic Dinner, Cincinnati, Ohio (October 6, 1960).

440. "[T]the present Cuba is gone. Our policies of neglect and indifference have let it slip behind the Iron Curtain — and for the present no magic formula will bring it back. [T]he time to save Cuba was some time ago. Hopefully, events may once again bring us an opportunity to bring our influence strongly to bear on behalf of the cause of freedom in Cuba. But in the meantime we can constantly express our friendship for the Cuban people — our sympathy with their economic problems — our determination that they will again be free." Speech by Senator John F. Kennedy, Democratic Dinner, Cincinnati, Ohio (October 6, 1960).

441. "[O]nly if we extend the hand of American friendship in a common effort to wipe out the poverty and discontent and hopelessness on which communism feeds — only then will we drive back tyranny until it ultimately perishes in the streets of Havana." Speech by Senator John F. Kennedy, Democratic Dinner, Cincinnati, Ohio (October 6, 1960).

442. "Mr. Castro is only a symptom. He is not a freak. He is the kind of problem we are going to face in country after country in the next 10 years." Remarks of Senator John F. Kennedy, Butler, Pennsylvania (October 15, 1960).

443. "We cannot write the Cuban people off as lost. Neither should we drive them inextricably into Soviet hands. [L]et us make the American Revolution the chief import of Latin America, not the Cuban Revolution. And if we do so then some day on the island of Cuba itself, there will be a government constituted to secure the rights of life, liberty, and the pursuit of happiness." Remarks by Senator John F. Kennedy, Johnstown, Pennsylvania (October 15, 1960).

444. "[N]o amount of oratory ... can hide the harsh facts ... that our prestige has never been lower and that of the Communists never higher. [T]he basic facts [cannot be hidden] that American strength in relation to that of the Sino-Soviet bloc relatively has been slipping, and communism has been steadily advancing until now it rests 90 miles from this city of Miami." Speech by Senator John F. Kennedy, American Legion Convention, Miami Beach, Florida (October 18, 1960).

445. "Our objection with Cuba is not over the people's drive for a better life. Our objection is to their domination by foreign and domestic tyrannies.... Questions of economic and trade policy can always be negotiated. But Communist domination in this Hemisphere can never be negotiated." Annual Message to the Congress on the State of the Union (January 30, 1961).

446. "[A]lthough Castro and his fellow dictators may rule nations, they do not rule people; [t]hey may imprison bodies, but they do not imprison spirits; [t]hey may destroy the exercise of liberty, but they cannot eliminate the determination to be free. And by helping to free [Cuba], the United States has been given the opportunity to demonstrate once again that all men who fight for freedom are our brothers, and shall be until your country and others are free." Remarks in Miami at the Presentation of the Flag of the Cuban Invasion Brigade (December 29, 1962).

447. "The Cuban people were promised by the revolution political liberty, social justice, intellectual freedom, land for the campesinos, and an end to economic exploitation. They have received a police state, the elimination of the dignity of land ownership, the destruction of free speech and of free press, and the complete subjugation of individual human welfare to the service of the state and of foreign states." Remarks in Miami at the Presentation of the Flag of the Cuban Invasion Brigade (December 29, 1962).

448. "[I]t is the strongest wish of the people of this country [the United States] ... that Cuba shall one day be free again...." Remarks in Miami at the Presentation of the Flag of the Cuban Invasion Brigade (December 29, 1962).

Cuban Missile Crisis

449. "[U]nmistakable evidence has established the fact that a series of offensive missile sites is now in preparation on that imprisoned island [Cuba]. The purpose of these bases can be none other than to provide a nuclear strike capability against the Western Hemisphere." Radio and Television Report to the American People on the Soviet Arms Buildup in Cuba (October 22, 1962).

450. "This urgent transformation of Cuba into an important strategic base — by the presence of these large, long-range, and clearly offensive weapons of sudden mass destruction — constitutes an explicit threat to the peace and security of all the Americas This action also contradicts the repeated assurances ... that the Soviet Union had no need or desire to station strategic missiles on the territory of any other nation." Radio and Television Report to the American People on the Soviet Arms Buildup in Cuba (October 22, 1962).

451. "We no longer live in a world where only the actual firing of weapons represents a sufficient challenge to a nation's security to constitute maximum peril. Nuclear weapons are so destructive and ballistic missiles are so swift, that any substantially increased possibility of their use or any sudden change in their deployment [as in Cuba] may well be regarded as a definite threat to peace." Radio and Television Report to the American People on the Soviet Arms Buildup in Cuba (October 22, 1962).

452. "The 1930s taught us a clear lesson: aggressive conduct, if allowed to go unchecked and unchallenged, ultimately leads to war. This nation is opposed to war.... Our policy has been one of patience and restraint, as befits a peaceful and powerful nation ... [b]ut now further action is required.... We will not prematurely or unnecessarily risk the costs of worldwide nuclear war in which even the fruits of victory would be ashes in our mouth — but neither will we shrink from that risk at any time it must be faced." Radio and Television Report to the American People on the Soviet Arms Buildup in Cuba (October 22, 1962).

453. "The American people have good reason to recall with pride their conduct throughout that harrowing week [during the Cuban missile crisis]. For they neither dissolved in panic nor rushed headlong into reckless belligerence. [T]hey ... refused to tolerate the Soviets' attempt to place nuclear weapons in this hemisphere, but recognized at the same time that our preparations for the use of force necessarily required a simultaneous search for fair and peaceful solutions." Address at the University of Maine (October 19, 1963).

454. "Some hail it [the Soviet's removal of missiles from Cuba] as the West's greatest victory, others as a bitter defeat. Some mark it as a turning point in the cold war, others as proof of its permanence. Some attribute the Soviet withdrawal of missiles to our military actions alone, while some credit solely our use of negotiations. Some view the entire episode as an example of Communist duplicity, while some others abroad have accepted the assertion that it indicated the Soviets' peaceful intentions. While only the passage of time and events can reveal in full the true perspective of last October's drama, it is already clear that no single, simple view of this kind can be wholly accurate...." Address at the University of Maine (October 19, 1963).

DEMOCRACY

455. "A democracy is the most difficult kind of government to operate. It represents the last flowering, really of the human experience. The Communist system really is as old as Egypt, and we represent really the most modern and evolutionary development of the human experience." Speech of Senator John F. Kennedy, High School Auditorium, Pocatello, Idaho (September 6, 1960).

456. "Democracy demands more of us than any other system of education, character, self-restraint, self-discipline." Remarks of Senator John F. Kennedy, New Fieldhouse, Moline, Illinois (October 24, 1960).

457. "Our greatness is based on the final premise that the people themselves, working among themselves, making their final decision, will make a judgment which fits the best interest of our country. If we did not accept that premise, then the whole concept upon which a democracy is based would be hollow." Remarks of Senator John F. Kennedy, Lord & Taylor Shopping Center, Philadelphia, Pennsylvania (October 29, 1960).

458. "We preach the doctrine of democracy. It is the most difficult of all doctrines. But we have to live up to it. We have to practice what we preach, and that is what we are going to do." Remarks of Senator John F. Kennedy, Elks Auditorium, Los Angeles, California (November 1, 1960).

459. "I know that many people feel that a democracy is a divided system, that where the Communists are certain in purpose and certain in execution, we debate and talk and are unable to meet their consistency and their perseverance. I do not hold that view. There are many disadvantages which a free society bears with it in a cold war struggle, but I believe over the long run that people do want to be free, that they desire to develop their own personalities and their own potentials, that democracy permits them to do so." Remarks at George Washington University Upon Receiving an Honorary Degree (May 3, 1961).

460. "The dynamic of democracy is the power and the purpose of the individual...." Annual Message to the Congress on the State of the Union (January 11, 1962).

461. "What we do here in this country, and what we are, what we want to be, represents really a great experiment in a most difficult kind of self-discipline, and that is the organization and maintenance and development of the progress of free government." Remarks on the 20th Anniversary of the Voice of America Remarks on the 20th Anniversary of the Voice of America (February 26, 1962).

462. "[W]hile there may be some who say that the business of government is so important that it should be confined to those who govern, in this free society of ours the consent and ... support of the citizens of this country is essential if ... any other piece of progressive legislation is going to be passed. Make no mistake about it — make no mistake about it." Address at a New York Rally in Support of the President's Program of Medical Care for the Aged (May 20, 1962).

463. "[T]o maintain a free democratic government is difficult for us in this country — and we've been very generously blessed by nature. In countries which have not had such resources placed at their disposal ... this is an extraordinary task...." Toast of the President at a Luncheon in Honor of President Arosemena [of Panama] (July 23, 1962).

464. "[O]ur political structure ... is not perhaps the most efficient in the world. And indeed it was developed in a sense to be inefficient in order to protect the rights of the individual. Winston Churchill once said that democracy is the worst form of government, except for all of the other systems that have been tried. It is among the most difficult." Remarks to Delegates Attending the World Youth Forum (March 7, 1963).

465. "[Democracy] is most difficult. It places upon those who are governed ... the most heavy obligations not only to improve through a system of freedom the life of their people but also to bear the heavy burdens which go with maintaining the freedom in a difficult and hazardous world." Toasts of the President and President Radhakrishnan [of India] (June 3, 1963).

466. "Democracy is a difficult kind of government. It requires the highest qualities of self-discipline, restraint, a willingness to make commitments and sacrifices for the general interest, and also it requires knowledge." Remarks at a Civic and Academic Reception in St. Patrick's Hall, Dublin Castle [Ireland] (June 28, 1963).

467. "We ... believe in democracy at what Americans call 'the grass roots'—placing the individual ahead of the state, the community ahead of the party, and public interests ahead of private." Remarks at a Dinner Given in His Honor by President Segni [of Italy] (July 1, 1963).

468. "Democracy involves delays and debates and dissension. It requires men to think as well as believe, to look ahead as well as back, to give up narrow views or interests that retard their nation's progress. But given an opportunity to work, it completely contradicts and isolates the false appeals of the extremists who would destroy democracy." Remarks at a Dinner Given in His Honor by President Segni [of Italy] (July 1, 1963).

469. "The achievement of justice is an endless process—democracy must be a daily way of life." Remarks at a Dinner Given in His Honor by President Segni [of Italy] (July 1, 1963).

470. "It is an unfortunate fact ... that the number of people who are able to maintain this sensitive system of democracy and individual liberty are rather limited. It has been confined, on the whole, to a relatively few areas of the world. Most of the world moves through a far more centralized system of authority which takes the ultimate responsibility upon the governors and not upon the people themselves." Remarks to Student Participants in the White House Seminar in Government (August 27, 1963).

471. "If we in the West find it [self-government] so difficult, imagine how complicated it is for the newly developing countries which lack this long [democratic] tradition, which lack this happy balance of economic and political power which we have been able to develop in this country." Remarks to a Group Attending the Convention of the International Federation of Catholic Universities (September 4, 1963).

472. "[T]he free, democratic system of government which places more burdens on the individual than any other system, must depend in its final analysis upon an informed citizenry." Remarks at the Cheney Stadium in Tacoma, Washington (September 27, 1963).

473. "There can be no progress and stability if people do not have hope for a better life tomorrow. That faith is undermined when men seek the reins of power and ignore the restraints of constitutional procedures. They may even do so out of a sincere desire to benefit their own country. But democratic governments demand that those in opposition accept the defects of today and work towards remedying them within the machinery of peaceful change. Otherwise, in return for momentary satisfaction, we tear apart the fabric and the hope of lasting democracy." Address in Miami Before the Inter-American Press Association (November 18, 1963).

DOMESTIC SOCIAL ISSUES

General

474. "We cannot continue to allow millions of Americans to work for substandard wages and live in substandard houses. This gap between our national wealth and the poverty of too many citizens has reached the crisis stage...." Remarks of Senator John F. Kennedy, Roosevelt Birthday Ball, Salt Lake City, Utah (January 30, 1960).

475. "[We] have not yet achieved a decent home in a decent neighborhood for every American family. We have not yet made retirement a period of health and dignity and freedom from economic want for every aging or disabled worker. Our minimum wage laws are out-of-date. Our unemployment insurance is outmoded.... [I]t is clear that there is much to be done — that our work is cut out." Remarks of Senator John F. Kennedy, District Democratic Committee Dinner, South Bend, Indiana (April 8, 1960).

476. "It is no answer to say that there is no poverty in your own community — that there are no slums in your neighborhood. For this is one nation of one people. The poorly educated may be voting for your President. The unemployed and needy may be using your tax dollars. The ill and the delinquent may be moving into your area.... Our prosperity must be prosperity for all. Our growth should leave no group behind." Remarks of Senator John F. Kennedy, Phoenix, Arizona (April 9, 1960).

477. "We are going to make the vision of Franklin Roosevelt — the vision of a decent life with dignity for all men — ... a reality for the America of the sixties. And we are not going to be held back by the cries of the budget cutters ... or the doubts of the fearful." Remarks of Senator John F. Kennedy, Jefferson-Jackson Dinner, Minneapolis, Minnesota (June 4, 1960).

478. "[W]e must modernize and extend the great social welfare programs of the New Deal — expanded social security benefits, medical care for the aged, higher minimum wages, adequate unemployment compensation — a decent life for our workers, food for our hungry, and an opportunity to achieve a decent life under freedom for all Americans. This is the heritage ... which we must and shall carry on." Remarks of Senator John F. Kennedy at Essex County Democratic Dinner, Spring Lake, New Jersey (June 22, 1960).

479. "The American economy is interdependent, and a decline in one area inevitably brings a decline in another ... [but] when one section and another section join together, then the economy of this country begins to move forward." Remarks of Senator John F. Kennedy, Farmers Union Gta [Grain Terminal Association] Convention, St. Paul, Minnesota (October 2, 1960).

480. "[I]t is the function of government to use our resources to the fullest, to use our natural and material and human resources to the fullest, to educate our children, to build a stronger economy, to provide medical care for our aged under social security, to use to the fullest those [resource schools and hospitals and libraries, inadequate recreation, the breakdown of mass transportation, polluted air and water, juvenile delinquency." Speech by Senator John F. Kennedy Delivered Before the Urban Affairs Conference, Pittsburgh, Pennsylvania (October 10, 1960).

481. "[W]e must get moving on policies designed to strengthen our economy and society in every segment — helping the young in need of education, the aged in need of medical care, the small businessman in need of credit, [c]hildren whose education suffers from overcrowded classrooms or underpaid teachers [and who] can never gain back what they have lost ... [and] [w]age earners who must help their aged parents bear the high cost of drugs and medical bills — because they would never require their parents to take a Republican pauper's oath — [to] have less money to build a future for themselves and their families." Speech of Senator John F. Kennedy, Fair Grounds, Louisville, Kentucky (October 5, 1960).

482. "Aristotle said, 'Men come together in cities in order to live; they remain together in order to live the good life.' The good life is still just a dream for too many of the people who live in cities." Speech by Senator John F. Kennedy Delivered Before the Urban Affairs Conference, Pittsburgh, Pennsylvania (October 10, 1960).

483. "What stands between our people and the good life ... is not any lack of ability to produce consumer goods. That problem, for America, has been solved. What have not been solved are those problems which lie largely in the realm of public action — bad housing, poverty, recessions, unemployment, discrimination, crowded and obsolete schools and hospitals and libraries, inadequate recreation, the breakdown of mass transportation, polluted air and water, juvenile delinquency." Speech by Senator John F. Kennedy Delivered Before the Urban Affairs Conference, Pittsburgh, Pennsylvania (October 10, 1960).

484. "[I] am concerned with what is on the other side of the moon, but I am also concerned ... with the condition or life of the man or woman on the other side of the street." Speech by Senator John F. Kennedy, National Conference on Constitutional Rights and American Freedom, Park-

Sheraton Hotel, New York, New York (October 12, 1960).

485. "I do not suggest ... that the problem of maintaining full employment, the problem of solving automation, the problem of stimulating our housing industry, the problem of increasing educational opportunities, the problem of caring for our aged, the problem of balancing supply and demand in agriculture.... I do not suggest that there are easy answers to the most difficult and complicated problems that this country has ever faced." Remarks of Senator John F. Kennedy, Capitol Steps, Lansing, Michigan (October 14, 1960).

486. "[T]he responsibilities which we will meet in the sixties [fall] into two categories. The first ... is to attempt to bring up to date those pieces of social legislation passed in the 1930s which still have great significance in the lives of our citizens today, and [the second is the problem] of housing and social security, unemployment compensation, [and] minimum wages...." Speech by John F. Kennedy, Boys' Gymnasium, Montgomery-Blair High School, Silver Spring, Maryland (October 16, 1960).

487. "[T]he great domestic issue which goes to ... the kind of society that we can build here ... [is whether] we [can] as a free society maintain full employment for our people, educate our children, provide security for our older citizens, provide equality of opportunity for all Americans, regardless of their race, their origin, or the circumstances of their birth. Can we, in other words, build the kind of society which we promised to build in all of the great statements of our leaders...." Remarks of Senator John F. Kennedy, Trade Union Council of Liberal Party, New York, New York (October 27, 1960).

488. "All of this [Kennedy's goals] will not be finished in the first one hundred days. Nor will it be finished in the first one thousand days, nor in the life of this Administration, nor even perhaps in our lifetime on this planet. But let us begin." Inaugural Address (January 20, 1961).

489. "[A] strong America cannot neglect the aspirations of its citizens — the welfare of the needy, the health care of the elderly, the education of the young. For we are not developing the Nation's wealth for its own sake. Wealth is the means — and people are the ends. All our material riches will avail us little if we do not use them to expand the opportunities of our people." Annual Message to the Congress on the State of the Union (January 11, 1962).

490. "A strong America depends on its cities — America's glory, and sometimes America's shame." Annual Message to the Congress on the State of the Union (January 11, 1962).

491. "All of these [domestic social] programs have been written into the statute books of nearly every country in Western Europe. And yet they are regarded with concern because they are new — and because they may be somewhat different. We have to decide, and this is the issue, not so much [between] parties, but between those who feel we should stand still and those who feel we should move ahead." Address in Milwaukee at the Jefferson-Jackson Dinner (May 12, 1962).

492. "[T]here are a good many things still left to do in this country ... vital measures which make the difference between prosperity and recession — between a man having a decent job and not having one — between a man being able to send his children to college and not being able to do so — between a man being able to retire with a decent expectation of dignity and not being able to do so. These ... issues ... may not be perhaps as dramatic as they were 30 years ago, but they are just as important." Remarks with David McDonald Recorded for the United Steelworkers Convention at Miami Beach (September 17, 1962).

493. "There is universal agreement that the two key objectives of an effective [illegal drug] program are the elimination of illicit traffic in drugs and, secondly, the rehabilitation and restoration to society of drug addicts." Remarks to the White House Conference on Narcotic and Drug Abuse (September 27, 1962).

494. "One problem meriting special attention deals with the growing abuse of non-narcotic drugs, including barbiturates and amphetamines. Society's gains will be illusory if we reduce the incidence of one kind of drug dependence, only to have new kinds of drugs substitute." Remarks to the White House Conference on Narcotic and Drug Abuse (September 27, 1962).

495. "The campaign of 1960 ... reminded this Nation that even in America people through no fault of their own have had to live lives of hardship and want, and that even in America communities, through no fault of their own, have suffered from stagnation and age, and it reminded this Nation that an affirmative and progressive Government could do something about it." Remarks at the Wheeling Stadium, Wheeling, West Virginia (September 27, 1962).

496. "Unless we are strong here in this country, unless we are moving ahead, unless our people can find work, unless we're educating our children, unless we're providing the kind of society where every person has an opportunity, regardless of his race or his creed or his color, to develop their resources, this country fails." Remarks at the Hippodrome Arena in St. Paul, Minnesota (October 6, 1962).

497. "[T]he most exciting adventure ... in our own cities ... in our own country, [is] to make it possible for every American to live a rich and fruitful and productive and prosperous life. That is a challenge which carries with it the greatest responsibility, the greatest burdens, and the greatest opportunities for us all." Remarks at a Columbus Day Celebration in Newark, New Jersey (October 12, 1962).

498. "I don't know why ... expenditures which deal with the enforcement of the minimum wage, that deal with the problem of school dropouts, of retraining of workers, of unskilled labor, all the problems that are so much with us ... why they are always regarded as the waste in the budget, and expenditures for defense are always regarded as the untouchable item in the budget." Remarks at a Dinner Celebrating the 50th Anniversary of the Department of Labor (March 4, 1963).

499. "I am astonished, as President of the United States ... to see how difficult it is for us to pass assistance to education so that your children and the children of fellow Americans can go to college in 1970 ... that it is so difficult for us to provide transit so our people and our workers can go to work ... [and] that it is so difficult for us to provide ... assistance for our youth who are out of work, who are pouring into our labor markets.... [I] am very conscious, as President of this country, that this is a rich and prosperous and growing country, but I do think that we have an obligation to those who have not shared in that prosperity." Remarks at the 75th Anniversary Banquet of the International Association of Machinists (March 5, 1963).

500. "To retrain a man, to educate a child, to give security to an older citizen, to find jobs for those who want to work — this country of ours is rich and can afford to do it. We can afford to do it, and I am confident [we] will do it because the people of this country cannot possibly turn their backs upon history and expect ... to continue to be the leader of the free world, unless we make this society of ours a dynamic one." Remarks in Hollywood at a Breakfast with Democratic State Committeewomen of California (June 8, 1963).

501. "[A] matter which concerns us all, and that is, how the American people can live more happily and more securely together." Remarks Upon Arrival at Honolulu International Airport (June 8, 1963).

502. "This country is very strong. It is, on the whole, rich ... [and] [t]here have been a number of explanations for that, but I think probably the most important was the solid framework of legislation established in the thirties which has put a platform under the lives of most Americans, whether it is minimum wage or social security or unemployment compensation or housing, urban renewal, protection of the bank deposits, all the rest." Remarks to Delegates to a Conference on Voter Registration Sponsored by the AFL-CIO's Committee on Political Education (September 18, 1963).

503. "This country cannot afford to move and limp from recession to recession, with increased numbers of people unemployed, with a fifth of our population on the bottom end, passing on ... from generation to generation a lack of education, a lack of opportunity, a lack of hope...." Address in Duluth to Delegates to the Northern Great Lakes Region Land and People Conference (September 24, 1963).

504. "[I]t is our responsibility as a nation to master our domestic problems so that we are able to carry our responsibilities abroad, so that we can continue to live here at home in peace." Address in Duluth to Delegates to the Northern Great Lakes Region Land and People Conference (September 24, 1963).

505. "All these subjects [poverty, unemployment, and inadequate education] do not have the drama of the great struggle over the nuclear test ban treaty, but these are the hard jobs of Government...." Address in Duluth to Delegates to the

Northern Great Lakes Region Land and People Conference (September 24, 1963).

506. "We can ... solve a good many of our problems. [T]hey are man-made and they can be solved by man. And I think we must not keep our attention so fixed on those great issues of war and peace, which are perhaps the most desperate and the most serious ... but [we must] also concern ourselves with what happens in the United States, and particularly in those areas of the United States which have been left behind." Address in Duluth to Delegates to the Northern Great Lakes Region Land and People Conference (September 24, 1963).

507. "This rich country of ours must fulfill its promise to all of our citizens, and that can only be done by a national commitment to use all of our energy and all of our talents so that we can produce all of the things that we are capable of doing in order to meet our responsibility to ourselves and to those who look to us for leadership." Remarks at the Cheney Stadium in Tacoma, Washington (September 27, 1963).

508. "[H]ere at home what we are trying to do is all so simple, though its execution is difficult: that is to educate our children so that they are able to maintain themselves and their families and this free system, to find jobs for them when they have graduated from school or college, to make it possible for them to lead fruitful lives, and then in their older age to live in security." Remarks in Tampa on the 50th Anniversary of Scheduled Air Service (November 18, 1963).

509. "[E]very American has the right to a decent life for himself and a better life for his children." Address in Miami Before the Inter-American Press Association (November 18, 1963).

Automation and Its Effects

510. "[O]ur next President must face the crisis of automation — the replacement of men by machines — the replacement of established industries by new products. We can smile today at the plight of the blacksmith when the automobile replaced the horse and buggy. But coal miners, sheep-growers, railroad workers, telephone operators, office employees, auto workers, and millions of other Americans are not smiling at the threat of their own replacement by modern machines." Remarks of Senator John F. Kennedy, Roosevelt Birthday Ball, Salt Lake City, Utah (January 30, 1960).

511. "We must welcome this revolution [of automation] and its promise of a better life. But at the same time we cannot continue to forget our unemployed workers and our depressed areas. We must re-train those out of work — we must rehabilitate our depressed cities and towns — and, if we are to increase our economic growth — we must make sure that the technological advances of the future are made available to the people and not locked away in either private or Pentagon vaults." Remarks of Senator John F. Kennedy, Roosevelt Birthday Ball, Salt Lake City, Utah (January 30, 1960).

512. "We cannot — and we would not — halt the steady advance of technology with its promise of economic growth and increased productivity for the future. [But] government, industry and labor must collaborate in planning for the important social and economic changes which automation is certain to bring. Workers must be retrained — factories must be relocated — and, above all, we must be certain that the worker himself shares in the fruits of his increased productivity — in terms of greater leisure and higher income." Remarks of Senator John F. Kennedy, Weyerhaeuser Lumber Company, Eugene, Oregon (May 17, 1960).

513. "It [automation] is a problem which is now on the horizon no bigger than a man's hand. But it is a problem which will disturb the lives of all of us in the next decade unless we move to it at once." Remarks of Senator John F. Kennedy, United Chemical Workers Convention, Ambassador Hotel, Atlantic City, New Jersey (September 19, 1960).

514. "[T]he problem for ... those of us who serve in the Government ... is how we can maintain full employment ... how we can provide for the orderly transition from present production methods into new production methods without displacing our workers ... how we can provide labor-saving machinery at the same time maintaining full employment, ... making sure that those machines produce a better life rather than a life of unemployment for so many of our citizens." Remarks of Senator John F. Kennedy, United Chemical Workers Convention, Ambassador Hotel, Atlantic City, New Jersey (September 19, 1960).

515. "[T]he problem of automation is not a problem for a family or even for a company, or even for an industry. The problem of automation is a national problem, and I think it is incumbent [that all of us] ... try to bring better relief to our people, so that new machinery means better life rather than people out of work." Speech by Senator John F. Kennedy, Civic Center, Charleston, West Virginia (September 19, 1960).

516. "The problem of automation is to make sure that machines make our lives easier, not harder, for those who are thrown out of work." Remarks of Senator John F. Kennedy, Municipal Auditorium, Canton, Ohio (September 27, 1960).

517. "We need people who are well trained, well qualified. This is not the 1900s, when millions of immigrants came in with no skills except an ability to lift. Now we can lift ourselves with machines." Remarks in Hollywood at a Breakfast with Democratic State Committeewomen of California (June 8, 1963).

518. "In the aftermath of all the changes which are taking place in science and technology, no American can expect that any skill which he now has can carry him throughout his life. This is a time of change, and a time of opportunity. [W]e have to concern ourselves not only with the education of our children, but also with the education and the retraining of those who are already at work." Address in Duluth to Delegates to the Northern Great Lakes Region Land and People Conference (September 24, 1963).

Housing

519. "It is hard to realize that in this, the richest country on earth, we have not yet reached that goal [of 'a decent home in a suitable environment for every American family']. The housing problem is not merely an economic problem. It is not merely a political issue. It is a human problem." Remarks of Senator John F. Kennedy, Democratic State General Committee Luncheon, Roseburg, Oregon (February 9, 1960).

520. "I believe in an America where every family can live in a decent home in a decent neighborhood; where children can play safely; where no home is unsafe or unsanitary...." Speech by Senator John F. Kennedy, Convention Hall, Philadelphia, Pennsylvania (October 31, 1960).

521. "Public housing, urban renewal, private housing, all of this represents a basic aspiration of American families to house themselves securely." Remarks at the Swearing In of Robert C. Weaver as Housing and Home Finance Administrator (February 11, 1961).

522. "These [Federal Housing] programs, old and new, offer ... the opportunity and the challenge to build the cities of tomorrow where families can live in dignity, free from both the squalor of the slums and the unbroken monotony of suburban sprawl...." Remarks Upon Signing the Housing Act (June 30, 1961).

523. "I believe that every American family should live in a decent home, in a decent neighborhood." Remarks in Philadelphia at a Dinner Sponsored by the Democratic County Executive Committee (October 30, 1963).

Juvenile Delinquency

524. "The future of our country depends upon our younger people who will occupy positions of responsibility and leadership in the coming days. Yet for 11 years juvenile delinquency has been increasing.... This is a matter of national concern and requires national action." Remarks Upon Signing the Juvenile Delinquency and Youth Offenses Control Act (September 22, 1961).

525. "[T]his problem of what we call juvenile delinquency, which is really perhaps not the most descriptive phrase, [is] really a question of young people and their opportunity...." Remarks Upon Receiving Report of the President's Committee on Juvenile Delinquency and Youth Crime (May 31, 1962).

526. "[Juvenile delinquency is] an area not just in law enforcement but it is also recreation, counseling and guidance, better schools, better education — an attempt through the churches, community efforts, to instill better motivations and an opportunity to work and find useful employment. [I]t requires an attack on many areas, and it requires the cooperation, the hard work of the community, and of course the individual families — the community, the city, the State, and the National Government." Remarks Upon Receiving Report of the President's Committee on Juvenile Delinquency and Youth Crime (May 31, 1962).

527. "[Solving the problem of youth unemployment] represents one of the most serious challenges which this country faces, the ability to use our most valuable resource, which is our young people, in a way which serves their interest in the country and does not permit them to live in a social exile which denies them an opportunity to participate usefully in the growth of our society." Remarks to the Committee on Youth Employment in Response to Its Report (April 24, 1963).

Minimum Wage

528. "Substandard wages inevitably take their toll in poor health, low efficiency, and great personal tragedy. This is a price we cannot afford to pay. Our greatest asset in the worldwide struggle for industrial supremacy — and in our own fight for a decent way of life for all Americans — is a strong, healthy and vital labor force. To secure such a labor force, Congress must provide our workers with the important protection of a decent minimum wage." Remarks of Senator John F. Kennedy, Androy Hotel Reception, Superior, Wisconsin (March 18, 1960).

529. "I don't think $1.25 an hour for somebody who works in a business which makes $1 million a year is an extreme wage...." Remarks of Senator John F. Kennedy, Entrance of Union Hall, New York, New York (October 19, 1960).

530. "I am not satisfied ... to see people who want to work can't find a job. I do not believe it saps the initiative of any American to pay him $1.25 minimum wage." Address in Chicago at a Dinner of the Democratic Party of Cook County [Illinois] (April 28, 1961).

531. "I don't believe that there's any American who believes that any man or woman should have to work in interstate commerce, in companies of substantial size, for less than a dollar twenty-five cents an hour, or fifty dollars a week. That itself is a very minimum wage...." Remarks Upon Signing the Minimum Wage Bill (May 5, 1961).

532. "Why it is so difficult to secure passage of a minimum wage paying somebody in interstate commerce a dollar or a dollar ten and fifteen cents, I do not understand, but it is regarded in some circles as highly radical and highly inflationary. I think that this country must pay people adequately. How else are we going to be able to buy the cars and the refrigerators and the television sets which we produce in such mass?" Address in Atlantic City at the Convention of the United Auto Workers (May 8, 1962).

Unemployment

533. "[T]he extension of unemployment compensation — essential as that is ... does not strike at the causes of unemployment.... Some areas have been hurt by shifts in plant locations and the closing down of local factories — others have exhausted their natural resources ... still others have been hurt by fluctuating demand for their products — and others by automation or technological change. It is no answer to say that the unemployed workers and their families in these areas should move elsewhere.... Many do. But many ... lack the skills necessary for a new job in a new area — many lack the funds to travel to another state — many are women unwilling to leave their homes. Moreover, is it not natural that they should want to hold on to their roots and try to 'stick it out'? ... Solutions can be found. Each community and state must bear the major responsibility. But Congress has a responsibility also — for this is a national problem." Remarks of Senator John F. Kennedy, La Crosse, Wisconsin (March 9, 1960).

534. "It is a double failure of our civilization if we cannot permit them [unemployed workers] to pay their bills and feed their families while looking for another job. [We need] nationwide standards for unemployment compensation — to make sure that every worker ... can draw [enough] to really tide him over until he can find work." Remarks of Senator John F. Kennedy, Clarksburg, West Virginia (April 18, 1960).

535. "[L]et us never forget those who will never go back to work — those who are too old, too sick or disabled. There is a song about them: 'Who will take care of you, how'll you get by, when you're too old to work and you're too young

to die?'" Remarks of Senator John F. Kennedy, Clarksburg, West Virginia (April 18, 1960).

536. "I am confident that the American people are not going to tolerate pockets of poverty and chronic unemployment in this land, the waste of idle men and women who are ready, willing, and able to work, or the decline of our farms." Speech by Senator John F. Kennedy, Cadillac Square, Detroit, Michigan (September 5, 1960).

537. "[To enable people to] find work at decent wages ... must be a basic policy for the Government and for the free enterprise system here in this country, to make sure that everyone who wants to find a job can find one. Whether they work in organized labor or whether they are teachers or doctors or nurses, whatever they may be, the chance to work at decent wages must be a basic, fundamental premise upon which our society must be based." Speech by Senator John F. Kennedy, Multnomah Hotel, Portland, Oregon (September 7, 1960).

538. "As long as there are Americans who want to work and can't find it ... as long as some of our brightest children never get to realize their opportunities, as long as there are some Americans who, because of their race or their color, are denied their chance to develop their talents ... I believe there is need for action here in the United States...." Remarks of Senator John F. Kennedy, Courthouse Steps, Dayton, Ohio (October 17, 1960).

539. "If a free society cannot help the many who are poor, it cannot save the few who are rich." Inaugural Address (January 20, 1961).

540. "In this free society we want to make it possible for everyone to find a job who wants to work and support their families...." Remarks Upon Signing the Area Redevelopment Act (May 1, 1961).

541. "[W]e recognize that in our time ... there is still a good deal of unfinished business: to provide more security for our younger people who want jobs and can't find them; [and] to provide more security ... for those particularly who are unemployed chronically and who have families who depend upon them, who exhaust their unemployment compensation ... and who now want to work and find themselves having to turn to inadequate public assistance." Remarks on the 50th Anniversary of the First State Workmen's Compensation Law (August 31, 1961).

542. "I believe that this country has an obligation to those who want to work and can't find it, to make it possible for them to maintain themselves and their families.... We may not get it this year [a permanent unemployment insurance program], but we are going to get it, because it is fair." Address in Atlantic City at the Convention of the United Auto Workers (May 8, 1962).

543. "[O]ur effort ... [must be] to try to arrange and develop policies which will maintain our economic momentum, the thrust of our growth which will deal with the problems of chronic unemployment, which will deal with the problems of the chronic business cycle, [and] which will provide equality of opportunity for all Americans. That is what we are attempting to do...." Remarks to Delegates to a Conference on Voter Registration Sponsored by the AFL-CIO's Committee on Political Education (September 18, 1963).

544. "The one thing we will not need in the next 7, or 8, or 9 years is unskilled labor." Address in Duluth to Delegates to the Northern Great Lakes Region Land and People Conference (September 24, 1963).

545. "I [believe] in America where work [is] available to those who were willing and able to work, where the waste of idle men and machines [can] be avoided, and where greater economic growth [can] provide the new jobs and the new markets that our growing Nation needed." Remarks in Philadelphia at a Dinner Sponsored by the Democratic County Executive Committee (October 30, 1963).

546. "This Nation needs ... [broad civil rights legislation] if we are to fulfill our constitutional obligations, but no one gains from a fair employment practice bill if there is no employment to be had; no one gains by being admitted to a lunch counter if he has no money to spend. No one gains from attending a better school if he doesn't have a job after graduation. No one thinks much of the right to own a good home and to sleep in a good hotel or go to the theater if he has no work and no money. The civil rights legislation is important. But to make that legislation effective we need jobs in the United States." Remarks in New York City at the AFL-CIO Convention (November 15, 1963).

ECONOMIC POLICIES

General

547. "I preach the doctrine of interdependence of the American economy, because this country cannot be prosperous unless the farmers and the workers are prosperous together." Remarks of Senator John F. Kennedy, Michigan State Fair, Detroit, Michigan (September 5, 1960).

548. "[I]f our agriculture is prosperous, we will be prosperous in our cities. If our cities are prosperous, we will be prosperous, we will be prosperous in our country. A rising tide lifts all the boats...: A strong America from one shore to the other, north and south, east and west, in which all Americans share their prosperity." Remarks of Senator John F. Kennedy, State Fair, Nashville, Tennessee (September 21, 1960).

549. "We are not 50 separate States; we are not 6 different regions of the United States. We are one country with one great problem, and that is to [e]nsure the prosperity of our people and their security in the days ahead...." Speech by Senator John F. Kennedy, National Plowing Contest, Sioux Falls, South Dakota (September 22, 1960).

550. "If we are moving ahead ... in the West, if we are moving ahead in agriculture ... in industry, if we have an administration that looks ahead, then the country prospers. But if one ... section of the country is standing still, then sooner or later a dropping tide drops all the boats, whether the boats are in Boston or whether they are in this community." Remarks of Senator John F. Kennedy, Frontier Park, Cheyenne, Wyoming (September 23, 1960).

551. "Unless the economy is functioning properly, our people will not be employed at good wages, our businessmen will not produce efficiently and profitably, our farmers will not receive fair prices, and our Nation will lack funds for defense, schools, roads and other public services, and the means to help strengthen the cause of world freedom." Speech by Senator John F. Kennedy at the Associated Business Publications Conference, Biltmore Hotel, New York, New York (October 12, 1960).

552. "[R]easonable stability in the price level is a vital goal of economic policy. By pursuing this goal we keep faith with those who save; we protect those who live on a fixed income; and we build world confidence in the soundness and integrity of the dollar. It is equally urgent that we do not achieve this kind of stability at the expense of any one group in the economy ... or at the price of recessions, unemployment, and stagnation." Speech by Senator John F. Kennedy, Associated Business Publications Conference, Biltmore Hotel, New York, New York (October 12, 1960).

553. "[I]n order to meet our obligations at home and abroad ... [w]e need a strong economy.... We need a strong economy if we are going to meet our obligations to the underdeveloped world, to maintain our defenses, to meet our needs in education and health and housing. I consider this to be ... the No. 1 domestic problem the next President will face." Speech by Senator John F. Kennedy, Fieldhouse, University of Wisconsin, Madison, Wisconsin (October 23, 1960).

554. "The key to the future of the United States, the key to our foreign policy, the key to our national defense depends on our maintaining full employment in the United States, depends on our using our facilities and our manpower." Speech by Senator John F. Kennedy, Chicago Auditorium, Chicago, Illinois (November 4, 1960).

555. "Economic prophecy is at best an uncertain art...." Annual Message to the Congress on the State of the Union (January 30, 1961).

556. "We have two tasks in economic policy: to create demand so that we will have a market for all that we can produce, and to avoid inflation. To return to a policy of halting inflation by curbing demand would be self-defeating — but to expand the forces of demand by feeding the fires of inflation would be equally dangerous and delusive." Address in Atlantic City at the Convention of the United Auto Workers (May 8, 1962).

557. "So [the challenge is to] ... look at things as they are, not through party labels, or through position labels, but as they are and figure out how we can maintain this economy so that it moves ahead?" Remarks to Members of the White House Conference on National Economic Issues (May 21, 1962).

558. "What is at stake in our economic decisions today is not some grand warfare of rival ideologies which will sweep the country with passion but the practical management of a modern economy. What we need is not labels and clichés but more basic discussion of the sophisticated and technical questions involved in keeping a great economic machinery moving ahead." Commencement Address at Yale University (June 11, 1962).

559. "The national interest lies in high employment and steady expansion of output, in stable prices, and a strong dollar. The declaration of such an objective is easy; their attainment in an intricate and interdependent economy and world is a little more difficult. To attain them, we require not some automatic response but hard thought." Commencement Address at Yale University (June 11, 1962).

560. "[S]tatistics and details of the economy may sometimes seem dry, but the economy and economic statistics are really a story of all of us as a country, and these statistics tell whether we are going forward or standing still or going backward. They tell whether an unemployed man can get a job or whether a man who has a job can get an increase in salary or own a home or whether he can retire in security or send his children to college. These are the people and the things behind the statistics." Radio and Television Report to the American People on the State of the National Economy (August 13, 1962).

561. "I don't hold the Marxist view that economics is at the bottom of all human affairs, but it's an important element in human affairs." Toasts of the President and Prince Albert of Belgium (February 26, 1963).

562. "[E]very effort must be made ... to strengthen the economy so that we can find work for the people who want it. This involves ... our position of leadership in the world. Mr. Khrushchev has said that the hinge of history would move when he was able to demonstrate that his system could out-produce ours. The hinge of history will move if we are not able to find jobs for our people, not only during recessions but also during periods of prosperity." Remarks at a Civic Luncheon in Chicago (March 23, 1963).

Economic Growth

563. "[Our challenge is] whether we can spur the nation's economic growth to provide a more secure life for all Americans, regardless of race, creed or national origin, including a high wage, better social security, medical care for the aged, and a better break for the mentally ill." Indiana Primary Announcement of Senator John F. Kennedy, Indianapolis, Indiana (February 4, 1960).

564. "[A]s long as our national assets are squandered or neglected ... with no investment in the future ... we have no right to boast about efficiency and economy in government. Ignoring the problems of growth that are staring us in the face is not efficiency. Destroying the hopes of tomorrow by short-sighted restrictions today is not economical. There is no real savings in permitting more streams to be polluted, more mines to close, more farms to be sold, more small businesses to fail, more children to receive an inadequate education. That is not real efficiency. That is not real economy." Remarks of Senator John F. Kennedy, Phoenix, Arizona (April 9, 1960).

565. "Our problems are problems which affect the growth of our economy. In the next 10 years we are going to have to find 25,000 new jobs a week ... in order to provide full employment, in order to get jobs for your sons and daughters.... We are going to have to make our economy grow." Remarks of Senator John F. Kennedy, Harrisburg, Illinois (October 3, 1960).

566. "This country rises or falls based upon its economic growth, its economic vitality." Remarks of Senator John F. Kennedy, Anderson, Indiana (October 5, 1960).

567. "Economic growth is not a technical term. It goes to the kind of profit which businessmen make. It goes to the question of whether our children will get jobs. It goes to the question of whether there will be full employment.... This is a tremendously difficult challenge for us all.... [I]t is a very important matter, because it goes to the future of our position around the world. Now the question is what can we do to stimulate our growth." Speech by Senator John F. Kennedy, Luncheon, Biltmore Hotel, Dayton, Ohio (October 17, 1960).

568. "[T]he whole question of economic growth ... is not an argument which is of interest only to economists. It concerns the job of every man and woman...." Remarks of Senator John F. Kennedy, Aurora, Illinois (October 25, 1960).

569. "I do not equate recovery with growth. But it is an essential first step. Only by putting millions of people back to work can we expand purchasing power and markets. Only by higher income and profits can we provide the incentive and the means for increased investment. And only when we are using our plant at near capacity can we expect any solid expansion." Address at a Luncheon Meeting of the National Industrial Conference Board (February 13, 1961).

570. "Economic growth has come to resemble the Washington weather — everyone talks about it, no one says precisely what to do about it, and our only satisfaction is that it can't get any worse." Address in New York City to the National Association of Manufacturers (December 6, 1961).

571. "[O]ur primary challenge is not how to divide the economic pie, but how to enlarge it. To fight now over larger slices of the existing pie, by seeking higher margins on lower volume, or higher wages ahead of productivity, can only weaken our effort to expand the economy of the United States." Address Before the United States Chamber of Commerce on Its 50th Anniversary (April 30, 1962).

572. "It is a simple, inescapable, economic truth that increases in productivity ... set the outer limits of our [Nation's] economic progress.... No financial sleight of hand can raise real wages and profits faster than productivity without defeating their own purpose through inflation." Address in Atlantic City at the Convention of the United Auto Workers (May 8, 1962).

573. "The mere absence of recession is not growth." Annual Message to the Congress on the State of the Union (January 14, 1963).

574. "I do not see anything abstract or academic about economic growth. It means finding ... additional jobs every year for the men and women pouring into our labor market ... [it means] ending the persisting slack which has kept our unemployment rate at 5 percent ... [and it means] pushing our economy to 4 percent instead of 3 percent...." Remarks and Question and Answer Period at the American Bankers Association Symposium on Economic Growth (February 25, 1963).

575. "[T]he growth of our free enterprise economy under a free political system ... has brought our citizens to an unprecedented standard of living ... an unparalleled position in the world, as the world's foremost banker, merchant, manufacturer, and consumer. [I]t has demonstrated the power of freedom for all to see, and sustained the cause of freedom through hot wars and cold, at home and abroad." Remarks and Question and Answer Period at the American Bankers Association Symposium on Economic Growth (February 25, 1963).

576. "I want to see this country provide an economic growth rate to make it possible for all those people, who want to find a job, to work." Remarks Upon Arrival at Miami International Airport (November 18, 1963).

Government's Role

577. "The Government cannot legislate a balance between supply and demand." Remarks of Senator John F. Kennedy, Shawano, Wisconsin (March 11, 1960).

578. "[T]here is a ... major place for private responsibility and for individual enterprise. It is the system upon which our country is founded. It provides great prosperity, and it provides great freedom. But there is also a responsibility for the people, working as a whole, if they are going to develop the resources of our country ... provide employment for our people ... provide homes for our people, and Federal policy affects that program as sharply as any other factor." Remarks of Senator John F. Kennedy, United Brotherhood of Carpenters & Joiners of America, Special Convention, Chicago, Illinois (September 26, 1960).

579. "Economic policy can result from governmental inaction as well as governmental action." Speech by Senator John F. Kennedy, Associated Business Publications Conference, Biltmore Hotel, New York, New York (October 12, 1960).

580. "[T]here is no inevitable clash between the public and the private sectors — or between investment and consumption — nor, as I have said, between Government and business. All elements in our national economic growth are interdependent. Each must play its proper role...." Address at a Luncheon Meeting of the National Conference Board (February 13, 1961).

581. "A free government in a free society has only a limited influence — provided that they are above the minimum — over prices and wages freely set and bargained for by free individuals and free enterprises. And this is as it should be if our economy is to remain free." Address at a Luncheon Meeting of the National Industrial Conference Board (February 13, 1961).

582. "We want to keep our economy free — we want labor to be free — we want management to be free — and we want to keep the Federal Government in its proper role." Remarks at a Meeting of the President's Advisory Committee on Labor-Management Policy (March 21, 1961).

583. "We have many burdens in Washington — we do not want the added burden of determining individual prices for individual products. We seek instead an economic climate in which an expanding concept of business and labor responsibility, an increasing awareness of world commerce and the free forces of domestic competition will keep the price level stable and keep the Government out of price-setting." Address Before the United States Chamber of Commerce on Its 50th Anniversary (April 30, 1962).

584. "Our domestic programs call for substantial increases in employment, but it is business, not Government, who must actually perform these jobs. While Government economists can point out the necessity of increasing the rates of investment, of modernizing plant and productivity, while Washington officials may urge responsible collective bargaining and responsible wage-price decisions, we also recognize that beneath all the laws and guidelines and tax policies and stimulants we can provide, these matters all come down, quite properly in the last analysis, to private decision by private individuals." Address Before the United States Chamber of Commerce on Its 50th Anniversary (April 30, 1962).

585. "This administration ... will not undertake to fix prices and wages in this economy.... [W]e possess and seek no powers of compulsion, and must rely primarily on the voluntary efforts of labor and management to make sure that their sense of public responsibility ... that in this kind of world, fulfilling our role, that the national interest is preserved." Address in Atlantic City at the Convention of the United Auto Workers (May 8, 1962).

586. "I know that frequently businessmen talk about 'We wish the Government would stay out — would mind its own business,' even though the Government's business has not been defined. But then on the other hand, they look to Washington for action whenever a crisis takes place." Remarks to Members of the Brookings Institution's Public Policy Conference for Business Executives (June 7, 1962).

587. "I don't think we can merely sell ... the idea that competitive factors will protect completely the public interests. If we felt that, we never would have had an Antitrust Division or a federal Trade Commission.... So we want private enterprise to function effectively, and I think it is our job to assist by making it difficult for those who seek to defraud, those who are less concerned about safety, those who seem to exploit the private enterprise system, in a sense, by being less responsible." Remarks at a Meeting with the Consumers' Advisory Council (July 19, 1962).

588. "[T]o increase demand and lift the economy, the Federal Government's most useful role is not to rush into a program of excessive increases in public expenditures, but to expand the incentives and opportunities for private expenditures." Address and Question and Answer Period at the Economic Club of New York (December 14, 1962).

589. "No doubt a massive increase in Federal spending could also create jobs and growth-but, in today's setting, private consumers, employers, and investors should be given a full opportunity first." Annual Message to the Congress on the State of the Union. (January 14, 1963).

590. "[T]he leadership of Franklin Roosevelt [and the] great New Deal for the United States ... demonstrated in those great years the immense power of affirmative, free government, the power which adds the idea of social responsibility to individual liberty." Remarks at the University of Costa Rica in San Jose (March 20, 1963).

591. "[G]overnment ... has [a] long recognized ... obligation and contribution ... that Federal monetary and fiscal policies can and must supplement the decisions of the marketplace in determining the course of the economy; that interest rates must be adjusted up and down; budgets into deficits and surpluses to fit the needs of the time.... [A] certain amount of intelligent Federal planning [is desirable]." Address and Question and Answer Period at the 20th Anniversary Meeting of the Committee for Economic Development (May 9, 1963).

592. "[W]hile the battles may be somewhat quieter in Washington in some ways than they might have been in the early thirties, nevertheless what we are trying to do is to carry on the concept of the Federal Government meeting its responsibilities to keep this economy of ours moving ahead." Remarks to Members of the Amalgamated Meat Cutters and Butcher Workmen of North America (May 16, 1963).

593. "The free enterprise system ... is primarily a system which depends upon the judgment of the private citizens of this country, their judgment in the market, the businessmen, the workingmen, all the rest, but the Federal Government does have, though it seems to be regarded as somewhat controversial, an important role to play." Remarks to the National Advisory Council of the Small Business Administration (May 16, 1963).

594. "We bear under the Constitution as well as the statutes of the Congress ... a very clear responsibility in the National Government for the state of the national economy. "Remarks to Delegates to the Young Presidents" Conference (October 24, 1963).

595. "Our policies and our objective ... though the means of carrying them out are complicated, are quite simple — to assist in providing an atmosphere and environment for a steadily rising economy which can absorb the millions of people who are coming into the labor market, those who are being displaced by machines, by automation, and those who are unemployed." Remarks to Delegates to the Young Presidents' Conference (October 24, 1963).

596. "The primary effort [in building the economy] falls on [American business], but ... in our monetary policy, our fiscal legislation, our social legislation, we have a good deal to do here in Washington. I would hope that that relationship would be ... as compatible as possible [but] [t]here may be occasions when the interest of business and Government may be somewhat in conflict. [I]n in the larger sense, [however] ... [y]our success makes the country's success." Remarks to Delegates to the Young Presidents' Conference (October 24, 1963).

597. "Things don't happen, they are made to happen." Remarks in Tampa to Members of the United Steelworkers (November 18, 1963).

EDUCATION

598. "I am convinced that American education and American science, given the necessary funds and effort and leadership, can work.... But it will take a new administration to do the job — an administration that puts education ahead of larger tail-fins and bigger refrigerators — and administration that puts national needs first...." Remarks of Senator John F. Kennedy, Testimonial

Dinner, Nashua, New Hampshire (March 5, 1960).

599. "[W]e cannot fail education much longer without failing our future as well." Remarks of Senator John F. Kennedy, Bethany College, Bethany, West Virginia (April 19, 1960).

600. "[O]ur great, rich nation ... [must] ensure that poverty will not be a bar to higher education for any talented student." Remarks of Senator John F. Kennedy, Bethany College, Bethany, West Virginia (April 19, 1960).

601. "[M]ost Americans, including educators, are not accustomed to thinking of us politicians as educated men. We may be experienced, or cynical, or skillful, or shrewd or even fluent — but no more education is required for this kind of success, it is assumed, than how to find one's way around a smoke-filled room.... But under our form of government, we must put our ultimate faith in ordinary men, not machines or experts. In the words of Thomas Jefferson: 'If we think them not enlightened enough to exercise their control with a wholesome discretion, (then) the remedy is not to take it from them — but to inform their discretion by education.'" Remarks of Senator John F. Kennedy, Concord College, Athens, West Virginia (April 27, 1960).

602. "It is not enough ... that our schools merely be great centers of learning, without concerning themselves with the uses to which that learning is put in the years that follow graduation. Indeed, care must be taken to see that it is not all left behind upon graduation." Remarks of Senator John F. Kennedy, Concord College, Athens, West Virginia (April 27, 1960).

603. "A free society is the most difficult of all kinds of government to maintain, and it can only be done if we have the best educated and the best trained citizens." Remarks of Senator John F. Kennedy, Courthouse Square, Eugene, Oregon (September 7, 1960).

604. "[O]ur brightest children, in the top half of your high school classes, do not go to college ... [b]ecause ... we have not been able to work out a system where the best can be educated, and in these changing times, when science and automation and technology is changing the face of our country.... I believe we have to recognize the new problems and those new responsibilities." Remarks of Senator John F. Kennedy, Public Square, Youngstown, Ohio (October 9, 1960).

605. "Growth requires that we have the best trained and best educated labor force in the world. Investment in manpower is just as important as investment in facilities. Yet today we waste precious resources when the bright youngster, who should have been a skilled draftsman or able scientist or engineer must remain a pick-and-shovel worker because he never had a chance to develop his talents. It is time we geared our educational systems to meet the increased demand of modern industry — strengthening our public schools, our colleges, and our vocational programs for retraining unemployed workers." Speech by Senator John F. Kennedy, Associated Business Publications Conference, Biltmore Hotel, New York, New York (October 12, 1960).

606. "I believe that the United States must have an educational system second to none, and I believe that the Federal Government has a responsibility in this area for school construction and for teachers' salaries...." Remarks of Senator John F. Kennedy, Kalamazoo, Michigan (October 14, 1960).

607. "[T]he Federal Government should ... give funds to local communities and they should make the judgment how the money should be spent in cooperation with their own expenditures [and] [I] believe the Federal Government must [also] provide loan funds for students who wish to go to college." Remarks of Senator John F. Kennedy, Kalamazoo, Michigan (October 14, 1960).

608. "If the boys and girls of this country are going to meet their responsibilities as Americans, if they are going to find employment and decent wages, if they are going to maintain the freedoms of this country we are going to have to have the best educational system in the world." Remarks of Senator John F. Kennedy, Kalamazoo, Michigan (October 14, 1960).

609. "[A] university stands for freedom, for intellectual freedom, for the search for the truth, and we are all engaged in that great endeavor, and perhaps lastly because if this country is going to not only survive, to endure, but to prevail, at least its system, then there must be the closest cooperation between our universities and our politicians, between our academicians and intellectuals and those who guide our governmental life." Speech by Senator John F. Kennedy, Wittenburg College Stadium, Springfield, Ohio (October 17, 1960).

610. "Every child ... deserves to be well educated, because as Thomas Jefferson said, 'If you hope that people will be free and ignorant, you hope for what never was and never will be.' In order to maintain a free society, in order that we can maintain our independence ... we have to have the best educated citizens in the world. That involves a responsibility of the people ... the Governor of the State, and ... the National Government, because all must work together for this great objective." Remarks of Senator John F. Kennedy, Meadowdale Shopping Center, Carpentersville, Illinois (October 25, 1960).

611. "We can't waste [our children's] talent. We need all the talent we can get. So [we must provide] scholarships and loans for students who want to go to college but can't afford it. We need them and they have a right to have an education." Remarks of Senator John F. Kennedy, Meadowdale Shopping Center, Carpentersville, Illinois (October 25, 1960).

612. "Any time that a child grows up without the best education, he dooms himself to a life of economic hardship in many ways. His children's chances are not so good, and it passes on generation after generation. A good education is the most valuable resource that you can pass on to your children." Remarks of Senator John F. Kennedy, Meadowdale Shopping Center, Carpentersville, Illinois (October 25, 1960).

613. "[W]e have a right to expect that our teachers will be well trained, will be imaginative, will be dedicated." Speech by Senator John F. Kennedy, Beverly Hilton Hotel, Los Angeles, California (November 2, 1960).

614. "We ... have a right to expect that every high school in the country will meet high school standards, and will make it possible for any child ... who has talent, who has ability, who has motivation, who desires to go to college, will have the skills [and] study [habits developed in] them in their earlier years so that they are able to make the grade when they enter college." Speech by Senator John F. Kennedy, Beverly Hilton Hotel, Los Angeles, California (November 2, 1960).

615. "Colleges and universities and schools are the basic strength of this society. The kind of jobs that [our] children will get in the next 10 years will depend in great measure as industry and technology changes — will depend in great measure on the kind of education that [we] give them...." Speech by Senator John F. Kennedy, Commack Arena, Commack, Long Island, New York (November 6, 1960).

616. "There is no doubt that the maximum impact of a reducing economy falls upon those who are at the bottom of the educational ladder. The first people unemployed are those with the least education, the last people to be hired back are those with the least education." Address at a Luncheon Meeting of the National Industrial Conference Board (February 13, 1961).

617. "As our own history demonstrates so well, education is in the long run the chief means by which a young nation can develop its economy, its political and social institutions and individual freedom and opportunity." Remarks at a Meeting with the Board of Foreign Scholarships and the U.S. Advisory Commission on Educational Exchange (February 27, 1961).

618. "I want our educational system to be the best in the world, because the responsibility upon the graduates of our schools is greater than it is upon any other society." Address in Chicago at a Dinner of the Democratic Party of Cook County (April 28, 1961).

619. "Our goal ... is not simply to provide an adequate educational system — or even a merely good educational system. Our goal must be an educational system that will permit the maximum development of the talents of every American boy and girl." Message to the Members of the National Education Association Meeting in Atlantic City (June 25, 1961).

620. "Whatever decisions we make, whatever events occur in our time, the students of today and tomorrow will face in their time a host of decisions so critical and complex as to demand a degree of wisdom and dedication never previously reached. Thus, to a large extent, the success of freedom then depends upon the success of free education now." Message to the Members of the National Education Association Meeting in Atlantic City (June 25, 1961).

621. "In the last analysis, no amount of federal aid, no amount of new classrooms, no amount of state and local support can succeed without ... [the] daily efforts [of America's teachers] to improve the minds of our children." Message to the Members of the National Education Association Meeting in Atlantic City (June 25, 1961).

622. "[We must] make every effort and meet every challenge to build this Nation's most fundamental resource: the human mind." Message to the Members of the National Education Association Meeting in Atlantic City (June 25, 1961).

623. "[T]hese schools [the nation's land grant colleges] are not maintained ... in order to merely give the graduates of these schools an economic advantage in the life struggle. Rather ... our people realize that this country has needed in the past, and needs today as never before, educated men and women who are committed to the cause of freedom." Address in Seattle at the University of Washington's 100th Anniversary Program (November 16, 1961).

624. "It's not enough that our own home town has a good school, we want the United States as a country to be among the best educated in the world." Address in Miami at the Opening of the AFL-CIO Convention (December 7, 1961).

625. "I believe that it is essential that we recognize ... our obligation to make it possible for any young man or woman of talent and motivation to secure an education and advance their life and interest." Remarks in Columbus at a Birthday Dinner for Governor DiSalle (January 6, 1962).

626. "If this Nation is to grow in wisdom and strength, then every able high school graduate should have the opportunity to develop his talents.... [T]his Nation cannot afford to maintain its military power and neglect its brainpower." Annual Message to the Congress on the State of the Union (January 11, 1962).

627. "There is ... a great tendency ... to consider education important but perhaps not so vital. We are so concerned ... with the problems that are coming today, next year, and the year after — and it does take 5 or 10 or 15 years to educate a boy or girl — and therefore there is a tendency to concentrate available resources on the problems we face now...." Remarks to a Group of Visiting Foreign Educators (February 16, 1962).

628. "[The] purpose of education is not merely to advance the economic self-interest of its graduates ... [but also because of] how important it is to the maintenance of a free society that its citizens be well educated." Address in Berkeley at the University of California (March 23, 1962).

629. "In a time of turbulence and change, it is more true than ever that knowledge is power; for only by true understanding and steadfast judgment are we able to master the challenge of history. If this is so, we must strive to acquire knowledge — and to apply it with wisdom." Address in Berkeley at the University of California (March 23, 1962).

630. "In looking at the long-range or the next decade's needs in manpower, the one thing we are going to need less and less of is unskilled labor. What we are going to need more and more of are educated men and women who are able, technically as well as generally, to handle the increasing complexities of modern industrial life." Remarks on the 50th Anniversary of the Children's Bureau (April 9, 1962).

631. "[I]n order to maintain our position in the world, [America is going to need] the best schools and the best colleges, and the best research centers and the best engineers, and the best scientists — and the best citizens that a free democracy can possibly produce. Those who have these skills, those who are willing to apply themselves to developing their talents, will have the brightest future." Remarks in New Orleans at a Civic Reception (May 4, 1962).

632. "[We] honor all the thousands of other teachers upon whom the future of our country so much depends. We entrust to our teachers our most valuable resource, our children, for very vital years. And what happens to them, really, depends upon [our teachers]." Remarks at Ceremonies Honoring the Teacher of the Year. (May 14, 1962).

633. "[It is a] self-evident truth that a great university is always enlisted against the spread of illusion and on the side of reality." Commencement Address at Yale University (June 11, 1962).

634. "[N]o free society can possibly survive unless it has an educated citizenry." Remarks at the Swearing In of Francis Keppel as Commissioner of Education (December 10, 1962).

635. "There are a good many millions of Americans who live in a family atmosphere which denies them equality of opportunity [to obtain an adequate education], not by law ... but by the very force of economic pressure upon them." Remarks at the 50th Anniversary Luncheon of the Delta Sigma Theta Sorority (January 12, 1963).

636. "The future of any country which is dependent upon the will and wisdom of its citizens is damaged, and irreparably damaged, whenever any of its children is not educated to the full extent of his talent, from grade school through graduate school." Annual Message to the Congress on the State of the Union (January 14, 1963).

637. "Investment in education yields a substantial return in new research, new products, new techniques, in higher wages and purchasing power, and a greater supply of college-trained manpower.... We must improve the quantity and the quality of our education if we are to have growth." Remarks and Question and Answer Period at the American Bankers Association Symposium on Economic Growth (February 25, 1963).

638. "Our national tradition of variety in higher education shows no sign of weakening, and it remains the task of each of our institutions to shape its own role among its differing sisters." Address at the Boston College Centennial Ceremonies (April 20, 1963).

639. "[W]herever we turn, in defense, in space, in medicine, in industry, in agriculture, and most of all in basic science, itself, the requirement is for better work, deeper understanding, higher education. And while I have framed this comment in the terms of the natural sciences ... at every level of learning there must be an equal concern for history, for letters and the arts, and for man as a social being in the widest meaning of Aristotle's phrase." Address at the Boston College Centennial Ceremonies (April 20, 1963).

640. "Men can no longer know everything themselves; the 20th century has no universal man. All men today must learn to know through one another — to judge across their own ignorance — to comprehend at second hand. These arts are not easily learned. Those who would practice them must develop intensity of perception, variety of mental activity, and the habit of open concern for truth in all its forms. Where can we expect to find a training ground for this modern maturity, if not in our universities?" Address at the Boston College Centennial Ceremonies (April 20, 1963).

641. "[E]verything changes but change itself. We live in an age of movement and change, both evolutionary and revolutionary, both good and evil — and in such an age a university has a special obligation to hold fast to the best of the past and move fast to the best of the future." Remarks in Nashville at the 90th Anniversary Convocation of Vanderbilt University (May 18, 1963).

642. "[L]iberty and learning will be and must be the touchstones of ... any free university in this country or the world. I say two touchstones, yet they are almost inseparable, inseparable if not indistinguishable, for liberty without learning is always in peril, and learning without liberty is always in vain." Remarks in Nashville at the 90th Anniversary Convocation of Vanderbilt University (May 18, 1963).

643. "The creation and maintenance of ... all great universities has required considerable effort and expenditure, and I cannot believe that all of this was undertaken merely to give [those schools'] graduates an economic advantage in the life struggle." Remarks in Nashville at the 90th Anniversary Convocation of Vanderbilt University (May 18, 1963).

644. "If the pursuit of learning is not defended by the educated citizen, it will not be defended at all. For there will always be those who scoff at intellectuals, who cry out against research, who seek to limit our educational system. Modern cynics and skeptics see no more reason for landing a man on the moon ... than the cynics and skeptics of half a millennium ago saw for the discovery of this country. They see no harm in paying those to whom they entrust the minds of their children a smaller wage than is paid to those to whom they entrust the care of their plumbing." Remarks in Nashville at the 90th Anniversary Convocation of Vanderbilt University (May 18, 1963).

645. "[O]nly an educated and informed people will be a free people ... the ignorance of one voter in a democracy impairs the security of all...." Remarks in Nashville at the 90th Anniversary Convocation of Vanderbilt University (May 18, 1963).

646. "No country can possibly move ahead, no free society can possibly be sustained, unless it has an educated citizenry whose qualities of mind and heart permit it to take part in the complicated and increasingly sophisticated decisions that pour not only upon the President and upon the Congress, but upon all the citizens who exercise the ultimate power." Commencement Address at San Diego State College (June 6, 1963).

647. "[A]n uneducated child makes an uneducated parent who, in many cases, produces another uneducated child...." Commencement Address at San Diego State College (June 6, 1963).

648. "There is nothing more wasteful than to lose the opportunity to educate a boy or girl. He then is in the labor market for 30 or 40 years, frequently on relief, frequently in trouble, frequently living in a depressed section of your community, costing this country millions of dollars in the final analysis ... and bringing up children themselves who are also uneducated. And so it follows generation after generation, and we never catch up." Address in Honolulu Before the United States Conference of Mayors (June 9, 1963).

649. "[E]very university ... must be interested in turning out citizens of the world, men who comprehend the difficult, sensitive tasks that lie before us as free men and women, and men who are willing to commit their energies to the advancement of a free society." Address at the Free University of Berlin (June 26, 1963).

650. "We depend upon education ... [and] what really challenges us ... is the ability of the great mass of the people to make judgments about increasingly complicated and sophisticated questions.... Experts disagree. New data crowds upon us. Research opens up wide horizons, and if we believe in a free society, we believe in the ability of people to make an intelligent judgment.... They can't do that without the best education, and they can't get the best education without the best teachers." Remarks to a Group of Fulbright-Hays Exchange Teachers (August 23, 1963).

651. "[E]ducation is not merely a means and an end, and not merely a technique, but also a way to the good life which is a way to a more secure and afterlife." Remarks to a Group Attending the Convention of the International Federation of Catholic Universities (September 4, 1963).

652. "There is really not much use in having science and its knowledge confined to the laboratory unless it comes out into the mainstream of American and world life, and only those who are trained and educated to handle knowledge and the disciplines of knowledge can be expected to play a significant part in the life of their country." Address at the University of Wyoming (September 25, 1963).

653. "What we seek to advance, what we seek to develop in all of our colleges and universities, are educated men and women who can bear the burdens of responsible citizenship, who can make judgments about life as it is, and as it must be...." Address at the University of North Dakota (September 25, 1963).

654. "[H]ere in this richest of all countries, the country which spreads the doctrine of freedom and hope around the globe, we permit our most valuable resource, our young people, their talents to be wasted by leaving their schools. So I think we have to save them. I think we have to insist that our children be educated to the limit of their talents...." Address in Salt Lake City at the Mormon Tabernacle (September 26, 1963).

655. "[We have] to make sure that they [America's children] are the best educated citizens in the world ... so that they can develop their own resources ... develop their own talents to the extent that they have those talents, [and] so that they can make something of themselves.... And we ought to try to develop in this country the kind of educational system ... which ornaments the cause of freedom. That is our most important job of conservation and development." Remarks at the Convention Center in Las Vegas, Nevada (September 28, 1963).

656. "[C]ritics of our modern universities have often accused them of producing either too little loyalty or too little learning. But I cannot agree with either charge. I am convinced that our universities are an invaluable national asset which must be observed, conserved, and expanded." Address at the University of Maine (October 19, 1963).

657. "[W]hat good is a private college or university unless it is serving a great national purpose? ... [I]t seems to me incumbent upon ... [those] schools' graduates to recognize their responsibility to the public interest. [W]ith privilege goes responsibility." Remarks at Amherst College Upon

Receiving an Honorary Degree (October 26, 1963).

658. "I believe in an America which provide[s] the maximum amount of education to the maximum number of our children, an America [that] no longer den[ies] a college education to one-third of our brightest students ... [and an America where] it [is] possible for every child of every State and station to attend a well-equipped school under well-trained and well-paid teachers...." Remarks in Philadelphia at a Dinner Sponsored by the Democratic County Executive Committee (October 30, 1963).

659. "Education is a key to the growth of this country. We must educate our children as our most valuable resource." Remarks in New York City at the AFL-CIO Convention (November 15, 1963).

ENERGY POLICY

660. "Without doubt, this nation's vast coal reserves are among our most important assets. And without doubt, no resource has been subjected to more government indifference, short-sightedness and even hostility than these same coal reserves." Remarks of Senator John F. Kennedy, Fairmont, West Virginia (April 18, 1960).

661. "We must embark on a bold, new program of coal research which will find new uses for coal, broaden existing uses, and decrease the cost of coal distribution [a]nd we must stimulate the increased use of 'coal by wire'— the construction of steam plants which will transform coal power into electric power and carry it to the homes of America, vastly increasing coal consumption." Remarks of Senator John F. Kennedy, Charleston, West Virginia (April 20, 1960).

662. "[T]he coal industry is not a defeated industry. Nor is it looking for charity or handouts. It only seeks an equal opportunity in our free enterprise system — a chance to reach its full potential of growth and strength — and to put an end to the discrimination and indifference which is destroying it. For the coal industry today is the most modern and progressive industry in the world ... and it's coal reserves provide an enormous source of fuel for America's future. Remarks of Senator John F. Kennedy, Logan, West Virginia (April 25, 1960).

663. "[T]he coal industry does not want charity — and it does not need charity. It wants and deserves equal treatment — for with such treatment coal will prosper — men will go back to work in the mines — dignity and decent living will be restored to thousands — and America itself will grow stronger." Remarks of Senator John F. Kennedy, Logan, West Virginia (April 25, 1960).

664. "[T]he development of the peaceful use of atomic energy ... can make atomic energy not merely a burden for mankind but a blessing." Speech by Senator John F. Kennedy, High School Auditorium, Pocatello, Idaho (September 6, 1960).

665. "So we [must] use nuclear power for peaceful purposes and power. We [must] use new techniques to develop new kinds of coal and oil from shale ... and ... from the sun we are going to find more and more uses for that energy...." Remarks at the Hanford, Washington, Electric Generating Plant (September 26, 1963).

666. "[W]e must hasten the development of low-cost atomic power. I think we should lead the world in this." Remarks at the Hanford, Washington, Electric Generating Plant (September 26, 1963).

667. "[W]e must maintain an aggressive program to use our hydro resources to the fullest.

Every drop of water which goes to the ocean without being used for power or used to grow, or being made available on the widest possible basis is a waste, and I hope that we will do everything we can to make sure that nothing runs to the ocean unused and wasted." Remarks at the Hanford, Washington, Electric Generating Plant (September 26, 1963).

ENVIRONMENT

668. "[W]e are in the midst of a depression — a depression in the handling of our natural resources. This is not a depression of scarcity — it is not caused by a lack of water or power or land. It is due to despoilment, under-development and neglect — it is due to a lack of vision and a lack of faith — it is due to a reluctance to make the effort needed to transform our untapped abundance into the raw materials required for today's needs and tomorrow's goals. Every day in which we lack leadership — every day in which no plans are drawn or efforts made — plunges us deeper into this depression." Remarks of Senator John F. Kennedy, Western Conference, Albuquerque, New Mexico (February 7, 1960).

669. "[E]very dollar spent on flood control, on reclamation, on power, on increasing water supplies, not only contributes immeasurable to national welfare, but returns many fold to the Federal treasury." Remarks of Senator John F. Kennedy, Western Conference, Albuquerque, New Mexico (February 7, 1960).

670. "[I]n an age of science, the newest of man's tools must be applied to the oldest of man's problems — the development of his natural resources." Remarks of Senator John F. Kennedy, Western Conference, Albuquerque, New Mexico (February 7, 1960).

671. "In twenty years we will almost double our need for water. We will need the fantastic total of 600 billion gallons a day.... The answer — of course — is the re-use of the water which we already have. But water pollution is the obstacle to this easy and effective solution. Almost all of the country's rivers are affected by water pollution — and polluted water cannot be reused. [W]e must halt the destructive filthying of our water if we are to provide the resources on which a sound economy and a healthy population depends." Remarks of Senator John F. Kennedy, Fond du Lac, Wisconsin (February 17, 1960).

672. "[O]ur great national rivers flow past hundreds of cities and towns carrying with them the refuse and the filth of all they touch. The need for healthy water goes beyond political boundaries — it is a national need — and our nation's welfare and our nation's health are gravely affected." Remarks of Senator John F. Kennedy, Fond du Lac, Wisconsin (February 17, 1960).

673. "We ... need increased research and development — to find new methods of conserving and using our great national forests ... as well as to find new methods of exploiting our vast mineral resources — and of developing sources of water in the sea.... [We also need] ... science and technology to find new sources of natural resources, and to develop new uses for those resources which we already have." Remarks of Senator John F. Kennedy, Reception, Madison, Wisconsin (February 24, 1960)

674. "[T]he conservation of our great natural resources — those resources on which much of your economy depends — is a matter of vital interest to all ... a vital national problem." Remarks of Senator John F. Kennedy, Appleton, Wisconsin (March 11, 1960).

675. "[W]e must have vision and strength — we must summon all our resources — the resources of mind and will — and the resources which lie beneath the earth, and in our forests, and in our great rivers and lakes — those resources on which we have built a great nation, those resources on which our continued greatness depends." Remarks of Senator John F. Kennedy, Appleton, Wisconsin (March 11, 1960).

676. "Our forests are one of our most vital assets — they contain ... commercial timber ... they provide recreation for millions — they are the major source of water for more than 1600 cities and towns — they drive more than 600 hydroelectric projects —[and] they are necessary to the control of destructi[ve] floods.... [W]e must our great woodlands as a source of strength for the nation's future." Remarks of Senator John F. Kennedy, Democratic Luncheon, Tucson, Arizona (April 9, 1960).

677. "[W]e must act immediately to stop the destructive filthying of our lakes and rivers — a growing contamination, which is destroying vitally, needed recreational areas ... [a]nd is ... menacing all the major waterways of our country." Remarks of Senator John F. Kennedy, Hinton, West Virginia (April 27, 1960).

678. "[I] know enough about the history of the world to know that water is the key to the development of the United States...." Rear Platform Remarks of Senator John F. Kennedy, Redding, California (September 8, 1960).

679. "[W]e must bring to bear the best minds that this country has on the development of our natural resources.... [W]e have to recognize that in other centuries, in other areas of the world, great countries which ignored their natural resources now lie buried under sand." Rear Platform Remarks of Senator John F. Kennedy, Redding, California (September 8, 1960).

680. "I don't think that there can be any greater disservice to the cause of the United States and the cause of freedom than for any political party at this watershed of history to put forward a policy for developing the resources of the United States of no new starts." Remarks of Senator John F. Kennedy, Frontier Park Cheyenne, Wyoming (September 23, 1960).

681. "We are going to have to make sure that we pass on to our children a country which is using natural resources given to us by the Lord to the maximum; that every drop of water that flows to the ocean first serves a useful and beneficial purpose; that the resources of the land are used, whether it is agriculture or whether it is oil or minerals...." Remarks of Senator John F. Kennedy, Frontier Park Cheyenne, Wyoming (September 23, 1960).

682. "We do not have the right to exploit the natural resources of this country unless we make provision for the 300 million people who are going to live in the United States by the year 2000." Remarks of Senator John F. Kennedy, Civic Center, Denver, Colorado (September 23, 1960).

683. "The pollution of our air and water has reached the proportions of a national disgrace. It endangers our health. It limits our business opportunities. It destroys recreation.... [There must be] national leadership to develop comprehensive conservation plans for all of our great interstate river basins." Speech by Senator John F. Kennedy, Urban Affairs Conference, Pittsburgh, Pennsylvania (October 10, 1960).

684. "[I]f we are to bequeath our full national estate to our heirs — [we must establish] a new long-range conservation and recreation program — [an] expansion of our superb national parks and forests — [and a] preservation of our authentic wilderness areas...." Annual Message to the Congress on the State of the Union (January 11, 1961).

685. "[I]t is our task in our time and in our generation, to hand down undiminished to those who come after us, as was handed down to us by those who went before, the natural wealth and beauty which is ours. To do this will require constant attention and vigilance — sustained vigor and imagination." Remarks at the Dedication of the National Wildlife Federation Building. (March 3, 1961).

686. "I think it is very important to all of us in this generation to pass on and perhaps even better the position of all the natural resources that we have...." Remarks Upon Signing the Federal Water Pollution Control Act Amendments (July 20, 1961).

687. "[H]arnessing science to conservation is going to be the great contribution of our day...." Remarks to the White House Conference on Conservation (May 25, 1962).

688. "[M]any years ago a distinguished French marshal, Marshal Lyautey, asked his gardener to plant a tree, and the gardener said, 'Well, this won't flower for a hundred years.' And he said, 'In that case, plant it this afternoon.' That's the way we all feel about conservation — it won't come this afternoon, but we ought to get started this afternoon, if it's ever going to come." Remarks to the White House Conference on Conservation (May 25, 1962).

689. "What this country needs is a broad, new conservation effort, worthy of the two Roosevelts ... [and] an effort to build up our resource heritage so that it will be available to those who come after us." Remarks in Los Banos, California, at the Ground-Breaking Ceremonies for the San Luis Dam (August 18, 1962).

690. "[It is important] to preserve our Nation's great natural beauty areas to [e]nsure their existence and enjoyment by the public in the decades and centuries to come ... especially those areas close to the major centers of population." Remarks Upon Signing Bill to Establish the Point Reyes National Seashore, California (September 13, 1962).

691. "If we do not plan today for the future growth of these and other great natural assets — not only parks and forests but wildlife and wilderness preserves, and water projects of all kinds — our children and their children will be poorer in every sense of the word." Annual Message to the Congress on the State of the Union (January 14, 1963).

692. "[It is necessary] for us not to take any of our great natural resources for granted. They require very dedicated work ... by all ... who are attempting to protect really our most valuable national heritage which is going to be increasingly endangered by the increase in population and the number of industrial developments in our country." Remarks to Leaders of Twelve National Conservation Organizations (May 20, 1963).

693. "Today's conservation movement must ... embrace disciplines unknown in the past. It must marshal our vast technological resources in behalf of our resource supplies.... Government must provide a national policy framework ... but in the final analysis it must be done by the people themselves." Address at the Pinchot Institute for Conservation Studies, Milford, Pennsylvania (September 24, 1963).

694. "The American people are not by nature wasteful. They are not unappreciative of our inheritance. But unless we, as a country, [act now] ... we are going to leave an entirely different inheritance in the next 25 years than the one we found." Address at the Pinchot Institute for Conservation Studies, Milford, Pennsylvania (September 24, 1963).

695. "It is not always the other person who pollutes our streams, or litters our highways, or throws away a match in a forest.... [A]ll of us therefore must commit ourselves ... to a determined effort to preserve what is left, to develop what we have, to make the most effective use of all the resources that have been given to us." Address at the Pinchot Institute for Conservation Studies, Milford, Pennsylvania (September 24, 1963).

696. "[R]ecreational activities and new national park, forest, and recreation areas can bolster [our] economy and provide pleasure for millions of people in the days to come. If we do what is right now ... we must set aside substantial areas of our country for all the people who are going to live in it by the year 2000.... [W]e have to provide for them, as Theodore Roosevelt, and Franklin Roosevelt, and the others provided for us." Remarks Upon Arrival at the Airport, Ashland, Wisconsin (September 24, 1963).

697. "[W]ith the proper spirit and effort of the people living ... in this country, we can do in the 1960s what was done at the turn of the century, and that is, make this great country of ours more beautiful for those who are here now and those who come after us." Remarks Upon Arrival at the Airport, Ashland, Wisconsin (September 24, 1963).

698. "The fact of the matter is that conservation ... has changed. Before, it was just preserving what the Lord gave us. Now it is using science and technology to find new uses for materials which, a few short years ago, were wasted." Remarks Upon Arrival at the Airport in Cheyenne (September 25, 1963).

699. "[T]here is some feeling in many parts of the country ... that we can afford to waste what we have. I don't believe that at all. I think what we have to decide is how we can put it to best use, how we can ... use of our natural and scientific and technological advances so that in the years to come the 350 million people who will live in the United States in the year 2000 can enjoy a much richer and happier life than we do today." Address at the University of North Dakota (September 25, 1963).

700. "[T]he management of our natural resources instead of being primarily a problem of conserving them ... now requires the scientific application of knowledge to develop new resources. We have come to realize ... that resources are not passive. Resources are not merely something that was here, put by nature. [P]reviously valueless materials ... now can be among the most valuable natural resources of the United States. And that is the most significant fact in conservation now...." Address at the University of Wyoming (September 25, 1963).

701. "A conservationist's first reaction ... [in the early 1900s] was to preserve ... to protect every non-renewable resource. It was the fear of resource exhaustion which caused the great conservation movement of the 1900s.... [B]ut today that approach is out of date.... It is both too pessimistic and too optimistic. We need no longer fear that our resources and energy supplies are a fixed quantity that can be exhausted in accordance with a particular rate of consumption.... Our primary task now is to increase our understanding of our environment to a point where we can ... maintain a living balance between man's actions and nature's reactions, for this Nation's great resources are as elastic and productive as our ingenuity can make them." Address at the University of Wyoming (September 25, 1963).

702. "I hope ... that we will take this rich country of ours, given to us by God and by nature, and improve it through science and find new uses for our natural resources, to make it possible for us to sustain ... a steadily increasing standard of living...." Remarks at the High School Memorial Stadium, Great Falls, Montana (September 26, 1963).

703. "There are two points on conservation.... One is the necessity for us to protect what we already have, what nature gave to us, and use it well ... so that it will be available to those who come in the future. That is the traditional concept of conservation.... But the other part of conservation is the newer part, and that is to use science and technology to achieve significant breakthroughs ... to conserve the resources which 10 or 20 or 30 years ago may have been wholly unknown." Remarks at the Hanford, Washington, Electric Generating Plant (September 26, 1963).

704. "[T]he United States ... bear[s] the burdens which go with being the most powerful country in the free world. And one of those decisions involves the wise use of what nature gave us and also putting science and technology to work to develop new uses ... which can mean so much to the people who come after us." Remarks at the Cheney Stadium in Tacoma, Washington (September 27, 1963).

705. "This is a great country that was given to us and a great land. It is our job, it seems to me, to make the most of it, [to] do in our time to the extent that we can what Franklin Roosevelt did in his time and, before him, what Theodore Roosevelt did in his time — to make sure that we take those steps now which will make it possible for those who come after us to have a better life." Remarks in Heber Springs, Arkansas, at the Dedication of Greers Ferry Dam (October 3, 1963).

706. "The earth can be an abundant mother to all of the people that will be born in the coming years if we learn to use her with skill and wisdom, to heal her wounds, replenish her vitality, and utilize her potentialities.... This seems to me the greatest challenge to science in our times...." Address at the Anniversary Convocation of the National Academy of Sciences (October 22, 1963).

EQUAL OPPORTUNITY AND CIVIL RIGHTS

General

707. "Our job is to turn the American vision of a society in which no man has to suffer discrimination based on race into a living reality.... [W]e must secure to every American equal access to all parts of our public life — to the voting booth, to the schoolroom, to jobs, to housing, to all public facilities including lunch counters. Let us trust no one who offers slick and easy answers — for the only final answer will come from the work of thousands of individual answers, large and small...." Remarks of Senator John F. Kennedy, NAACP Rally, Los Angeles, California (July 10, 1960).

708. "[T]his is one nation and we are all one great people. Our origins may be different but our destiny is the same, our aspirations are identical — there can be no artificial distinctions, no arbitrary barriers, in securing these [civil] rights.... These are not minority rights or even merely civil rights — they are the goals desired and required for every American. There is nothing complicated about these goals, however difficult their achievement. There is nothing unreasonable or unusual about these goals, however much some may resist them. But they will not be achieved without leadership...." Remarks of Senator John F. Kennedy, NAACP Rally, Los Angeles, California (July 10, 1960).

709. "[T]he average American of Caucasian descent does not realize that it is he who is a member of a minority race — and a minority religion — and a minority political system — and that he is regarded with some suspicion, if not hostility, by most of that restless, envious, surging majority. The tide of human dignity is world-wide — and the eyes of that world are upon us." Remarks of Senator John F. Kennedy, NAACP Rally, Los Angeles, California (July 10, 1960).

710. "I am confident that all of us here, as descendants of immigrants, are ready to renew our hospitality to the homeless, the tired, and the poor, from other lands, without discrimination as to national origin." Speech by Senator John F. Kennedy, Cadillac Square, Detroit, Michigan (September 5, 1960).

711. "[W]e believe in the right of every American to stand up for his rights, even if to do so he has to sit down for them." Speech by Senator John F. Kennedy, Civic Auditorium, Oakland, California (September 8, 1960).

712. "Can we honestly say that it doesn't affect our security and the fight for peace when Negroes and others are denied their full constitutional rights ... when we in this country who are a white minority around the world, are asking for the friendship of Negroes and colored people stretching all around the globe, whose good will, whose support, whose common interest we seek to develop in the coming years?" Speech of Senator John F. Kennedy, Shrine Auditorium, Los Angeles, California (September 9, 1960).

713. "[A]s a legislative leader, the President must give us the legal weapons necessary to carry on and enforce the constitutional rights of every American. We must wipe out discriminatory poll taxes, we must provide effective anti-bombing and anti-lynching legislation — and we must continually strengthen the legal framework which permits us all to move forward toward our full constitutional, economic, and political rights." Speech of Senator John F. Kennedy, Shrine Auditorium, Los Angeles, California (September 9, 1960).

714. "[T]he next President must be prepared to put an end to racial and religious discrimination in every field of Federal activity — by issuing the long-delayed Executive Order to put an end to racial discrimination in federally subsidized and supported housing, by revitalizing and making significant the [requirement] ... that those who receive contracts from the Federal Government shall not at the same time practice discrimination in the hiring and in their employing." Speech by Senator John F. Kennedy, Shrine Auditorium, Los Angeles, California (September 9, 1960).

715. "[T]he next President must play his role in interpreting the great moral issues ... our crusade for human rights. He must exert the great moral and educational force of his office to help bring equal access to public facilities from churches to lunch counters.... For only the President ... can create the understanding and tolerance necessary as the spokesman for all the American people, as the symbol of the moral imperative upon which any free society is based." Speech of Senator John F. Kennedy, Shrine Auditorium, Los Angeles, California (September 9, 1960).

716. "This [civil rights] is a great issue ... whether we believe the precepts upon which this democracy was founded ... [whether] we honestly believe what the Declaration of Independence said, that all men are created equal? That they are endowed not by the Constitution and not by the Supreme Court, they are endowed by their Creator with these rights?" Speech of Senator John F. Kennedy, Shrine Auditorium, Los Angeles, California (September 9, 1960).

717. "I want to see an America which is free for everyone, which develops the constitutional rights of all Americans, which will serve as our own symbol, our own identification, with the cause of freedom." Remarks of Senator John F. Kennedy, Riverside Drive Rally, Memphis, Tennessee (September 21, 1960).

718. "You cannot possibly maintain your families unless you get a decent education. You cannot possibly live in decent homes unless you are treated fairly and secure a decent job. As it is now, the first to be fired at the time a recession comes are mostly those who are Negroes, because they have not had a chance to finish school and because they have not had a chance to learn skills." Remarks of Senator John F. Kennedy, Lake Meadow Shopping Center, Chicago, Illinois (October 1, 1960).

719. "We waste our people. There are people born in this country that because of their color do not get as good a job, do not go to as good a school, do not have as good teachers, do not get to go to college, do not get to be professional men, do not get to own their house. I consider that waste, too." Remarks of Senator John F. Kennedy, Marion County Court House, Marion, Illinois (October 3, 1960).

720. "Every American's talents are not equal. Every American will not finish school or college or own a house, but that should be on the basis of his contribution to society, his energy, his vitality, his intelligence, his motivations, not based on the color of his skin. That is the goal of the society which I think we should work toward in the 1960s." Remarks of Senator John F. Kennedy, Howard University, Washington, D.C. (October 7, 1960).

721. "[I]f we are to have progress in this area [civil rights], and [if we are] to be true to our ideals and responsibilities, then Presidential leadership is necessary so that every American can enjoy his full constitutional rights." Speech by Senator John F. Kennedy, State House, Columbia, South Carolina (October 10, 1960).

722. "In America there must be only citizens, not divided by grade, first and second, but citizens...." Speech of Senator John F. Kennedy, National Conference on Constitutional Rights and American Freedom, Park-Sheraton Hotel, New York, New York (October 12, 1960).

723. "[W]e [must] make the best possible use of our people, and that is wherever they may live, and regardless of their race or their creed. We have to use all the talent that we have in this country.... There is no reason at all that a young boy or girl of talent, merely because their skin is a different color, should be denied an opportunity to realize their talents." Speech by Senator John F. Kennedy, Fair Grounds, Saginaw, Michigan (October 14, 1960).

724. "[I]f we are to open employment opportunities in this country for members of all races and creeds, then the Federal Government must set an example.... The President himself must set the key example. I am not going to promise a Cabinet post or any other post to any race or ethnic group. That is racism in reverse at its worst. So I do not promise to consider race or religion in my appointments if I am successful." Speech of Senator John F. Kennedy, Wittenburg College Stadium, Springfield, Ohio (October 17, 1960).

Equal Opportunity/Rights

725. "[I] [see] no reason why, if a Negro baby and a white baby were born side by side, that white baby had twice as much chance of finishing high school as the Negro baby; he had three times as much chance of getting to college as the Negro baby; he had four times as much chance, the white baby did, of having a job and of being a professional man as that Negro baby, and that Negro baby was four times more likely to be unemployed in his life than that white baby. I don't say that all people have equal talent, but what I do say is that everyone should have their chance to develop their talent equally...." Remarks of Senator John F. Kennedy, Fulton and Nostrand, Brooklyn, New York (October 20, 1960).

726. "I want it said at the end of our administration, if we are successful, that every American had an equal chance, every American had a fair chance to develop his talents, and that is all we ask and that is all that any American asks." Remarks of Senator John F. Kennedy, Fulton and Nostrand, Brooklyn, New York (October 20, 1960).

727. "When an African diplomat comes here and can't find decent housing in Washington, it isn't because he is an African; it is because he is a Negro.... Well, we can do better and we are going to have to do better if we are going to survive." Remarks of Senator John F. Kennedy, Fulton and Nostrand, Brooklyn, New York (October 20, 1960).

728. "[T]he longest problem [facing the Nation] ... which is a problem and an opportunity which has been with us since our country was founded ... and that is to make good on the commitments of the Constitution and the Declaration of Independence that all men are created equal, that they are endowed by their Creator with certain inalienable rights, that they are entitled to fairness and justice and equal opportunity, and it is the responsibility of the people speaking through their National Government, speaking through their President, to accord them those rights. That is the first opportunity and the first responsibility of the President of the United States." Speech of Senator John F. Kennedy, Fieldhouse, University of Wisconsin, Madison, Wisconsin (October 23, 1960).

729. "[I]f there are going to be inequalities [among people], it should be on the grounds of their ability and dedication, not on the grounds of their color. That is what we wish to wipe out." Speech of Senator John F. Kennedy, Fieldhouse, University of Wisconsin, Madison, Wisconsin (October 23, 1960).

730. "I want to see America where there are no statistics, Negro and white, but all men, regardless." Speech by Senator John F. Kennedy, Detroit Coliseum, Michigan State Fair, Detroit, Michigan (October 26, 1960).

731. "I don't think ... this country or this society of ours will move ahead until every child who has the talent to develop a superior intelligence, capability, or skill, is given a chance to do it, regardless of his race or his color." Remarks of Senator John F. Kennedy, Johnston Hall, Moravian College, Bethlehem, Pennsylvania (October 27, 1960).

732. "I believe in an America where every child is educated not according to his means or his race, but according to his capacity; where there are no longer literacy tests for voting, because there are no illiterates...." Speech by Senator John F. Kennedy, Convention Hall, Philadelphia, Pennsylvania (October 31, 1960).

733. "If human rights and human dignity are not shared by every American, regardless of his race or his color, then those in other lands of other creeds and other colors, and they are in the majority, will treat our claims of a great democracy with suspicion and indifference." Speech by Senator John F. Kennedy, Convention Hall, Philadelphia, Pennsylvania (October 31, 1960).

734. "[F]ederal money should not be spent in any way which encourages discrimination, but rather should be spent in such a way that it encourages the national goal of equal opportunity. And when Federal budgets are as large as they are ... this quite obviously can be a very effective instrument to carry out a national objective." Remarks at the First Meeting of the President's Committee on Equal Employment Opportunity (April 11, 1961).

735. "I don't think there's any more important domestic effort [equal employment opportunity] in which we could be engaged." Remarks at the First Meeting of the President's Committee on Equal Employment Opportunity (April 11, 1961).

736. "We cannot be satisfied until, first, everyone who wants a job can find it, and also everyone who wants a job will find that job based on their own native ability and desire for work, and not because of their racial or religious extraction." Address in Los Angeles at a Dinner of the Democratic Party of California (November 18, 1961).

737. "[T]hose who are first discharged and the last to be rehired too often are among those who are members of our minority groups. We want everyone to have a chance, regardless of their race or color, to have an opportunity to make a life for themselves and their families, to get a decent education so they have a fair chance to compete, and then be judged on what's in here [on the inside] and not on what's on the outside." Address in Miami at the Opening of the AFL-CIO Convention (December 7, 1961).

738. "America stands for progress in human rights as well as economic affairs, and a strong America requires the assurance of full and equal rights to all its citizens, of any race or of any color." Annual Message to the Congress on the State of the Union (January 11, 1962).

739. "[E]veryone should have the right to develop his talents freely without regard to any other factor. That is what all of us believe in." Remarks at Ceremony on the Signing of Equal Opportunity Agreements by Leading Employers (February 7, 1962).

740. "[Working women] have a primary obligation to their families and to their homes ... [but they should be] able to move ahead and perform their functions [in the work world] ... and ... receive compensation and receive a response from [their] work completely in accord with the work which [they do].... [Working women should be] ... receiving compensation in accordance with the service they render, [and they should be] ... protected in their promotion rights, and all the rest." Remarks to the Members of the President's Commission on the Status of Women (February 12, 1962).

741. "We shall not have fulfilled our obligation as a people unless our children, regardless of the circumstances of their birth, regardless of geography, regardless of their color, have the opportunity to grow to wholesome, self-sustaining adulthood and make something of their lives." Remarks on the 50th Anniversary of the Children's Bureau (April 9, 1962).

742. "[H]owever fortunate our own children may be, we are not fulfilling our obligation as parents until other children have the same opportunities." Remarks on the 50th Anniversary of the Children's Bureau (April 9, 1962).

743. "We must eliminate racial barriers. There is no reason why if your skin is colored you have twice as much chance to be unemployed, about a half as much chance to own your house, about a half or a third as much chance of your son or daughter going to college. This country is a free society, in which everyone can succeed or fail based on what they have inside of them, not what they have outside." Address in Atlantic City at the Convention of the United Auto Workers (May 8, 1962).

744. "[A]ll of us as Americans have a very definite obligation to secure adequate employment opportunities for all of our citizens. The whole essence of our country is the idea that the competition for talent and those that have it, those who have ability, those who are highly motivated, those who work hard, will have a chance to advance ... and that therefore the matter of color or racial origin, religion, and all the rest of it, should not be involved in a society based on the principles which ours is." Remarks to Participants in the Signing of Equal Opportunity Agreements (June 22, 1962).

745. "We cannot have ... important segments of our population who are out in the cold, while opportunities are given to those who are in, based on what we would consider extraneous conditions." Remarks to Participants in the Signing of Equal Opportunity Agreements (June 22, 1962).

746. "The number of school dropouts, the lack of skills [among too many young black people] — this is a real problem.... [Business] may have a good many jobs that [it] would be glad to give to members of minority groups, but [businesses] can't find the people who have the skill ... because they have not had the training and that starts away back before they might have come into [businesses'] sphere of interest. So this is a very long job requiring the efforts of ... all of us ... in an attempt to focus national attention on this matter."

Remarks to Participants in the Signing of Equal Opportunity Agreements (June 22, 1962).

747. "We in the United States are committed to a better life for our people, for no nation can seek social justice abroad that does not practice it at home." Address by the President at a Luncheon Given in His Honor by President Lopez Matcos (June 29, 1962).

748. "I recognize that the present period of transition and adjustment in our Nation's Southland is a hard one for many people. Neither Mississippi nor any other southern State deserves to be charged with all the accumulated wrongs of the last 100 years of race relations. To the extent that there has been failure, the responsibility for that failure must be shared by us all, by every State, by every citizen." Report to the Nation on the Situation at the University of Mississippi (September 30, 1962).

749. "The problem of housing for members of minority groups is a challenge of a special kind. It tests not only our planning skills and productive capacity, but also our sense of fairness; and it is a challenge that must be met if we are to carry out the national policy of a decent home and a suitable living environment for every American family." Filmed Message to the Chicago Convention and Exposition of the National Association of Home Builders (December 12, 1962).

750. "The right to competent counsel must be assured to every man accused of crime in Federal court, regardless of his means." Annual Message to the Congress on the State of the Union (January 14, 1963).

751. "This [racial discrimination] is a national problem. We cannot permit ... an important segment of our population to be denied an opportunity to find decent jobs, to be the first to be unemployed and the last to be rehired, and to be at the bottom of the ladder, and regard that as an acceptable situation. It is a fact today that they are the first to be thrown out and the last to be rehired." Remarks to Participants in the Signing of Equal Opportunity Agreements (January 17, 1963).

752. "It [bringing minorities into the workforce] will require some effort on your [American business'] part. I don't think it is just a question of signing the certificates and indicating a willingness to accept people if they have the talent. I think we probably have to do more than that. You really have to go out and look for them because they won't be able in sufficient cases to find you. I think you have to find them." Remarks to Participants in the Signing of Equal Opportunity Agreements (January 17, 1963).

753. "Too many of the bonds of restriction still exist. The distance still to be traveled one hundred years after the signing of the Emancipation Proclamation is at once a reproach and a challenge. It must be our purpose to continue steady progress until the promise of equal rights for all has been fulfilled." Remarks Upon Receiving Civil Rights Commission Report "Freedom to the Free" (February 12, 1963).

754. "[A]n opportunity and a challenge [exists] for us all of making sure that the American Indians have every chance to develop their lives in the way that best suits their customs and traditions and interests, is a matter which has been of concern to the Government of the United States for many years." Remarks to Representatives of the National Congress of American Indians (March 5, 1963).

755. "[We must] make sure that our private schools are increasingly representative of the diversity of American life. These schools will not survive if they become the exclusive possession of a single class or creed or color. They will enlarge their influence only as they incorporate within themselves the variety which accounts for so much of the drive and the creativity of the American tradition." Recorded Message to the Alumni of the Choate School, Wallingford, Connecticut (May 4, 1963).

756. "No one can deny the complexity of the problems involved in assuring to all of our citizens their full fights as Americans. But no one can gainsay the fact that the determination to secure these rights is in the highest traditions of American freedom. In these moments of tragic disorder, a special burden rests on the educated men and women of our country to reject the temptations of prejudice and violence, and to reaffirm the values of freedom and law on which our free society depends." Remarks in Nashville at the 90th Anniversary Convocation of Vanderbilt University (May 18, 1963).

757. "If our Nation is to meet the goal of giving every American child a fair chance ... we must move ahead swiftly ... [a]nd we must recognize that segregation and education, and I mean de facto segregation in the North as well as the proclaimed segregation in the South, brings with it serious handicaps to a large proportion of the population. It does no good ... to say that that is the business of another State. It is the business of our country...." Commencement Address at San Diego State College (June 6, 1963).

758. "There is a good deal of unfinished business which we have inherited and about which perhaps we have done too little. But I think at least it is understood ... that we are going to meet our responsibility in the 1960s to provide equality of opportunity, to give every child, regardless of his color, a fair chance." Remarks in Hollywood at a Breakfast with Democratic State Committeewomen of California (June 8, 1963).

759. "[A] problem which is not local, but national, not northern or southern, eastern or western, but a national problem, a national challenge, a problem and challenge, and responsibility, and opportunity ... [is] the problem of race relations, the relations of one American to another, wherever he may live and wherever he may work." Address in Honolulu Before the United States Conference of May (June 9, 1963).

760. "[W]herever we are, we must all, in our daily lives, live up to the age-old faith that peace and freedom walk together. In too many of our cities today, the peace is not secure because freedom is incomplete." Commencement Address at American University in Washington (June 10, 1963).

761. "[It is an] unconscionable practice [to] ... [pay] female employees less wages than male employees for the same job." Remarks Upon Signing the Equal Pay Act (June 10, 1963).

762. "[W]hen Americans are sent to Viet-Nam..., we do not ask for whites only. It ought to be possible, therefore, for American students of any color to attend any public institution they select without having to be backed up by troops ... for American consumers of any color to receive equal service in places of public accommodation, such as hotels and restaurants ... without being forced to resort to demonstrations in the street, and ... for American citizens of any color to register and to vote in a free election without interference or fear of reprisal. It ought to be possible, in short, for every American to enjoy the privileges of being American without regard to his race or his color.... But this is not the case." Radio and Television Report to the American People on Civil Rights (June 11, 1963).

763. "If an American, because his skin is dark, cannot eat lunch in a restaurant open to the public, if he cannot send his children to the best public school available, if he cannot vote for the public officials who represent him, if, in short, he cannot enjoy the full and free life which all of us want, then who among us would be content to have the color of his skin changed and stand in his place? Who among us would then be content with the counsels of patience and delay?" Radio and Television Report to the American People on Civil Rights (June 11, 1963).

764. "[T]his Nation, for all its hopes and all its boasts, will not be fully free until all its citizens are free." Radio and Television Report to the American People on Civil Rights (June 11, 1963).

765. "We preach freedom around the world, and we mean it, and we cherish our freedom here at home, but are we to say to the world, and much more importantly, to each other that this is a land of the free except for the Negroes; that we have no second-class citizens except Negroes; that we have no class or cast system, no ghettoes, no master race except with respect to Negroes? Now the time has come for this Nation to fulfill its promise." Radio and Television Report to the American People on Civil Rights (June 11, 1963).

766. "[W]e are trying to erase for all time the injustices and inequalities of race and color in order to [en]sure all Americans a fair chance to fulfill their lives and their opportunity as Americans, and as equal children of God." Remarks at a Dinner Given in His Honor by President Segni [of Italy] (July 1, 1963).

767. "I can neither conceal nor accept the discrimination now suffered by our Negro citizens in many parts of the country; and I am determined to obtain both public and private action to end it." Remarks at a Dinner Given in His Honor by President Segni [of Italy] (July 1, 1963).

768. "I sometimes wonder whether we make as much use of all of our talent that we have in this country as we should. I think particularly of the hundreds of thousands and millions of women teachers, doctors, flyers, a whole variety of skills which they possess which I think we should use to the maximum." Remarks to Members of the "99 Club" of Women Pilots Following Issuance of an Amelia Earhart Commemorative Stamp (July 26, 1963).

769. "[The United States] has launched a determined effort to rid our Nation of discrimination which has existed far too long in education, in housing, in transportation, in employment, in the civil service, in recreation, and in places of public accommodation. And therefore, in this [the United Nations] or any other forum, we do not hesitate to condemn racial or religious injustice, whether committed or permitted by friend or foe." Address Before the 18th General Assembly of the United Nations (September 20, 1963).

770. "We are opposed to apartheid and all forms of human oppression. We do not advocate the rights of black Africans in order to drive out white Africans. Our concern is the right of all men to equal protection under the law...." Address Before the 18th General Assembly of the United Nations (September 20, 1963).

771. "[L]et us remember that the Mormons of a century ago were a persecuted and prosecuted minority, harried from place to place, the victims of violence and occasionally murder, while today, in the short space of 100 years, their faith and works are known and respected the world around, and their voices heard in the highest councils of this country." Address in Salt Lake City at the Mormon Tabernacle (September 26, 1963).

772. "[Today's] view of the South may be distorted by headlines and headline-seekers. The old South has its problems and they are not yet over, nor are they over in the rest of the country. But there is rising every day, I believe, a new South...." Remarks at the Arkansas State Fairgrounds in Little Rock (October 3, 1963).

773. "This used to be an old story, that a civilization could be judged on how it treated its elderly people. But I think it can also be judged on its opportunities for women." Remarks at Presentation of the Final Report of the President's Commission on the Status of Women (October 11, 1963).

774. "I believe in an America where [civil] rights ... are enjoyed by all regardless of their race or their creed or their national origin. While our gains in this area have been considerable ... that issue is still very much with us, and it will continue to be with us until all Americans of every race can regard one another with ... brotherly love. This is not a partisan issue or a Republican or Democratic issue. It is a matter of concern to all Americans...." Remarks in Philadelphia at a Dinner Sponsored by the Democratic County Executive Committee (October 30, 1963).

African American Leadership

775. "[A] far greater responsibility rests upon the Negro leadership than it does upon the leadership of almost any other group...." Remarks of Senator John F. Kennedy, Howard University, Washington, D.C. (October 7, 1960).

776. "Every educated man or woman who is a Negro has not only the opportunity to advance their own private interests — and I think this is true of every American — but they have the obligation to advance the common cause, advance the interests of their own people because in doing that I think they advance the interests of their country." Remarks of Senator John F. Kennedy, Howard University, Washington, D.C. (October 7, 1960).

777. "Looking back at this period [the 100 years since the signing of the Emancipation Proclamation], one must observe two remarkable facts. The first is that despite humiliation and deprivation, the Negro retained his loyalty to the United States and to democratic institutions.... The second is that ... the Negro has never stopped working for his own salvation." Remarks Recorded for the Ceremony at the Lincoln Memorial Commemorating the Centennial of the Emancipation Proclamation (September 22, 1962).

778. "There is no more impressive chapter in our history than the one in which our Negro fellow citizens sought better education for themselves and their children, built better schools and better houses, carved out their own economic opportunities, enlarged their press, fostered their arts, and clarified and strengthened their purpose

as a people." Remarks Recorded for the Ceremony at the Lincoln Memorial Commemorating the Centennial of the Emancipation Proclamation (September 22, 1962).

779. "It can be said, I believe, that Abraham Lincoln emancipated the slaves, but that in this century since, our Negro citizens have emancipated themselves." Remarks Recorded for the Ceremony at the Lincoln Memorial Commemorating the Centennial of the Emancipation Proclamation (September 22, 1962).

780. "He [the American Negro] has not ... been alone in this struggle. Men and women of every racial and religious origin have helped. But ... it is the Negroes themselves, by their courage and steadfastness, who have done most to throw off their legal, economic, and social bonds which, in holding back part of our Nation, have compromised the conscience and haltered the power of all the Nation. In freeing themselves, the Negroes have enlarged the freedoms of all Americans." Remarks Upon Receiving Civil Rights Commission Report "Freedom to the Free" (February 12, 1963).

781. "[A]merican Negroes have never succumbed to defeatism but have worked bravely and unceasingly to secure the rights to which as American citizens they are entitled." Remarks Upon Receiving Civil Rights Commission Report "Freedom to the Free" (February 12, 1963).

782. "[A]t a time of change in the country ... when the Negro community is looking forward to fuller participation in the life of this country [t]here isn't any doubt that education is the key, knowledge is power, and these [Negro] colleges are going to have as undergraduates, and will have a chance to mold as undergraduates, the young men and women who will be the very significant and important leaders of the future." Remarks to Leaders and Members of the United Negro Colleges Development Campaign (September 12, 1963).

Civil Rights Protests

783. "Justice cannot wait for too many meetings. It cannot wait for the action of the Congress or the courts. [M]en of generosity and vision must make themselves heard in every section of this country." Address in Honolulu Before the United States Conference of Mayors (June 9, 1963).

784. "The Federal Government does not control [civil rights] demonstrations. It neither starts them, directs them, nor stops them. What we can do is seek through legislation and Executive action to provide peaceful remedies for the grievances which set them off, to give all Americans, in short, a fair chance for an equal life." Address in Honolulu Before the United States Conference of Mayors (June 9, 1963).

785. "It is clear to me that the time for token moves and talk is past, if we are going to meet this problem [of ensuring equal civil rights for all Americans] and master it, that these rights are going to be won, and that it is our responsibility ... to see that they are won in a peaceful and constructive way, and not won in the streets." Address in Honolulu Before the United States Conference of Mayors (June 9, 1963).

786. "The fires of frustration and discord are burning in every city, North and South, where legal remedies are not at hand. Redress is sought in the streets.... We face ... a moral crisis as a country and as a people. It cannot be met by repressive police action [or] be left to increased demonstrations in the streets. It cannot be quieted by token moves or talk. It is a time to act ... above all, in all of our daily lives.... A great change is at hand, and our task ... is to make that revolution, that change, peaceful and constructive for all. Those who do nothing are inviting shame as well as violence. Those who act boldly are recognizing right as well as reality." Radio and Television Report to the American People on Civil Rights (June 11, 1963).

787. "We have a right to expect that the Negro community will be responsible, will uphold the law, but they have a right to expect that the law will be fair, that the Constitution will be color blind.... This is what we are talking about and this is a matter which concerns this country and what it stands for...." Radio and Television Report to the American People on Civil Rights (June 11, 1963).

788. "This is one country ... because all of us ... who came here had an equal chance to develop their talents. We cannot say to 10 percent of the population that you can't have that right; that your children can't have the chance to develop whatever talents they have; that the only way that they are going to get their rights is to go into the streets and demonstrate. I think we owe them and we owe ourselves a better country than that." Radio and Television Report to the American People on Civil Rights (June 11, 1963).

Federal Intervention

789. "[O]ur Nation is founded on the principle that observance of the law is the eternal safeguard of liberty and defiance of the law is the surest road to tyranny. The law which we obey includes the final rulings of the courts, as well as the enactments of our legislative bodies. Even among law-abiding men few laws are universally loved, but they are uniformly respected and not resisted." Radio and Television Report to the Nation on the Situation at the University of Mississippi (September 30, 1962).

790. "Americans are free ... to disagree with the law but not to disobey it.... [N]o man, however prominent or powerful, and no mob, however unruly or boisterous, is entitled to defy a court of law. If this country should ever reach the point where any man or group of men by force or threat of force could long defy the commands of our court and our Constitution, then no law would stand free from doubt, no judge would be sure of his writ, and no citizen would be safe from his neighbors." Report to the Nation on the Situation at the University of Mississippi (September 30, 1962).

791. "[T]he most effective means of upholding the law is not the State policeman or the marshals or the National Guard. It is you. It lies in your courage to accept those laws with which you disagree as well as those with which you agree. The eyes of the Nation and of all the world are upon you and upon all of us...." Report to the Nation on the Situation at the University of Mississippi (September 30, 1962).

792. "This Government will do whatever must be done to preserve order, to protect the lives of its citizens, and to uphold the law of the land." Radio and Television Remarks Following Renewal of Racial Strife in Birmingham (May 12, 1963).

793. "The Federal Government will not permit it [the Birmingham Agreement which, *inter alia,* called for the desegregation of public accommodations] to be sabotaged by a few extremists on either side who think they can defy both the law and the wishes of responsible citizens by inciting or inviting violence." Radio and Television Remarks Following Renewal of Racial Strife in Birmingham (May 12, 1963).

794. "[L]aw is the adhesive force in the cement of society, creating order out of chaos and coherence in place of anarchy. [F]or one man to defy a law or court order he does not like is to invite others to defy those which they do not like, leading to a breakdown of all justice and all order. [E]very fellowman is entitled to be regarded with decency and treated with dignity." Remarks in Nashville at the 90th Anniversary Convocation of Vanderbilt University (May 18, 1963).

795. "Certain other societies may respect the rule of force — we respect the rule of law." Remarks in Nashville at the 90th Anniversary Convocation of Vanderbilt University (May 18, 1963).

796. "[T]o uphold the law ... is the obligation of every citizen in a free and peaceful society — but the educated citizen has a special responsibility by the virtue of his greater understanding. For whether he has ever studied history or current events, ethics or civics, the rules of a profession or the tools of a trade, he knows that only a respect for the law makes it possible for free men to dwell together in peace and progress." Remarks in Nashville at the 90th Anniversary Convocation of Vanderbilt University (May 18, 1963).

Voting Rights

797. "[P]erhaps the most important — the right of every citizen to vote must be assured. That right is the precondition of all other rights. It is through the exercise of political power that all other rights can — in the last analysis — be protected. And if the right to vote is denied ... if men are not allowed to choose their elected officials — then the very fabric of democratic society is threatened — and no person and no place is secure." Remarks of Senator John F. Kennedy, Reception, Jewish Community Center, Milwaukee, Wisconsin (March 23, 1960).

798. "There is no need for providing the right to vote in some States where Negroes are denied the vote unless they vote to the fullest ... [and] are given their rights to participate in the political process ... as free individuals, not part of some great organization or other, but speaking as individuals, giving their considered judgment on what is best for their country and what is best for themselves and what is best for the cause of freedom." Remarks of Senator John F. Kennedy, Howard University, Washington, D.C. (October 7, 1960).

799. "[L]et me make it clear.... I believe that every American, regardless of their race, their creed, or their color is entitled not only to vote, but to hold office in our country." Speech of Senator John F. Kennedy, Wittenburg College Stadium, Springfield, Ohio (October 17, 1960).

800. "We believe in a maximum extension of the right to vote. We believe in participation. We believe that everyone should vote...." Remarks of Senator John F. Kennedy, Auditorium, Union Hall, New York, New York (October 19, 1960).

801. "The denial of constitutional rights to some of our fellow Americans on account of race — at the ballot box and elsewhere — disturbs the national conscience, and subjects us to the charge of world opinion that our democracy is not equal to the high promise of our heritage." Annual Message to the Congress on the State of the Union (January 30, 1961).

802. "[T]he most precious and powerful right in the world, the right to vote in a free American election, must not be denied to any citizen on grounds of his race or color. I wish that all qualified Americans permitted to vote were willing to vote, but surely in this centennial year of Emancipation all those who are willing to vote should always be permitted." Annual Message to the Congress on the State of the Union (January 14, 1963).

803. "This afternoon, following a series of threats and defiant statements, the presence of Alabama National Guardsmen was required on the University of Alabama to carry out the final and unequivocal order of the United States District ... call[ing] for the admission of two clearly qualified young Alabama residents who happened to have been born Negro.... I hope that every American, regardless of where he lives, will stop and examine his conscience about this and other related incidents." Radio and Television Report to the American People on Civil Rights (June 11, 1963).

FOREIGN ASSISTANCE

804. "[F]arm abundance should be treated as a blessing and not as a curse. There are still more than one billion 800 million people in other lands trying to get by on less than a subsistence diet. There are still tremendous possibilities for using food as a means of capital investment in underdeveloped countries...." Remarks of Senator John F. Kennedy, Stutusman County Democratic Committee Dinner, Jamestown, North Dakota (February 6, 1960).

805. "To us the challenge is not one of preserving our wealth and our civilization — it is one of extension. Actually, they are the same challenge. To preserve, we must extend. And if the scientific, technical and educational benefits of the West cannot be extended to all the world, our status will be preserved only with great difficulty — for the balance of power is shifting, shifting into the hands of the two-thirds of the world's people who want to share what the one-third has already taken for granted." Remarks of Senator John F. Kennedy at Student Convocation, Stanford University, Palo Alto, California (February 12, 1960).

806. "America's great storehouses are overflowing with the great abundance of our land ... food which we cannot consume here at home.

Foreign Assistance

Only America has too much food in a hungry world." Remarks of Senator John F. Kennedy, Howard County Court House, Indiana (April 29, 1960).

807. "Th[e] vast world-wide shortage of food is one of the major obstacles to world peace. Hunger, and the disease it produces, create disillusionment and discontent among the underdeveloped nations ... which provide a fertile breeding ground for communist revolution.... It is time, therefore, for this nation to try a bold new expansion of our food for peace program — with new goals ... to relieve our farm surpluses, and to turn our great agricultural abundance into a blessing — for ourselves, and for all the world." Remarks of Senator John F. Kennedy, Howard County Court House, Indiana (April 29, 1960).

808. "Norman Cousins has written that 'when I enter my home I enter with the awareness that my table is only half set, for half the men on this earth know the emptiness of want....' Tonight all the tables in America are only half set in this sense — and they remain half set until we can begin to use our richness, our abundance and our great resources to drive want away from the tables of men everywhere." Remarks of Senator John F. Kennedy, Howard County Court House, Indiana (April 29, 1960).

809. "[I]t is not enough merely to provide sufficient money. Equally important is our attitude and our understanding. For if we undertake this effort [foreign assistance] in the wrong spirit, or for the wrong reasons, or in the wrong way, then any and all financial measures will be in vain." Remarks of Senator John F. Kennedy, District Hood College, Frederick, Maryland (May 13, 1960).

810. "Let us ... stress our positive interest in, and moral responsibility for, relieving misery and poverty, and acknowledge to ourselves and the world that, communism or no communism, we cannot be an island unto ourselves." Remarks of Senator John F. Kennedy, District Hood College, Frederick, Maryland (May 13, 1960).

811. "[W]e must undertake this effort [foreign assistance] in a spirit of generosity, motivated by a desire to help our fellow citizens of the world — not as narrow bankers or self-seeking politicians." Remarks of Senator John F. Kennedy, U.S. Senate (June 14, 1960).

812. "[I] am confident that, as citizens of one world, we are willing to share our plenty with our brothers in the new states of Asia and Africa, and with those in Europe and Latin America, who need our help and our friendship." Speech by Senator John F. Kennedy, Cadillac Square, Detroit, Michigan (September 5, 1960).

813. "Our purpose [in foreign assistance] is not to buy friends or hire allies. Our purpose is to defeat poverty. Our primary weapons must be long-term loans, technical assistance, and regional development plans, and our goal is to again influence history instead of merely observing it." Speech by Senator John F. Kennedy, Democratic Women's Luncheon, Commodore Hotel, New York, New York (September 14, 1960).

814. "[W]e must help the developing and newly emerging nations of the world to achieve the economic progress on which their political freedom depends. We must be sure that they are strong and stable enough to resist the steady and ruthless infiltration of Communist subversion. We must be ready with bold and imaginative new programs to help eliminate poverty and hunger throughout the world." Speech of Senator John F. Kennedy, Coliseum, Raleigh, North Carolina (September 17, 1960).

815. "I do not regard the distribution of food around the world as a great burden upon us. I regard it as an opportunity, to use our assets in a way which will attract people to the cause of freedom. I am glad that this is our problem and not starvation. I am glad we can produce more than we can consume, if we can share it usefully, for we are our brother's keeper, and if we have great assets in this country, I believe we should hold out the hand of friendship.... I want to help people and I want the United States to be identified with that cause...." Speech by Senator John F. Kennedy, National Plowing Contest, Sioux Falls, South Dakota (September 22, 1960).

816. "[T]here is a world around us which is hungry.... I believe in putting our bread on the water, and I think it will come back to us many times over. I cannot believe that the best use for food is letting it rot in storehouses. I think it should serve people. I think it should serve the cause of peace. I think it should serve us and serve freedom." Remarks of Senator John F. Kennedy,

Marion County Court House, Marion, Illinois (October 3, 1960).

817. "[We must] take a new look at our programs of economic aid. I firmly support such aid — but we must be sure that it is well and efficiently used — and increasingly, we must make assistance to the under-developed nations a cooperative endeavor of the well-to-do developed lands ... those lands we assisted after World War II.... Today, could we not fairly ask our friends ... to carry, according to their ability, a larger share of the financial burden of defending the free world and aiding the underdeveloped nations? Speech by Senator John F. Kennedy, to the Associated Business Publications Conference, Biltmore Hotel, New York, New York (October 12, 1960).

818. "I believe if the United States is going to speak with vigor and strength abroad, it must not only carry on the struggle against the Communists, but it must also identify itself with the people around the globe against poverty, misery, disease, and ignorance." Speech of Senator John F. Kennedy, Commack Arena, Commack, Long Island, New York (November 6, 1960).

819. "I cannot understand those who are the most vigorous in wishing to stem the tide of communism around the world and who are at the same time bombarding the Congress and the Administration with attacks on this [foreign assistance] program. We all get used to paradoxes, but I must say that in all my political life that is one of the most extreme. This is a program which does offer hope of stemming the [communist] advance." Remarks at the Eighth National Conference on International Economic and Social Development (January 16, 1961).

820. "To those peoples in the huts and villages of half the globe struggling to break the bonds of mass misery, we pledge our best efforts to help them help themselves, for whatever period is required — not because the communists may be doing it, not because we seek their votes, but because it is right." Inaugural Address (January 20, 1961).

821. "If we can work closely together to make our food surpluses a blessing instead of a curse, no man, woman or child need go hungry. And if each of the more fortunate nations can bear its fair share of the effort to help the less-fortunate — not merely those with whom we have traditional ties, but all who are willing and able to achieve meaningful growth and dignity — then this decade will surely be a turning-point in the history of the human family." Address Before the Canadian Parliament in Ottawa (May 17, 1961).

822. "[N]o Western nation on its own can help those less-developed lands to fulfill their hopes for steady progress." Address Before the Canadian Parliament in Ottawa (May 17, 1961).

823. "[W]here the contest is one of human liberty and economic growth — and I tie them both together ... because ... economic growth and productivity and material well-being are the handmaidens of liberty — we have the resources ... [and] we have an opportunity in our time to fulfill our responsibilities." Remarks and Question and Answer Period at the Press Luncheon in Paris (June 2, 1961).

824. "The easy work and the popular work ... can be left to many hands. But this work [international economic and social development] requires the effort of committed and dedicated citizens." Remarks at the Eighth National Conference on International Economic and Social Development (June 16, 1961).

825. "[T]he efforts to seize power ... particularly in those countries where poverty and ignorance and illiteracy are the order of the day — can be stemmed only by one thing. And that is governments which are oriented and directed towards assisting the people and identified with causes which mean a better life for the people of those countries." Remarks at the Eighth National Conference on International Economic and Social Development (June 16, 1961).

826. "[T]here's no point in speaking out against the spread of communism unless we are willing to do our part in giving those who are fighting communism the weapon [economic assistance] to fight it. There's no point in calling for vigorous action to protect our security if we're unwilling to pay the price and maintain the burden which are necessary for that security...." Remarks at the Eighth National Conference on International Economic and Social Development (June 16, 1961).

827. "We cannot live in an isolated world. And I would much rather give our assistance in this way — and a large part of it consists of food, defense support as well as long-term economic loans — I would much rather have us do it this way than have to send American boys to have to do it." Remarks to the Citizens Committee for International Development (July 10, 1961).

828. "[We] must not divert our eyes or our energies from the harsh realities that face our fellow men. Political sovereignty is but a mockery without the means of meeting poverty and literacy and disease. Self-determination is but a slogan if the future holds no hope." Address in New York City Before the General Assembly of the United Nations (September 25, 1961).

829. "[F]ree world development will ... be an uphill struggle. Government aid can only supplement the role of private investment, trade expansion, commodity stabilization, and, above all, internal self-improvement. The processes of growth are gradual — bearing fruit in a decade, not a day." Annual Message to the Congress on the State of the Union (January 14, 1962).

830. "It makes little sense for us to assail ... the horrors of communism ... and then to begrudge spending, largely on American products ... to help other nations strengthen their independence and cure the social chaos in which communism always has thrived." Annual Message to the Congress on the State of the Union (January 14, 1962).

831. "Wherever nations are willing to help themselves, we stand ready to help them build new bulwarks of freedom. We are not purchasing votes for the cold war; we have gone to the aid of imperiled nations, neutrals and allies alike. What we do ask — and all that we ask — is that our help be used to best advantage...." Annual Message to the Congress on the State of the Union (January 14, 1962).

832. "[A]s an American I am proud of the effort that this country has made. It is almost unprecedented. We don't seek satellites but friends. None of our efforts [in promoting freedom and prosperity overseas] ... is directed to an economic advantage to us. We seek the association of others. We welcome them. We ... recognize ... that if a few [nations] are prosperous and many are poor, the stability of the world will be endangered." Remarks at the 18th Annual Washington Conference of the Advertising Council (March 7, 1962).

833. "[W]e all know that no matter what contribution the United States may make, the ultimate responsibility for success lies within the developing nation itself. For only [that nation] ... can mobilize the resources, make the reforms, set the goals and provide the energies which will transform [America's] ... external assistance into an effective contribution.... Only [the developing nation] ... can create the economic confidence which will encourage the free flow of capital, both domestic and foreign — the capital which, under conditions of responsible investment and together with public funds, will produce permanent economic advance." Address on the first Anniversary of the Alliance for Progress (March 13, 1962).

834. "None of us feels very happy at having food stored away while others need it, and the way that we can solve that problem is a very human one which transcends national frontiers." Remarks to Participants in the World Food Forum (May 17, 1962).

835. "Aid, the concept of foreign assistance, is not a popular program in the United States. That's a well-known fact.... But I cannot think of any action which is more important [than working with less developed countries] ... in developing the economic thrust of their country so that they ... can solve their problems without resorting to totalitarian control, and becoming part of the [Communist] bloc." Remarks to a Group of Overseas Mission Directors of the Agency for International Development (June 8, 1962).

836. "[Foreign aid] represents a very essential national commitment. It is a burden, but far less than the burden that would be involved to us directly if we did not have this program.... This is a tremendous source of influence for a President of the United States, in exerting the power of this country in a way which serves our security.... If we did not have this program our voice would not be as distinct." Remarks to a Group of Overseas Mission Directors of the Agency for International Development (June 8, 1962).

837. "I don't always know why we have so much difficulty explaining [foreign aid] ... because the arguments are rather easy to make, and they do not require much thought.... But the American people, though they may not like it, in my judgment they support it." Remarks to a Group of

Overseas Mission Directors of the Agency for International Development (June 8, 1962).

838. "[If we can] keep these [less developed] countries free, then we can keep the peace and keep our own freedom. That's what this aid fight is all about.... This way we can defeat communism. This is the way to victory. And I hope that however fatigued we may get with this program or carrying these burdens, the Communists aren't tired, we mustn't be tired, because we can win this way." Broadcast Remarks on Trade and Foreign Aid (September 23, 1962).

839. "One of the most significant contributions that we can make to the underdeveloped countries is to pass on to them the techniques which we in this country have developed and used successfully." Remarks at the Signing of a Contract to Aid Electrification of Underdeveloped Countries (November 1, 1962).

840. "[W]e [the United States and Western Europe] are a relatively small island of prosperity in a very dark sea of poverty. And unless we can adjust our affairs so that the power of the West is brought to bear on the great desperate areas of the world, particularly to the south of us, quite obviously we are going to fail." Toasts of the President and Prince Albert of Belgium (February 26, 1963).

841. "Our growth, private enterprise system, the governmental relationship to it — particularly the governmental relationship which has developed over the last 50 years — represents a very special blend of our population, our skills, our natural resources. It is very difficult to transfer our particular circumstances to another country...." Remarks to a Group of Economics Students from Abroad (April 10, 1963).

842. "No foreign aid program, of course, can and should substitute for private initiative, but it can assist in breaking the path...." Address Before the White House Conference on Exports (September 17, 1963).

843. "Every nation has its own traditions, its own values, its own aspirations. Our assistance from time to time can help other nations preserve their independence and advance their growth, but we cannot remake them in our own image. We cannot enact their laws, nor can we operate their governments or dictate our policies." Address in Salt Lake City at the Mormon Tabernacle (September 26, 1963).

844. "Too often we advance the need of foreign aid only in terms of our economic self-interest. To be sure, foreign aid is in our economic self-interest.... But [also] ... [t]he gulf between rich and poor ... is an invitation to agitators, subversives, and aggressors. It encourages the ambitions of those who desire to dominate the world, which threatens the peace and freedom of us all." Remarks at the Dinner of the Protestant Council of the City of New York (November 8, 1963).

845. "[T]here are still those who ... find it politically convenient to denounce foreign aid on the one hand, and in the same sentence to denounce the Communist menace. I do not say it has purchased for us lasting popularity or servile satellites. I do say it is one essential instrument in the creation of a better, more peaceful world. I do say that it has substituted strength for weakness all over the globe, encouraging nations struggling to be free to stand on their own two feet. And I do not say that merely because others may not bear their share of the burden that it is any excuse for the United States not to meet its responsibility." Remarks at the Dinner of the Protestant Council of the City of New York (November 8, 1963).

FOREIGN POLICY

General

846. "We must encourage, not hamper, the tidal waves of nationalism sweeping Africa and Asia, so that each emerging nation knows that America, not Russia or China, is the home of the Declaration of Independence." Remarks of Senator John F. Kennedy, New Mexico State Democratic Convention, New Mexico (June 4, 1960).

847. "[I]n this country a very valuable national asset ... is the connection with the past; that is the connection with foreign languages. The knowledge of foreign languages, the knowledge of foreign cultures, the knowledge of foreign history, is really the most important asset that we, as a nation, have in our relations with countries abroad." Remarks of Senator John F. Kennedy, Overseas Press, New York, New York (August 5, 1960).

848. "If we present ... an image to the world of hostility, of saying that one country is better than another, by writing that into our national immigration laws, I think we do a disservice to our people and to our country." Remarks of Senator John F. Kennedy, Overseas Press, New York, New York (August 5, 1960).

849. "I[t] is essential on the pathway to peace that the United States associate itself with other countries who also desire to live in peace. We cannot protect the security of the free world by ourselves. We have to join with others ... as leaders of the free world, not dominating [them] but joining it together in a common interest in a desire to be free and independent and live in peace." Rear Platform Remarks of Senator John F. Kennedy, "Pathways to Peace," Fresno, California (September 9, 1960).

850. "Americans cannot stand alone as a tiny minority in a hostile world, without friends and allies.... [I]f we want the support and cooperation of others, we must earn that friendship and respect. We must consider their problems as well as ours, and joined by other free nations of the West ... we must help strengthen the political, economic, and social independence of those countries in the bottom half of the globe who are now emerging on the road to independence, to prevent those countries from succumbing to the chaos and despair which comes with poverty, with no hope of release." Speech by Senator John F. Kennedy, Democratic Women's Luncheon, Commodore Hotel, New York, New York (September 14, 1960).

851. "You cannot separate a strong foreign policy from a strong vigorous domestic economy." Remarks by Senator John F. Kennedy, Columbia Park, Pennsylvania (September 16, 1960).

852. "[W]e have not associated ourselves strongly enough ... with this tremendous force [the desire for freedom] which is sweeping the world. [I]n Indochina ... in north Africa [and] ... in all of Africa [t]hese people may not be able successfully to maintain the kind of democracy that we have, but their desire to be free is our most valuable weapon. We do not wish to dominate them; the Communists do." Remarks of Senator John F. Kennedy, Sioux City, Iowa Remarks of Senator John F. Kennedy, Sioux City, Iowa (September 22, 1960).

853. "These people of the underdeveloped world are not naive. They don't expect the United States to sustain them and I don't think we should. But I do think that they hope ... that we [will] ... work with them in cooperation, not seeking allies in a cold war struggle, but sharing a desire which we have with them to maintain free and independent countries around the world." Remarks of Senator John F. Kennedy, War Memorial Building, Rochester, New York (September 28, 1960).

854. "I have never defended Western colonialism.... The British, the French, the Belgians, however unfortunate their record may have been in the past, at least [the] countries ... they once held are moving into the sunlight of freedom.... Now we ask the Soviet Union to do the same." Speech of Senator John F. Kennedy, Polish-American Congress, Chicago, Illinois (October 1, 1960).

855. "I think the American people in 1960 want somebody who is liberal at home and who is careful abroad. I think they want somebody who builds the strength of this country, who carries a big stick and speaks softly around the world." Speech by Senator John F. Kennedy, Syria Mosque, Pittsburgh, Pennsylvania (October 10, 1960).

856. "I do not think the American people ... will support ... trigger-happy leadership. I believe they want peace — that they want us to make only these commitments which can be honored, which our allies will support, and which we have the arms to back up." Speech by Senator John F. Kennedy, Democratic National and State Committees Dinner, Waldorf-Astoria Hotel, New York, New York (October 12, 1960).

857. "This Nation is clearly pledged to that defense [of Formosa and the Pescadores], and I want to make it clear that if I have anything to say about it, the next administration will stand by that pledge. For there our security is clearly involved. There our prestige is clearly at stake. There our commitment is precise." Speech by Senator John F. Kennedy, Democratic National and State Committees Dinner, Waldorf-Astoria Hotel, New York, New York (October 12, 1960).

858. "The Red Chinese ... are going through a dangerous, aggressive, Stalinist phase. We are not going to let them dominate the Far East — we are not going to appease or retreat under pressure...." Speech by Senator John F. Kennedy, Democratic National and State Committees Dinner, Waldorf-Astoria Hotel, New York, New York (October 12, 1960).

859. "I want [immigration policies that] ... set an image of America that is fair, that stands for the torch of freedom, that encourages [people] to unite their families." Remarks of Senator John F. Kennedy, Banner Democratic Club, 12th District, Brooklyn, New York (October 27, 1960).

860. "[T]oo many ambassadors have been chosen who are ill equipped and ill briefed. Campaign contributions have been regarded as a substitute for experience. Men who lack compassion for the needy here ... were sent abroad to represent us in countries which were marked by disease and poverty and illiteracy and ignorance.... Men who do not even know how to pronounce the name of the head of the country to which they are accredited ... have been sent to important countries ... in the struggle between East and West. How can they compete with Communist emissaries long trained and dedicated and committed to the cause of extending communism in those countries?" Speech by Senator John F. Kennedy, Cow Palace, San Francisco, California (November 2, 1960).

861. "To those old allies whose cultural and spiritual origins we share, we pledge the loyalty of faithful friends. United, there is little we cannot do in a host of cooperative ventures. Divided, there is little we can do — for we dare not meet a powerful challenge at odds and split asunder." Inaugural Address (January 20, 1961).

862. "Let both sides [the United States and the Soviet Union] seek to invoke the wonders of science instead of its terrors. Together let us explore the stars, conquer the deserts, eradicate disease, tap the ocean depths and encourage the arts and commerce." Inaugural Address (January 20, 1961).

863. "[I]f a beach-head of cooperation may push back the jungle of suspicion, let both sides join in creating a new endeavor, not a new balance of power, but a new world of law, where the strong are just and the weak secure and the peace preserved." Inaugural Address (January 20, 1961).

864. "We shall not always expect to find them [former European colonies] supporting our view. But we shall always hope to find them strongly supporting their own freedom — and to remember that, in the past, those who foolishly sought power by riding the back of the tiger ended up inside." Inaugural Address (January 20, 1961).

865. "My fellow citizens of the world: ask not what America will do for you, but what together we can do for the freedom of man." Inaugural Address (January 20, 1961).

866. "[I] think in these days where hazard is our constant companion, that friends are a very good thing to have." Address Before the Canadian Parliament in Ottawa (May 17, 1961).

867. "[I]n the end, we live on one planet and we are part of one human family; and whatever the struggles that confront us, we must lose no chance to move forward towards a world of law and a world of disarmament." Address Before the Canadian Parliament in Ottawa (May 17, 1961).

868. "The foreign policy of the United States is founded upon concern for the welfare of man." Remarks to the National Advisory Council for the Peace Corps (May 22, 1961).

869. "I do not believe that meetings between heads of state ... are designed to solve a series of specific problems or bring about a fundamental change in relationships. [O]nly changes in the realities which underlie the relations between nations, shifts in power, the pressure of events, revisions of policies which reflect new needs, fresh assessments, and the change in power balances within the countries ... leave a permanent mark on the prospects for peace. And while meetings of Presidents and Premiers can sometimes help in fulfilling such changes, they rarely initiate them." Remarks at the Democratic National Committee Dinner in Honor of the President's 44th Birthday (May 27, 1961).

870. "In a fast-moving and revolutionary world where new crises and threats occur almost daily, where the power to make decisive and perhaps irrevocable decisions rests in a few hands, where calculation of how others will react is often a decisive factor in decisions — in such a world I believe it is indispensable for leaders of nations to have an understanding of men with whom they must deal." Remarks at the Democratic National Committee Dinner in Honor of the President's 44th Birthday (May 27, 1961).

871. "Two aims of American foreign policy, above all others [are] ... the unity of the free world, whose strength is the security of us all, and the eventual achievement of a lasting peace." Radio and Television Report to the American People on Returning from Europe (June 6, 1961).

872. "My country favors a world of free and equal states ... [and while much has been done], I do not ignore the remaining problems of traditional colonialism.... Those problems will be solved, with patience, good will, and determination.... [M]y country intends to be a participant and not merely an observer, in the peaceful, expeditious movement of nations from the status of colonies to the partnership of equals." Address in New York City Before the General Assembly of the United Nations (September 25, 1961).

873. "We must work with certain countries lacking in freedom in order to strengthen the cause of freedom. We find some who call themselves neutral who are our friends and sympathetic to us, and others who call themselves neutral who are unremittingly hostile to us." Address in Seattle at the University of Washington's 100th Anniversary Program (November 16, 1961).

874. "[A]s the most powerful defender of freedom on earth, we find ourselves unable to escape the responsibilities of freedom, and yet unable to exercise it without restraints imposed by the very freedoms we seek to protect." Address in Seattle at the University of Washington's 100th Anniversary Program (November 16, 1961).

875. "[W]e must face the fact that the United States is neither omnipotent or omniscient ... that we cannot impose our will upon the ... [rest] of mankind — that we cannot right every wrong or reverse each adversity — and that therefore there cannot be an American solution to every world problem." Address in Seattle at the University of Washington's 100th Anniversary Program (November 16, 1961).

876. "We possess weapons of tremendous power — but they are least effective in combating the weapons most often used by freedom's foes: subversion, infiltration, guerrilla warfare, civil disorder. We send arms to other peoples — just as we send them the ideals of democracy in which we believe — but we cannot send them the will to use those arms or to abide by those ideals." Address in Seattle at the University of Washington's 100th Anniversary Program (November 16, 1961).

877. "[L]et us not heed these counsels of fear and suspicion. Let us concentrate more on keeping enemy bombers and missiles away from our shores, and concentrate less on keeping neighbors away from our shelters. Let us devote more energy to organizing the free and friendly nations of the world, with common trade and strategic goals, and devote less energy to organizing armed bands of civilian guerrillas that are more likely to supply local vigilantes than national vigilance." Address in Los Angeles at a Dinner of the Democratic Party of California (November 18, 1961).

878. "[A]n alliance is an extremely difficult system to operate. The interests of all must be considered. It is far easier for our adversaries to move with speed, commanding as they do their satellites. We are all sovereign and allied, and we are therefore interdependent as well as independent." Toasts of the President and Chancellor Adenauer [of Germany] (November 21, 1961).

879. "We must reject over-simplified theories of international life — the theory that American power is unlimited, or that the American mission is to remake the world in the American image. We must seize the vision of a free and diverse world — and shape our policies to speed progress toward a more flexible world order. This is the unifying spirit of our policies in the world today." Address in Berkeley at the University of California (March 23, 1962).

880. "Our task [America's and other free countries'] ... is to prove that the free life and the abundant life go hand in hand. And that is the central responsibility ... of those who occupy positions of responsibility ... to prove that prosperity and the fruitful experience go hand in hand with liberty. If we can do that, we shall have succeeded. If we cannot do that, then of course our failure will be most awesome." Toasts of the President and President Goulart [of Brazil] (April 3, 1962).

881. "In the life of every nation, as in the life of every man, there comes a time when a nation stands at the crossroads; when it can either shrink from the future and retire into its shell, or can move ahead — asserting its will and its faith in an uncertain sea. I believe that we stand at such a juncture in our foreign economic policy. And I ... believe [that] the United States [chose] to move ahead in 1962." Address in New Orleans at the Opening of the New Dockside Terminal (May 4, 1962).

882. "Let us remember that we are working with allies, with equals — and [we] ... have a responsibility to speak frankly as well as constructively on all issues affecting the West. If the [Western] Alliance were to ... pursue a policy of merely patching over the status quo with the lowest common denominator of generalities, no doubt all disagreements could be avoided or postponed. But dissent does not mean disunity — and disagreement can surely be healthy, so long as we avoid, on both sides of the Atlantic, any ill-tempered or ill-conceived remarks which may encourage those who hope to divide and conquer." Address Before the Conference on Trade Policy (May 17, 1962).

883. "We recognize the right of every nation to order its own affairs, to formulate its own policies, to decide upon its own actions, subject only to the obligations of international law and the rights of other nations." Address by the President at a Luncheon Given in His Honor by President Lopez Matcos [of Mexico] (June 29, 1962).

884. "If change were easy, everybody would change. But if you did not have change, you would have revolution. I think that change is what we need in a changing world, and therefore when we embark on new policies, we drag along all the anchors of old opinions and old views." Address at a Meeting of the American Foreign Service Association (July 2, 1962).

885. "[I]t is our national obligation and in our national interest and security to work for a world in which there is a chance for national sovereignty and national independence." Remarks Upon Signing the Foreign Assistance Act (August 1, 1962).

886. "When burdens are shared, there is no undue burden on any nation. When risk is shared, there is less risk for all. And cooperative efforts to ... share ... responsibilities are not, therefore, based on appeals to gratitude or even friendship, but on the hard and factual grounds of self-interest and common-sense." Remarks to the Board of Governors of the World Bank and the International Monetary Fund (September 20, 1962).

887. "[I]t's most appropriate and important that close allies who are separated by nearly half the globe should have the dearest and most intimate understanding of each other's problems and challenges and opportunities." Remarks of Welcome to President Ayub Khan of Pakistan at Quonset Point, Rhode Island (September 24, 1962).

888. "The United States ... bears responsibilities ... to contain the expansion of communism ... but we are only 180 million people. We are spread very thin around the world. There are a billion people in the Communist empire operating from central lines and in a belligerent phase of their national development. So that I think this is a period of great danger...." Remarks at a Luncheon in Honor of a Japanese Trade Delegation (December 3, 1962).

889. "Alliances are difficult to hold together. Communities of interest — unless there is great, overt danger from the outside, communities of interest are liable to split ... apart." Remarks Upon Presenting the Distinguished Service Medal to Gen. Lauris Norstad (January 9, 1963).

890. "[W]e seek not the worldwide victory of one nation or system but a worldwide victory of man. The modern globe is too small, its weapons are too destructive, and its disorders are too contagious to permit any other kind of victory." Annual Message to the Congress on the State of the Union (January 14, 1963).

891. "[T]he road to world peace and freedom is still long, and there are burdens which only full partners can share — in supporting the common defense, in expanding world trade, in aligning our balance of payments, in aiding the emergent nations, in concerting political and economic policies, and in welcoming to our common effort other industrialized nations...." Annual Message to the Congress on the State of the Union (January 14, 1963).

892. "[L]et our adversaries choose. If they choose peaceful competition, they shall have it. If they come to realize that their ambitions cannot succeed — if they see their 'wars of liberation' and subversion will ultimately fail ... and if they are willing to turn their energies, as we are, to the great unfinished tasks of our own peoples — then, surely, the areas of agreement can be very wide indeed...." Annual Message to the Congress on the State of the Union (January 14, 1963).

893. "[I]n these difficult and dangerous days ... it is of vital importance to the maintenance of freedom that the United States and Canada, Great Britain, the members of the Commonwealth and Western Europe should, joining together, serve as a core of freedom, and spreading out from that core [e]nsure a free world." Remarks of Welcome at the White House to Grand Duchess Charlotte and Prince Jean of Luxembourg (April 30, 1963).

894. "[I]n the nuclear age ... there are no purely political decisions or purely military decisions ... every problem is a mixture of both...." Remarks at Colorado Springs to the Graduating Class of the U.S. Air Force Academy (June 5, 1963).

895. "We live in a world ... where the principal problems that we face are not susceptible to military solutions alone. The role of our military power, in essence, is, therefore, to free ourselves and our allies to pursue the goals of freedom without the danger of enemy attack...." Remarks at Colorado Springs to the Graduating Class of the U.S. Air Force Academy (June 5, 1963).

896. "[W]e do not have a separate military policy, and a separate diplomatic policy, and a separate disarmament policy, and a separate foreign aid policy, all unrelated to each other. They are all bound up together in the policy of the United States." Remarks at Colorado Springs to the Graduating Class of the U.S. Air Force Academy (June 5, 1963).

897. "[W]e can seek a relaxation of tensions without relaxing our guard. [W]e do not need to use threats to prove that we are resolute. We do not need to jam foreign broadcasts out of fear our faith will be eroded. We are unwilling to impose our system on any unwilling people — but we are willing and able to engage in peaceful competition with any people on earth." Commencement Address at American University in Washington (June 10, 1963).

898. "We are bound to many nations by alliances. Those alliances exist because our concern and theirs substantially overlap.... The United States will make no deal with the Soviet Union at the expense of other nations and other peoples, not merely because they are our partners, but also because their interests and ours converge." Commencement Address at American University in Washington (June 10, 1963).

899. "[T]he United States has interpreted its own welfare and its own security in very broad terms since 1945. We have felt that the security and freedom of other countries provided for our freedom and security. [I]nstead of following a national, narrow policy, we have held out our hand and associated ourselves with countries all around the globe in the attempt to build a whole system of free societies...." Remarks to the American Embassy Staff at Bad Godesberg [Germany] (June 23, 1963).

900. "It is not easy to maintain friends in personal life or in international life. There are many things that can disturb us, and [become] highly developed and become well known ... [so] that it requires a good deal of understanding to maintain friendly relations over a long period of time." Remarks to the American Embassy Staff at Bad Godesberg [Germany] (June 23, 1963).

901. "These are the critical days because whether the world survives or not is a matter that comes before us for judgment, at least once every year, and I suppose it is going to go on that rather doleful path." Toasts of the President and Chancellor Adenauer [of Germany] at a Dinner at the American Embassy Club in Bad Godesberg [Germany] (June 24, 1963).

902. "Against the hazards of division and lassitude, no lesser force will serve. History tells us that disunity and relaxation are the great internal dangers of an alliance." Address in the Assembly Hall at the Paulskirche in Frankfurt [Germany] (June 25, 1963).

903. "[W]e live in an age of interdependence as well as independence — an age of internationalism as well as nationalism." Address in the Assembly Hall at the Paulskirche in Frankfurt [Germany] (June 25, 1963).

904. "[T]ruth ... requires us to face the facts as they are, not to involve ourselves in self-deception; to refuse to think merely in slogans. If we are to work for the future ... let us deal with the realities as they actually are, not as they might have been, and not as we wish they were." Address at the Free University of Berlin [Germany] (June 26, 1963).

905. "[I] am proud ... of my own country [because] [m]y country welcomed so many sons and daughters of so many countries, Irish and Scandinavian, Germans, Italian, and all the rest, and gave them a fair chance and a fair opportunity." Remarks at Redmond Place in Wexford (Ireland) (June 27, 1963).

906. "[N]o nation, large or small, can be indifferent to the fate of others, near or far. Modern economics, weaponry and communications have made us realize more than ever that we are one human family and this one planet is our home." Address Before the Irish Parliament in Dublin (June 28, 1963).

907. "[A]cross the gulfs and barriers that now divide us, we must remember that there are no permanent enemies. Hostility today is a fact, but it is not a ruling law. The supreme reality of our time is our indivisibility as children of God and our common vulnerability on this planet." Address Before the Irish Parliament in Dublin (June 28, 1963).

908. "We believe the world is one, that East and West can learn to live together under law, that war is not inevitable, and that an effective end to the arms race would offer greater security than its indefinite continuation, that such progress requires clarity, firmness, against threats from those who make themselves our adversary." Remarks at a Dinner Given in His Honor by President Segni [of Italy] (July 1, 1963).

909. "I believe strongly that the Atlantic Ocean should be to all of us, on the east and the west side of it, a *mare nostrum*, that it should be a common bond, and that it is essential for the maintenance of freedom in both of our continents and, indeed, around the world, that the United States and Canada, and Europe, should work in the closest harmony." Remarks at the Campidoglio in Rome (July 1, 1963).

910. "Nations which agree in applying at home the principles of freedom and justice are better able to understand each other and work together in world affairs." Remarks in Naples at NATO Headquarters (July 2, 1963).

911. "[T]he unity of the West can lead to the unity of East and West, until the human family is truly a 'single sheepfold' under God." Remarks in Naples at NATO Headquarters (July 2, 1963).

912. "It is easy to divide people. It is easy to divide countries. But ... when we look at the world around us and what is at issue today, and what we stand for ... I think it is important that we work together. And I admire those who seek to strengthen that cooperation...." Remarks to a Group from the Military Schools of Brazil (August 27, 1963).

913. "[We] determined in the years following the Second World War ... that our security was best served in a world of diversity. If there could be a whole variety of sovereign states stretching around the world, living ... in ... freedom, not part of the Communist bloc ... it would be impossible for any group to mobilize sufficient force to imperil the United States. Our basic objective has [thus] been to maintain the security and interest of the United States by maintaining the freedom of other countries." Address in Duluth [Minnesota] to Delegates to the Northern Great Lakes Region Land and People Conference (September 24, 1963).

914. "[W]e are trying to assist the hundred-odd countries which are now independent to maintain their independence. We do that not only because we wish them to be free, but because it serves our own national interest. As long as there are all of these countries separate, free, and independent, and not part of one great monolithic bloc which threatens us, so long we are free and independent." Remarks at the Yellowstone County Fairgrounds, Billings, Montana (September 25, 1963).

915. "One central theme has run through the foreign policy of the United States, and that is, in a dangerous and changing world it is essential that the 180 million people of the United States throw their weight into the balance in every struggle, in every country on the side of freedom." Remarks at the High School Memorial Stadium, Great Falls, Montana (September 26, 1963).

916. "[F]oreign policy in the modern world does not lend itself to easy, simple black and white solution. If we were to have diplomatic relations only with those countries whose principles we approved of, we would have relations with very few countries in a very short time. If we were to withdraw our assistance from all governments who are run differently from our own, we would relinquish half the world immediately to our adversaries. If we were to treat foreign policy as merely a medium for delivering self-righteous sermons to supposedly inferior people, we would give up all thought of world influence or world leadership." Address in Salt Lake City at the Mormon Tabernacle (September 26, 1963).

917. "[T]he purpose of foreign policy is not to provide an outlet for our own sentiments of hope or indignation; it is to shape real events in a real world. We cannot adopt a policy which says that if something does not happen, or others do not do exactly what we wish, we will return to 'Fortress America.' That is the policy ... of retreat, not of strength." Address in Salt Lake City at the Mormon Tabernacle (September 26, 1963).

918. "I think it is most important that we have — across the distance of water and across perhaps a difference in political philosophy — that we have an understanding of the basic policies and objectives of the countries through the globe so that danger may be lessened." Remarks of Welcome at the White House to President Tito of Yugoslavia (October 17, 1963).

Europe

919. "[W]e must never, at the summit, in any treaty declaration, in our words or even in our minds, recognize the Soviet domination of eastern Europe as permanent. We must never do it." Speech of Senator John F. Kennedy, Polish-American Congress, Chicago, Illinois (October 1, 1960).

920. "[T]he hope of freedom in Eastern Europe, the hope of stalemating the Communist advance and turning it, depends not upon goodwill missions.... It depends on one thing, the power, vitality, conviction, direction, and perseverance of the great Republic of the United States. That is what counts — what we do." Remarks of Senator John F. Kennedy, Hartford Times Steps, Hartford, Connecticut (November 7, 1960).

921. "[O]ur security is inevitably tied up with the security of Europe. The United States cannot look forward to a free existence if Western Europe is not free." Remarks in Paris Before the North Atlantic Council (June 1, 1961).

922. "The United States cannot withdraw from Europe, unless and until Europe should wish us gone. We cannot distinguish its defenses from our own.... [O]ur policies in Europe today are founded on one deep conviction: that the threat to Western Europe and freedom [are] basically indivisible, as is the Western deterrent to that threat.... The United States, therefore, is committed to the defense of Europe, by history as well as by choice." Address Before the Conference on Trade Policy (May 17, 1962).

923. "We have no wish to join, much less to dominate, the European community. We have no intention of interfering in its internal affairs. But neither do we hope or plan to please all of our European allies, who do not always agree with each other, on every topic of discussion — or to base those decisions which affect the long run state of the common security on the short-term state of

924. "As long as the United States is staking its own national security on the defense of Europe ... we will continue to participate in the great decisions affecting war and peace in that area. A coherent policy cannot call for both our military presence and our diplomatic absence." Address Before the Conference on Trade Policy (May 17, 1962).

925. "We cannot and do not take any European ally for granted — and I hope no one in Europe would take us for granted either. Our willingness to bear our full share of Western defenses is deeply felt — but it is not automatic. American public opinion has turned away from isolation — but its faith must not be shattered. Our commitment ... is to a common united defense, in which every member of the Western Community plays a full and responsible role, to the limit of his capability and in reliance on the strength of others — and it is that commitment which will be fulfilled." Address Before the Conference on Trade Policy (May 17, 1962).

926. "We do not regard a strong and united Europe as a rival but as a partner. To aid its progress has been the basic object of our foreign policy for years. We see in such a Europe a partner with whom we can deal on a basis of full equality in all the great and burdensome tasks of building and defending a community of free nations." Address at Independence Hall, Philadelphia (July 4, 1962).

927. "Our old dangers are not gone beyond return, and any division among us [the United States and Europe] would bring them back in doubled strength. Our defenses are now strong — but they must be made stronger. Our economic goals are now clear — but we must get on with their performance. And the greatest of our necessities, the most notable of our omissions, is progress toward unity of political purpose." Address in the Assembly Hall at the Paulskirche in Frankfurt [Germany] (June 25, 1963).

928. "[I] believe so strongly that the great power of Europe should be harnessed to the great power of the United States, and together both Europe and the United States should concern themselves not merely with the business of our own immediate interests, but with the business of the free world's interest all around the globe." Remarks to the American Embassy Staff at the Ambassador's Residence in Rome [Italy] (July 1, 1963).

929. "There will always be honest differences among friends [the United States and Europe]; and they should be freely and frankly discussed. But these are differences of means, not ends. They are differences of approach, not spirit." Remarks in Naples at NATO Headquarters (July 2, 1963).

930. "We did not assist in the revival of Europe to maintain its dependence on the United States.... We welcome a stronger partner. For today no nation can build its destiny alone; the age of self-sufficient nationalism is over. The age of interdependence is here. The cause of Western European unity is based on logic and common sense. It is based on moral and political truths. It is based on sound military and economic principles. And it is based on the tide of history." Remarks in Naples at NATO Headquarters (July 2, 1963).

Israel and the Middle East

931. "We must give our support to programs to help people instead of regimes — to work in terms of their problems, not ours — and seek a permanent settlement among Arabs and Israelis based not on an armed truce but on mutual self-interest. Guns and anti-communist pacts and propaganda and the traditional piecemeal approach are not enough — refugee resettlement and a regional resources development fund in full partnership with the Middle Eastern nations, are all parts of a long-range strategy which is both practical and in the best interests of all concerned." Remarks of Senator John F. Kennedy, U.S. Senate (June 14, 1960).

932. "Peace is our primary objective in the Middle East — and peace is partly our responsibility. 'Seek peace, and pursue it' commands the psalmist. And that we must do. With open minds, open hearts, and the priceless asset of our American heritage, we shall seek peace in the Middle East, as elsewhere. And when history writes its verdict, let it be said that we pursued the peace with all the courage, all the strength, and all the resourcefulness at our command." Speech by Senator John F. Kennedy, Zionists of America Convention, Statler Hilton Hotel, New York, New York (August 26, 1960).

933. "[I] have always believed that there is no real conflict or contradiction between the genuine aspirations of the Arab nations and the genuine aspirations of Israel. The Arab peoples rose to freedom and independence in the very years which saw the rise of Israel. From the cooperation of these two awakened nationalisms could come a new golden age for the Middle East. But from their destructive vendetta can come nothing but misery and poverty and the risk of war." Speech by Senator John F. Kennedy, Zionists of America Convention, Statler Hilton Hotel, New York, New York (August 26, 1960).

934. "Time will judge whether Israel will continue to exist. But I wish I could be as sure of all my prophecies as I am of my flat prediction that Israel is here to stay. For Israel was not created in order to disappear—Israel will endure and flourish. It is the child of hope and the home of the brave. It can neither be broken by adversity nor demoralized by success. It carries the shield of democracy and it honors the sword of freedom; and no area of the world has ever had an overabundance of democracy and freedom." Speech by Senator John F. Kennedy, Zionists of America Convention, Statler Hilton Hotel, New York, New York (August 26, 1960).

935. "[O]ur national policy ... [has been one] of extending the hand of friendship to all those nations, independent, who desire to be free, who desire to associate with us in a great international effort to extend freedom to all people." Remarks of Senator John F. Kennedy, Bonds for Israel Dinner, Philadelphia, Pennsylvania (October 31, 1960).

936. "I hope that the United States will hold out the hand of friendship to Israel. I hope that we will make it clear that we stand by our commitments and by our friends and by the United Nations, that we will defend those who wish to be free and independent; that we will work for peace; that we will use our influence through the United Nations, through the World Bank, through our own effort, to provide for the spreading of peace in the Middle East." Remarks of Senator John F. Kennedy, Bonds for Israel Dinner, Philadelphia, Pennsylvania (October 31, 1960).

937. "The Bible says, 'Blessed are the peacemakers.' We shall pursue peace, and that shall be our objective, here in the United States, in the Middle East, in the relationship which Israel has with the surrounding countries. Justice and peace is our objective, and those who share those objectives in their domestic and foreign policy shall find friendship here in the United States." Remarks of Senator John F. Kennedy, Bonds for Israel Dinner, Philadelphia, Pennsylvania (October 31, 1960).

Latin America

938. "[T]he major issue is the fight against communism, but to them, those who live to the south of us, the fighting is against poverty and disease and illiteracy and ignorance. Each time they feel that we seek to gain their friendship in order to secure a new recruit in a battle against the communism, and each time we dismiss anti-American agitators as tools of the Communists, or condemn neutrals out of hand, our prestige will suffer and our relations with those with whom we wish to be friends will worsen." Speech of Senator John F. Kennedy, Civic Auditorium, Portland, Oregon (September 7, 1960).

939. "[T]he people of Latin America upon whom our security depends, just as upon our freedom their security depends, have turned increasingly away from the good neighbor policy which once was a source of comfort and satisfaction both to the North and to the South [because we] failed to recognize ... the necessity of holding out a hand of friendship until Castro's actions forced us to do so.... I don't want to see the United States do anything in Latin America at the point of Castro's pistol. I want us to do it because we believe in it." Remarks of Senator John F. Kennedy, the Alamo, San Antonio, Texas (September 12, 1960).

940. "[T]here [is] no security for the United States unless there was a happy atmosphere existing, a good neighbor policy existing between Latin America and the United States.... We together with Latin America are one. When the

United States moves in a different direction from Latin America, we adversely affect the security of every American." Remarks of Senator John F. Kennedy, Cortez Hotel Plaza, El Paso, Texas (September 12, 1960).

941. "[I]f we are to halt the advance of Latin communism, we must create a Latin America where freedom can flourish — where long enduring people know, at last, that they are moving toward a better life for themselves and their children — where steady economic advance is a framework for stable, democratic Government — and where tyranny, isolated and despised, eventually withers on the vine." Speech by Senator John F. Kennedy, Democratic Dinner, Cincinnati, Ohio (October 6, 1960).

942. "If we continue to repeat our past errors — if we continue to care more for the support of regimes than the friendship of people — if we continue to devote greater effort to the support of dictators than to the fight against poverty and hunger — then rising discontent will provide fertile ground for Castro and his Communist friends." Speech by Senator John F. Kennedy, Democratic Dinner, Cincinnati, Ohio (October 6, 1960).

943. "The perils and hardships [throughout Latin America] will be many. But here in America we pledge ourselves to raise high the light of freedom — until it burns brightly from the Arctic to Cape Horn — and one day that light will shine again." Speech by Senator John F. Kennedy, Democratic Dinner, Cincinnati, Ohio (October 6, 1960).

944. "Let all our neighbors know that we shall join with them to oppose aggression or subversion anywhere in the Americas. And let every other power know that this Hemisphere intends to remain the master of its own house." Inaugural Address (January 20, 1961).

945. "[T]his New World of ours is not a mere accident of geography. Our continents are bound together by a common history, the endless exploration of new frontiers. Our nations are the product of a common struggle, the revolt from colonial rule. And our people share a common heritage, the quest for the dignity and the freedom of man." Address at a White House Reception for Members of Congress and for the Diplomatic Corps of the Latin American Republics (March 13, 1961).

946. "[P]olitical freedom [throughout Latin America] must be accompanied by social change. For unless necessary social reforms, including land and tax reform, are freely made — unless we broaden the opportunity for all of our people — unless the great mass of Americans share in increasing prosperity — then our alliance, our revolution, our dream, and our freedom will fail." Address at a White House Reception for Members of Congress and for the Diplomatic Corps of the Latin American Republics (March 13, 1961).

947. "The Organization of American States represents a great dream of those who believe that the people of this hemisphere must be bound more closely together." Remarks at the Protocolary Session of the Council of the Organization of American States (April 14, 1961).

948. "[The] Alliance for Progress is more than a doctrine of development — a blueprint of economic advance.... [I]t is an expression of the noblest goals of our society. It says that want and despair need not be the lot of free men ... that no society is free until all its people have an equal opportunity to share the fruits of their own land and their own labor [a]nd that material progress is meaningless without individual freedom and political liberty. It is a doctrine of the freedom of man in the most spacious sense of that freedom." Address on the first Anniversary of the Alliance for Progress (March 13, 1962).

949. "[T]he course of rational social change is even more hazardous for those progressive governments who often face entrenched privilege of the right and subversive conspiracies on the left." Address on the First Anniversary of the Alliance for Progress (March 13, 1962).

950. "[T]he United States of America is committed to ... work together ... with all the other nations of the inter-American system, to create a society in which all men have equal access to land, to jobs, and to education — a society in which no man is exploited for the enrichment of a few, and in which every arm of the Government is dedicated to the welfare of all the people." Address by the President at a Luncheon Given in His Honor by President Lopez Matcos [of Mexico] (June 29, 1962).

951. "[W]e in this hemisphere are not merely against something; we are strongly for something, and that is the opportunity to provide, through freedom, a better life for our people. So that as long as we are free, as long as we are able to maintain that freedom, we have to use that freedom ... to provide internally a more equitable and more fruitful life for the people...." Remarks to Students and Members of the Faculty of the Brazilian Escola Superior de Guerra (October 30, 1962).

952. "[A]ll of the members of this hemisphere are involved in a great enterprise, which is to demonstrate that countries facing ... very serious problems ... can through a system of freedom and a system of democracy successfully solve these problems and demonstrate that not only can people live more happily in freedom, but can also live more prosperously." Toasts of the President and President Alessandri [of Chile] (December 11, 1962).

953. "If we can demonstrate in this [Western] hemisphere that through democratic means, through progressive means, that we can solve the problems of this hemisphere then, of course, this battle [with Communism] will be won." Remarks of Welcome at the White House to President Betancourt of Venezuela (February 19, 1963).

954. "We have a good deal of unfinished business in this [Western] hemisphere and I think it's important that in the days to come as we attempt to protect this hemisphere from foreign subversion and foreign activities directed against the liberties of this hemisphere...." Remarks to a Group of Staff Members and Students of the Argentine War College (March 1, 1963).

955. "[I]t is our responsibility in this [Western] hemisphere ... to demonstrate that economic prosperity is the handmaiden of political liberty. That is the responsibility of all of us. If we meet that responsibility, then [all countries] ... will remain free. If we do not meet this responsibility, then their inevitable fate will be one of enslavement by those who already have indicated their desire to crush out independence...." Remarks Upon Arrival at the Airport, San Jose, Costa Rica (March 18, 1963).

956. "Our great effort, in [Latin America] ... must be to help construct democratic, responsible, and stable governments which provide an ever-increasing standard of living for the people of their countries. That is our objective.... That is the meaning of the Alliance for Progress." Remarks to Members of the American Colony in San Jose [Costa Rica] (March 18, 1963).

957. "[T]oday we are faced not merely with the protection of new nations, but with the remolding of ancient societies — not only with the destruction of political enemies, but with the destruction of poverty, hunger, ignorance, and disease — not [only] with the creation of national dignity but with the preservation of human dignity. To meet this enormous challenge, the peoples of the Americas have fashioned an Alianza para el Progreso...." Address at the Teatro Nacional in San Jose [Costa Rica] Upon Opening the Presidents' Conference (March 18, 1963).

958. "[U]nless those of us now making an effort are willing to redouble our efforts, unless the rich are willing to use some of their riches more wisely, unless the privileged are willing to yield up their privileges to a common good, unless the young and the educated are given opportunities to use their education, and unless governments are willing to dedicate themselves tirelessly to the tasks of governing efficiently and developing swiftly, then ... our Alianza [para el Progresso] will fail, and with it will fall the society of free nations which our forefathers labored to build." Address at the Teatro Nacional in San Jose [Costa Rica] Upon Opening the Presidents' Conference (March 18, 1963).

959. "[N]o man's job is done until every man in this [Western] hemisphere shares an equal opportunity to pursue his hopes as far as his capacities will carry him. That is the commitment of this country [Costa Rica] and my own...." Remarks at El Bosque Housing Project Near San Jose [Costa Rica] (March 19, 1963).

960. "The more we can do to link the sister republics of this [Western] hemisphere in one great community, the stronger we will all be, the greater we will serve our national interests, and the more abundant we will make the life of our people." Remarks to the Delegates to the Pan American Highway Congress (May 7, 1963).

961. "We want a fairer distribution of the wealth of Latin America, because we think that a degree of equality of economic opportunity is essential for political stability and for a system of freedom." Remarks to a Group of Student Leaders from Brazil (July 30, 1963).

962. "[T]he United States values its relations with the countries of Latin America because of historical reasons, cultural reasons, hemispheric ties, geography, and all the rest, probably more warmly than it does any of its obligations and responsibilities around the world." Toasts of the President and President Paz [of Bolivia] at a Luncheon at the White House (October 22, 1963).

963. "Time may not always be our friend. [T]his decade must mark a major effort by the United States, in association with the other countries of this [Western] hemisphere, in attacking the problems of poverty, misery and disease, and lack of opportunity." Toasts of the President and President Paz at a Luncheon at the Bolivian Embassy (October 23, 1963).

964. "[T]he goals and the methods of the Alliance [for Progress], represent the only hope whereby men of good will can obtain progress without despotism, social justice without social terror. And it is on the Alliance for Progress that we base our common hope for the future." Address in Miami Before the Inter-American Press Association (November 18, 1963).

965. "Whatever may be the case in other parts of the world, this [the Western Hemisphere] is a hemisphere of free men capable of self-government. It is in accordance with this belief that the United States will continue to support the efforts of those seeking to establish and maintain constitutional democracy." Address in Miami Before the Inter-American Press Association (November 18, 1963).

Southeast Asia

966. "South Viet-Nam is already under attack — sometimes by a single assassin, sometimes by a band of guerrillas, recently by full battalions. The peaceful borders of Burma, Cambodia, and India have been repeatedly violated. And the peaceful people of Laos are in danger of losing the independence they gained not so long ago. No one can call these 'wars of liberation.' For these are free countries living under their own governments. Nor are these aggressions any less real because men are knifed in their homes and not shot in the fields of battle." Address in New York City Before the General Assembly of the United Nations (September 25, 1961).

967. "The systematic aggression now bleeding that country [Viet-Nam] is not a 'war of liberation' — for Viet-Nam is already free. It is a war of attempted subjugation — and it will be resisted." Annual Message to the Congress on the State of the Union (January 11, 1962).

968. "Chairman Khrushchev and I ... have committed [ourselves] to the goal of the maintenance of a neutral and independent Laos. If this goal ... can be successfully implemented ... the chances of a peaceful relationship between great powers with great military capacities will be substantially increased ... at a very critical time in history.... If our common efforts and commitments in Laos fail, then the future not only of Laos but of a good deal of the rest of the world becomes darker." Toasts of the President and Prince Souvanna Phouma, Prime Minister of Laos (July 27, 1962).

969. "We are assisting the people of Viet-Nam.... If we stop helping them, they stand on the razor edge today. If we stop helping them, they will become ripe for internal subversion and a Communist takeover." Broadcast Remarks on Trade and Foreign Aid (September 23, 1962).

970. "[W]hen you ask why are we in Laos, or Viet-Nam, or the Congo, or why do we support the Alliance for Progress in Latin America, we do so because we believe that our freedom is tied up with theirs, and if we can develop a world in which all the countries are free, then the threat to the security of the United States is lessened. So we have to stay at it. We must not be fatigued." Remarks at the High School Memorial Stadium, Great Falls, Montana (September 26, 1963).

FOUNDING FATHERS

971. "During the Constitutional Convention there was behind the desk of General Washington a painting of a sun low on the horizon, and many of the delegates wondered during the debate whether it was a rising or a setting sun. At the conclusion, Benjamin Franklin stood up. He said, 'Because of what we have done here, we now know that it is a rising sun, and the beginning of a great new day.'" Remarks of Senator John F. Kennedy, Eastern Carolina Stadium, Greenville, North Carolina (September 17, 1960).

972. "[A]ll of us as Americans are constantly bemused and astounded by this extraordinary golden age in our history which produced so many men of exceptional talent. I have not heard, nor I suppose is there a rational explanation for the fact that this small country, possessed of a very limited population, living under harsh circumstances, produced so ... many brilliant and extraordinary figures who set the tone for our national life and who really represent the most extraordinary outpouring of human ability devoted to government, really, than any time since the days of Greece." Remarks at a Luncheon Marking the Publication of the First Four Volumes of the Adams Papers (October 3, 1961).

973. "[T]he people who wrote the Declaration of Independence from the beginning recognized ... that they were not advancing a theory of government merely for the people of the United States, but for the people around the world. [The Founding Fathers] all emphasized that this spirit which had motivated the Declaration of Independence represented the basic concept which should govern around the world, of the relationship between the Government and the people." Remarks at an Independence Day Celebration with the American Community in Mexico City [Mexico] (June 30, 1962).

974. "[T]hey [the signers of the Declaration of Independence] gathered to affix their names to a document which was, above all else, a document not of rhetoric but of bold decision. It was, it is true, a document of protest — but protests had been made before. It set forth their grievances with eloquence — but such eloquence had been heard before. But what distinguished this paper from all the others was the final irrevocable decision that it took — to assert the independence of free States in place of colonies, and to commit to that goal their lives, their fortunes, and their sacred honor." Address at Independence Hall, Philadelphia, Pennsylvania (July 4, 1962).

975. "The men who first shaped the democratic legacy ... were filled with a sense of excitement and of wonder at the importance of the events in which they were participating. It was not only ... that they were to have the unique opportunity to write a new Constitution and form a new government and begin a new nation; it was also the deep conviction ... that here we have planted the standard of freedom, and here we will test the capacities of men for self-government." Remarks at the 50th Annual Meeting of the Anti-Defamation League of B'nai B'rith (January 31, 1963).

976. "It is an extraordinary fact of history ... unmatched since the days of early Greece, that this country should have produced during its [founding] days ... such an extraordinary range of scholars and creative thinkers who helped build this country — Jefferson, Franklin ... and all the rest. This is a great tradition which we must maintain in our time with increasing strength and increasing vigor." Commencement Address at San Diego State College (June 6, 1963).

977. "The more we can know what they [the Founding Fathers] really thought, the more we can follow their extraordinary careers, almost day by day, [and] the more ... the American people are given a certain sense of confidence in their past which in turn gives them confidence in their future." Remarks at a Luncheon for Sponsors and Editors of Historical Publications (June 17, 1963).

978. "[I]t is well to remember that this Nation's first great leaders, our founders — Jefferson, Madison, Monroe, Jay, Mason, Bryan, and all the rest — were not only the political leaders of this country, but they were also among the most educated citizens that this country had ever produced." Remarks at the Cheney Stadium in Tacoma, Washington (September 27, 1963).

FREE ENTERPRISE SYSTEM

979. "[I] believe a strong America is a growing America, a nation that is developing all of its resources to the fullest possible potential, human, scientific, economic, and natural, and developing these resources under a free enterprise system that looses the energy of our people." Remarks of Senator John F. Kennedy, Memorial Auditorium Dallas, Texas (September 13, 1960).

980. "I believe in an America where the free enterprise system flourishes for all other systems to see and admire — where no businessman lacks either competition or credit — and where no monopoly, no racketeer, no government bureaucracy can put him out of business that he built up with his own initiative." Speech by Senator John F. Kennedy, Convention Hall, Philadelphia, Pennsylvania (October 31, 1960).

981. "We cannot afford to waste idle hours and empty plants while awaiting the end of the recession. We must show the world what a free economy can do — to reduce unemployment, to put unused capacity to work, to spur new productivity, and to foster higher economic growth...." Annual Message to the Congress on the State of the Union (January 30, 1961).

982. "If we can provide a strong economy here at home, with steadily improving life for all of our people, then we can maintain our position abroad with more effectiveness, and we can demonstrate what a free system can do in this competing world." Remarks by Telephone to the First White House Regional Conference Meeting in Chicago [Illinois] (November 7, 1961).

983. "[A] free economy need not be an unstable economy ... a free system need not leave men unemployed — and ... a free society is not only the most productive but the most stable form of organization yet fashioned by man." Annual Message to the Congress on the State of the Union (January 11, 1962).

984. "We want prosperity and in a free enterprise system there can be no prosperity without profit. We want a growing economy, and there can be no growth without the investment that is inspired and financed by profit." Address Before the United States Chamber of Commerce on Its 50th Anniversary (April 30, 1962).

985. "Those who preach the doctrine of the inevitability of the class struggle and of the Communist success, should realize ... that the great effort which has been made to unify economically the countries of the free World, offers far greater promise than the sterile and broken promises of the Communist system." Address in New Orleans at the Opening of the New Dockside Terminal (May 4, 1962).

986. "We all would endorse ... the concept of a free economy. But what we want to hear from you [business, labor, and academic leaders] is how we can make this free economy work, how we can make it work at full capacity, how we can provide adequate profits in return for labor, how we can provide adequate demand for all that we can produce." Remarks to Members of the White House Conference on National Economic Issues (May 21, 1962).

987. "We all believe in the free enterprise system and the competition in the market place, and we believe from that competition comes the advancement of the general interest from the clash of private interests and public interests to serve."

Remarks at a Meeting with the Consumers' Advisory Council (July 19, 1962).

988. "I believe that the free enterprise system means that there will be an opportunity for all people who want to work to find a job...." Remarks at the Wheeling Stadium, Wheeling, West Virginia (September 27, 1962).

989. "[T]he growth of our free enterprise economy under a free political system ... has brought our citizens to an unprecedented standard of living ... an unparalleled position in the world, as the world's foremost banker, merchant, manufacturer, and consumer. [I]t has demonstrated the power of freedom for all to see, and sustained the cause of freedom through hot wars and cold, at home and abroad." Remarks and Question and Answer Period at the American Bankers Association Symposium on Economic Growth (February 25, 1963).

990. "[T]he central question which faces [many countries], my own country ... is whether, under a system of political liberty, we can solve the economic problems that press upon our people ... [whether we can] ... demonstrat[e] to a watching world that free men can conquer the ancient enemies of man, poverty, ignorance, and hunger; of protecting freedom against those who would destroy it; of bringing hope to those who search for hope; of extending liberty to those who lack it." Remarks at the University of Costa Rica in San Jose (March 20, 1963).

991. "Mr. Khrushchev has said that the hinge of history would move when the Soviet Union was able to out-produce the United States. [A]s the leader of the free world ... [and] the country upon which the cause of freedom and its survival in the world and its ultimate success finally depends, I think it most important that we develop for our own people not only a more fruitful and productive life, but that we also demonstrate to the world that a system of freedom offers an example which they can hopefully follow." Remarks and Question and Answer Period Before the American Society of Newspaper Editors (April 19, 1963).

FREEDOM AND LIBERTY

992. "[T]he cause of freedom, the cause of free men and women everywhere, is tied up with the future of a free country, and therefore we are ready to assume our burdens of being the leaders of the free world in a time of great danger, in a time of great peril." Text of Telephone Address by Senator John F. Kennedy to Amvet Convention, Miami Beach, Florida (August 26, 1960).

993. "[W]e are willing to bear any burden on behalf of our country.... [W]e want a defense second to none ... an economic growth second to none ... a scientific effort second to none, [and] an educational system that turns out the brightest of hard-working boys and girls in the world ... in other words, to demonstrate that a free society is also a vital society and that the future belongs to us. I believe it does. I believe that our country is willing to assume any burdens in order to maintain its freedom." Text of Telephone Address by Senator John F. Kennedy to Amvet Convention, Miami Beach, Florida (August 26, 1960).

994. "[W]e believe that this is the greatest country in the world, because we believe it has the greatest potential for growth, because we want it to be in the future as it has been in the past — the greatest hope for freedom." Remarks of Senator John F. Kennedy, Airport Rally, Presque Isle, Maine (September 2, 1960).

995. "In many ways, I think that the years will be as difficult in the 1960s as they were after the election 100 years ago of President Lincoln. In that election, Lincoln said that this Nation cannot exist half slave and half free. The question for the 1960s following this election will be whether the world can exist half slave and half free." Speech by Senator John F. Kennedy, Civic Auditorium, Portland, Oregon (September 7, 1960).

996. "[T]o those who believe in the cause of freedom ... we are the great hope for freedom. If we fail in this country, the cause of freedom fails. If we succeed, if we make this a better country, if we make this a better place for everyone to live in ... then we strengthen the United States, and we strengthen the cause of freedom." Remarks of Senator John F. Kennedy, Lockheed Air Terminal, Burbank, California (September 9, 1960).

997. "The United States is the great defender of freedom. If we fail, the cause of freedom fails. If we succeed, the cause of freedom succeeds." Rear Platform Remarks of Senator John F. Kennedy, Merced, California (September 9, 1960).

998. "[F]reedom is not licensed, and ... liberty calls for certain qualities of self-restraint and character which go with self-government...." Speech by Senator John F. Kennedy, Shrine Auditorium, Los Angeles, California (September 9, 1960).

999. "[W]e are free, and it is worth an effort to maintain it." Remarks of Senator John F. Kennedy, Senior Citizens Rally, City Center, New York, New York (September 14, 1960).

1000. "[I]f the United States is not the great defender of freedom, no other country is. If we fail, the cause of freedom fails; if we succeed, the cause of freedom succeeds." Remarks of Senator John F. Kennedy, Lebanon, Pennsylvania (September 16, 1960).

1001. "I hold the view that the Constitution is the most revolutionary document with the Declaration of Independence, ever written, and it should to the new countries serve as a source of stimulation and enterprise to them. We hold the view that the people will come first, not the government. We hold the view that every American, regardless of his religion or his race is entitled to his constitutional rights. We hold the view that the people make the best judgment in the long run. That is a revolutionary document." Remarks of Senator John F. Kennedy, Airport Rally, Greensboro, North Carolina (September 17, 1960).

1002. "[T]he American Constitution [is] the best and most happy way for the organization of our life, and I think our great ambition is to see the blessings of freedom spread, [not] only in our own country, but around the world. A strong America, believing in freedom for all our citizens I think offers the best hope of freedom to all those who look to us with confidence and hope." Remarks of Senator John F. Kennedy, Eastern Carolina Stadium, Greenville, North Carolina (September 17, 1960).

1003. "[O]ur own greatness is living proof that the road to abundance is freedom's road." Speech by Senator John F. Kennedy, Coliseum, Raleigh, North Carolina (September 17, 1960).

1004. "I think the free system happens to fit the best with the desires of the people every place.... We have seen it in our own history. We have seen it in Latin America. How can people who desire to be free and independent, who will stop at nothing to gain their own independence, how can they possibly submit themselves to the tyranny of the Communists...? I consider this desire to be independent the strongest force for freedom of our security in the world." Remarks of Senator John F. Kennedy, Sioux City, Iowa (September 22, 1960).

1005. "I want people to say the way of the future is freedom. I want people to say that we want to travel on freedom's road. The Communist system will be dead ... if we meet our responsibilities by the turn of the century. It does not represent, as we do, a basic aspiration of the human nature." Remarks of Senator John F. Kennedy, Armory, Akron, Ohio (September 27, 1960).

1006. "The desire to be free and independent. This is the greatest and most heartening event in world history." Remarks of Senator John F. Kennedy, Schenectady, New York (September 29, 1960).

1007. "I do not believe there is a more valuable exposition of the vitality of freedom ... than ... to see the United States involved in a great free election, to have an opportunity to make a freedom of choice, to have the issues presented honestly to the American people, so that they can make their judgment...." Remarks of Senator John F. Kennedy, State Capitol, Albany, New York (September 29, 1960).

1008. "As long as this country lives, what Thomas Jefferson called the disease of liberty will be catching." Remarks of Senator John F. Kennedy, City Hall, Chicago, Illinois (October 1, 1960).

1009. "How can we possibly be indifferent and stand for an important principle which is the right of people to be free unless we did it regardless of whether it be a friend or a foe? The principle is the important thing. The principle serves us. The principle serves the cause of freedom." Speech by Senator John F. Kennedy, Polish-American Congress, Chicago, Illinois (October 1, 1960).

1010. "Our task is to encourage and pursue a policy of patiently encouraging freedom and carefully pressuring tyranny, a policy that looks to evolution and not toward immediate revolution." Speech by Senator John F. Kennedy, Polish-American Congress, Chicago, Illinois (October 1, 1960).

1011. "The unfinished business of this society is the maintenance of freedom here and around the world. Thomas Paine said during the American Revolution, 'The cause of America is the cause of all mankind.' I think in 1960 the cause of all mankind is the cause of America." Remarks of Senator John F. Kennedy, Bean Feed, Minneapolis, Minnesota (October 1, 1960).

1012. "[T]o protect individual liberties [we] must be strong as a nation. And ... to be strong we must protect individual liberties." Speech by Senator John F. Kennedy, Chase Hotel, St. Louis, Missouri (October 2, 1960).

1013. " I believe that this generation of Americans has the same rendezvous with destiny as that generation of Americans in 1936 to whom Franklin Roosevelt addressed those words, that that generation had a rendezvous with destiny. I believe we do, too. The rendezvous was the question of whether freedom could be maintained here in the United States. Our destiny is to determine whether freedom can be maintained throughout the world, whether a house divided against itself can survive, whether a world can exist half slave and half free. I think we will move in the direction of freedom." Remarks of Senator John F. Kennedy, Belleville, Illinois (October 3, 1960).

1014. "The hard tough question for the next decade ... is whether this country, with its freedom of choice, its breadth of opportunity, its range of alternatives, whether that country ... can successfully, over a long period of time, compete with a totalitarian state, where the total resources of the state ... are harnessed to the service of the state. How can we, over a long period of time, maintain our position, our strength, our leadership, relative to that of the Communist world? That is the question which faces ... America and which faces all who believe in the cause of freedom." Speech by Senator John F. Kennedy, Southern Illinois University Stadium, Carbondale, Illinois (October 3, 1960).

1015. "[It is] the American Revolution — not the Russian — which began man's struggle for national independence and individual liberty. When the African national congress in Northern Rhodesia called for reform and justice, it threatened a 'Boston Tea Party,' not a Bolshevik bomb plot ... invok[ing] the 'American Dream'— not the Communist manifesto. And in the most remote bush lands of central Africa there are children named Thomas Jefferson and George Washington — but there are none named Lenin or Stalin or Trotsky." Speech by Senator John F. Kennedy, National Council of Women, Inc., Waldorf-Astoria Hotel, New York, New York (October 12, 1960).

1016. "Freedom is indivisible ... in all its aspects. To provide equal rights for all requires that we respect the liberties of speech and belief and assembly, guaranteed by the Constitution, and these liberties in turn are hollow mockeries unless they are maintained also by a decent economic life.... Those who are too poor, uninformed, too uneducated to enjoy their constitutional freedoms of choice, do not really possess those freedoms.... These are the indispensible foundations of a free society...." Speech by Senator John F. Kennedy, National Conference on Constitutional Rights and American Freedom, Park-Sheraton Hotel, New York, New York (October 12, 1960).

1017. "[America] is a country which is the chief defender of freedom, and upon us and upon our willingness to meet our responsibilities rests not only our own security, but rests the hope of freedom all around the globe." Remarks of Senator John F. Kennedy, Shopping Center, Levittown, New Jersey (October 16, 1960).

1018. "The strength of freedom in the world and its vitality rests upon the economic productivity of the United States...." Remarks of Senator John F. Kennedy, New Fieldhouse, Moline, Illinois (October 24, 1960).

1019. "As long as the United States lives, so freedom lives." Remarks of Senator John F. Kennedy, Keyworth Stadium, Hamtramck, Michigan (October 26, 1960).

1020. "[T]he best service that we can render to the cause of freedom is to build a strong and vital society here that spreads its influence around the world and demonstrates to the Communists that we represent the way of the future, that their system is doomed to die...." Speech by Senator John F. Kennedy, Sunnyside Gardens, Queens, New York (October 27, 1960).

1021. "Our function and responsibility as the chief defenders of freedom is to build a strong and shining society here in the United States a society with purpose, a society with strength, and then hold out hope to all those hundreds of millions of people stretching around the globe who want to live their lives in freedom." Remarks of Senator John F. Kennedy, Upper Darby, Pennsylvania (October 29, 1960).

1022. "If there is any fact that has emerged from the stream of history, whether it is East Germany, Hungary, or Poland against the Communists or the experience of Africa against Western colonialism, it is the desire of people to be independent. We know it from our history." Remarks of Senator John F. Kennedy, Upper Darby, Pennsylvania (October 29, 1960).

1023. "One of the great sources of strength of the United States has been that the people who came to this country to establish their homes all came seeking freedom and opportunity...." Remarks of Senator John F. Kennedy, Bonds for Israel Dinner, Philadelphia, Pennsylvania (October 31, 1960).

1024. "I believe in an America where ... every citizen is free to think and speak as he pleases and write and worship as he pleases — and where every citizen is free to vote as he pleases, without instructions from anyone, his employer, the union leader or his clergyman." Speech by Senator John F. Kennedy, Convention Hall, Philadelphia, Pennsylvania (October 31, 1960).

1025. "If we succeed, freedom succeeds. If we fail, freedom fails. That is the sober and awesome responsibility which events and our own choice have put upon our shoulders." Speech by Senator John F. Kennedy, Faneuil Hall, Boston, Massachusetts (November 7, 1960).

1026. "Thomas Jefferson at the beginning of this country once said the disease of liberty is catching, but if it is going to catch, if it is going to spread around the world, then we here in the United States must meet our responsibilities. We must recognize there are no shortcuts, no easy way, no overnight, weekend meetings, which will bring a change in the balance of power in the world." Remarks of Senator John F. Kennedy, City Hall, Providence, Rhode Island (November 7, 1960).

1027. "In the long history of the world, only a few generations have been granted the role of defending freedom in its hour of maximum danger. I do not shrink from this responsibility — I welcome it. I do not believe that any of us would exchange places with any other people or any other generation. The energy, the faith, the devotion which we bring to this endeavor will light our country and all who serve it — and the glow from that fire can truly light the world." Inaugural Address (January 20, 1961).

1028. "My fellow citizens of the world: ask not what America will do for you, but what together we can do for the freedom of man." Inaugural Address (January 20, 1961).

1029. "Let every nation know, whether it wishes us well or ill, that we shall pay any price, bear any burden, meet any hardship, support any friend, oppose any foe to assure the survival and the success of liberty." Inaugural Address (January 20, 1961).

1030. "It is one of the ironies of our time that the techniques of a harsh and repressive system should be able to instill discipline and ardor in its servants — while the blessings of liberty have too often stood for privilege, materialism and a life of [ease]." Annual Message to the Congress on the State of the Union (January 30, 1961).

1031. "Liberty is not easy to find. It is a search that takes us on a hard road." Remarks at the Presentation of the Medal of Freedom to Paul Henri Spaak, Secretary General of NATO (February 21, 1961).

1032. "This [living in freedom] has been a long tradition of this country, stretching back to our earliest beginnings. We ourselves are a revolutionary people, and we want to see for other people what we have been able to gain for ourselves." Remarks on Introducing President Nkrumah [of Ghana] to the Press (March 8, 1961).

1033. "[The] rights [of the individual] do not come to us because of the generosity of the state." Remarks on the Occasion of the Celebration of the Centennial of Italian Unification (March 16, 1961).

1034. "[T]he preoccupation of the United States with the cause of freedom not only here but around the world has been one of the most important facets of our national life.... I think all of us who believe in freedom feel a sense of community with all those who are free, but I think we also feel an even stronger sense of community with those who are not free but who some day will be free." Remarks at a Reception Marking African Freedom Day (April 15, 1961).

1035. "I believe that the future can belong to those who are free, because I believe it must belong to those who are free." Address in Chicago at a Dinner of the Democratic Party of Cook County [Illinois] (April 28, 1961).

1036. "We are prepared to meet our obligations, but we can only defend the freedom of those who are determined to be free themselves. We can assist them — we will bear more than our share of the burden, but we can only help those who are ready to bear their share of the burden themselves." Address in Chicago at a Dinner of the Democratic Party of Cook County (April 28, 1961).

1037. "We are a people of strong faith in ourselves and in our institutions. We believe that our freedom and our liberty are worth protecting." Remarks Recorded for Broadcast During the Annual Civil Defense Exercises (April 28, 1961).

1038. "It is difficult for me to believe that any young man or woman, or any citizen who understands the real meaning of freedom, who recognizes that freedom is at issue around the globe, could possibly hold that view [that 'the discipline of the totalitarian system has some attraction']." Address at the 39th Annual Convention of the National Association of Broadcasters (May 8, 1961).

1039. "[O]ur nation is on the side of man's desire to be free, and the desire of nations to be independent. And thus we are allied ... with the strongest force in the world today." Address at the 39th Annual Convention of the National Association of Broadcasters (May 8, 1961).

1040. "The great inner resource of freedom, the resource which has kept the world's oldest democracy continually young and vital, the resource which has always brought us our greatest exploits in time of our greatest need, is the very fact of the open society." Address at the 39th Annual Convention of the National Association of Broadcasters (May 8, 1961).

1041. "No man can hope to prophesy with precision the outcome of the great struggle in which our generation is now engaged. Yet we do know that the cause of human freedom has been threatened on many occasions since the system of free choice and democracy was developed in sunlit Greece more than twenty-four hundred years ago. And yet from each threat and indeed from each defeat ... it has ultimately emerged unconquered." Address at the 39th Annual Convention of the National Association of Broadcasters (May 8, 1961).

1042. "At the conference table and in the minds of men, the Free World's cause is strengthened because it is just." Address Before the Canadian Parliament in Ottawa (May 17, 1961).

1043. "[I]t is clear that no free nation can stand alone to meet the threat of those who make themselves our adversaries — that no free nation can retain any illusions about the nature of the threat — and that no free nation can remain indifferent to the steady erosion of freedom around the globe." Address Before the Canadian Parliament in Ottawa [Canada] (May 17, 1961).

1044. "[O]ur historic task in this embattled age is not merely to defend freedom. It is to extend its writ and strengthen its covenant — to peoples of different cultures and creeds and colors, whose policy or economic system may differ from ours, but whose desire to be free is no less fervent than our own." Address Before the Canadian Parliament in Ottawa (May 17, 1961).

1045. "[I]t is my judgment that when the time comes to write the story of the 20th century, the dominant fact will be that liberty grew and spread around the world." Remarks at the Democratic National Committee Dinner in Honor of the President's 44th Birthday (May 27, 1961).

1046. "I shall tell those who do not agree with us that our desire for peace is matched by our determination to resist all those who seek the destruction of freedom. And I shall tell the world that ... American men and women are calling forth all the great resources and untapped power of this country, providing strength for that faith in the freedom of man which will be the silent guest at every conference table." Remarks at the Democratic National Committee Dinner in Honor of the President's 44th Birthday (May 27, 1961).

1047. "We go to many countries but we sing the same song. And that is, this country wants peace and this country wants freedom." Remarks at a Dinner of the Eleanor Roosevelt Cancer Foundation in New York City (May 30, 1961).

1048. "What counts, of course, is not merely the words, but the meaning behind them. We believe in liberty and equality and fraternity. We believe in life and liberty and the pursuit of happiness. And we believe that the rights of the individual are preeminent, not merely the slogans and the mottoes which are invoked across the globe by those who make themselves our adversary. We believe in the significance behind these great ideas." Toasts of the President and President de Gaulle [of France] at the Formal Dinner in the Elysee Palace (May 31, 1961).

1049. "The Government of the United States ... or the President, cannot possibly in a free society command, or should they, those actions [that contribute to 'the maintenance of our country'] for the benefit of the state which our adversaries are able to do with ease. These things must be done in a voluntary manner. And they must be done by our own individual impulse." Remarks at a Dinner of the Big Brothers of America (June 7, 1961).

1050. "[C]olonialism in its harshest forms is not only the exploitation of new nations by old, of dark skins by light, or the subjugation of the poor by the rich. My Nation was once a colony, and we know what colonialism means; the exploitation and subjugation of the weak by the powerful, of the many by the few, of the governed who have given no consent to be governed, whatever their continent, their class, or their color." Address in New York City Before the General Assembly of the United Nations (September 25, 1961).

1051. "It is not free societies which bear within them the seeds of inevitable disunity." Annual Message to the Congress on the State of the Union (January 11, 1962).

1052. "[S]ome people cannot bear the responsibility of a free choice which goes with self-government [a]nd ... shrinking from choice, they turn to those who prevent them from choosing, and thus find in a kind of prison, a kind of security, [but] [w]e believe that people are capable of standing the burdens and the pressures which choice places upon them...." Remarks on the 20th Anniversary of the Voice of America (February 26, 1962).

1053. "A free society is a critical society...." Remarks at the White House to Members of the American Legion (March 1, 1962).

1054. "It is far more difficult to be a self-governing and free country. This [independence] represents the ultimate challenge to any choice — it presents ... a free choice — and choice is always difficult." Remarks of Welcome to President Olympio of Togo at the Washington National Airport (March 20, 1962).

1055. "[T]he revolution of national independence is a fundamental fact of our era. This revolution will not be stopped. As new nations emerge from the oblivion of centuries, their first aspiration is to affirm their national identity. Their deepest hope is for a world where ... every country can solve its own problems according to its own traditions and ideals." Address in Berkeley at the University of California (March 23, 1962).

1056. "Wisdom requires the long view. And the long view shows us that the revolution of national independence is a fundamental fact of our era. This revolution will not be stopped. As new nations emerge from the oblivion of centuries, their first aspiration is to affirm their national identity. Their deepest hope is for a world where, within a framework of international cooperation, every country can solve its own problems according to its own traditions and ideals." Address in Berkeley at the University of California (March 23, 1962).

1057. "[T]he strongest force in the world today [i]s the desire for national independence, reaching well beyond any ideology or really any national power." Remarks of Welcome to the Shah and the Empress of Iran at the Washington National Airport (April 11, 1962).

1058. "To run a free society is very difficult.... It is not easy." Remarks at a Reception for Foreign Students on the White House Lawn (May 10, 1962).

1059. "[T]he fact of political freedom, means very little to the man who is not yet independent of poverty and illiteracy and disease. New factories and machinery mean little to the family without a home, to the student without a meal, to the farmer who even gives up hope of finally owning the land that he tills." Address by the President at a Luncheon Given in His Honor by President Lopez Matcos [of Mexico] (June 29, 1962).

1060. "[P]olitical freedom ... does not reach its full significance until there is also economic participation in the life of the country by the people themselves. Housing, education, jobs, and security go hand in hand with the real concepts of political equality and freedom." Remarks at the Unidad Independencia Housing Project in Mexico City (June 30, 1962).

1061. "For 186 years this doctrine of national independence [as enshrined in the Declaration of Independence] has shaken the globe — and it remains the most powerful force anywhere in the world today. There are those struggling to eke out a bare existence in a barren land who have never heard of free enterprise, but who cherish the idea of independence." Address at Independence Hall, Philadelphia (July 4, 1962).

1062. "If there is a single issue that divides the world today, it is independence...." Address at Independence Hall, Philadelphia (July 4, 1962).

1063. "[T]he Constitution of the United States ... stresse[s] not independence but interdependence — not the individual liberty of one but the indivisible liberty of all." Address at Independence Hall, Philadelphia [Pennsylvania] (July 4, 1962).

1064. "The cost of freedom is always high — but Americans have always paid it. And one path we shall never choose, and that is the path of surrender or submission. Our goal is not the victory of might, but the vindication of right — not peace at the expense of freedom, but both peace and freedom, here ... around the world. God willing, that goal will be achieved." Radio and Television Report to the American People on the Soviet Arms Buildup in Cuba (October 22, 1962).

1065. "The mere accumulation of wealth and power is available to the dictator and the democrat alike. What freedom alone can bring is the liberation of the human mind and spirit which finds its greatest flowering in the free society." Remarks at a Close[d] Circuit Television Broadcast on Behalf of the National Cultural Center (November 29, 1962).

1066. "We believe strongly in democracy and personal freedom, but I also strongly believe ... that through a system of national sovereignty and personal independence and personal liberty we can best advance the interest of all of our people." Toasts of the President and President Alessandri [of Chile] (December 11, 1962).

1067. "[A] free society places greater burdens upon every citizen than any other kind of system. It requires an ability to make a choice, to have those qualities of judgment and self-restraint which permit a democracy to operate." Remarks at the 50th Anniversary Luncheon of the Delta Sigma Theta Sorority (January 12, 1963).

1068. "[T]he unity of freedom has never relied on uniformity of opinion." Annual Message to the Congress on the State of the Union (January 14, 1963).

1069. "[T]he American Hemisphere is not a fertile ground for foreign tyranny, and ... any effort to spread such rule will meet with fierce and unyielding resistance. For Americans will not yield up those freedoms which they shed so much blood to achieve." Address at the Teatro Nacional in San Jose [Costa Rica] Upon Opening the Presidents' Conference (March 18, 1963).

1070. "[W]e know that our enjoyment of freedom is not so much a gift from the past as a challenge for the future, not so much a reward for old victories, but a goal for new struggles, not so much an inheritance from our forefathers as an obligation to those of us who follow, for democracy is never a final achievement. It is a call to effort, to sacrifice, and a willingness to live and to die in its defense." Remarks at El Bosque Housing Project Near San Jose [Costa Rica] (March 19, 1963).

1071. "One of our great challenges [in promoting freedom] has been to develop ... a greater dedication, a greater willingness to work, a greater organizational sense, and a willingness to undertake all the laborious tasks which go with maintaining freedom and which are more important than all the speeches." Remarks at the Ambassador's Residence, San Jose [Costa Rica], in Response to a Welcoming Declaration by Christian Democratic Youth (March 20, 1963).

1072. "[I]f the task of progress with freedom is more complex, more subtle, and more difficult than the promise of progress without freedom, we are unafraid of that challenge." Remarks at the University of Costa Rica in San Jose (March 20, 1963).

1073. "[E]very individual citizen [has the right] to political liberty, the right to speak his own views, to worship God in his own way, to select the government which rules him, and to reject it when it no longer serves the need of a nation." Remarks at the University of Costa Rica in San Jose (March 20, 1963).

1074. "[Every citizen has] the right to social justice, the right ... to participate in the progress of his nation [which] ... means land for the landless, and education for those who are denied their education today.... It means that ancient institutions which perpetuate privilege must give way. It means that rich and poor alike must bear the burden and the opportunity of building a nation. It will not be easy to achieve social justice, but freedom cannot last without it." Remarks at the University of Costa Rica in San Jose (March 20, 1963).

1075. "It is no accident that men of genius in music like Paderewski or Chopin should also have been great patriots. You have to be a free man to be a great artist." Remarks at the Dedication of a Marker to Identify the Grave of Ignace Jan Paderewski (May 9, 1963).

1076. "Disagreement and dissent are fundamental to a free society." Address and Question and Answer Period at the 20th Anniversary Meeting of the Committee for Economic Development (May 9, 1963).

1077. "[U]nless liberty flourishes in all lands, it cannot flourish in one." Address in the Assembly Hall at the Paulskirche in Frankfurt [Germany]. (June 25, 1963).

1078. "[W]e live in an age of interdependence as well as independence — an age of internationalism as well as nationalism." Address in the Assembly Hall at the Paulskirche in Frankfurt [Germany] (June 25, 1963).

1079. "[G]oethe tells us in his greatest poem that Faust lost the liberty of his soul when he said to the passing moment: 'Stay, thou art so fair.' And our liberty, too, is endangered if we pause for the passing moment, if we rest on our achievements, if we resist the pace of progress. For time and the world do not stand still. Change is the law of life. And those who look only to the past or the present are certain to miss the future." Address in the Assembly Hall at the Paulskirche in Frankfurt [Germany] (June 25, 1963).

1080. "[F]reedom is more than the rejection of tyranny ... prosperity is more than an escape from want—[and] ... partnership is more than a sharing of power. These are, above all, great human adventures. They must have meaning and conviction and purpose — and because they do ... we are called to a great new mission. It is not a mission of self-defense alone.... It is not a mission of arbitrary power for we reject the idea of one nation dominating another. The mission is to create a new social order, founded on liberty and justice, in which men are the masters of their fate, in which states are the servants of their citizens, and in which all men and women can share a better life for themselves and their children." Address in the Assembly Hall at the Paulskirche in Frankfurt [Germany] (June 25, 1963).

1081. "If there is any myth that has been destroyed in the last 10 years, it has been the concept that communism and economic welfare go hand in hand. [O]ur times have shown that freedom is the handmaiden of economic advancement, that through a system of freedom, through a system of progress, through a system of responsibilities within a free society, that is the best way that people can live, not only peacefully ... but also can enjoy an increasingly high standard of living." Remarks in Berlin to the Trade Union Congress of German Construction Workers (June 26, 1963).

1082. "Freedom has many difficulties and democracy is not perfect, but we have never had to put a wall up to keep our people in, to prevent them from leaving us." Remarks in the Rudolph Wilde Platz, Berlin [Germany] (June 26, 1963).

1083. "Freedom is indivisible, and when one man is enslaved, all are not free." Remarks in the Rudolph Wilde Platz, Berlin [Germany] (June 26, 1963).

1084. "The strongest force in the world today has been the strength of the state, of the idea of nationalism of a people; and ... all around the globe, new countries have sprung into existence determined to maintain their freedom. This has been one of the strongest forces on the side of freedom. And it is a source of satisfaction to me...." Address at the Free University of Berlin [Germany] (June 26, 1963).

1085. "[W]hile freedom is an end in itself, it is also a means." Remarks in Berlin to the Trade Union Congress of German Construction Workers (June 26, 1963).

1086. "[F]reedom must mean more than an absence of tyranny; ... it must have internal meaning as well; ... it must provide not only for theoretical rights, but for solid economic and social progress towards the enjoyment of those rights by all of its citizens." Remarks at a Dinner Given in His Honor by President Segni [of Italy] (July 1, 1963).

1087. "[L]et us build sturdy mansions of freedom, mansions that all the world can admire and copy but that no tyrant can ever enter." Remarks at a Dinner Given in His Honor by President Segni [of Italy] (July 1, 1963).

1088. "[W]ithout the United States they [Europe] would not be free and with the United States they are free, and it is the United States which stands on guard all the way from Berlin to Saigon." Remarks to Delegates to the 18th Annual American Legion "Boys Nation" (July 24, 1963).

1089. "We are the keystone in the arch of freedom. If the United States were to falter, the whole world, in my opinion, would inevitably begin to move toward the Communist bloc." Remarks at the High School Memorial Stadium, Great Falls, Montana (September 26, 1963).

1090. "[B]ecause of the effort of the American people stretching back to all of the days since 1945, under three different administrations, of different political parties — because of that great effort, there are dozens of countries, which would long ago have been overrun, which are now free and independent." Remarks in Boston [Massachusetts] at the "New England's Salute to the President" Dinner (October 19, 1963).

GOD AND COUNTRY

1091. "The motto of the State of South Dakota is 'Under God the People Rule.' The motto of the United States could be the same. I hope in the next 10 or 20 years when historians write of our times that they will write that that cause of the people ruling under God spread in these years and became stronger, increased in strength, increased in substance." Remarks of Senator John F. Kennedy, Corn Palace, Mitchell, South Dakota (September 22, 1960).

1092. "Many a great nation has been torn by religious feuds and holy wars — but never the United States of America. For here diversity has led to unity — liberty has led to strength." Speech by Senator John F. Kennedy, Mormon Tabernacle, Salt Lake City, Utah (September 23, 1960).

1093. "Here in our land church and state are separate and free — in their [Communist] lands neither is free, and the church lives in constant fear of the state. In our land the diversity of equality brings strength to our spiritual ties — in their lands the terror of tyranny drives hope and will from the hearts of men." Speech by Senator John F. Kennedy, Mormon Tabernacle, Salt Lake City, Utah (September 23, 1960).

1094. "In 1860 when ... the question of whether the world would exist and this country would exist half slave and half free, Lincoln wrote to a friend, 'I know there is a God and that He hates [in]justice. I see the storm coming and I know is hand and is in it, but, if He has a place and a part for me, I believe that I am ready.' Now, 100 years later, we know there is a God and we know He hates injustice and we see the storm coming and we see His hand in it, but, if he has a place and a part for us, I believe that we are ready." Speech by John F. Kennedy, Montgomery-Blair High School, Silver Spring, Maryland (October 16, 1960).

1095. "[T]he same revolutionary beliefs for which our forebears fought are still at issue around the globe — the belief that the rights of man come not from the generosity of the state but from the hand of God." Inaugural Address (January 20, 1961).

1096. "With a good conscience our only sure reward, with history the final judge of our deeds, let us go forth to lead the land we love, asking His blessing and His help, but knowing that here on earth God's work must truly be our own." Inaugural Address (January 20, 1961).

1097. "[Y]ou can't have religious freedom without political freedom." Remarks on Greeting Representatives of the Baptist World Alliance at the White House (February 2, 1961).

1098. "[O]ne of the great ironies is that the Communists have been able to secure great devotion to their program and too often our people are identified with a devotion to material things." Remarks on Greeting Representatives of the Baptist World Alliance at the White House (February 2, 1961).

1099. "While they came from a wide variety of religious backgrounds and held a wide variety of religious beliefs, each of our Presidents in his own way has placed a special trust in God. Those who were strongest intellectually were also strongest spiritually." Remarks at the Dedication Breakfast of International Christian Leadership, Inc. (February 9, 1961).

1100. "No man who enters upon the office to which I have succeeded can fail to recognize how every President of the United States has placed special reliance upon his faith in God. Every President has taken comfort and courage when told, as we are told today, that the Lord 'will be with thee. He will not fail thee nor forsake thee. Fear not — neither be thou dismayed.'" Remarks at the Dedication Breakfast of International Christian Leadership, Inc. (February 9, 1961).

1101. "This country was founded by men and women who were dedicated or came to be dedicated to two propositions: first, a strong religious conviction, and secondly a recognition that this conviction could flourish only under a system of freedom." Remarks at the Dedication Breakfast of International Christian Leadership, Inc. (February 9, 1961).

1102. "It is an ironic fact that in this nuclear age, when the horizon of human knowledge and human experience has passed far beyond any that any age has ever known, that we turn back at this time to the oldest source of wisdom and strength, to the words of the prophets and the saints, who tell us that faith is more powerful than doubt, that hope is more potent than despair, and that only through the love that is sometimes called charity can we conquer those forces within ourselves and throughout all the world that threaten the very existence of mankind." Remarks at the Dedication Breakfast of International Christian Leadership (February 9, 1961).

1103. "The guiding principle and prayer of this Nation has been, is now, and shall ever be 'In God We Trust.'" Remarks at the Dedication Breakfast of International Christian Leadership (February 9, 1961).

1104. "We have a great advantage ... in having such common roots, and therefore though our convictions may take us in different directions in our faith, nevertheless the basic presumption of the moral law, the existence of God, man's relation to Him — there is generally consensus on those questions." Remarks to the Officers of the National Conference of Christians and Jews (November 21, 1961).

1105. "With thanks to Almighty God for seeing us through a perilous passage [Cuban missile crisis], we ask His help anew in guiding the 'Good Ship Union.'" Annual Message to the Congress on the State of the Union (January 14, 1963).

1106. "[A]ll of us believe in and need prayer." Remarks at the 11th Annual Presidential Prayer Breakfast (February 7, 1963).

1107. "The problems we face are complex ... the limits of mere human endeavor [have] become more apparent than ever. We cannot depend solely on our material wealth, on our military might, or on our intellectual skill or physical courage to see us safely through.... Along with all of these we need faith ... the faith with which our first settlers crossed the sea to carve out a state in the wilderness, a mission they said ... [was] undertaken for the glory of God. We need the faith with which our Founding Fathers proudly proclaimed the independence of this country ... with a firm reliance on the protection of divine providence. We need the faith which has sustained and guided this Nation for 175 long and short years." Remarks at the 11th Annual Presidential Prayer Breakfast (February 7, 1963).

1108. "We are all builders of the future, and whether we build as public servants or private citizens, whether we build at the national or the local level, whether we build in foreign or domestic affairs, we know the truth of the ancient Psalm, 'Except the Lord build the house, they labour in vain that build it.'" Remarks at the 11th Annual Presidential Prayer Breakfast (February 7, 1963).

1109. "This country has carried great responsibilities ... and I think that willingness to assume those responsibilities has come in part from the strong religious conviction which must carry with it a sense of responsibility to others if it is genuine, which has marked our country from its earliest beginnings, when the recognition of our obligation to God was stated in nearly every public document, down to the present day." Remarks at the 11th Annual Presidential Prayer Breakfast (February 7, 1963).

1110. "[T]he strong commitment to the good life and also the strong feeling of communication which so many of our citizens have with God, and the feeling that we are under His protection ... is, I think, a source of strength to us all." Remarks at the 11th Annual Presidential Prayer Breakfast (February 7, 1963).

1111. "No one can tell in the future whether there is a storm coming for all of us, but what we can be sure of is that no matter what happens, we believe in God and we are ready." Remarks at the Romerberg in Frankfurt [Germany] (June 25, 1963).

GOVERNMENT

General

1112. "The idea of a perfect Union has been one which has inspired this country from our earliest days. It is not achieved — and in a sense probably it is a goal to which we will always be working to reach — but it is a goal which is worthy of our effort." Remarks of Senator John F. Kennedy, Overseas Press Club, New York, New York (August 5, 1960).

1113. "[A]ll of us who work for the Government in one service or another ... have a great and common interest in ... the advancement of the interest of the United States, to increase its power and prestige, to make it more secure, to make it possible in a dangerous world ... to make it possible for us to move safely ahead in a world of peace, protecting not only the security of the United States, but holding out the hand of friendship to all those who wish to be associated with us." Remarks at State Office Building, Trenton, New Jersey (September 15, 1960).

1114. "All States are equal, and therefore, the responsibility on the people of [each state] ... is to make sure that they send Members to the U.S. Senate who speak not only for [their state] ... who serve not only as ambassadors from [their state] ... but also speak for the United States and speak for the public interest...." Remarks at Frontier Park, Cheyenne, Wyoming (September 23, 1960).

1115. "I believe ... that it is the function of government not to dominate but to serve. I don't believe ... in big government, but I believe in government meeting its responsibilities." Remarks at Municipal Auditorium, Canton, Ohio (September 27, 1960).

1116. "Every governmental action affects our lives for good or for bad. Every movement forward moves us all forward. A rising tide lifts all the boats." Remarks of Senator John F. Kennedy, Augustine's Restaurant, Belleville, Illinois (October 3, 1960).

1117. "I do not believe that Washington should be the center of all action. We do not know as much about your problems as you do." Speech by Senator John F. Kennedy, State House, Columbia, South Carolina (October 10, 1960).

1118. "I believe not in big government for big government's sake, but I believe in effective government, and I believe there is a responsibility for the National Government. The farmers ... who grow cotton ... cannot protect themselves without a national policy. The textile workers ... cannot protect themselves against the imports that may destroy them, without national action.... There is a place for action on every level, and those who say that they are against action, I believe, are against the United States moving ahead...." Speech by Senator John F. Kennedy, State House, Columbia, South Carolina (October 10, 1960).

1119. "None of us attaches any magic to dollars that go to Washington and return, if local and private efforts can do the job." Speech by Senator John F. Kennedy, the Little White House, Warm Springs, Georgia (October 10, 1960).

1120. "Franklin Roosevelt did not believe there was any magic in tax money flowing from ... [any state] to be spent. He did not believe that Government should do things that the people or local government or local community could do better. But he believed that there were some things that must be done by the people, acting together, for the very simple reason, he said, that if the Government does not do it, nobody else can or will." Speech by Senator John F. Kennedy, the Little White House, Warm Springs, Georgia (October 10, 1960).

1121. "[I am] ... opposed to excessive, unjustified or unnecessary government intervention in the economy — to needlessly unbalanced budgets and centralized government. I do not believe that Washington should do for the people what they can do for themselves through local and private effort." Speech by Senator John F. Kennedy, Associated Business Publications Conference, Biltmore Hotel, New York, New York (October 12, 1960).

1122. "I believe in an America with a government of men devoted solely to the public interests — men of ability and dedication, free from conflict or corruption or other commitment — a responsible government that is efficient and economical ... a government willing to entrust the people with the facts that they have — not a businessman's government, with business in the saddle ... not a labor government, not a farmer's government, not a government of one section of the country or another, but a government of, for and by the people." Speech by Senator John F. Kennedy, Convention Hall, Philadelphia, Pennsylvania (October 31, 1960).

1123. "We are an open and free society. All of our strengths and all of our weaknesses are on display. They are a matter of discussion. Those of us who hold high office and high responsibilities are subject to all of the scrutiny — the careful scrutiny — which comes from a free press and a free people, operating within an open society. That is the way this country was planned, and ... this diversity, this division, in some cases this dissension, is not a source of weakness but is a source of strength." Remarks on the White House Lawn at a Reception for Foreign Students (May 10, 1961).

1124. "The Constitution of the United States did not make the President or the Congress powerless. It gave them definite responsibilities to advance the general welfare...." Address at a New York Rally in Support of the President's Program of Medical Care for the Aged (May 20, 1962).

1125. "[T]he most basic power which is contained in the Constitution of the United States and the Declaration of Independence [is] the right of a citizen to petition his Government." Address at a New York Rally in Support of the President's Program of Medical Care for the Aged (May 20, 1962).

1126. "There has come ... a substitute for direct participation and that has been the organizations ... which are active here in Washington and which represent the interests of various groups. They fulfill a very important function, particularly of bringing to bear on any piece of legislation the viewpoint of those who might be affected. [Because] the subjects that we deal with are very complicated ... it's essential that we have that viewpoint. The difficulty, however, arises in that they take what's known as organization positions ... and it's difficult for us to know frequently what people who are in positions of responsibility are really thinking." Remarks to Members of the White House Conference on National Economic Issues (May 21, 1962).

1127. "Now there are those who say that the federal Government, the National Government, ought to mind its own business. I think the business of the people is the people's business, and as long as we have these problems which are so much a part of our lives, which are all around us, then we have to try to do something about it." Remarks to Participants in the Campaign Conference for Democratic Women (May 22, 1962).

1128. "The truth about big government is the truth about any other great activity — it is complex. Certainly it is true that size brings dangers — but it is also true that size can bring benefits." Commencement Address at Yale University (June 11, 1962).

1129. "There are too few people in this country who understand how the Congress works." Remarks Upon Presenting Certificates to Graduates of the Capitol Page School (June 12, 1962).

1130. "The indestructible union of indestructible States, created by the Constitution, has been envied and imitated by many other nations. It is the best system yet devised. But we have to make it work. It should have constant attention." Telephone Remarks to the 5th Annual National Conference of State Legislative Leaders (September 21, 1963).

1131. "The seniority system ... provides that if a district elects a Congressman or a Senator long enough and they stay in the same party long enough that they will become the ... chairman of their committee in the House and Senate. This has, on occasion, in all frankness, produced very dubious results, but it has also on many other occasions produced rather extraordinary results." Remarks in Heber Springs, Arkansas, at the Dedication of Greers Ferry Dam (October 3, 1963).

1132. "I think that our objective today is simple ... and that is to provide for our people a rising rate of well-being, to make it possible for all of our people to develop all of their talents in a growing and fruitful society, and for us around the world to continue to bear, as we have for 18 years [since the end of World War II], the great burdens of maintaining the security and peace of the world." Remarks in Boston at the "New England's Salute to the President" Dinner (October 19, 1963).

1133. "What we are attempting to do in the United States in 1963, both at home and abroad, is relatively simple, and that is to maintain the peace, to maintain the vital interests of the United States, to maintain the economy of the United States moving ahead fast enough to absorb the millions of people who are coming into the labor market every year.... I think their execution is difficult. But what we are trying to do is simple." Remarks in Tampa on the 50th Anniversary of Scheduled Air Service (November 18, 1963).

1134. "The Federal Government has no desire to expand the size and scope of its activities merely for the sake of expansion. Many tasks would never have been taken on by the Congress had they been able to be fulfilled at the State and local level." Address and Question and Answer Period in Tampa Before the Florida Chamber of Commerce (November 18, 1963).

Building for the Future

1135. "We cannot simply sit by and watch on the sidelines. There are no sidelines. Under the laws of physics, in order to maintain the same relative position to a moving body, one cannot stand still. As others change, so must we, if we wish to maintain our relative political or economic position." Remarks of Senator John F. Kennedy, Student Convocation, Stanford University, Palo Alto, California (February 12, 1960).

1136. "We compete not merely with the Soviet Union, but we compete with ourselves, to make this a better country, to make this a stronger country, to make sure that those who come after us enjoy the same benefits that we enjoy." Remarks of Senator John F. Kennedy, Courthouse Square, Eugene, Oregon (September 7, 1960).

1137. "I don't think there is anyone ... who can say that all the things that had to be done were done in the past administrations. I think that in our generation as Franklin Roosevelt said about his generation, we also have a rendezvous with destiny." Remarks of Senator John F. Kennedy, City Hall, Newark, New Jersey (September 15, 1960).

1138. "We are a great and strong country — perhaps the greatest and strongest in the history of the world. But greatness and strength are not our natural right. They are not gifts which are automatically ours forever. It took toil and courage and determination to build this country — and it will take those same qualities if we are to maintain it. For, although a country may stand still, history never stands still." Speech by Senator John F. Kennedy, Coliseum, Raleigh, North Carolina (September 17, 1960).

1139. "What does this country want? Does this country want a government frozen in the ice of its own indifference, or do we want a government that will move, that will care for our people, that will set before the American people the unfinished business of our society." Remarks at Municipal Auditorium, Canton, Ohio (September 27, 1960).

1140. "Anybody who says that there is nothing left for us to do has not read the paper, doesn't know what is left for the United States to do in its unfinished business here at home." Remarks of Senator John F. Kennedy, Main Intersection, East St. Louis, Illinois (October 2, 1960).

1141. "Anybody who says that we have to do nothing now, that all we have to do is realize the opportunities which Franklin Roosevelt and Truman presented, is wrong. We in our time have our own responsibility. We have to build homes. We have to get our mills moving again. We have to provide employment for our people. We have to protect the constitutional rights of all Americans. We have to build a stronger America." Remarks of Senator John F. Kennedy, Venice, Illinois (October 3, 1960).

1142. "[W]e can do better, [and] unless we are willing to recognize that a great country must be greater, unless we in our day and generation recognize that we have unfinished business, then we will not be true to this country, we will not maintain our freedom, we will not meet our responsibilities, and history will record that in the 1960s when the world exploded and when the world moved, the United States stood still." Speech by Senator John F. Kennedy, the Little White House, Warm Springs, Georgia (October 10, 1960).

1143. "[I]f we are going to maintain in this country and around the world the cause of freedom, if we are going to defend ourselves and all those who look to us for help, we have to be strong, we have to be moving ahead here at home. We have to be developing our resources, we have to be educating our children. We have to be meeting the problems of our older citizens. We have to find jobs for our people...." Remarks of Senator John F. Kennedy, Sharon, Pennsylvania (October 15, 1960).

1144. "[A]s long as we are not developing our resources, rebuilding our cities, moving our economy ahead, as long as we are not giving the same effort to disarmament and nuclear controls that we are to arms and war, as long as science and technology and space and the earth are not being used to make men's lives more secure, in my judgment we are not meeting our full potential, our full capacity." Remarks of Senator John F. Kennedy, Reyburn Plaza, Philadelphia, Pennsylvania (October 31, 1960).

1145. "[W]e have to begin another great movement forward. [W]e have to build in this country a strong and vital and progressive society, one that ornaments the cause of freedom, one that demonstrates what freedom can do, one that holds out a helping hand to all those who desire to be free." Remarks of Senator John F. Kennedy, South Bay Shopping Center, Redondo Beach, California (November 1, 1960).

1146. "[T]he Bible tells us that 'there is a time for every purpose under the heaven ... a time to cast away stones and a time to gather stones together.' And ... I believe it is time for us all to gather stones together to build this country as it must be built in the coming years." Address Before the United States Chamber of Commerce on Its 50th Anniversary (April 30, 1962).

1147. "[I] don't think we should be worried about progress. I think we should make up our minds that this great country of ours [has] ... many tasks still undone, and we can do them." Address in Milwaukee at the Jefferson-Jackson Dinner (May 12, 1962).

1148. "There is an old Chinese saying that each generation builds a road for the next. The road has been well built for us, and I believe it incumbent upon us, in our generation, this year of 1962, to build our road for the next generation." Address Before the Conference on Trade Policy (May 17, 1962).

1149. "If you want to have equal opportunity for all Americans ... if we want to make this country as wonderful a place as it can be for the 300 million people who will live in this country within 40 years, then we have to do our task today. It is the task of every generation to build a road for the next generation." Remarks in New York City at the Dedication of the Penn Station South Urban Renewal Project (May 19, 1962).

1150. "There are those who say that the job is done, that the function of the federal Government is not to govern, that all the things that had to be done were done in the thirties and the forties, and that now our task is merely to administer. I do not accept that view at all, nor can any American who sees what we still have left to do." Remarks in New York City at the Dedication of the Penn Station South Urban Renewal Project (May 19, 1962).

1151. "Every day I am reminded of how many things were left undone.... Anyone who says that Woodrow Wilson, as great a President as he was, and Franklin Roosevelt and Harry Truman, that they did it all and we have nothing left to do now, is wrong." Address at a New York Rally in Support of the President's Program of Medical Care for the Aged (May 20, 1962).

1152. "All the great revolutionary movements of the Franklin Roosevelt administration in the thirties we now take for granted. [I] refuse to see us live on the accomplishments of another generation. I refuse to see this country ... shrink from these struggles which are our responsibility in our time." Address at a New York Rally in Support of the President's Program of Medical Care for the Aged (May 20, 1962).

1153. "And I do not take the view that everything that had to be done was done by those who went before us, and that ... our [job] is now merely to pass through our political period and occupy positions of public significance and not do anything." Remarks to Participants in the Campaign Conference for Democratic Women (May 22, 1962).

1154. "Anything we begin today is for those who come after us. And just as those who began something years ago make it possible for us to be here, I hope we'll fulfill our responsibility to the next generation that's going to follow us." Remarks in Pueblo, Colorado Following Approval of the Fryingpan-Arkansas Project (August 17, 1962).

1155. "[L]iberty ... is endangered if we pause for the passing moment, if we rest on our achievements, if we resist the pace of progress. For time and the world do not stand still. Change is the law of life. And those who look only to the past or the present are certain to miss the future." Address in the Assembly Hall at the Paulskirche in Frankfurt [Germany] (June 25, 1963).

1156. "[I] think it is essential that we, in the 1960s, take steps to provide for the kind of country ... that we are going to have 20 years from now, so that we do for our children the same thing that was done for us." Remarks in Salt Lake City [Utah] at the Dedication by Remote Control of Flaming Gorge Dam (September 27, 1963).

1157. "[T]hose ... who are young, I think, can look forward to a day when we shall have no South, no North, no East, no West, but 'one nation under God, indivisible, with liberty and justice for all.' That is what we are building in this country today." Remarks at the Arkansas State Fairgrounds in Little Rock (October 3, 1963).

1158. "[I]t is no accident — it didn't just merely happen that this country has steadily increased in wealth and strength in the years from 1945 on. It is because of the steps that were taken in the thirties to lay the foundation for progress in the forties and fifties and sixties.... And our obligation in the 1960s is to do those things ... which will make it possible for others in the 1970s and 1980s to continue to live in prosperity." Remarks in New York City at the AFL-CIO Convention (November 15, 1963).

Checks and Balances

1159. "[A] Congress in the hands of one party and an administration in the hands of another party, with threats of vetoes, with party war in the most dangerous time in the life of our country [is not a 'happy experience']. I think it is time to move. I think this country wants to go ahead.... [G]ive us [the Democrats] the responsibility or give the Republicans the responsibility. But don't divide it and end up with no one responsible." Speech by Senator John F. Kennedy, Democrat Rally, George Washington High School Stadium, Alexandria, Virginia (August 24, 1960).

1160. "[A] divided government with neither party bearing responsibility and both parties sharing power [would be 'unfortunate'].... There is not any doubt in my mind that our system of checks and balances, which I strongly support, cannot work effectively unless the House, the Senate, and the Presidency are working together for the general interest. [A] Democratic President, a Democratic House and a Democratic Senate ... can begin to move [the country ahead] again...." Speech by Senator John F. Kennedy, Multnomah Hotel, Portland, Oregon (September 7, 1960).

1161. "James Madison and John Quincy Adams and Benjamin Franklin wrote sufficient checks and balances into the American constitutional system without adding another one of a Republican President and a Democratic Congress. Everyone who wants to stand still, everyone who wants to look back, everyone who feels that everything that could be done has been done, that the best government is that which does not govern, they should vote for a system like that." Speech by Senator John F. Kennedy, Houston Coliseum, Houston, Texas (September 12, 1960).

1162. "[T]he Constitution of the United States confines and limits the power of Senators. We are given the right to approve Presidential nominations, and to ratify treaties. But the House of Representatives is given the two great powers which are the hallmark of a self-governing society: One, the power to appropriate money, and the second is the power to levy taxes." Remarks of Senator John F. Kennedy, Frontier Park, Cheyenne, Wyoming (September 23, 1960).

1163. "Our Constitution wisely assigns both joint and separate roles to each branch of the government; and a President and a Congress who hold each other in mutual respect will neither permit nor attempt any trespass." Annual Message to the Congress on the State of the Union (January 30, 1961).

1164. "What we are now talking about is whether the United States ... shall have such a balance of power in the Congress and in the Executive that nothing will be done. That's the simple and clear issue.... [A]s long as we have so many issues facing us ... so much unfinished business involving all kinds of issues which go to the well-being of our people, as long as we have a necessity for action as the leader of the free world, I believe we should have the opportunity and not have the kind of balance [of power] in the Congress which will mean two — many more years of inertia and inaction. That's why this is an important election." Remarks in Response to New York's Birthday Salute to the President (May 19, 1962).

1165. "Our Founding Fathers, concerned about the centralization of authority, which they were revolting against, wrote very careful safeguards, checks, and balances into the American constitutional system. This provides great protection for individual liberty and right, but it also places a heavy burden on the men and women who must make this system operate. The division of powers between the Executive, the Congress, the Courts, the divisions between the National Government and the State government requires the greatest comity between the various bodies if our system is to function effectively." Remarks at the Cornerstone — Laying Ceremonies of the Rayburn House Office Building (May 24, 1962).

1166. "[O]ur system is designed to encourage both differences and dissent, because its checks and balances are designed to preserve the rights of the individual and the locality against preeminent central authority." Address at Independence Hall, Philadelphia (July 4, 1962).

Modern-Day Complexities

1167. "So these [modern-day economic challenges] are all matters which I think are extremely complicated. In many ways they move beyond the problems which the New Deal and the Fair Deal faced in their days. They are new problems that require new solutions...." Speech by Senator John F. Kennedy, Multnomah Hotel, Portland, Oregon (September 7, 1960).

1168. "The problems we face now are entirely new. Nothing that has happened in the last two or three decades gives us any assurances for the future. Therefore, I put my confidence in those who are ready and who have shown their willingness to face the future and to seed it and to make it ours." Remarks of Senator John F. Kennedy, Airport Rally, Fargo, North Dakota (September 22, 1960).

1169. "[T]he next President of the United States will deal with problems far more complicated, far more difficult of solution, requiring greater judgment, greater responsibility, than any President of the United States in history." Remarks of Senator John F. Kennedy, Corn Palace, Mitchell, South Dakota (September 22, 1960).

1170. "[T]he problems which our country will face of economic growth, of development of our resources, of the development of outer space ... of the undeveloped world and its economic development, of the peaceful use of the atom, the control of atomic weapons, the developments in the camps of our adversaries between the Russians and the Chinese ... all those are entirely new problems, requiring new people, new solutions, new ideas, and requiring above all a sense of dedication to the cause of freedom." Remarks of Senator John F. Kennedy, Roosevelt Field, Norristown, Pennsylvania (October 29, 1960).

1171. "All the problems which the next President of the United States is going to face are complicated; technical, they involve economic growth ... automation ... countries around the world, and people, facing staggering problems of poverty and ignorance and decline, how they can maintain freedom and how we can head a world torn by conflict, in many cases by poverty, fighting against an enemy who is unrelenting in his attacks on freedom and upon the United States. The United States in the 1960s will be meeting its great time of challenge, and also its great time of opportunity." Remarks of Senator John F. Kennedy, Court House, Toledo, Ohio (November 4, 1960).

1172. "We have ... issues which arouse powerful feeling among specific groups, but among the general public many of the issues which in the thirties [generated strong feelings] ... now ... are sophisticated, technical questions which affect our economy and on which we ought to work in the closest concert." Remarks to Members of the White House Conference on National Economic Issues (March 21, 1962).

1173. "Most of us are conditioned ... to have a political viewpoint, Republican or Democratic — liberal, conservative, moderate ... [but] most of the problems ... that we now face are technical problems, are administrative problems. They are very sophisticated judgments which do not lend themselves to the great sort of 'passionate movements' which have stirred this country so often in the past. Now they deal with questions which are beyond the comprehension of most men, most governmental administrators, over which experts may differ, and yet we operate through our traditional political system." Remarks to Members of the White House Conference on National Economic Issues (May 21, 1962).

1174. "[W]e cannot understand and attack our contemporary problems ... if we are bound by traditional labels and worn-out slogans of an earlier era. [T]he unfortunate fact of the matter is that our rhetoric has not kept pace with the speed of social and economic change. Our political debates, our public discourse — on current domestic and economic issues — too often bear little or no relation to the actual problems the United States faces." Commencement Address at Yale University (June 11, 1962).

1175. "The central domestic issues of our time are more subtle and less simple [than the great issues of the preceding century]. They relate not to basic clashes of philosophy or ideology but to ways and means of reaching common goals — to research for sophisticated solutions to complex and obstinate issues." Commencement Address at Yale University (June 11, 1962).

1176. "I have tried to say recently that the slogans and clichés and the political arguments which so suited an earlier generation are not particularly adapted to the kinds of problems which we have now. Most of our problems are technical, administrative, sophisticated, and merely being a member of one or the other political party does not offer you a solution to the problem." Remarks of Welcome to Participants in the Summer Intern Program for College Students (June 20, 1962).

1177. "[The problems that the nation faces] are all very sophisticated and technical problems, and the great sort of passions and movements of the early part of this century — William Jennings Bryan and all the rest — are not involved today because now it requires the finest judgments upon which even experts differ, and to bring a solution to these kinds of problems in the midst of a very turbulent and large country involved in more traditional political dialogs requires the best of all of us." Remarks of Welcome to Participants in the Summer Intern Program for College Students (June 20, 1962).

1178. "Every generation faces different problems and every generation must come up with new solutions." Remarks at City Hall, McKeesport, Pennsylvania (October 13, 1962).

1179. "Each generation of public officials, each generation of citizens faces new problems. The solution of every problem brings with it a response which presents new difficulties to our country." Remarks to Participants in the Senate Youth Program (February 1, 1963).

1180. "[W]e have a complicated economy, a rich and prosperous country, but we have serious problems which many of our citizens do not notice, but which press upon us and ... [which require] new tools because the problems are new." Remarks in Hollywood at a Breakfast with Democratic State Committeewomen of California (June 8, 1963).

1181. "[T]he problems which now face us and their solution are far more complex, far more difficult, far more subtle, require a far greater skill and discretion of judgment, than any of the problems that this country has faced in its comparatively short history, or any, really, that the world has faced in its long history." Address at the University of Wyoming (September 25, 1963).

1182. "We are bound to grope for a time as we grapple with problems without precedent in human history. But wisdom is the child of experience." Address at the Anniversary Convocation of the National Academy of Sciences (October 22, 1963).

Working Together

1183. "Why should one state of the nation suffer while another prospers? ... This is one nation, under God. Depression in one area hurts all areas. Depression in one industry hurts all industries." Remarks of Senator John F. Kennedy, Reception, Beckley, West Virginia (April 11, 1960).

1184. "The problems facing this country in the challenging sixties are by no means exclusively Federal problems. There are enough to go around for every level of government — Federal, State and local." Text of the Telephone Message to the National Association of County Officials Meeting, Miami, Florida (August 17, 1960).

1185. "We don't have coal and iron and oil [in New England], but we have human talent. We can clean our rivers, we can provide an atmosphere for business to move ahead. We can reform our transportation system. We can protect our textile and shoe industries. We can bring in new industries. We can perfect our educational system to have the best-trained people. All these things can be done in partnership of the State and the Government working together." Remarks of Senator John F. Kennedy, Airport Rally, Manchester, New Hampshire (September 2, 1960).

1186. "[T]he fundamental responsibility of all of us ... [is to] demonstrate ... that a government and the people can work together." Statewide TV

Speech, Zembo Mosque Temple, Harrisburg, Pennsylvania (September 15, 1960).

1187. "I think the fundamental responsibility of all of us who wish to survive, who wish to live our lives in peace, who wish to see the influence of the United States extend around the world as a vital and vigorous society, whose brightest days are ahead, whose economic growth is increasing, whose devotion to the public interest is being maintained ... is ... that we ... demonstrate as Franklin Roosevelt did in his day, and Wilson in his day, and Truman in his day, that a government and the people can work together." Statewide TV Speech, Zembo Mosque Temple, Harrisburg, Pennsylvania (September 15, 1960).

1188. "This community [Schenectady], like the cities of my own State, Massachusetts, can fight against recession. They can build their own economies. They can try to bring business in here. But if there isn't business growing in all parts of the United States, every effort which Schenectady may make ... isn't enough. If there isn't enough to go around, no city of the United States can rebuild itself by its own effort. It requires the cooperative effort of the people of this city, of labor and management, and of economic policies which stimulate our economy carried on by the Federal Government. It is a joint effort by us all if we are going to bring the tide up." Remarks of Senator John F. Kennedy, Schenectady, New York (September 29, 1960).

1189. "[T]here is a proper function for individual effort, for community government, for State government, and for National Government, and unless each group is meeting its responsibilities toward the community as a whole and toward the country, this country does not go ahead." Remarks of Senator John F. Kennedy, Schenectady, New York (September 29, 1960).

1190. "[New] problems [now] swarm across the desk of the political leaders of this country: monetary and fiscal policy, the control of outer space, disarmament, nuclear cessations, control of agricultural surpluses, control of business cycles, automation, stimulation of our economy, the extension of the franchise to our citizens, the extension of our influence around the world, the struggle for a better world, the struggle for a stronger America, and unless there is the most intimate association between those who look to the far horizons and those who deal with our daily problems, then quite obviously we shall not pass through these stormy times with success...." Speech by Senator John F. Kennedy, Wittenburg College Stadium, Springfield, Ohio (October 17, 1960).

1191. "[We are] in an hour of national peril and national opportunity. Before my term has ended, we shall have to test anew whether a nation organized and governed such as ours can endure. The outcome is by no means certain. The answers are by no means clear. All of us together — this Administration, this Congress, this nation — must forge those answers." Annual Message to the Congress on the State of the Union (January 30, 1961).

1192. "[W]e recognize that in our time ... there is still a good deal of unfinished business: to provide more security for our younger people who want jobs and can't find them; to provide more security for those who are unemployed — for those particularly who are unemployed chronically ... [and] who now want to work and find themselves having to turn to inadequate public assistance." Remarks on the 50th Anniversary of the First State Workmen's Compensation Law. (August 31, 1961).

1193. "Let our patriotism be reflected in the creation of confidence in one another, rather than in crusades of suspicion. Let us prove we think our country great, by striving to make it greater. And, above all, let us remember, however serious the outlook, however harsh the task, the one great irreversible trend in the history of the world is on the side of liberty — and we, for all time to come, are on the same side." Address in Los Angeles at a Dinner of the Democratic Party of California (November 18, 1961).

1194. "[T]he Constitution makes us [the President and the Congress] not rivals for power but partners for progress. We are all trustees for the American people, custodians of the American heritage." Annual Message to the Congress on the State of the Union (January 11, 1962).

1195. "[T]he best interests of the National Government and the country are tied to the enlightened best interests of its most important segments.... [A]ll the segments, including the National Government, must operate responsibly in terms of each other, or the balance which sustains the general welfare will be lost." Address Before the United States Chamber of Commerce on Its 50th Anniversary (April 30, 1962).

1196. "[T]hose who say that what we are now talking about [government involvement] spoils our great pioneer heritage should remember that the West was settled with two great actions by the National Government; one, in President Lincoln's administration, when he gave a homestead to everyone who went West, and in 1862 [when] he set aside Government property to build our land grant colleges. This cooperation between an alert and Progressive citizen and a progressive Government is what has made this country great...." Address at a New York Rally in Support of the President's Program of Medical Care for the Aged (May 20, 1962).

1197. "[T]he prosperity of this country depends on the assurance that all major elements within it will live up to their responsibilities. If business were to neglect its obligations to the public, if labor were blind to all public responsibility, above all, if government were to abandon its ... duty of watchful concern for our economic health — if any of these things should happen, then confidence might well be weakened and the danger of stagnation would increase.... The solid ground of mutual confidence is the necessary partnership of government with all of the sectors of our society in the steady quest for economic progress." Commencement Address at Yale University (June 11, 1962).

1198. "If a contest in angry argument were forced upon it, no administration could shrink from response, and history does not suggest that American Presidents are totally without resources in an engagement forced upon them because of hostility in one sector of society. But in the wider national interest, we need not partisan wrangling but common concentration on common problems." Commencement Address at Yale University (June 11, 1962).

1199. "The necessity for comity between the National Government and the several States is an indelible lesson of our long history." Address at Independence Hall, Philadelphia [Pennsylvania] (July 4, 1962).

1200. "Our system and our freedom permit the legislative to be pitted against the executive, the State against the Federal Government, the city against the countryside, party against party, interest against interest, all in competition ... with another. Our task ... is to weave from all these tangled threads a fabric of law and progress. We are not permitted the luxury of irresolution. Others may confine themselves to debate, discussion, and that ultimate luxury — free advice. Our responsibility is one of decision — for to govern is to choose." Address at Independence Hall, Philadelphia (July 4, 1962).

1201. "The home is the basis of our society, and it has been through the happy cooperation of the National Government, private enterprise and ... the citizens of our country who desire to own their own homes that we've had this extraordinary gain in private ownership ... which I think ornaments our society." Remarks Upon Presenting the President's Awards for Distinguished Federal Civilian Service (August 7, 1962).

1202. "This country would still be in the dark ages economically if we permitted [the] opponents of progress and defenders of special privileges and interests to veto every forward move. [T]he President of the United States ... and the Congress ... must be committed to action in our time. Other Congresses and other Presidents were committed to other action in their time." Radio and Television Report to the American People on the State of the National Economy (August 13, 1962).

1203. "What I preach is the interdependence of the United States. We are not 50 countries — we are one country of 50 States and one people. And I believe that those programs which make life better for some of our people will make life better for all of our people." Remarks in Pueblo, Colorado Following Approval of the Fryingpan-Arkansas Project (August 17, 1962).

1204. "We cannot permit, as a country, public and private power interests to veto each other's projects, or one region to say another region shall not develop. If we do that, we shall stand still and forget the lesson that our history has told us." Remarks at the Dedication of the Oahe Dam, Pierre, South Dakota (August 17, 1962).

1205. "We are 180 million different people, with very different ideas on what we should do and how this country should be run, and where we should go, and what are our responsibilities and obligations, [and] I think it is important that we recognize how often we [have] worked together to accomplish great results...." Remarks at the Dedication of the Oahe Dam, Pierre, South Dakota (August 17, 1962).

1206. "Nothing could be more disastrous for this country than for the citizens of one part of the State to feel that everything that they have is theirs and it should not be shared with other citizens of this State.... That is the way to stand still. The way to move ahead is to realize that we are citizens of one country who can freely move from one State to another, and as one State does well, so do the others, and if one State stands still, so do all the rest." Remarks in Los Banos, California, at the Ground-Breaking Ceremonies for the San Luis Dam (August 18, 1962).

1207. "Progress represents the combined will of the American people, and [it is achieved] only when they are joined together for action, instead of standing still and thinking that everything that had to be done has been done. It's only when they join together in a forward movement that this country moves ahead and that we prepare the way for those who come after us...." Remarks in Los Banos, California, at the Ground-Breaking Ceremonies for the San Luis Dam (August 18, 1962).

1208. "From time to time statements are made labeling the Federal Government an outsider, an intruder, an adversary. In any free federation of States, of course differences will arise and difficulties will persist. But ... the United States Government is not a stranger or not an enemy. It is the people of 50 States joining in a national effort to see progress in every State of the Union." Remarks at Muscle Shoals, Alabama, at the 30th Anniversary Celebration of TVA (March 18, 1963).

1209. "[T]he Federal Government is not a remote bureaucracy. It must seek to meet those needs of the individual, the family, and the community which can best be met by the nationwide cooperation of all, and which cannot be met by State and local governments." Remarks and Question and Answer Period Before the American Society of Newspaper Editors (April 19, 1963).

1210. "This idea that we are 50 separate countries, that the Federal Government does not have a responsibility to set a tone and a standard and example, whether it is in transit, or libraries, or retardation, or education, whether it is in space, or on the ground, or under the earth, the National Government, representing the will of 180 million people, must move ahead, must meet its responsibilities. And all those who say 'go home' are those who have permitted this country to stagnate during the years of our past history...." Remarks in Hollywood at a Breakfast with Democratic State Committeewomen of California (June 8, 1963).

1211. "Too often it is suggested that the Federal Government and the State governments are competitors.... Instead, we must work closely together for the benefit of our country which all of us seek to serve. [W]e in Washington know that the success of any program or effort depends upon local control and local support. Our system of intergovernmental relations works best when there is complete coordination and cooperation between every level of government." Telephone Remarks to the 5th Annual National Conference of State Legislative Leaders (September 21, 1963).

1212. "These are the problems which face this great democracy of ours. They cannot be solved by turning away, but can be solved, I believe, by the united, intelligent effort of us all." Address at the University of North Dakota (September 25, 1963).

1213. "We hear a good deal about the rights of States, and they are important. But we should remember how easily and quickly our people move from one State to another." Remarks at the Convention Center in Las Vegas, Nevada (September 28, 1963).

1214. "[T]he partnership between the Federal Government and the States ... is essential to the progress of all of our people...." Remarks at the Dedication of the Delaware-Maryland Turnpike (November 14, 1963).

HEALTHCARE

1215. "The prospects of any President ever receiving for his signature a bill providing foreign aid funds for birth control are very remote indeed. It is hardly the major issue some have suggested." Remarks of Senator John F. Kennedy, American Society of Newspaper Editors, Washington, D.C. (April 21, 1960).

1216. "[A] diet which does not permit a healthy, decent existence — a diet which is causing malnutrition, chronic diseases and physical handicaps — [such] a diet ... is a disgrace to a country which has the most abundant and richest food supply in the history of the world." Remarks of Senator John F. Kennedy, Glenwood Park, West Virginia (April 26, 1960).

1217. "Illness is a national problem. It recognizes no barriers of race or religion or region, and its conquest must be a national effort benefiting all Americans — for the protections of our Government in every field must be extended without regard to artificial distinctions, and full participation in our national life must be open to all." Speech by Senator John F. Kennedy, the Little White House, Warm Springs, Georgia (October 10, 1960).

1218. "In no area is progress more vitally needed than the area of health. The cost of medical care has skyrocketed beyond the reach of many citizens, particularly our older citizens.... There are too few doctors, too few nurses, and too few hospitals. Too few of our handicapped are being rehabilitated — too many medical research projects are financially starved — too many rivers are dangerously polluted. Drugs are too expensive — insurance plans are too limited." Speech by Senator John F. Kennedy, the Little White House, Warm Springs, Georgia (October 10, 1960).

1219. "[P]rovid[ing] loans and scholarships for medical students ... grants for renovating our older hospitals ... long-term grants for increased medical research, including basic research, [and grants] for expand[ing] our efforts for rehabilitation ... is not a program for socialized medicine — it is a program to prevent socialized medicine, by meeting our critical needs in a manner consistent with our obligation to freedom and the doctor's obligation to humanity." Speech by Senator John F. Kennedy, the Little White House, Warm Springs, Georgia (October 10, 1960).

1220. "[T]he field of health ... [requires] cooperative effort by the private sources of this country and also by the National Government. Illness is a national problem. It knows neither barriers of region or race or religion or creed, for the protections of our Government must be given to every American who needs the attention of our people, who needs the attention of vigorous national action." Speech by Senator John F. Kennedy, the Little White House, Warm Springs, Georgia (October 10, 1960).

1221. "Medical research has achieved new wonders — but these wonders are too often beyond the reach of too many people, owing to a lack of income (particularly among the aged), a lack of hospital beds, a lack of nursing homes and a lack of doctors and dentists. Measures to provide health care for the aged under Social Security, and to increase the supply of both facilities and personnel, must be undertaken...." Annual Message to the Congress on the State of the Union (January 30, 1961).

1222. "[W]e ... recognize the great need that lies before us to deal more satisfactorily with the question of health in our society; most particularly and immediately is the health of our older citizens, those who are chronically ill, those who come to the end of their working lives with inadequate resources stored away in spite of many years of devoted labor — inadequate resources to meet their medical bills." Remarks on the 50th Anniversary of the First State Workmen's Compensation Law (August 31, 1961).

1223. "[Mental retardation] is a matter which I think should be brought out into the sunlight and given a full national commitment.... It is high time that the country gives its time and attention to this." Remarks to the Members of the Panel on Mental Retardation. (October 18, 1961).

1224. "[M]edical care ... is the only issue which arouses powerful feelings among the general public." Remarks to Members of the White House Conference on National Economic Issues (March 21, 1962).

1225. "I am hopeful that the fact that so many outstanding doctors who believe in the responsibilities of the profession very strongly and ... support ... this concept of medical care for the aged through social security will cause other doctors ... to examine and reexamine their own positions." Remarks Upon Receiving a Statement by a Group of Physicians on Medical Care for the Aged (March 27, 1962).

1226. "[Mental illness and mental retardation] ha[ve] been tolerated too long. It has troubled our national conscience, but only as a problem unpleasant to mention, easy to postpone, and despairing of solution. The time has come for a great national effort." Remarks on Proposed Measures to Combat Mental Illness and Mental Retardation (February 5, 1963).

1227. "Enactment of this legislation [new program of comprehensive maternity and infant care, aimed directly at preventing mental retardation] ... is ... an important landmark.... We can say with some assurance that, although children may be the victims of fate, they will not be the victims of our neglect." Remarks Upon Signing the Maternal and Child Health and Mental Retardation Planning Bill (October 24, 1963).

1228. "This is a very rich and prosperous country. There is no reason why our standards [in mental health care] in this country should be below other countries.... There is no reason why we should be. [T]his is one of the areas ... that has somewhat darkened our national life...." Remarks Upon Signing the Maternal and Child Health and Mental Retardation Planning Bill (October 24, 1963).

1229. "Albert Einstein once said that it would be a great cause of regret and would put all mankind into jeopardy if the life sciences did not keep up with the tremendous advances of the physical sciences. This is nowhere more apparent than in the field of mental retardation. We have conquered the atom, but we have not yet begun to make a major assault upon the mysteries of the human mind." Remarks at the 13th Annual Convention of the National Association for Retarded Children (October 24, 1963).

1230. "It was said, in an earlier age, that the mind of a man is a far country which can neither be approached nor explored. But, today, under present conditions of scientific achievement, it will be possible for a nation as rich in human and material resources as ours to make the remote reaches of the mind accessible. The mentally ill and the mentally retarded need no longer be alien to our affections or beyond the help of our communities." Remarks Upon Signing Bill for the Construction of Mental Retardation Facilities and Community Mental Health Centers (October 31, 1963).

HUMAN RIGHTS

1231. "Let the word go forth from this time and place, to friend and foe alike, that the torch has been passed to a new generation of Americans — born in this century, tempered by war, disciplined by a hard and bitter peace, proud of our ancient heritage — and unwilling to witness or permit the slow undoing of those human rights to which this nation has always been committed, and to which we are committed today at home and around the world." Inaugural Address (January 20, 1961).

1232. "[W]e support ... the right of free elections and the free exercise of basic human freedoms. We support land reform and the right of every campesino to own the land he tills. We support the effort of every free nation to pursue programs of economic progress. We support the right of every free people to freely transform the economic and political institutions of society so that they may serve the welfare of all." Remarks in Miami at the Presentation of the Flag of the Cuban Invasion Brigade (December 29, 1962).

1233. "An injury to one, whether it's a man, woman, or country, is of concern to us all here and around the world." Remarks at a Dinner Celebrating the 50th Anniversary of the Department of Labor (March 4, 1963).

1234. "The cause of human rights and dignity, some two centuries after its birth, in Europe and the United States, is still moving men and nations with ever-increasing momentum.... The truth doesn't die. The desire for liberty cannot be fully suppressed." Address at the Free University of Berlin (June 26, 1963).

1235. "[H]uman rights ... are not respected when a Buddhist priest is driven from his pagoda, when a synagogue is shut down, when a Protestant church cannot open a mission, when a Cardinal is forced into hiding, or when a crowded church service is bombed. The United States of America is opposed to discrimination and persecution on grounds of race and religion anywhere in the world, including our own Nation." Address Before the 18th General Assembly of the United Nations (September 20, 1963).

INTERNATIONAL RELATIONS

1236. "If there is one area in the world which demonstrates the truth of Jefferson's observation that 'the disease of liberty is catching,' that area is Africa. For, in the past few years, freedom has spread from one end of that continent to the other — until there is hardly a corner of Africa which is not independent or about to become independent. Everywhere the old colonial empires are dissolving as the African peoples take up the reins of self-government." Remarks of Senator John F. Kennedy, Saint Anselm's College, Manchester, New Hampshire (March 5, 1960).

1237. "Tom Paine wrote during the American Revolution, 'a flame has arisen not to be extinguished.' That flame — the flame of hope — of freedom — of progress — now burns brightly across all of Africa. It is we Americans — as leaders of the western world — who have the great responsibility of keeping it alight." Remarks of Senator John F. Kennedy, Saint Anselm's College, Manchester, New Hampshire (March 5, 1960).

1238. "[A]rgentina ... is not ... a country with a consistent tradition of freedom. It is a land where democracy is struggling for existence, after the long years of a dictatorship which wasted the nation's resources — which almost destroyed its economy — and which left seeds of unrest and discontent which will trouble the development of Argentina for generations to come. It is also a graphic illustration of how American support of dictators has harmed the cause of freedom.... I do not say that we should have tried to tell the Argentines what form of government to have — but neither should we have embarked on such an open and friendly support of the brutal and repressive Peron dictatorship." Remarks of Senator John F. Kennedy, Dartmouth College, Hanover, New Hampshire (March 6, 1960).

1239. "It is Brazil's destiny to become the other great power of the Western Hemisphere. And why not? Brazil is larger than the continental United States — rich in natural resources — with a vigorous and rapidly expanding population.... In many ways Brazil is like the United States of 100 years ago." Remarks of Senator John F. Kennedy, Dartmouth College, Hanover, New Hampshire (March 6, 1960).

1240. "Chile ... [is] a nation devoted to democracy—a country which has gone through a series of political and economic crises which would have brought dictatorship to almost any other country in Latin America—but a country which, through every emergency, has clung to its democratic way of life as the only true solution to its pressing problems." Remarks of Senator John F. Kennedy, Dartmouth College, Hanover, New Hampshire (March 6, 1960).

1241. "Uruguay ... has a durable democratic tradition—since 1904 its government has been devoted to political and personal freedom—and under that democracy—a democracy long the object of the hostility of surrounding dictators—the Uruguayans have built a highly diversified economy." Remarks of Senator John F. Kennedy, Dartmouth College, Hanover, New Hampshire (March 6, 1960).

1242. "Whatever battles may be in the headlines, no struggle in the world deserves more time and attention ... than ... the battle between India and China.... And that is the struggle between India and China for the economic and political leadership of the East ... for the opportunity to demonstrate whose way of life is the better.... India follows a route in keeping with human dignity and individual freedom. Red China represents the route of regimented controls and ruthless denial of human rights." Remarks of Senator John F. Kennedy, University of New Hampshire, Durham, New Hampshire (March 7, 1960).

1243. "Unless India can compete equally with China, unless she can show that her way works as well or better than dictatorship, unless she can make the transition from economic stagnation to economic growth ... the entire Free World will suffer a serious reverse. India herself will be gripped by frustration and political instability—its role as a counter to the Red Chinese in Asia would be lost—India herself and then most of Asia would later—and Communism would have won its greatest bloodless victory." Remarks of Senator John F. Kennedy, University of New Hampshire, Durham, New Hampshire (March 7, 1960).

1244. "[W]e should not now recognize Red China or agree to its admission to the United Nations without a genuine change in her belligerent attitude toward her Asian neighbors and the world ... [but] we must nevertheless work to improve at least our communications with mainland China." Remarks of Senator John F. Kennedy, U.S. Senate (June 14, 1960).

1245. "[J]ust as America provided the spark which helped bring freedom to Africa—we must also do our part in helping to create the economic conditions which are essential to freedom's continued existence. We must do this, not because we wish to use the African nations as pawns in the cold war ... [but] because the ultimate survival of the Free World depends upon our ability to help construct a community of stable and independent governments—where human rights are valued and protected—and where people are given the opportunity to choose their own national course...." Remarks of Senator John F. Kennedy, Luncheon in Honor of the African Diplomatic Corps., Washington, D.C. (June 24, 1960).

1246. "Poland is a satellite government, but the Poles are not a satellite people." Speech by Senator John F. Kennedy, Polish-American Congress, Chicago, Illinois (October 1, 1960).

1247. "[I]f Columbus discovered one continent—his journey—in large measure—resulted in the loss of another.... With the discovery of America, the kings, the generals, and the traders turned westward, leaving Africa to become the neglected and undeveloped province of a few European nations. Today, more than four centuries later ... [t]he nations of the West once more look toward Africa. And Africa itself is struggling for the freedom and the economic progress which centuries of neglect have denied it." Speech by Senator John F. Kennedy, National Council of Women, Inc., Waldorf-Astoria Hotel, New York, New York (October 12, 1960).

1248. "The new nations of Africa are determined to emerge from the poverty and hunger which now blanket much of that vast continent. They are determined to build a modern and growing economy.... They are determined to educate their people—maintain their independence—and receive the respect of all the world. There can be no question about this determination. The only real question is whether these new nations will look West or East — to Moscow or Washington — for sympathy, help, and guidance in their great effort to recapitulate, in a few decades, the entire history of modern Europe and America." Speech by Senator John F. Kennedy, National Council of Women, Inc., Waldorf-Astoria Hotel, New York, New York (October 12, 1960).

1249. "We want an Africa which is made up of a community of stable and independent governments — where the human rights of Negroes and white men alike are valued and protected — where men are given the opportunity to choose their own national course, free from the dictates or coercion of any other country We want an Africa which is not a pawn in the cold war.... And this too is what the African people want." Speech by Senator John F. Kennedy, National Council of Women, Inc., Waldorf-Astoria Hotel, New York, New York (October 12, 1960).

1250. "As long as countries in Africa ... feel that the future belongs to the Communists and not to us ... as long as they begin to fear the Russians more than they trust us ... as long as they think we regard them merely as pawns in the cold war, then they begin to wonder whether they should do what Castro has done." Remarks of Senator John F. Kennedy, Shopping Center, Levittown, New Jersey (October 16, 1960).

1251. "All over Africa there are children named George Washington, Thomas Jefferson, Abraham Lincoln, Woodrow Wilson, Franklin Roosevelt.... There are none yet called Lenin or Stalin, and we don't want them to be. We want those people to be associated with the cause of freedom because they are impressed by what we have done here...." Remarks of Senator John F. Kennedy, Truman Shopping Center, Grand View, Missouri (October 22, 1960).

1252. "I think that [Israel] serve[s] the United States, and the cause of freedom generally around the world...." Remarks of Senator John F. Kennedy, Bonds for Israel Dinner, Philadelphia, Pennsylvania (October 31, 1960).

1253. "It is an extraordinary fact in history that so much of what we are and so much of what we believe had its origin in this rather small spear of land stretching into the Mediterranean. All in a great sense that we fight to preserve today had its origins in Italy, and earlier than that in Greece." Remarks on the Occasion of the Celebration of the Centennial of Italian Unification (March 16, 1961).

1254. "The tide of foreign affairs flows swiftly in and out. New nations arise, old empires vanish, alliances come and go, but through it all the historic friendship of your nation [Canada] and mine has stood firm. Together we have worked for peace, together we have stood in war, and now in this long twilight era that is neither peace nor war, we must stand together even more firmly than ever before." Remarks Upon Arrival at the Royal Canadian Air Force Uplands Airport in Ottawa (May 16, 1961).

1255. "Geography has made us neighbors. History has made us friends. Economics has made us partners. And necessity has made us allies. Those whom nature hath so joined together, let no man put asunder." Address Before the Canadian Parliament in Ottawa (May 17, 1961).

1256. "[T]he present relationship between France and the United States is essential for the preservation of freedom around the globe." Remarks Upon Arrival at Orly Airport in Paris [France] (May 31, 1961).

1257. "[F]rance ... is America's oldest friend." Remarks Upon Arrival at Orly Airport in Paris [France] (May 31, 1961).

1258. "[I]t is not difficult for this President of the United States to come to France. I sleep in a French bed. In the morning my breakfast is served by a French chef. I go to my office, and the bad news of the day is brought to me by my Press Secretary, Pierre Salinger, not in his native language, and I am married to a daughter of France." Toasts of the President and President de Gaulle at the Formal Dinner in the Elysee Palace (May 31, 1961).

1259. "[F]rance is more than the sum of its parts. This long influence which stretches around the globe, which is a part of your tradition, is a source of strength to us today, and that great interest in common, more than any of the ties of the past, that great hope for the future is what makes inevitable the intimate and constant association of France and the United States." Remarks at a

Civic Reception for President Kennedy at the Hotel de Ville (June 1, 1961).

1260. "[England is an] ancient country from which so many of our great traditions in my own country have sprung." Remarks Upon Arrival at the London Airport (June 4, 1961).

1261. "Our obligations to them [the British] for the beneficial influences that they have had in the development of our great political structure I think are known to every American." Remarks to the Staff of the U.S. Embassy in London [England] (June 5, 1961).

1262. "We believe in this country that the Pacific Ocean does not separate Japan and the United States. Rather, it unites us. And we have the greatest admiration for this extraordinary people, who have conquered the sea and the land and in the most energetic and productive way have built a life for themselves."Toasts of the President and Prime Minister Ikeda of Japan (June 21, 1961).

1263. "[F]inland and the Finnish people are identified in the minds of the people of the United States with those qualities of courage and fortitude and perseverance which have made the reputation of your country and people second to none here in the United States." Remarks of Welcome to the President of Finland at Andrews Air Force Base (October 16, 1961).

1264. "Africa, in a sense, is a newly discovered continent for the people of America, and we are attempting to learn, and to join in every possible way, to associate ourselves with the best in Africa." Toasts of the President and President Ahidjo [of Cameroon] (March 13, 1962).

1265. "Brazil and the United States have been very intimately bound together, [not] ... so much by geography because, after all, we are separated by great distances, nor ... by a common cultural experience, because our cultural experience has been somewhat different. I think what has bound us together is the sense of great adventure by those who settled both our countries, in coming to the New World for a similar purpose which was a free life." Toasts of the President and President Goulart [of Brazil] (April 3, 1962).

1266. "The interest of both of us [the United States and Iran] is the same: to maintain our freedom, to maintain the peace, and to provide a better life for our people. That is the purpose of your visit, Your Majesty, as to how we can jointly concert that effort." Remarks of Welcome to the Shah and the Empress of Iran at the Washington National Airport (April 11, 1962).

1267. "Were it not for the leadership that [the Shah of Iran] has given, in identifying himself with the best aspirations of his people ... we are quite aware that this vital area of the world, which has been ... a vital matter of concern to the Soviet Union ... would long ago have collapsed. So, when we welcome the Shah here, we welcome a friend and a very valiant fighter. We do not live in easy times ourselves. But we do not live in the belly of the bear. But he does — and has done it for years, and his country is still free." Remarks of Welcome to the Shah and the Empress of Iran at the Washington National Airport (April 11, 1962).

1268. "We regard the Atlantic as uniting us, not separating us [the United States and Great Britain]." Remarks of Welcome to Prime Minister Macmillan at Andrews Air force Base (April 27, 1962).

1269. "To those who may wonder what we find to talk about on these occasions (summit meetings between the United States and the Great Britain], I suggest they take a map of the world and trace those countries scattered around the globe whose integrity, security, and freedom both the United States and Great Britain are committed to maintain. In ... dozens of areas, Great Britain and the United States work shoulder to shoulder." Remarks of Welcome to Prime Minister Macmillan at Andrews Air force Base (April 27, 1962).

1270. "It is almost 'sad' that there are so few issues which are causing intense controversy between Norway and the United States — an unaccustomed feeling...." Toasts of the President and Prime Minister Gerhardsen of Norway (May 9, 1962).

1271. "[The] relations between Mexico and the United States ... should be constantly worked on and not merely be permitted to be assumed...." Remarks to Visiting Members of the Mexican Congress (May 14, 1962).

1272. "Panama has been very generous to the United States. And we are quite aware that whatever contribution or whatever blessings the Canal gives to Panama, it gives great blessings to the United States and is very essential to our security and also to the economy and security of so much of the world." Toasts of the President and President Chiari of Panama (June 12, 1962).

1273. "[T]here is so much which unites this great country [Mexico] with my own. We share a border of 2,000 miles. Over 3 million of our citizens in the United States are descended from your citizens. Most of all, we are both children of revolution, [a] ... revolution in our country and, in a sense, in yours, [that] was primarily political, a declaration of political liberty." Remarks Upon Arrival at the Airport in Mexico City [Mexico] (June 29, 1962).

1274. "While geography has made us [the United States and Mexico] neighbors, tradition has made us friends. Economics has made us partners. And necessity has made us allies — in a vast Alianza para el Progreso. Those whom nature has so joined together, let no man put asunder." Address by the President at a Luncheon Given in His Honor by President Lopez Matcos [of Mexico] (June 29, 1962).

1275. "It is our responsibility [the United States and Mexico] ... and the responsibilities of others in our sister republics in this great hemisphere, to recognize that there is also a necessity for an economic revolution, if political independence, political equality, national sovereignty are all to have true significance and true meaning." Remarks Upon Arrival at the Airport in Mexico City (June 29, 1962).

1276. "[A]ustralia [is comprised of an] extraordinary group of men and women ... who have demonstrated on many occasions, on many fields ... that they are the most extraordinary athletic group in the world today, and that this extraordinary demonstration of physical vigor and skill has come not by the dictates of the State, because the Australians are among the freest citizens in the world, but because of their choice." Remarks in Newport at the Australian Ambassador's Dinner for the America's Cup Crews (September 14, 1962).

1277. "Nature has tied us [Brazil and the United States] together. In a sense we are all the objects or the subjects of a most extraordinary historic experience, and we are, it seems to me, bound together essentially today in the preservation of the freedom of our hemisphere." Remarks to Students and Members of the Faculty of the Brazilian Escola Superior de Guerra (October 30, 1962).

1278. "I hope that ... thought can be given to what role we can play as partners [Japan and the United States] ... to attempt to prevent the domination of Asia by a Communist movement which is in its essence today a believer in not only the class struggle, but also in the international class struggle of a third world war." Remarks at a Luncheon in Honor of a Japanese Trade Delegation (December 3, 1962).

1279. "Our two nations [the United States and France] have fought on the same side in four wars during a span of the last 185 years. Each has been delivered from the foreign rule of another by the other's friendship and courage. Our two revolutions helped define the meaning of democracy and freedom which are so much contested in the world today." Remarks at the National Gallery of Art Upon Opening the Mona Lisa Exhibition (January 8, 1963).

1280. "The United States and Italy as allies, members of NATO ... have a good many matters of common concern, of common policies to develop and coordinate in defense and economic policy and political matters. Indeed, all the subjects which go to the defense of the West and the defense of the free world properly concern the United States and Italy." Remarks of Welcome at the White House to Prime Minister Fanfani of Italy (January 16, 1963).

1281. "[T]here is no country or people for whom my countrymen have a stronger feeling of admiration for than the people of Poland." Remarks to the Boys' and Men's Choir of Poznan, Poland (March 11, 1963).

1282. "[I] know of no more vital, energetic, warmhearted, vigorous, hopeful people than the great citizens of this great democracy [Costa Rica]." Remarks at El Coco Airport, Costa Rica, Upon Leaving for the United States (March 20, 1963).

1283. "We [and Canada] share more than geography — a history, a common commitment to freedom, and a common hope for the future, and it is my strong conviction and that of my fellow countrymen that in this great cause [defeating

Communism], Canada and the United States should stand side by side." Remarks of Welcome at Otis Air Force Base, Falmouth, Massachusetts, to Prime Minister Pearson of Canada (May 10, 1963).

1284. "[India is] the largest democracy in the world ... a country which has occupied a position of moral leadership during the difficult days which have followed the end of the Second World War; a country which is on the other side of the globe but with which we [feel] bound by the closest ties of a common commitment to the independence of our countries and the integrity of our individual citizens." Remarks of Welcome at the White House to President Radhakrishnan of India (June 3, 1963).

1285. "[W]hen I leave the office of the White House, whenever that may be, I am going to leave an envelope in the desk for my successor. And it will say, 'To be opened only in saddest moments.' So it will have only the words written, 'Go visit Germany.'" Remarks at a Reception in Wiesbaden [Germany] (June 25, 1963).

1286. "[E]ight of my grandparents left these shores [of Ireland] ... and came to the United States. No country in the world ... has endured the hemorrhage which this island endured over a period of a few years for so many of her sons and daughters. These sons and daughters are scattered throughout the world, and they give this small island a family of millions upon millions who are scattered all over the globe, who have been among the best and most loyal citizens of the countries that they have gone to, but have also kept a special place in their memories, in many cases their ancestral memory, of this green and misty island." Remarks Upon Arrival at Dublin [Ireland] Airport (June 26, 1963).

1287. "[O]ur two nations [the United States and Ireland], divided by distance, have been united by history. No people ever believed more deeply in the cause of Irish freedom than the people of the United States. And no country contributed more to building my own than your sons and daughters." Address Before the Irish Parliament in Dublin [Ireland] (June 28, 1963).

1288. "This has never been a rich or powerful country, and yet, since earliest times, its influence on the world has been rich and powerful. No larger nation did more to keep Christianity and Western culture alive in their darkest centuries. No larger nation did more to spark the cause of independence in America, indeed, around the world. And no larger nation has ever provided the world with more literary and artistic genius. This is an extraordinary country." Address Before the Irish Parliament in Dublin [Ireland] (June 28, 1963).

1289. "[I]reland is a very special place. It has fulfilled in the past a very special role. It is in a very real sense the mother of a great many people, a great many millions of people, and in a sense a great many nations. And what gives me the greatest satisfaction and pride, being of Irish descent, is the realization that even today this very small island still sends thousands, literally thousands, of its sons and daughters to the ends of the globe to carry on an historic task which Ireland assumed 1400 or 1500 years ago." Remarks at Shannon [Ireland] Airport Upon Leaving for England (June 29, 1963).

1290. "Italy occupies a position of strategic importance, vital to the security of Europe, vital to the security of the United States. In the heart of Europe, reaching down into the Mediterranean towards Africa, the maintenance of a free democracy here in Italy is of great interest, of vital interest, not only to your own people, but also to all of us who believe in freedom." Remarks Upon Arrival at Fiumicino Airport, Rome [Italy] (July 1, 1963).

1291. "Millions of my fellow countrymen left these [Italian] shores. They occupy positions of the highest responsibility in the United States ... and most importantly, perhaps, of all, they have raised large families and have been productive and responsible citizens." Remarks Upon Arrival at Fiumicino Airport, Rome [Italy] (July 1, 1963).

1292. "[T]he relationship between Australia and the United States is based not so much on sentiment and not only on self-interest—although there are, of course, those factors—but I think our confidence in Australia was built during two world wars ... and in the days that have followed when the United States and Australia have moved in such concert together." Toasts of the President and Prime Minister Menzies of Australia (July 8, 1963).

1293. "Fate and geography and time and necessity have made the United States and Ethiopia very closely associated in the years since the end of the Second World War. We value that association. We value the position of responsibility and leadership which His Majesty [Emperor Haile Selassie] occupies." Toasts of the President and the Emperor of Ethiopia at a Dinner at the White House (October 1, 1963).

1294. "Ireland is not a major participant in the cold war struggle, as size goes, but it is a fact that in the struggle for peace and order, which is of very much interest to all of us who believe in freedom, Ireland is playing a role beyond her size." Toasts of the President and Prime Minister Lemass (October 15, 1963).

1295. "[W]hile there are differences in viewpoint which separate our governments [the United States and Yugoslavia], nevertheless, this administration and my two predecessors, President Eisenhower and President Truman, all believed strongly in the independence of [Yugoslavia] and all appreciated the extraordinary efforts you [President Tito] are making to maintain that independence, situated as you are in an area of great importance." Toasts of the President and President Tito (October 17, 1963).

1296. "Because of the places from whence the American people originally came, we have ordinarily looked east to Europe and south to Latin America. I think it is most important that we also look west across the Pacific, which can be a bridge rather than a barrier, and, particularly, that we look to the very vital, vigorous, progressive nation of Japan." Remarks to a Group from the Second U.S.—Japan Conference on Educational and Cultural Interchange (October 18, 1963).

INTERNATIONAL TRADE

1297. "[T]here [must be a] proper concern about our balance of payments.... It is vital that we keep our exports well ahead of our imports in order to cover our commitments abroad—our military forces around the world, our diplomatic obligations, our military aid, and our assistance to underdeveloped nations." Speech by Senator John F. Kennedy, Associated Business Publications Conference, Biltmore Hotel, New York, New York (October 12, 1960).

1298. "[W]e need [foreign] imports if other nations are to have the money to buy our exports and the incentive to lower their own tariff barriers.... We need those imports to give our consumers a wide choice of goods at competitive prices ... to give our industries ... the raw materials they require at prices they can afford—to keep a healthy pressure on our own producers and workers to improve efficiency, [to] develop better products, and [to] avoid the inflation that could price us out of markets vital to our own prosperity." Address in New York City to the National Association of Manufacturers (December 6, 1961).

1299. "[I]f we cannot increase our sales abroad, we will diminish our stature in the Free World. Economic isolation and political leadership are wholly incompatible." Address in New York City to the National Association of Manufacturers (December 6, 1961).

1300. "Capitalism is on trial as we debate these [free trade] issues. [W]e have boasted of the virtues of the marketplace under free competitive enterprise ... of the vitality of our system in keeping abreast with the times. Now the world will see whether we mean it or not—whether America will remain the foremost economic power in the world—or whether we will evacuate the field of power before a shot is fired, or go forth to meet new risks and tests of our ability. The hour of decision has arrived." Address in New York City to the National Association of Manufacturers (December 6, 1961).

1301. "Let me repeat: If we cannot maintain the balance of trade in our favor ... and indeed increase it, then this country is going to face most serious problems.... The solution rests with increasing our export trade, with remaining competitive, with our businesses selling abroad, finding new markets, and keeping our people working at home and around the world." Address in Miami [Florida] at the Opening of the AFL-CIO Convention (December 7, 1961).

1302. "[The United States and the European Common Market] ... face a common challenge: to enlarge the prosperity of free men everywhere — to build in partnership a new trading community in which all free nations may gain from the productive energy of free competitive effort." Annual Message to the Congress on the State of the Union (January 11, 1962).

1303. "We spend a large sum of money, three billion dollars a year, in maintaining our defense forces abroad [and] [w]e have to earn that money through a balance of trade in our favor...." Remarks at the Conference Opening the 1962 Savings Bond Campaign (January 19, 1962).

1304. "[T]he necessity for the United States to maintain an ever-increasing export trade ... is tied directly to our security. If we can continue to build our exports then we can continue to finance our security obligations overseas. If we don't, then quite obviously we are going to have to lessen those commitments." Remarks Upon Presenting "E" Awards for Exports Promotion (March 28, 1962).

1305. "I do not mean to say that we have priced ourselves out of world markets. [W]e have not.... But if we are to stem the gold outflow ... eliminate the deficit in our balance of payments, and continue ... to discharge our far-flung international obligations, we must avoid inflation, modernize American industry, and improve our relative position in the world markets." Address Before the United States Chamber of Commerce on Its 50th Anniversary (April 30, 1962).

1306. "[F]ighting for the re-establishment of the American character ... in our generation and time, is our responsibility.... And ... one facet of that character ... is trade. Because trade and competition and innovation have long been a significant part of the American character." Address in New Orleans at the Opening of the New Dockside Terminal (May 4, 1962).

1307. "[W]e stand at a great dividing point. We must either trade or fade. We must either go backward or go forward." Address in New Orleans at the Opening of the New Dockside Terminal (May 4, 1962).

1308. "Let us not avoid the fact: we cannot sell unless we buy. And there will be those who will be opposed to this competition. But, let those who believe in competition — those who welcome the challenge of world trade ... let them recognize ... that ... this exchange of goods ... will enrich the choice of consumers ... make possible a higher standard of living [and] help hold the lid on the cost of living." Address in New Orleans at the Opening of the New Dockside Terminal (May 4, 1962).

1309. "[Let] us not miss the main point: the new jobs opened through trade will be far greater than any jobs which will be adversely affected. And these new jobs will come in those enterprises that are today leading the economy of the country.... In short, trade expansion will emphasize the modern instead of the obsolete, the strong instead of the weak, the new frontiers of trade instead of the ancient strongholds of protection." Address in New Orleans at the Opening of the New Dockside Terminal (May 4, 1962).

1310. "[T]rade expansion program can benefit us all. I don't say that there won't be some changes in our economy which will require adjustment.... [W]e will be producing more of what we produce best, and others will be producing more of what they produce best. There'll be new employment in our growth industries — and this will come mostly in our high wage industries which are our most competitive abroad — and less new employment in some others." Address Before the Conference on Trade Policy (May 17, 1962).

1311. "America's free world leadership [is] a symbol of America's aim to encourage free nations to grow together, through trade and travel...." Address Before the Conference on Trade Policy (May 17, 1962).

1312. "[T]he Common Market, where we are going to have, instead of a number of different countries to trade with in Europe, one great unit ... can be a most powerful and prosperous and steadily growing economy which can bring the greatest results and strength to the United States in the entire free world." Broadcast Remarks on Trade and Foreign Aid (September 23, 1962).

1313. "[W]e cannot protect our economy by stagnating behind tariff walls.... [T]he best protection possible is a mutual lowering of tariff barriers among friendly nations so that all may benefit from a free flow of goods. Increased economic activity resulting from increased trade will provide more job opportunities for our workers." Remarks Upon Signing the Trade Expansion Act (October 11, 1962).

1314. "A vital expanding economy in the free world is a strong counter to the threat of the world Communist movement. [Greater trade among nations] is, therefore, an important new weapon to advance the cause of freedom." Remarks Upon Signing the Trade Expansion Act (October 11, 1962).

1315. "The relations between the expanding Common Market and the United States are going to be crucial to our economic progress in the sixties and also to our security, so closely linked is our security with the maintenance of an effective trade program." Remarks at the Swearing In of Christian Herter as Special Representative for Trade Negotiations (December 10, 1962).

1316. "We believe ... that closer economic ties among all free nations are essential to prosperity and peace. And neither we nor the members of the European Common Market are so affluent that we can long afford to shelter high cost farms or factories from the winds of foreign competition, or to restrict the channels of trade with other nations of the free world." Annual Message to the Congress on the State of the Union (January 14, 1963).

1317. "While each nation must naturally look out for its own interests, each nation must also look out for the common interest.... We must not return to the 1930s when we exported to each other our own stagnation. We must not return to the discredited view that trade favors some nations at the expense of others." Address in the Assembly Hall at the Paulskirche in Frankfurt [Germany] (June 25, 1963).

1318. "The Common Market was not designed by its founders, and encouraged by the United States, to build walls against other Western countries — or to build walls against the ferment and hope of the developing nations." Remarks in Naples at NATO Headquarters (July 2, 1963).

1319. "I hope that in making that economic judgment [about entering a foreign market], ... [America's companies] will also consider the national interest [because] [e]very dollar you earn abroad is in our interest. As long as we spend what we must spend to maintain our defenses ... assist those countries who are in the front line of freedom, [and] maintain our other obligations abroad, then we must earn our way. The Federal Government cannot earn the way for you. You have to do it yourselves. But earning your way, earning helps us." Address Before the White House Conference on Exports (September 17, 1963).

1320. "We are now committed ... to full participation in a world market of vast dimensions. We have left the house of partial protection and tariff stalemate to begin a much larger involvement in world trade. We ask other nations to do the same." Address Before the White House Conference on Exports (September 17, 1963).

1321. "[E]xport expansion means more jobs.... [B]y expanding our exports we can end the persistent deficits in our balance of payments program.... [I]ncreased exports mean increased profits, and profits are the basis of the free enterprise system, [a]nd finally, the entire free world will benefit from an expansion of our exports." Address Before the White House Conference on Exports (September 17, 1963).

1322. "We seek no unfair competition and no injury to others. [O]ur efforts rest on the fundamental principle that both parties to a transaction benefit from it. Increased trade increases international income. It sharpens efficiency and improves productivity and binds nations together." Address Before the White House Conference on Exports (September 17, 1963).

1323. "We do not seek by precipitous action to improve our [trade] position at the expense of others. We do seek by comprehensive effort, consistent with our international responsibilities, to reduce outflows which are weakening our capacity to serve the world community. In short, every nation in the world has a direct interest, for the dollar is an international currency. And the security of the dollar, therefore, involves the security of us all." Address at the Meeting of the International Monetary Fund (September 30, 1963).

1324. "The balance of payments is not a problem to be cured by a single all-purpose medicine. Each country is challenged to find the appropriate blend of fiscal, monetary, trade, and other policies that will enable it to play its proper role in sustaining rather than straining the system of international payments ... [b]ut [f]or us [the international community] to move in an opposite direction, of course, would be not only distressing but inimical to our common interest." Address at the Meeting of the International Monetary Fund (September 30, 1963).

1325. "Our balance of payments, the necessity for us to earn enough abroad to sustain our defense commitments around the globe, directly affects the national security of the United States. If we could increase our exports by 10 percent, we would have solved our balance of payments problem. That should be possible for a country as enterprising as the American people." Remarks to Members of the Illinois Trade Mission to Europe (October 18, 1963).

1326. "So this [international trade] is worth doing. This is very valuable for our country.... [H]owever happy we are at home, we must look abroad. Every dollar we can earn, that you [American business] can make, will go to increasing the security of our country." Remarks to Members of the Illinois Trade Mission to Europe (October 18, 1963).

KENNEDY ON KENNEDY

His Age

1327. "I read in this morning's newspaper a story that a great hero of my own home town, Ted Williams, was retiring. And I was also interested to read that he was too old at 42. Maybe experience isn't enough." Speech by Senator John F. Kennedy, Democratic Fund-Raising Dinner, Syracuse, New York (September 29, 1960).

1328. "It has recently been suggested that whether I serve one or two terms in the Presidency, I will find myself at the end of that period at what might be called the awkward age — too old to begin a new career and too young to write my memoirs." Address at a Luncheon Meeting of the National Industrial Conference Board (February 13, 1961).

1329. "[W]e are grateful to them, to Bobby Darin, and to Miss Carroll ... and to Miss Monroe who left a picture to come all the way East, and I can now retire from politics after having had 'Happy Birthday' sung to me in such a sweet [interrupted by audience laughter]." Remarks in Response to New York's Birthday Salute to the President (May 19, 1962).

Family

1330. "My wife is home in Massachusetts having a boy in November. I would like to have you meet my sister, Pat Lawford, who comes from California." Rear Platform Remarks of Senator John F. Kennedy, "Pathways to Peace," Fresno, California (September 9, 1960).

1331. "I have been presented with this donkey by two young ladies down there for my daughter. My daughter has the greatest collection of donkeys. She doesn't even know what an elephant looks like. We are going to protect her from that knowledge, too." Remarks of Senator John F. Kennedy, Sharon, Pennsylvania (October 15, 1960).

1332. "On this matter of experience, I had announced earlier this year that if successful I would not consider campaign contributions as a substitute for experience in appointing ambassadors. Ever since I made that statement I have not received one single cent from my father." Speech by Senator John F. Kennedy, Al Smith Memorial Dinner, Waldorf-Astoria Hotel, New York, New York (October 19, 1960).

1333. "I don't see anything wrong with giving him [brother Robert Kennedy] a little legal experience before he goes out to practice law." Remarks to Alfalfa Club in Washington, D.C. (January 21, 1961).

1334. "I am somewhat encouraged in saying a few words in French, from having had a chance to listen to the Prime Minister John G. [Deiefenbaker]. It's an unfortunate division of labor, that my wife who speaks so well should sit there without saying a word, while I get up and talk." Remarks Upon Arrival at the Royal Canadian Air Force Uplands Airport in Ottawa (May 16, 1961).

1335. "Somebody said ... the only thing keeping us going are not the programs but my wife and Caroline! But we believe that the programs are also important." Remarks to Participants in the Campaign Conference for Democratic Women (May 22, 1962).

1336. "In my own country it is sometimes said that there are too many Kennedys in American public life." Remarks at the Rathaus in Cologne [Germany] After Signing the Golden Book (June 23, 1963).

1337. "I first of all want to express my appreciation to my brother Teddy for his offering me his coattail. Teddy has been down in Washington and he came to see me the other day, and he said he was really tired of being referred to as the younger brother of the President, and being another Kennedy, and it is crowded in Washington, and that he was going to break loose and change his name. He was going out on his own. Instead of being Teddy Kennedy now, he is changing his name to Teddy Roosevelt." Remarks in Boston at the "New England's Salute to the President" Dinner (October 19, 1963).

1338. "My last campaign, I suppose, may be coming up very shortly — but Teddy is around and, therefore, these [Presidential] dinners can go on indefinitely." Remarks in Boston at the "New England's Salute to the President" Dinner (October 19, 1963).

Irish Heritage

1339. "There is an impression in Washington that there are no Kennedys left in Ireland, that they are all in Washington, so I wonder if there are any Kennedys in this audience. Could you hold up your hand so I can see? Well, I am glad to see a few cousins who didn't catch the boat." Remarks at Redmond Place in Wexford [Ireland] (June 27, 1963).

1340. "I don't want to give the impression that every member of this administration in Washington is Irish — it just seems that way." Remarks at the City Hall in Cork [Ireland] (June 28, 1963).

1341. "I am proud to be the first American President to visit Ireland during his term of office...." Address Before the Irish Parliament in Dublin [Ireland] (June 28, 1963).

1342. "This [Ireland] is not the land of my birth, but it is the land for which I hold the greatest affection...." Remarks at a Reception in Li [Ireland] (June 29, 1963).

Optimism and Aspirations

1343. "This is a great country. It can be greater. It is a powerful country. It can be more powerful." Remarks of Senator John F. Kennedy, Oakland Park, Pontiac, Michigan (September 5, 1960).

1344. "I look to the future of the United States with optimism.... The more I travel in this country, the more I see of it, the more optimistic I become. I think the future of the United States is unlimited...." Speech by Senator John F. Kennedy, High School Auditorium, Pocatello, Idaho (September 6, 1960).

1345. "Mr. Khrushchev has said that while we are Democrats and believe in freedom, that our children are going to be Communists. I don't believe this. I think we represent the best system, but I think it is up to us to do the best for our system and for our country. I don't hold the view that our best day is somewhere in the past and that the future belongs to the Communists. I think the future belongs to us." Remarks of Senator John F. Kennedy, Courthouse Square, Eugene, Oregon (September 7, 1960).

1346. "I don't take the view that we have never had it so good. I take the view that this is a great country, but it can be greater." Rear Platform Remarks of Senator John F. Kennedy, Sacramento, California (September 8, 1960).

1347. "I must say, looking at the power in this great country of ours, after having traveled in nearly every State in the last 12 months, and spending a great deal of time in some States in the primaries, I have come to have the greatest possible confidence, not only in our country, but in our system of government." Speech by Senator John F. Kennedy, Shrine Auditorium, Los Angeles, California (September 9, 1960).

1348. "[I]f we meet our responsibilities, if we measure up not only in the public sense, but in the private sense, to the opportunities that we have, if we recognize that freedom is not licensed, and that liberty calls for certain qualities of self-restraint and character which go with self-government, I am confident that the future can belong to those who believe in freedom." Speech by Senator John F. Kennedy, Shrine Auditorium, Los Angeles, California (September 9, 1960).

1349. "I think in a very real sense what we have here really is the final flowering of the human experience. I don't think the world is moving in the direction of communism. I think in time it will move in the direction that we have followed. I think that that is particularly true if we are willing to meet our responsibilities. If we recognize that what we have now is good, but that we can do better, if we recognize that our past experience is great but that our future possibilities are even greater...." Speech by Senator John F. Kennedy, Shrine Auditorium, Los Angeles, California (September 9, 1960).

1350. "In 1960, we believe there is a God, and we believe He hates injustice, and we see a storm coming, but I think [quoting Lincoln] 'If He has a place and a part for us, then we are ready.'" Rear Platform Remarks of Senator John F. Kennedy, Tulare, California (September 9, 1960).

1351. "[T]his is a difficult and trying time for us all, that ... calls for the best in the American Republic, the best spirit, the best determination, the feeling that the future can belong to us ... but ... we have the greatest possible confidence in the future of our country, in the future of the American people." Remarks of Senator John F. Kennedy, the Alamo, San Antonio, Texas (September 12, 1960).

1352. "I think our brightest days are ahead. I think it is incumbent upon us to demonstrate that this system of ours can work, that it can work in a period of danger, that it can work at a time when it is being challenged all over the globe, that we can hold out a hand of friendship to those ... [around the world] that we represent the way to the future, and that the Communist system is as old as Egypt." Remarks of Senator John F. Kennedy, Capitol Steps, Austin, Texas (September 13, 1960).

1353. "I do not accept the view that our high noon is in the past, and that we are moving into the late afternoon. I think our brightest days can be ahead. I think it is up to us to build the kind of country here, the kind of economic society, the kind of equality for all our citizens, regardless of their race or their religion, so that people around the world wish to move with us and not with our adversaries." Remarks of Senator John F. Kennedy, State Office Building, Trenton, New Jersey (September 15, 1960).

1354. "I feel a sense of kinship with the Pittsburgh Pirates. Like my candidacy, they were not given much chance in the spring. But fighting youth is winning out in the fall and neither of us is going to settle for second place." Statewide TV Speech by Senator John F. Kennedy, Zembo Mosque Temple, Harrisburg, Pennsylvania (September 15, 1960).

1355. "I think that this can be not a period of gloom for us. I have confidence in this country. I don't downgrade the United States. I say we can do better. I have more confidence in the United States and its potential than our adversaries who say what we are doing now is as much as we can do. I know we can do better...." Remarks of Senator John F. Kennedy, Tri-Cities Airport, Bristol, Virginia-Tennessee (September 21, 1960).

1356. "I don't want anyone 10 years from now, or any historian to write that these were the years when the balance of power began to turn against the United States; these were the years when the tide ran out for freedom.... I want historians to say that these were the years when the American people began to move again. These were the years when the United States met its responsibilities to freedom." Remarks of Senator John F. Kennedy, Mansfield, Ohio (September 27, 1960).

1357. "We have a form of government which every person in the world around us would most like to live under, given their free choice. We represent, in my judgment, the way of the future. I do not regard us as an extinct flowering of human experience. I regard us as the place where everyone ultimately wants to be." Remarks of Senator John F. Kennedy, Schenectady, New York (September 29, 1960).

1358. "[I] have great confidence in this Nation and in the American people ... that this Nation is strong enough to permit a free and open discussion of the great problems which face us in this difficult and somber time in the life of our country." Speech by Senator John F. Kennedy, Chase Hotel, St. Louis, Missouri (October 2, 1960).

1359. "I really believe that if the leadership sets before us the unfinished business of America, if we set before ourselves goals that we must achieve, if we are going to maintain our society free from being vulnerable, then I am confident that the power of this country can be unmatched." Speech by Senator John F. Kennedy, Auditorium (Coliseum), Indianapolis, Indiana (October 4, 1960).

1360. "I hold the greatest possible confidence in this country. I do not believe that there are any problems which once set before us cannot be met." Remarks of Senator John F. Kennedy, Courthouse Steps, Dayton, Ohio (October 17, 1960).

1361. "[America] is a great country, but I believe it must be greater, and it is a powerful country, but I believe it must be more powerful, and I believe that our responsibility in the 1960s is to restore to the world the image of America as a society on the move, a society whose high noon is just ahead, not a society which stands still, which begins to lose its vitality, which begins to lose its image as a moving society, a moving country." Remarks of Senator John F. Kennedy, 163d Street Shopping Center, North Miami Beach, Florida (October 18, 1960).

1362. "I [do not] wish to be the President of a nation which is being driven back, which is on the defensive, because of its unwillingness to face the facts of our national existence, to tell the truth, to bear the burdens which freedom demands, a nation which may be declining in relative strength, and with the world coming to an end, as T. S. Eliot said, 'Not with a bang, but with a whimper.'" Speech by Senator John F. Kennedy, American Legion Convention, Miami Beach, Florida (October 18, 1960).

1363. "I am confident that this country can meet its responsibilities. I see no peril, no burden that this country cannot sail through, unless we attempt to fool ourselves that these are easy, gentle, and prosperous times, without responsibility, without burden." Remarks of Senator John F. Kennedy, Roosevelt Field, Norristown, Pennsylvania (October 29, 1960).

1364. "I believe in an America where every man, or woman, who wants to work can find work—a full week's work for a full week's pay; where every man or woman of talent can use those talents; where the waste of idle men and idle machines, of steel mills half shut down, and coal mines boarded up ... can be limited; where a growing economy provides new jobs and new markets for a growing nation...." Speech by Senator John F. Kennedy, Convention Hall, Philadelphia, Pennsylvania (October 31, 1960).

1365. "I want historians to say a decade from now, these were the great years of the great Republic, these were the years when America began to move again. These were the years when the tide came in; these were the years when a free society demonstrated its vitality, when they brought people to Washington and sent them around the world, men who were committed to progress, men who could identify themselves with the basic aspiration of people everywhere." Remarks of Senator John F. Kennedy, Albuquerque, New Mexico (November 3, 1960).

1366. "If I am elected next Tuesday, I want to be a President known ... as one who not only held back the Communist tide but advanced the cause of freedom and rebuilt American prestige — not by words but by work — not by stating great aims merely as a good debater, but by doing great deeds as a good neighbor — not by tours and conferences abroad, but by vitality and direction at home.... I want to be a President who will regain that office for the people. I have no wish to be known as a narrowly partisan President, or as a private-interest President — I want to be President of all the people.... I want to be a President who has the confidence of the people — and who takes the people into his confidence — who lets them know what he is doing and where we are going, who is for his program and who is against.... I want to be a President who acts as well as reacts — who originates programs as well as study groups — who masters complex problems as well as one-page memorandums. I want to be a President who is the Chief Executive in every sense of the word — who responds to a problem, not by hoping his subordinates will act, but by directing them to act — a President who is willing to take the responsibility for getting things done, and take the blame if they are not done right." Remarks of Senator John F. Kennedy, New York Coliseum, New York, New York (November 5, 1960).

1367. "I believe that our future can be bright. I do not take a depressed view of our society here, or of our prospects around the world. I believe we live in a hard and difficult era of history. I believe that we are going to fail as well as succeed, but I believe that we are at least going to make the effort. I believe that we are going to try, and we will take our setbacks as well as our successes, and we will continue to move here, and around the world. We will continue to demonstrate that we desire ... the chance to build in this country a free society and under the shelter of our effort to permit others to do likewise." Address in Chicago at a Dinner of the Democratic Party of Cook County (April 28, 1961).

1368. "I do not believe the West is in decline. I believe the West is in the ascendancy." Remarks at a Civic Reception for President Kennedy at the Hotel de Ville [Paris, France] (June 1, 1961).

1369. "I am not an historical determinist, but I do believe that history is not moving against us, but in the long run is moving with us." Remarks in Paris Before the North Atlantic Council (June 1, 1961).

1370. "I want it to be said that this generation of Americans, jealous of its rights, conscious of its responsibilities, met its responsibility in the year 1961 and in the years to come — met it with all the resources and all the wisdom and all the judgment, and meeting it, prevailed." Remarks at the Eighth National Conference on International Economic and Social Development (June 16, 1961).

1371. "We bet on this country. We believe in its prospects, and we are ready to face what difficulties there are in our time." Remarks in Seattle at the Silver Anniversary Dinner Honoring Senator Magnuson (November 16, 1961).

1372. "[T]hose who see only hazard and do not recognize that on the other side of the coin is opportunity are wrong." Remarks in Columbus [Ohio] at a Birthday Dinner for Governor DiSalle (January 6, 1962).

1373. "This Administration was not elected to preside over the liquidation of American responsibility in these great years." Address in New Orleans at the Opening of the New Dockside Terminal (May 4, 1962).

1374. "I don't know with certainty what the future will bring, but I am certain that if we are willing to continue to play our proper part, that it can be happy for all of us." Address in Milwaukee at the Jefferson-Jackson Dinner (May 12, 1962).

1375. "I believe it is important that this country sail and not lie still in the harbors. Great opportunities lie before us and great responsibilities have been placed upon us. I believe we can meet them. We have in the past, we are going to today, and I know we will in the future." Radio and Television Report to the American People on the State of the National Economy (August 13, 1962).

1376. "I don't think in this administration or in our generation or time will this country be at the top of the hill, but some day it will be, and I hope when it is that they will think that we have done our part." Remarks at the Second Inaugural Anniversary Salute (January 18, 1963)

1377. "A man may die, nations may rise and fall, but an idea lives on. Ideas have endurance without death." Remarks Recorded for the Opening of a USIA Transmitter at Greenville, North Carolina (February 8, 1963).

1378. "[E]ven though the United States is, comparatively speaking, a young society we ... look to the future, not the past, and we look to that future with hope." Remarks of Welcome to a Group from Valdagno, Italy (May 17, 1963).

1379. "Our problems are manmade — therefore, they can be solved by man. And man can be as big as he wants. No problem of human destiny is beyond human beings. Man's reason and spirit have often solved the seemingly unsolvable — and we believe they can do it again." Commencement Address at American University in Washington, D.C. (June 10, 1963).

1380. "[W]e need not feel the bitterness of the past to discover its meaning for the present and the future." Address Before the Irish Parliament in Dublin [Ireland] (June 28, 1963).

1381. "[W]hen a judgment is rendered whether this generation of Americans took those steps at home and abroad to make it possible for those who came after us to live in greater security and prosperity, I am confident that history will write that in the 1960s we did our part to maintain our country and make it more beautiful." Remarks at the Yellowstone County Fairgrounds, Billings, Montana (September 25, 1963).

1382. "The solution of every problem brings with it other problems. And, therefore, this society of ours is, in a very real sense, in a race.... [I] want to see all of our children as well educated as possible. I want to see us protect our natural resources. I want to see us make our cities better places in which to live. I want this country, as I know you do, to be an ornament to the cause of freedom all around the globe, because as we go, so goes the cause of freedom. This is the obligation, therefore, of this generation of Americans." Remarks at the High School Memorial Stadium, Great Falls, Montana (September 26, 1963).

1383. "The fact of the matter is, as a general rule, every time we bet on the future of this country we win." Remarks at the Dedication of the Whiskeytown, California, Dam and Reservoir (September 28, 1963).

1384. "[I] I do not look to the future with gloom. I do not regard the efforts of the National Government, which represents the wishes of all of the people, as a failure. I think the United States here and abroad is moving into its brightest period, and I hope the people of the United States ... continue to make that choice as they have in the past — that they will continue to fulfill their responsibilities." Remarks in Boston at the "New England's Salute to the President" Dinner (October 19, 1963).

1385. "I look forward to a great future for America, a future in which our country will match its military strength with our moral restraint, its wealth with our wisdom, its power with our purpose ... an America which will not be afraid of grace and beauty, which will protect the beauty of our natural environment ... and which will build handsome and balanced cities for our future. I look forward to an America which will reward achievement in the arts as we reward achievement in business or statecraft ... to an America which will steadily raise the standards of artistic accomplishment and which will steadily enlarge cultural opportunities for all of our citizens. And I look forward to an America which commands respect throughout the world not only for its strength but for its civilization as well." Remarks at Amherst College Upon Receiving an Honorary Degree (October 26, 1963).

1386. "This country faces many serious problems at home and abroad, but I think we have a good deal to be thankful for. This is a rich country. We want those who come after us to have the same chance that those who came before us have had. We want them to live in a secure world. We want them to live in an America which is committed to progress." Remarks in Tampa to Members of the United Steelworkers (November 18, 1963).

Political Philosophy

1387. "I know no North and South, East or West. I believe in a party which stretches from Texas to Maine, from Florida to Washington, which stretches all the way across the country, representing all groups, speaking for the people. That is the kind of party which I believe in and that is the kind of party which can lead this country." Speech by Senator John F. Kennedy, Houston Coliseum, Houston, Texas (September 12, 1960).

1388. "My philosophy is a progressive one. I stand in direct succession to Woodrow Wilson and Franklin Roosevelt who in their day and generation recognized that there was a responsibility for the people as a whole, working through their government, to move this country ahead, and I stand in that tradition." Remarks of Senator John F. Kennedy, Battle Creek, Michigan (October 14, 1960).

1389. "I regard bipartisanship not as a means of stifling debate, not as a means of preventing discussion of the problems that face us, but I regard bipartisanship as putting the interest of our country first." Remarks of Senator John F. Kennedy, Grand Rapids, Michigan (October 14, 1960).

1390. "I never used to hear about the old Lincoln and the new Lincoln, the old Woodrow Wilson and the new Woodrow Wilson, the modern Franklin Roosevelt and the old-fashioned Franklin Roosevelt. I am a Democrat, without prefix or suffix." Remarks of Senator John F. Kennedy, New Castle, Pennsylvania (October 15, 1960).

1391. "I think they [the American [people] want a candidate who does not have to issue statements every day saying what he is and what he is not, depending on what section of the country he is in, and which audience he is talking to. I am a Democrat, east, west, north, south, a Democrat who stands in the tradition of Franklin Roosevelt, in Pennsylvania, in California in Georgia, in Massachusetts." Remarks of Senator John F. Kennedy, Breakfast, Sharon Inn, Sharon, Pennsylvania (October 15, 1960).

1392. "We have a chance to correct the future. We have a chance to participate in it. We have a chance to rejoin the world as a leader of the free world. We have a chance to build in this country the kind of society which people all over the world who want to be free say, 'This is the direction I want to go.' And it is on that basis, not saying that life is easy, not saying that if I am elected the problems will easily be solved, but promising that if I am elected this country will start to move again, this country will start to meet its responsibilities." Remarks of Senator John F. Kennedy, Capitol Steps, Columbus, Ohio (October 17, 1960).

1393. "This [the 1960 election] is not a fight between Republicans and Democrats: this is a fight between the comfortable and the concerned, between those who look forward and those who stand still, between those who believe that all we have to do is what we are doing now and more, and those who believe it is time for a great movement forward for our country again." Remarks of Senator John F. Kennedy, London, Ohio (October 17, 1960).

1394. "My disagreement is with those who run on slogans which do not represent the facts.... That is not the way we are going to survive. That is not the way we survived in the past. It has been on our willingness to face facts, to tell the truth, to tell the truth ... to stand for ... strengthening this country of ours, making it stronger here at home, building the kind of society in this country so that people around the world who wish to be free, wish to follow us, wish to identify themselves with us, wish to follow our leadership." Remarks of Senator John F. Kennedy, City Hall Steps, New York, New York (October 19, 1960).

1395. "I come here as the standard bearer of a party which in this century has run men like Woodrow Wilson and Franklin Roosevelt, and I run in their tradition." Remarks of Senator John F. Kennedy, Fulton and Nostrand, Brooklyn, New York (October 20, 1960).

1396. "[I] look not to the past, but to the future." Speech by Senator John F. Kennedy, Detroit Coliseum, Michigan State Fair, Detroit, Michigan (October 26, 1960).

1397. "I want to see the United States first, period." Remarks of Senator John F. Kennedy, Keyworth Stadium, Hamtramck, Michigan (October 26, 1960).

1398. "[I] believe [that] if we choose to look forward, if we choose to measure up to our responsibilities as Americans, as the chief defenders of freedom, and as progressive, forward looking strong people, in my judgment it can be a new day and the beginning of progress for the United States." Remarks of Senator John F. Kennedy, Wilkes-Barre, Pennsylvania (October 28, 1960).

Religious Faith

1399. "[W]hat has widely been called 'the religious issue' in American politics ... covers a multitude of meanings. There is no religious issue in the sense that any of the major candidates differ on the role of religion in our political life. Every Presidential contender, I am certain, is dedicated to the separation of church and state, to the preservation of religious liberty, to an end to religious bigotry, and to the total independence of the office-holder from any form of ecclesiastical dictation." Remarks of Senator John F. Kennedy, American Society of Newspaper Editors, Washington, D.C. (April 21, 1960).

1400. "I am not 'trying to be the first Catholic President,' as some have written. I happen to believe I can serve my nation as President — and I also happen to have been born a Catholic." Remarks of Senator John F. Kennedy, American Society of Newspaper Editors, Washington, D.C. (April 21, 1960).

1401. "I [do not] want anyone to support my candidacy merely to prove that this nation is not bigoted — and that a Catholic can be elected President. I have never suggested that those opposed to me are thereby anti–Catholic. There are ample legitimate grounds for supporting other candidates...." Remarks of Senator John F. Kennedy, American Society of Newspaper Editors, Washington, D.C. (April 21, 1960).

1402. "The Presidency is not ... the British Crown, serving a dual capacity in both church and state. The President is not elected to be protector of the faith — or guardian of the public morals. His attendance at church on Sunday should be his business alone...." Remarks of Senator John F. Kennedy, American Society of Newspaper Editors, Washington, D.C. (April 21, 1960).

1403. "I am fully aware of the fact that the Democratic Party, by nominating someone of my faith, has taken on what many regard as a new and hazardous risk — new, at least since 1928. But I look at it this way: the Democratic Party has once again placed its confidence in the American people, and in their ability to render a free, fair judgment. And you have, at the same time, placed your confidence in me, and in my ability to render a free, fair judgment — to uphold the Constitution and my oath of office — and to reject any kind of religious pressure or obligation that might directly or indirectly interfere with my conduct of the Presidency in the national interest." Address of Senator John F. Kennedy Accepting the Democratic Party Nomination for the Presidency of the United States, Memorial Coliseum, Los Angeles [California] (July 15, 1960.)

1404. "I hope that no American ... will waste his franchise by voting either for me or against me solely on account of my religious affiliation.... It is not relevant what abuses may have existed in other countries or in other times. It is not relevant what pressures, if any, might conceivably be brought to bear on me. I am telling you now what you are entitled to know: that my decisions on any public policy will be my own — as an American, a Democrat and a free man." Address of Senator John F. Kennedy Accepting the Democratic Party Nomination for the Presidency of the United States, Memorial Coliseum, Los Angeles (July 15, 1960.)

1405. "There is a question of do I believe all Protestants are heretics. No, and I hope you don't believe all Catholics are. May I say that it seems to me that the great struggle today is between those who believe in no God and those who believe in God. I really don't see why we should engage in close debate over what you may believe and what I may believe. That is my privilege and your privilege." Rear Platform Remarks of Senator John F. Kennedy, Modesto, California (September 9, 1960).

1406. "[B]ecause I am a Catholic, and no Catholic has ever been elected President, the real issues in this campaign have been obscured — perhaps deliberately, in some quarters.... So it is apparently necessary for me to state once again — not what kind of church I believe in, for that should be important only to me — but what kind of America I believe in. I believe in an America where the separation of church and state is absolute — where no Catholic prelate would tell the President (should he be Catholic) how to act, and no Protestant minister would tell his parishioners for whom to vote — where no church or church school is granted any public funds or political preference — and where no man is denied public office merely because his religion differs from the President who might appoint him or the people who might elect him. I believe in an America that is officially neither Catholic, Protestant nor Jewish — where no public official either requests or accepts instructions on public policy from the Pope, the National Council of Churches or any other ecclesiastical source — where no religious body seeks to impose its will directly or indirectly upon the general populace or the public acts of its officials — and where religious liberty is so indivisible that an act against one church is treated as an act against all." Speech by Senator John F. Kennedy, Greater Houston Ministerial Association, Rice Hotel, Houston, Texas (September 12, 1960).

1407. "[I] believe in an America where religious intolerance will someday end — where all men and all churches are treated as equal — where every man has the same right to attend or not attend the church of his choice — where there is no Catholic vote, no anti–Catholic vote, no bloc voting of any kind — and where Catholics, Protestants and Jews, at both the lay and pastoral level, will refrain from those attitudes of disdain and division which have so often marred their works in the past, and promote instead the American ideal of brotherhood. That is the kind of America in which I believe." Speech by Senator John F. Kennedy, Greater Houston Ministerial Association, Rice Hotel, Houston, Texas (September 12, 1960).

1408. "[The] Presidency ... [is] a great office that must neither be humbled by making it the instrument of any one religious group nor tarnished by arbitrarily withholding its occupancy from the members of any one religious group." Speech by Senator John F. Kennedy, Greater Houston Ministerial Association, Rice Hotel, Houston, Texas (September 12, 1960).

1409. "Whatever issue may come before me as President — in birth control, divorce, censorship, gambling or any other subject — I will make my decision in accordance with these [personal] views, in accordance with what my conscience tells me to be the national interest, and without regard to outside religious pressures or dictates. And no power or threat of punishment could cause me to decide otherwise. But if the time should ever come — and I do not concede any conflict to be even remotely possible — when my office would require me to either violate my conscience or violate the national interest, then I would resign the office; and I hope any conscientious public servant would do the same." Speech by Senator John F. Kennedy, Greater Houston Ministerial Association, Rice Hotel, Houston, Texas (September 12, 1960).

1410. "If I should lose [the 1960 presidential election] on the real issues, I shall return to my seat in the Senate, satisfied that I had tried my best and was fairly judged. But if this election is decided on the basis that 40 million Americans lost their chance of being President on the day they were baptized, then it is the whole Nation that will be the loser, in the eyes of Catholics and non–Catholics around the world, in the eyes of history, and in the eyes of our own people." Speech by Senator John F. Kennedy, Greater Houston Ministerial Association, Rice Hotel, Houston, Texas (September 12, 1960).

1411. "Some say that ... when the ballots are counted, that the religious convictions of the candidates will influence the outcome more than their convictions on the issues. But ... I do not believe [that]...." Speech by Senator John F. Kennedy, Al Smith Memorial Dinner, Waldorf-Astoria Hotel, New York, New York (October 19, 1960).

LABOR UNIONS

General

1412. "No union member should be denied the right to picket sites that require him to work side by side with [a] non-union member." Remarks of Senator John F. Kennedy, Sixth Annual National Legislative Conference Building and Construction Trades, Washington, D.C. (March 14, 1960).

1413. "The cause ... of labor has not been an easy one in the past few years. Unfortunately the headlines ... the attention has been largely focused on the few hoodlums and racketeers who have insinuated their way into the labor movement — plundering its members, destroying the hard won gains of the workers, and harming the reputation of ... organized labor. But these men are just the few parasites on the body of a great, vital group of men and women — a group that has contributed more to the economic health, the well-being and the strength of this country than any other organized group, in any other country, in any other period of human history." Remarks of Senator John F. Kennedy, Weyerhaeuser Lumber Company, Eugene, Oregon (May 17, 1960).

1414. "[T]he size of organized labor is a blessing — and its strength is a powerful force for the good of all America." Remarks of Senator John F. Kennedy, Weyerhaeuser Lumber Company, Eugene, Oregon (May 17, 1960).

1415. "[W]e must work to defeat legislation designed to repress labor — to destroy its power — and render the worker helpless to advance his own welfare.... [W]hatever office I shall hold — I shall always be unalterably opposed to so-called 'right-to-work' laws at any level, Federal or State. And I shall oppose ... any and all other such devices which are sure to spring from the fertile minds of labor's powerful foes." Remarks of Senator John F. Kennedy, Weyerhaeuser Lumber Company, Eugene, Oregon (May 17, 1960).

1416. "I know that the American labor movement wants for America what I want for America: the elimination of poverty and unemployment, the reestablishment of America's position of leadership in the world, the end of racial discrimination everywhere in our society. I know the American labor movement opposes what I oppose: complacency, unemployment, economic stagnation, and national insecurity. I believe in the things the labor movement believes in and fights for." Remarks of Senator John F. Kennedy via Telephone, New York State AFL-CIO (August 30, 1960).

1417. "[W]e share a deep-seated belief in free collective bargaining, and in the growth and development of free and responsible unions — and unlike our opponents, we do not believe in this only on Labor Day." Speech by Senator John F. Kennedy, Cadillac Square, Detroit, Michigan (September 5, 1960).

1418. "Our labor unions are not narrow, self-seeking groups. They have raised wages, shortened hours, and provided supplemental benefits. Through collective bargaining and grievance procedures, they have brought justice and democracy to the shop floor.... They have spoken, not for narrow self-interest, but for the public interest and for the people. For the labor movement is people. Our unions have brought millions of men and women together ... and given them common tools for common goals. Their goals are goals for all America — and their enemies are the enemies of all progress." Speech by Senator John F. Kennedy, Cadillac Square, Detroit, Michigan (September 5, 1960).

1419. "I think it can be said that the labor movement has concerned itself not only with the interest of its members, but also with the general public interest. Labor has identified itself with the fight for aid for education, with the fight for medical care for the aged under social security, with the fight for housing, the fight for a better system of social justice in this country, and for a stronger foreign policy abroad. They have been concerned with what concerns our country." Speech by Senator John F. Kennedy, Multnomah Hotel, Portland, Oregon (September 7, 1960).

1420. "[T]hose of you who are active in labor, those of you who lead organized labor movements ... know very well, perhaps better than anyone, that this country still has unfinished business, that we have to maintain full employment, that we have to advance the standards of living of our people, of better housing, of better minimum wage, of medical care for the aged." Remarks of Senator John F. Kennedy, Auditorium, Union Hall, New York, New York (October 19, 1960).

1421. "[The] labor movement ... [has] an obligation to participate in strengthening our country, making it work, making our system move, providing employment for our people, a better standard of living, setting an example to the world." Remarks of Senator John F. Kennedy, Auditorium, Union Hall, New York, New York (October 19, 1960).

1422. "I spent a month in a State which has a lot of miners in it, West Virginia. My own judgment is I know no tougher occupation in the world that to be a miner, lead, zinc, coal. I am always glad to meet them because I think they live with peril. They have as tough a life as there is. Every other one whose hand you shake has a finger off, a foot crushed, the chances of in 20 years their having a bad accident are more than any of the rest of us." Remarks of Senator John F. Kennedy Airport Rally, Joplin, Missouri (October 22, 1960).

1423. "It's no accident that Communists concentrate their attention on the trade union movement. They know that people — the working people — are frequently left out, that in many areas of the world they have no one to speak for them, and the Communists mislead them and say that they will protect their rights. So many go along. But ... because we have had a strong, free labor movement, the working people of this country have not felt that they were left out. And as long as the labor movement is strong and as long as it is committed to freedom, then I think that freedom in this country is strengthened ... and all around the world." Address in Miami at the Opening of the AFL-CIO Convention (December 7, 1961).

1424. "We want them [the people of other countries] to have the instruments of freedom to protect themselves and provide for progress in their country, and a strong, free labor movement can do it...." Address in Miami at the Opening of the AFL-CIO Convention (December 7, 1961).

1425. "I am a great believer in the contribution which the union movement can make, not only in this country in maintaining a progressive economy, but also the contribution which the union movement can make around the world." Remarks to the Policy Committee of the Communications Workers of America (February 14, 1962).

1426. "No greater service to the cause of the free world could possibly come forward than the development of effective, liberal, free trade unions in the newly emerging countries. These are the areas where the Communists concentrate. If they are able to have a great mass of people living in misery and a few in luxury, it suits them to a tee." Address in Atlantic City at the Convention of the United Auto Workers (May 8, 1962).

1427. "[I] [do not] believe in the philosophy that what is good for one company or one union is automatically good for the United States. I believe, instead, that what is good for the United States, for the people as a whole, is going to be good for every American company and for every American union." Address in Atlantic City at the Convention of the United Auto Workers (May 8, 1962).

1428. "We still have great areas of effort which are left for ... union[s] in protecting the welfare of [their] members. But it is also important to emphasize, and there is also a great opportunity open, to all unions across the country to participate in the strengthening of their country." Remarks in New York City at the Dedication of the Penn Station South Urban Renewal Project (May 19, 1962).

1429. "You cannot maintain a free society today ... unless you have a free trade union movement, and the trade union movement is effective not only because it is a means of securing a fair share of national productivity for the men and women who labor but it is also the means of supporting a broad program of social progress." Remarks to Students from Latin America and the Caribbean Attending the Institute for free Trade Union Development (August 8, 1962).

1430. "[T]he labor movement in this country has looked beyond its immediate responsibilities to its members and to its responsibilities to society as a whole, [and] I think it's fulfilled a great role in our country." Remarks to Students from Latin America and the Caribbean Attending the Institute for free Trade Union Development (August 8, 1962).

1431. "A strong trade union movement is essential for the maintenance of freedom...." Remarks to Students from Latin America and the Caribbean Attending the Institute for free Trade Union Development (August 8, 1962).

1432. "[S]ometimes we in Washington, dealing with larger issues, do not become as aware as we should be [of] ... the working conditions of men and women working in factories across the United States, men and women whose job security is vital to their survival, ... [and] the adjustments which are [being] made in their hours, and in their working conditions, by technological changes or by economic or monetary changes in the policy of the United States." Remarks at the Swearing In of Willard Wirtz as Secretary of Labor (September 25, 1962).

1433. "There are too many areas of our country where there isn't equal opportunity, where people aren't adequately paid, where they work too long, where their rights are not guaranteed. And as long as that's true, there's a need for the American labor movement." Remarks at the Signing of a Joint Statement on Fair Employment Practices (November 15, 1962).

1434. "The labor movement ... was originated by those who were being denied their equal opportunity. Whether it was because they were working 12 hours a day, 6 or 7 days a week, whether it was because they were immigrants, whether it was because of one reason or another, the labor movement began as a union of those who were the least privileged in our society." Remarks at the Signing of a Joint Statement on Fair Employment Practices (November 15, 1962).

1435. "[Those] who may find fault with the American labor movement today in the United States ... need only to look abroad ... in all parts of the world, and see labor unions controlled either by the Communists or by the government, or no labor unions, and ... they find inevitably poverty or totalitarianism. And therefore I think it is a [fair] judgment to make that a free, active, progressive trade union movement stands for a free, active, progressive country...." Remarks at the 75th Anniversary Banquet of the International Association of Machinists (March 5, 1963).

1436. "[T]he trade union movement ... is essential for a progressive democracy...." Remarks at the Ambassador's Residence, San Jose [Costa Rica], in Response to a Welcoming Declaration by Christian Democratic Youth (March 20, 1963).

1437. "It is no accident that ... the target of the Communist movement has been the destruction of the free trade union movement [because] [o]nce the free trade union movement is destroyed, once it is harnessed to the chariot of the state, once trade union leaders are nominated by the head of the state, once [trade union] meetings ... become formalities, endorsing the purposes of the state, the trade union movement is destroyed and so is democracy." Remarks in Berlin to the Trade Union Congress of German Construction Workers (June 26, 1963).

1438. "[T]he trade union movement ... [can] be an example to those who ... stand on the razor edge of moving into some kind of totalitarianism or developing a free, progressive society, where, through the trade union movement, the fruits of progress, the fruits of production, can be distributed fairly to the population — not by a leader, but by the people themselves." Remarks in Berlin to the Trade Union Congress of German Construction Workers (June 26, 1963).

1439. "[T]he right to work, the right to have a job in this country in a time of prosperity in the United States ... is the real right to work issue in 1963. [T]his country must move so fast to even stand still." Remarks in New York City at the AFL-CIO Convention (November 15, 1963).

Collective Bargaining

1440. "You get an agreement when there is a need for steel ... when the economy is moving ahead ... [when] there is incentive on both sides to sign a contract and get back to work.... As long as you have a slowdown in our economy, so long will you find it difficult to work out satisfactory collective bargaining procedures." Speech by Senator John F. Kennedy, United Steelworkers of America Convention, Convention Hall, Atlantic City, New Jersey (September 19, 1960).

1441. "[The] first line of defense against inflation is the good sense and public spirit of business and labor — keeping their total increases in wages and profits in step with productivity. There is no single statistical test to guide each company and each union. But ... for their country's interest, and for their own ... the test of the public interest [must be applied] to these transactions." Annual Message to the Congress on the State of the Union (January 11, 1962).

1442. "[T]he national interest can be protected and the interests of the industry and of the employees forwarded through free and responsible collective bargaining." Telephone Messages to Labor and Management Leaders following the Steel Settlement (March 31, 1962).

1443. "Union leaders' interests lie in the rate of return on labor for their members. To the extent that their efforts are devoted to securing equitable wages for their workers, our [the Federal Government's and organized labor's] interests are identical, because we must have consumers to absorb our vast productive capacity ... and [also because] the National Government also lives off personal income taxes." Address Before the United States Chamber of Commerce on Its 50th Anniversary (April 30, 1962).

1444. "[U]njustified wage demands which require price increases, and then other demands and then other price increases, are equally as contrary to the national interest as unjustified profit demands which require price increases." Address in Atlantic City at the Convention of the United Auto Workers (May 8, 1962).

1445. "What good is it to get an increase in wages if it is taken away by an increase in prices? What counts is the real increase in wages, which comes from increased productivity and technology." Address in Atlantic City at the Convention of the United Auto Workers (May 8, 1962).

1446. "[I]n general a wage policy which seeks its gains out of the fruits of technology instead of the pockets of the consumers is the one basic approach that can help every segment of the economy." Address in Atlantic City at the Convention of the United Auto Workers (May 8, 1962).

1447. "There are of course substantial differences of opinion between labor and management, particularly over the negotiating table — how shall it be divided, how much will go to profits and the stockholders, and how much to business. But there is an awful lot more that both labor and management have in common, because if we can operate this economy at full blast, then the division that comes out of that full blast is going to be a much easier task." Remarks to Members of the White House Conference on National Economic Issues (May 21, 1962).

NATIONAL SECURITY

General

1448. "[P]eace, not war, is the objective of our military policy." Remarks of Senator John F. Kennedy, Luncheon Meeting, Mauston, Wisconsin (March 9, 1960).

1449. "[I]t is an unfortunate fact that we can secure peace only by preparing for war. Winston Churchill said in 1949, 'We arm to parley.' ... I can imagine no more hazardous course than for the United States to gamble on its defenses, to take a chance that the Russians and the Chinese Communists will follow a peaceful role if we disarm ... or if we fail to maintain our strength. If we are strong, then peace will be our reward.... That requires only one kind of defense policy, a policy summed up in a single word 'first.' I do not mean 'first, if,' I do not mean 'first, but,' I do not mean 'first, when,' but I mean 'First, period.'" Speech by Senator John F. Kennedy, Civic Auditorium, Seattle, Washington (September 6, 1960).

1450. "[I]f we desire to live at peace, with the Russians and the Chinese, the United States must be strong; not 'Strong, if,' not 'Strong, when,' not 'Strong enough, but,' but 'Strong first,' first in the fight for survival, first in building our defenses." Rear Platform Remarks of Senator John F. Kennedy, "Pathways to Peace," Fresno, California (September 9, 1960).

1451. "I think the United States should be second to none [in the area of national defense] ... both because it provides for our own security and the security of those who look to us for protection, but also it represents the road to peace. If the United States is strong, then the Soviet Union or the Chinese Communists will not feel that the balance of power is moving in their direction but instead will make a determination that while other kinds of competition will go on, they will not be tempted to take a shortcut road to world domination." Remarks of Senator John F. Kennedy, U.S. Grant Hotel, San Diego, California (September 11, 1960).

1452. "[I] believe a strong America is a militarily secure America secure enough to convince any present or future enemy that an act aggression would be a mistake — his mistake — and to obtain that kind of strength requires two things: an invulnerable atomic striking force strong enough to persuade any aggressor that our force could survive in sufficient numbers and capable of penetrating his defense and retaliating on his country [and] a modern conventional force of sufficient strength, firepower, and mobility to intervene quickly and effectively before any brush fire war causes a holocaust." Remarks of Senator John F. Kennedy, Memorial Auditorium Dallas, Texas (September 13, 1960).

1453. "I think the most important issue is the security of the United States and the peace of the world. But I don't think we are going to be secure, and I don't think we are going to maintain our freedom unless we are building in this country a strong society on all fronts." Remarks of Senator John F. Kennedy, Treadway Inn, Niagara Falls, New York (September 28, 1960).

1454. "[I] will take whatever steps are necessary to defend our security and to maintain the cause of world freedom — but I will not risk American lives and a nuclear war by permitting any other nation to drag us into the wrong war at the wrong place at the wrong time through an unwise commitment that is unsound militarily, unnecessary to our security, and unsupported by our allies." Remarks of Senator John F. Kennedy, Democratic National and State Committees Dinner, Waldorf-Astoria Hotel, New York, New York (October 12, 1960).

1455. "We have only ourselves to depend on for our security. We have to build in this country a strong enough society so that we can protect our own people...." Remarks of Senator John F. Kennedy, Grand Rapids, Michigan (October 14, 1960).

1456. "Only if we are strong as a nation — strong economically, strong militarily, strong educationally, strong in heart and purpose — can we assure our peace and security in an age where our enemies are overtaking us in missile power ... have outshone our efforts in science and space, and have rolled the Iron Curtain to 90 miles from our shores onto the once friendly island of Cuba." Remarks of Senator John F. Kennedy, Johnstown, Pennsylvania (October 15, 1960).

1457. "On the Presidential Coat of Arms, the American eagle holds in his right talon the olive branch, while in his left he holds a bundle of arrows. We intend to give equal attention to both." Annual Message to the Congress on the State of the Union (January 30, 1961).

1458. "We live in a hazardous and dangerous time. I do not think it's possible to overstate it." Address in Chicago at a Dinner of the Democratic Party of Cook County [Illinois] (April 28, 1961).

1459. "[T]he story of Nehemias [from the Bible] ... tells us that when the children of Israel returned from captivity they determined to rebuild the wails of Jerusalem.... The wall was built and the peace was preserved. But it was written, 'Of them that built on the wall ... with one of his hands he did the work, and with the other he held the sword.' We hold the sword, and we are determined to maintain our strength and our commitments. But we also hold in our hand the trowel. We are determined to build in our own country, so that those who come after us ... will find available to them all of the great resources that we now have." Remarks at Big Cedar, Oklahoma, on the Opening of the Ouachita National Forest Road (October 29, 1961).

1460. "There is no way to maintain the frontiers of freedom without cost and commitment and risk. There is no swift and easy path to peace in our generation. No man who witnessed the tragedies of the last war, no man who can imagine the unimaginable possibilities of the next war, can advocate war out of irritability or frustration or impatience. But let no nation confuse our perseverance and patience with fear of war or unwillingness to meet our responsibilities." Remarks at the Veterans Day Ceremony at Arlington National Cemetery (November 11, 1961).

1461. "In the end, the only way to maintain the peace is to be prepared in the final extreme to fight for our country — and to mean it." Remarks at the Veterans Day Ceremony at Arlington National Cemetery (November 11, 1961).

1462. "As a nation, we have little capacity for deception. We can convince friend and foe alike that we are in earnest about the defense of freedom only if we are in earnest — and I can assure the world that we are." Remarks at the Veterans Day Ceremony at Arlington National Cemetery (November 11, 1961).

1463. "[W]hile we believe not only in the force of arms but in the force of right and reason, we have learned that reason does not always appeal to unreasonable men — that it is not always true that 'a soft answer turneth away wrath' — and that right does not always make might." Address in Seattle at the at the University of Washington's 100th Anniversary Program (November 16, 1961).

1464. "We increase our arms at a heavy cost, primarily to make certain that we will not have to use them. We must face up to the chance of war, if we are to maintain the peace." Address in Seattle at the University of Washington's 100th Anniversary Program (November 16, 1961).

1465. "There are two groups of these frustrated citizens, far apart in their views yet very much alike in their approach.... Each believes that we have only two choices: appeasement or war, suicide or surrender, humiliation or holocaust, to be either Red or dead.... The essential fact that both of these groups fail to grasp is that diplomacy and defense are not substitutes for one another. Either alone would fail. A willingness to resist force, unaccompanied by a willingness to talk, could provoke belligerence — while a willingness to talk, unaccompanied by a willingness to resist force, could invite disaster." Address in Seattle at the University of Washington's 100th Anniversary Program (November 16, 1961).

1466. "[T]he kind of aggression which we were threatened with 20 years ago ... is different from the kind of aggression and subversion which threatens ... today. We meet new techniques — though the general threat in a sense is unchanged. These new techniques require the most sophisticated, informed judgments; it requires a knowledge far beyond the usual technical subjects which occupy so much of our military studies, requires a knowledge of political, social, and economic conditions, requires a knowledge of the past as well as the future — so that this is a great challenge for us all." Remarks on the 20th Anniversary of the Inter-American Defense Board (March 29, 1962).

1467. "We are an open society, and all that we have is, in a sense, available to the world. We are in a struggle, though we do not wish it we accept it, with a closed system. Therefore, the ability to detect those developments which directly threaten our security [through aerial photographic reconnaissance] ... — this ability is essential to our survival, to the maintenance of our security and vital interests, and, in a very real sense, to the maintenance of peace." Remarks at Homestead Air Force Base, Florida, Upon Presenting Unit Awards (November 26, 1962).

1468. "[I]n an imperfect world where human folly has been the rule and not the exception, the surest way to bring on the war that can never happen is to sit back and assure ourselves it will not happen." Remarks at Colorado Springs to the Graduating Class of the U.S. Air Force Academy (June 5, 1963).

1469. "We maintain the peace by preparing for adversity...." Remarks to Allied and American Troops at Fliegerhorst Barracks Near Hanau [Germany] (June 25, 1963).

1470. "[I]t is very difficult for us to judge the present and the future, and there is a tendency in economics, and politics, and social sciences, as well as military life, to look to the past. I am sure we are all in a very good position to fight a war of the past today, but our wars, if they ever come, will be far more different, and therefore it requires, it seems to me, the broadest possible knowledge...." Remarks to Faculty and Students of the NATO Defense College (July 16, 1963).

1471. "The[re] are ... basic differences between the Soviet Union and the United States, and they cannot be concealed. So long as they exist, they set limits to agreement, and they forbid the relaxation of our vigilance. Our defense around the world will be maintained for the protection of freedom — and our determination to safeguard that freedom will measure up to any threat or challenge." Address Before the 18th General Assembly of the United Nations (September 20, 1963).

Armed Forces

1472. "It was West Virginians who led the American forces to France in World War I ... [and who] fought and bled on the far-flung battlefields of World War II ... [a]nd again ... in Korea, where a higher proportion of West Virginians shed their blood in the fight against Communism than those from any other state. [W]hen there were battles to be fought, when men were needed, when bravery and patriotism and strength were in demand, the nation turned to West Virginia." Remarks of Senator John F. Kennedy, Wheeling, West Virginia (April 19, 1960).

1473. "[We] ... know that what really counts is not the immediate act of courage or of valor, but those who bear the struggle day in and day out — not the sunshine patriots but those who are willing to stand for a long period of time. That is what constitutes, in my opinion, the real courage...." Remarks at the White House to Members of the American Legion (March 1, 1962).

1474. "I don't suppose there is any task in this country of ours that must be filled with more fairness and with a greater degree of confidence by the American people than the [the Selective Service System]." Remarks to State Directors of the Selective Service System (May 23, 1962).

1475. "No matter how complicated war has now become, we need a Navy which can take ships close in to shore; we need an Air force that can protect those ships; we need small boats that can take men on a beach; and we need men who will go ashore. The Marine Corps, the Navy, the Army, and the Air force do that." Remarks at the Evening Parade following an Inspection of the Marine Barracks (July 12, 1962).

1476. "[T]here are over a million Americans who are serving outside of their country, and ... since the beginning of recorded history there have been great periods where soldiers ... have served outside of their country..., but I know of no period in the history of the world or any nation that has done so in the defense of freedom and not made its object subjugation." Remarks in Key West Upon Presenting Unit Citations at the Boca Chica Naval Air Station (November 26, 1962).

1477. "Regardless of how persistent our diplomacy may be ... in the final analysis it rests upon the power of the United States, and that power rests upon the will and courage of our citizens and [our military].... The United States is the guarantor of the independence of dozens of countries stretching around the world. And the reason that we are able to guarantee the freedom of those countries ... is because of [America's servicemen] and [their] comrades in arms on a dozen different forts and posts, on ships at sea, planes in the air, all of you." Remarks at Fort Stewart, Georgia, to Members of the First Armored Division (November 26, 1962).

1478. "There are thousands of Americans who lie buried all around the globe who have been fighting for the independence of other countries and, in a larger sense, for the independence of their own...." Remarks at a Reception Honoring Medal of Honor Recipients (May 2, 1963).

1479. "[T]he responsibilities ... which we place upon our military today are really unprecedented.... Today it is not enough to know about the most advanced forms of weapons, the new weapons which have changed the whole theory of war, but we also have to be experts on the older traditional wars, guerrilla, paramilitary, subversive, and all the rest." Remarks to a Group of Foreign Military Officers (May 13, 1963).

1480. "The United States though a young country has an honorable and distinguished martial tradition stretching back to the Revolutionary War.... It has meant that every generation of Americans in our country's history has had to bear arms in defense of this country." Remarks in San Diego at the Marine Corps Recruit Depot (June 6, 1963).

1481. "[T]here are Americans on duty who help maintain the freedom of dozens of countries who might now be engulfed if it were not for this long, thin line which occupies such a position of responsibility, guarding so many gates where the enemy campfires in some cases can be seen from the top of the wall." Remarks to Allied and American Troops at Fliegerhorst Barracks Near Hanau [Germany] (June 25, 1963).

1482. "I sometimes think that the people of this country do not appreciate how secure we are because of the devotion of the men and their wives and children who serve this country in far off places, in the sea, in the air, and on the ground, thousands and thousands of miles away from this country, who make it possible for us all to live in peace each day [,but] [t]his country owes the greatest debt to our servicemen." Remarks at the U.S. Naval Academy (August 1, 1963).

1483. "[T]he fact that this country is secure and at peace, the fact that dozens of countries allied with us are free and at peace, has been due to the military strength of the United States. And that strength has been directly due to the men who serve in our Armed Forces." Remarks at the U.S. Naval Academy (August 1, 1963).

1484. "No country in the long history of the world has ever had such a proportion of its population serving outside of its native land without regard to conquest, without regard to material return, but in order to assist to maintain the freedom of countries stretching 10,000 miles away." Address in Duluth to Delegates to the Northern Great Lakes Region Land and People Conference (September 24, 1963).

1485. "Every citizen of this country owes them [members of the military] a greater debt than they realize, that they are able in a very prosperous and peaceful country to live as secure as they do because of the dedicated service of so many hundreds and thousands of our fellow citizens who serve in this country and all around the globe." Remarks Upon Signing the Uniformed Services Pay Raise Bill (October 2, 1963).

1486. "[W]hile we are all necessarily and properly respectful and impressed with the constantly more powerful weapons which are being developed, I think it is important that we realize that it is the men who must manage them, control them, and have the will to direct them." Remarks Upon Signing the Uniformed Services Pay Raise Bill (October 2, 1963).

1487. "The United States has one million of its citizens serving outside of its borders, a record unprecedented in history, not for the purposes of aggression and conquest, but for the purposes of liberation." Remarks Upon Leaving Westover Air Force Base, Massachusetts (October 26, 1963).

Military Strength

1488. "[W]e shall need [if we are to keep up with the Soviets] more missiles, more ships, planes and men, more atomic submarines and airlift mobility. [W]e are rapidly approaching the point where we will be unable to act as equals at the bargaining table — where we will be unable to seek arms control from a position of strength — where we will be unable to back up our position in Berlin, Formosa or the Middle East." Remarks of Senator John F. Kennedy, Jefferson-Jackson Day Dinner, Hartford, Connecticut (February 20, 1960).

1489. "We prepare for war — in order to deter war. We depend on the strength of armaments — to enable us to bargain for disarmament. We compare our military strength with the Soviets — not to determine whether we should use it — but to determine whether we can persuade them that to use theirs would be futile and disastrous — and to determine whether we can back up our own pledges in Berlin, Formosa and around the world." Remarks of Senator John F. Kennedy, Luncheon Meeting, Mauston, Wisconsin (March 9, 1960).

1490. "[T]hose of us who call for a higher defense budget are taking a chance on spending money unnecessarily. But those who oppose these expenditures are taking a chance on our very survival as a nation. The only real question is —

which chance, which gamble, do we take — our money or our survival?" Remarks of Senator John F. Kennedy, Luncheon Meeting, Mauston, Wisconsin (March 9, 1960).

1491. "We cannot avoid taking these measures [building up and modernizing America's military] any more than the average American can avoid taking out fire insurance on his home. We cannot be absolutely certain of the danger. But ... as individuals we are willing to pay for fire insurance — and, although we hope we never need it, we are surely equally prepared as a nation to pay every dollar necessary to take out this kind of additional insurance against a national catastrophe. I am calling, in short, for an investment in peace. Like any investment it will be a gamble with our money. But the alternative is to gamble with our lives." Remarks of Senator John F. Kennedy, Luncheon Meeting, Mauston, Wisconsin (March 9, 1960).

1492. "[W]hen we are in doubt, our allies are in doubt — and our enemy is in doubt — and such doubts are tempting to him. While those doubts persist, he will want to push, to probe and possibly to attack. He will not want to talk disarmament. He will not want to talk peace at the Summit." Remarks of Senator John F. Kennedy, Luncheon Meeting, Mauston, Wisconsin (March 9, 1960).

1493. "[I]t is an unfortunate fact that while peace is our goal, we need greater military security to prevent war ... to [be able to] bargain ... from a position of strength." Remarks of Senator John F. Kennedy, Washington College, Chestertown, Maryland (May 11, 1960).

1494. "[L]et us never ... [be] under the illusion that platitudes are a substitute for strength — or that personal goodwill can overcome irreconcilable conflicts of interest." Remarks of Senator John F. Kennedy, New Mexico State Democratic Convention, New Mexico (June 4, 1960).

1495. "[B]igger and better weapons, and faster and more effective armies are not enough. The needs of modern defense cut across the ancient and traditional service lines.... It is essential, therefore, that we ... reevaluat[e] ... our national defense organization, that we eliminate the wasteful duplication, the service rivalry, the competitive overlapping, that has consumed our money and prevented us from developing maximum strength; that we move forward toward a defense technology to meet the modern demands of the fight for peace." Speech by Senator John F. Kennedy, Civic Auditorium, Seattle, Washington (September 6, 1960).

1496. "The United States will never attack first. We always have to judge our defenses by what they would look like after the Soviet Union had made the initial attack. Would we have the capacity then to defend ourselves, to retaliate? If we have that capacity, then we have taken not a step toward war, but a step toward peace, and that is our objective." Remarks of Senator John F. Kennedy, U.S. Grant Hotel, San Diego, California (September 11, 1960).

1497. "America [requires] a military strength second to none — strength sufficient to convince any enemy that an attack would bring disaster. To do this we need two things: an invulnerable atomic striking force which can survive an enemy attack and still remain in possession of its ability to retaliate, and a modern conventional force of sufficient strength ... and mobility to intervene quickly and effectively to halt Communist aggression in any quarter of the globe. Only when we attain both of these objectives — and our enemies know and respect our strength — can we hope to talk successfully with Mr. Khrushchev about peace." Speech by Senator John F. Kennedy, Coliseum, Raleigh, North Carolina (September 17, 1960).

1498. "We must reverse the drift and complacency which has ... permitted our prestige and our strength to decline abroad.... We must reverse the policies which have confined Mr. Khrushchev to Manhattan — but which have not kept him from moving in Africa and Asia and Latin America. And we cannot do this by trading insults with Mr. Khrushchev or ... by talking tough.... We have talked tough about the need for disarmament — but the arms race is more intense than ever. We have a magnificent record of talking tough — but we do not have a magnificent record of halting the advance of communism and strengthening the spread of freedom. That will be done through the strength which alone can answer Mr. Khrushchev's threats and ambitions." Speech by Senator John F. Kennedy, Coliseum, Raleigh, North Carolina (September 17, 1960).

1499. "We pride ourselves on being the strongest power, and yet ... unless we are prepared to rebuild our strength, the United States will be in a position, I think of danger from an attack which could catch us in a position where we would be secure but not secure enough, where we would be strong but not strong enough." Speech by Senator John F. Kennedy, Memorial Auditorium, Buffalo, New York (September 28, 1960).

1500. "[A]ll those who agree that we never want to have a trial of strength agree that it is incumbent upon us to rebuild the strength of the United States." Speech by Senator John F. Kennedy, Chase Hotel, St. Louis, Missouri (October 2, 1960).

1501. "[T]he present rate of growth of the Soviet Union in military strength, particularly in long-range missiles, is greater than ours, and while I believe that today the United States is secure, I believe there is a danger in 1962, 1963 and 1964, that unless we move ahead at a greater rate, we won't meet it." Remarks of Senator John F. Kennedy, Kitanning, Pennsylvania (October 15, 1960).

1502. "[The] dangerous deterioration in our military strength has been the result of our willingness to cut our budget, to bear a much lower burden which is not large enough if we are going to maintain our freedom, and words are not a substitute for strength. These are the facts behind our speaking louder and louder while we carry a smaller and smaller stick." Speech by Senator John F. Kennedy, American Legion Convention, Miami Beach, Florida (October 18, 1960).

1503. "The implacable Communist drive for power takes many forms and works in many ways, but behind it all, behind every weapon that they have in their arsenal is one basic fact, and that is the military power of the Communist bloc, for it is here that the Communist advance and relative American decline can be most sharply seen, and it is here that the danger to our survival is the greatest." Speech by Senator John F. Kennedy, American Legion Convention, Miami Beach, Florida (October 18, 1960).

1504. "Talk is cheap, words are not enough, waving our finger under Khrushchev's face does not increase the strength of the United States, especially when you say to him ... as you wave your finger, 'You may be ahead of us in rockets, but we are ahead of you in color television.' I will take my television black and white." Speech by Senator John F. Kennedy, American Legion Convention, Miami Beach, Florida (October 18, 1960).

1505. "I have never believed in retreating under any kind of fire. And although I do not want to get into any comparison of military experience [with Vice President Nixon], I believe it clear that anyone who says the reverse is guilty of a malicious distortion. And I want Mr. Khrushchev and anyone else to understand that if the Democratic Party wins this [1960 Presidential] election, he will confront ... an America which is not only militarily strong, but which is waging the offensive for freedom all over the globe." Speech by Senator John F. Kennedy, American Legion Convention, Miami Beach, Florida (October 18, 1960).

1506. "[W]e [must] maintain our strength.... We cannot parley on the basis of equality with the Soviet unless we maintain a military position of equality with them, and that goes in the traditional weapons and in missiles and in outer space. One of the reasons why we have never been able to get an agreement on the disarmament of outer space is because we are second in outer space, and the Soviet Union will not give way their advantage. We arm to parley, and we must be strong if we are going to disarm and maintain our security." Remarks of Senator John F. Kennedy, Milwaukee, Wisconsin (October 23, 1960).

1507. "We dare not tempt them [America's adversaries] with weakness. For only when our arms are sufficient beyond doubt can we be certain beyond doubt that they will never be employed." Inaugural Address (January 20, 1961).

1508. "[B]oth the military and diplomatic possibilities require a Free World force so powerful as to make any aggression clearly futile." Annual Message to the Congress on the State of the Union (January 30, 1961).

1509. "We propose to see to it ... that our military forces operate at all times under continuous, responsible command and control from the highest authorities all the way downward—and we mean to see that this control is exercised before, during, and after any initiation of hostilities against our forces, and at any level of escalation. We believe in maintaining effective deterrent strength, but we also believe in making it do what we wish, neither more nor less." Remarks at the Opening Session of the Meeting of the Military Committee of NATO (April 10, 1961).

1510. "The United States no longer has a nuclear monopoly. The Soviet Union's possession of atomic and hydrogen weapons has increased its willingness to test and probe and push the West.... We must ... be constantly strengthening all of our forces of all kinds, at all levels, deterring war, and keeping the peace by making certain that those who would oppose us know that we are determined to resist aggression, whatever its force, and whatever kind of force is needed to resist it." Remarks and Question and Answer Period at the Press Luncheon in Paris (June 2, 1961).

1511. "[F]ew of the important problems of our time have, in the final analysis, been finally solved by military power alone." Remarks at Annapolis to the Graduating Class of the United States Naval Academy (June 7, 1961).

1512. "We believe in a strong country. We believe in a country which is militarily prepared." Remarks at the Airport at Fort Smith, Arkansas (October 29, 1961).

1513. "So long as fanaticism and fear brood over the affairs of men, we must arm to deter others from aggression." Annual Message to the Congress on the State of the Union (January 11, 1962).

1514. "Our foremost aim is the control of force, not the pursuit of force, in a world made safe for mankind. But whatever the future brings, I am sworn to uphold and defend the freedom of the American people — and I intend to do whatever must be done to fulfill that solemn obligation." Radio and Television Address to the American People: "Nuclear Testing and Disarmament" (March 2, 1962).

1515. "[I have] as an American a source of satisfaction to realize that we are the inheritors of [a] great martial tradition...." Remarks to a Group of Descendants of Civil War Medal of Honor Winners (April 28, 1962).

1516. "To meet the dangers of the world in which we live we are required to maintain a strong and versatile military force, one that can cover the broad spectrum of military operations. Because of this we are placing great emphasis ... on developing our special forces, which are well suited to assist those governments in maintaining their position against the threats of guerrillas and insurgents." Address by Telephone to the Convention of the American Veterans of World War II (August 23, 1962).

1517. "[We need] this [military] strength not to fight wars if we can help it, but to wage the peace...." Remarks at the Indianapolis Airport (October 13, 1962).

1518. "[T]here is no substitute for adequate defense, and no 'bargain basement' way of achieving it." Annual Message to the Congress on the State of the Union (January 14, 1963).

NATO (NORTH ATLANTIC TREATY ORGANIZATION)

1519. "NATO is remarkable among the alliances of history in its combination of political, military, economic, and even psychological components. What NATO is, at any time, depends not only upon its forces in being, but upon the resolution of its leaders, the state of mind of its people, and the view of all these elements which is held by those who do not always wish us well."

Remarks at the Opening Session of the Meeting of the Military Committee of NATO (April 10, 1961).

1520. "Our NATO alliance is still, as it was when it was founded, the world's greatest bulwark of freedom. But the military balance of power has been changing. Enemy tactics and weaponry have been changing. We can stand still only at our peril." Address Before the Canadian Parliament in Ottawa (May 17, 1961).

1521. "We are here with you [America's NATO allies], and as long as you are determined that our association with you is useful in the common cause, we shall remain, and we shall meet our commitments to the full, and we shall maintain our strength, and we shall continue to insist that here in this most ancient section of the civilized world springs the force, the vigor, the strength, and the commitment which can provide freedom, not only for this section of Europe, but also radiate around the globe." Remarks at SHAPE Headquarters in Paris (June 2, 1961).

1522. "[NATO is] an alliance of proud and sovereign nations, and works best when we do not forget it." Annual Message to the Congress on the State of the Union (January 14, 1962).

1523. "Our unity was forged in a time of danger; it must be maintained in a time of peace. Our Alliance was founded to deter a new war; it must now find the way to a new peace." Remarks Upon Arrival in Germany (June 23, 1963).

1524. "[T]he shores of history are dotted, with the shipwrecks of other alliances. If our [NATO] alliance is able to stand the lack of immediate outside pressure, we will be the exception. And, it seems to me, therefore, incumbent upon us ... to jointly consider ... how we can make this alliance work." Toasts of the President and Chancellor Adenauer at a Dinner at the Palais Schaumburg in Bonn [Germany] (June 23, 1963).

1525. "It is not always easy in times of calm to maintain the solidarity of an alliance. I believe that over a long period of years the members of NATO have set almost a unique example. It has been, really, an almost unprecedented act of history...." Remarks to Allied and American Troops at Fliegerhorst Barracks Near Hanau [Germany] (June 25, 1963).

1526. "The first task of the Atlantic Community was to assure its common defense. That defense was and still is indivisible. The United States will risk its cities to defend yours because we need your freedom to protect ours.... The purpose of our common military effort is not war but peace — not the destruction of nations but the protection of freedom." Address in the Assembly Hall at the Paulskirche in Frankfurt [Germany] (June 25, 1963).

1527. "NATO is one of the best and earliest examples of cooperation between Western Europe and the North American nations for the common good of freedom.... The NATO treaty pledges us all to the common defense — to regard an attack on one as an attack on all, and respond with all the force required — and that pledge is as strong and unshakable now as it was the day it was made." Remarks in Naples [Italy] at NATO Headquarters (July 2, 1963).

1528. "Alliances are very difficult organizations to maintain. Through history, in peacetime, they have disintegrated, sooner or later.... We have maintained this [NATO] alliance over a long period of time. It is my strong conviction that it should be maintained ... not only because of any military threats to Western Europe or the United States, but because we are involved in a struggle with an armed doctrine around the world. The closest concert among the Western powers on both sides of the Atlantic, it seems to me, is essential.... [I]f we can harness all that energy, all that power, all that knowledge, and all that vitality to the cause of freedom together, in the fight around the globe, I think we will certainly deserve well of our country and of history." Remarks to Faculty and Students of the NATO Defense College (July 16, 1963).

NEW FRONTIER

1529. "[I] stand tonight facing west on what was once the last frontier. From the lands that stretch three thousand miles behind me, the pioneers of old gave up their safety, their comfort and sometimes their lives to build a new world here in the West. They were not the captives of their own doubts, the prisoners of their own price tags. Their motto was not 'every man for himself' — but 'all for the common cause.' They were determined to make that new world strong and free, to overcome its hazards and its hardships, to conquer the enemies that threatened from without and within. Today some would say that those struggles are all over — that all the horizons have been explored — that all the battles have been won — that there is no longer an American frontier. But ... the problems are not all solved and the battles are not all won — and we stand today on the edge of a New Frontier — the frontier of the 1960s — a frontier of unknown opportunities and perils — a frontier of unfulfilled hopes and threats." Address of Senator John F. Kennedy Accepting the Democratic Party Nomination for the Presidency of the United States, Memorial Coliseum, Los Angeles [California] (July 15, 1960).

1530. "Woodrow Wilson's New Freedom promised our nation a new political and economic framework. Franklin Roosevelt's New Deal promised security and succor to those in need. But the New Frontier of which I speak is not a set of promises — it is a set of challenges. It sums up not what I intend to offer the American people, but what I intend to ask of them. It appeals to their pride, not to their pocketbook — it holds out the promise of more sacrifice instead of more security." Address of Senator John F. Kennedy Accepting the Democratic Party Nomination for the Presidency of the United States — Memorial Coliseum, Los Angeles [California] (July 15, 1960).

1531. "We have no time for complacency, timidity, or doubt. This is a time for courage and action. This is a time for strong leaders — leaders who are not afraid of New Frontiers — leaders who are not afraid of the facts — leaders who can turn our dreams into reality." Speech by Senator John F. Kennedy, Cadillac Square, Detroit, Michigan (September 5, 1960).

1532. "[T]he object of this [1960] campaign [is] to serve the American people and suggest a whole course of action in the various areas of the national effort so that we in this country can be secure and so the cause of freedom can be strengthened. I have called the challenge of the future the new frontier. I do not run for the Presidency emphasizing the services that I am going to bring to you. I run emphasizing the services which the American people must offer their country. My call is not to those who believe they belong to the past. My call is to those who believe in the future." Speech by John F. Kennedy, Civic Auditorium, Seattle, Washington (September 6, 1960).

1533. "When I talk about the new frontier, I don't mean just a physical reality, I mean all of those who believe that they want to serve our Government and serve our system, who want to join with us not because of what we are going to do for them, but for the opportunity that they will have to serve our country." Remarks of John F. Kennedy, Lincoln Monument Rally, Spokane, Washington (September 6, 1960).

1534. "I call for the new frontier and when I do so I don't say what I am going to promise to do for you, if I am elected. I promise that I will give you an opportunity to serve your country, to demonstrate that our cause and the cause of freedom all over the world are intertwined together." Remarks of John F. Kennedy, State Fairgrounds, Salem, Oregon (September 7, 1960).

1535. "I come in 1960 talking about the new frontier. The new frontier is not the things that I am promising to do for you if I am elected President. The new frontier consists of the things that we are asking all of us to do for this country in the 1960s. This is a great country, but it deserves the best that we have." Remarks of John F. Kennedy, Airport Rally, Bakersfield, California (September 9, 1960).

1536. "[The] journey to the new frontier recognize[es] that what we do here will finally determine the fate of freedom around the world." Speech by John F. Kennedy, Shrine Auditorium, Los Angeles, California (September 9, 1960).

1537. "The new frontier of which I speak does not consist of the things which we promise we will do for you. It consists of the things which you can do for your country, the opportunity for service, the opportunity to help this country realize its great potential, here and around the world." Remarks of John F. Kennedy, the Alamo, San Antonio, Texas (September 12, 1960).

1538. "I call upon all of you to join us in a journey to the new frontier. The voyage is a long and hazardous one, but we are all partners in a great and historic journey ... [and] in many ways ... the brightest days of this country can be ahead." Speech by Senator John F. Kennedy, IAM [International Association of Machinists] Convention, Kiel Auditorium, St. Louis, Missouri (September 14, 1960).

1539. "Woodrow Wilson stood for the New Freedom, Franklin Roosevelt for the New Deal, Harry Truman for the Fair Deal, Adlai Stevenson for the New America, and now I run on a platform which I call the New Frontier." Remarks of Senator John F. Kennedy, at York County Fair, York, Pennsylvania (September 16, 1960).

1540. "[T]he New Frontier ... represents — not the comforts we seek — but the tasks we must all perform, if we are to live up to our trust and our heritage." Speech by John F. Kennedy, Mormon Tabernacle, Salt Lake City, Utah (September 23, 1960).

1541. "The New Frontier represents all of the responsibilities which the American people must meet in the 1960s, and it represents all of the opportunities that are before us as a country and as a people.... That is the responsibility not of the next President, and not of the next Congress, and not of the House and the Senate — it is a responsibility in which all of us participate, in which all of us share." Remarks of Senator John F. Kennedy, at Lorain Stadium, Lorain, Ohio (September 27, 1960).

1542. "Our generation of Americans has a rendezvous with destiny just as much as the generation of 1933 whom Franklin Roosevelt addressed in his inaugural speech. The contribution of that generation was the maintenance of freedom here in the United States and the maintenance of the private enterprise system. I think the contribution of the next generation of Americans in the sixties and the seventies can be the maintenance of freedom here in the United States and also the maintenance of freedom around the world." Remarks of John F. Kennedy, War Memorial Building, Rochester, New York (September 28, 1960).

1543. "I am asking this generation of Americans ... to do in its time what those generations before us did, to maintain freedom and serve as an example and a bright light to the world around us. That is our opportunity, and I think that is our destiny." Remarks of Senator John F. Kennedy, State Capitol, Albany, New York (September 29, 1960).

1544. "I raise no call of alarm, of despair, of distress. I raise the call to rally to this country's behalf, and also to the cause of freedom, to serve it, to work for it, to move it, and in so doing that we serve and move and work for the cause of freedom." Remarks of Senator John F. Kennedy, Hibbing, Minnesota (October 2, 1960).

1545. "I cannot believe that the American people are going to say in 1960 that we have never had it so good, and we want more of the same. I think they are going to want to cross the new frontier." Speech by Senator John F. Kennedy, Chase Hotel, St. Louis, Missouri (October 2, 1960).

1546. "What are the new frontiers of the 1960s? ... First is the new frontier of population ... the largest 10-year growth in population [in the 1960s] in the history of the United States.... Second is the new frontier of longevity. [E]very year the percentage of our population that is over 65 is increasing.... The third opportunity is on the new frontier of education. Pouring into our schools in the next 10 years will be 51 million children who were born in this country between 1946 and 1956, a number greater than the entire population of the United States in 1880.... Fourth is the new frontier of suburbia, the fastest growing portion of the United States.... Fifth are the new frontiers of science and in space.... Sixth is the problem ... of automation.... Seventh, and finally, is the problem of what we are all going to do with our leisure time." Speech by Senator John F. Kennedy, Valley Forge Country Club, Valley Forge, Pennsylvania (October 29, 1960).

1547. "The new frontiers of which I speak call out for pioneers from every walk of life, from the White House in Washington and in the country at large. Their challenge can be concealed for a little while, but it cannot be ignored, it cannot be met by an easy complacency, a satisfaction with things as they are, a commitment of things done and not to be done, for as the Old Testament tells us, 'This challenge is not too hard for thee, neither is it far off. Who shall go over the sea for us and bring it on to us that we may do it, for the world is very near onto thee in thy mind and in thy heart.' The new frontier of which I speak is very near to you and to me. It is upon us. The only question is if the United States is ready for it." Speech by Senator John F. Kennedy, Valley Forge Country Club, Valley Forge, Pennsylvania (October 29, 1960).

1548. "We are the beneficiaries of the New Deal. I want to be sure in the 1970s that there are the people of this country who are the beneficiaries of what we did on the New Frontiers of 1962." Remarks at City Hall, McKeesport, Pennsylvania (October 13, 1962).

1549. "[T]he New Frontier ... is not a partisan term, and it is not the exclusive property of Republicans or Democrats. It refers, instead, to this Nation's place in history, to the fact that we do stand on the edge of a great new era, filled with both crisis and opportunity, an era to be characterized by achievement and by challenge. It is an era which calls for action and for the best efforts of all those who would test the unknown and the uncertain in every phase of human endeavor. It is a time for pathfinders and pioneers." Remarks in San Antonio at the Dedication of the Aerospace Medical Health Center (November 21, 1963).

NEWS MEDIA

1550. "The entire democratic system which depends for its success upon majority rule, and therefore for majority understanding, depends in a very real sense on information and communication — for our judgment is no better than our information." Remarks Recorded for a Television Program Marking Twenty-five Years of Publication of Life Magazine (March 2, 1961).

1551. "The very word 'secrecy' is repugnant in a free and open society; and we are as a people inherently and historically opposed to secret societies, to secret oaths and to secret proceedings. [T]he dangers of excessive and unwarranted concealment of pertinent facts far outweighed the dangers which are cited to justify it." Address "The President and the Press" Before the American Newspaper Publishers Association, New York City (April 27, 1961).

1552. "[T]here is little value in opposing the threat of a closed society by imitating its arbitrary restrictions ... there is little value in [e]nsuring the survival of our nation if our traditions do not survive with it. And there is very grave danger that an announced need for increased security will be seized upon by those anxious to expand its meaning to the very limits of official censorship and concealment." Address "The President and the Press" Before the American Newspaper Publishers Association, New York City (April 27, 1961).

1553. "Every newspaper now asks itself, with respect to every story: 'Is it news?' All I suggest is that you add the question: 'Is it in the interest of the national security?'" Address "The President and the Press" Before the American Newspaper Publishers Association, New York City (April 27, 1961).

1554. "[I]t is to the printing press — to the recorder of man's deeds, the keeper of his conscience, the courier of his news — that we look for strength and assistance, confident that with your help man will be what he was born to be: free and independent." Address "The President and the Press" Before the American Newspaper Publishers Association, New York City (April 27, 1961).

1555. "No President should fear public scrutiny of his program. For from that scrutiny comes understanding; and from that understanding comes support or opposition. And both are necessary." Address "The President and the Press" Before the American Newspaper Publishers Association, New York City (April 27, 1961).

1556. "The essence of free communication must be that our failures as well as our successes will be broadcast around the world." Address at the 39th Annual Convention of the National Association of Broadcasters (May 8, 1961).

1557. "[T]his is a free society, and ... we therefore take our chances out in the open, of success or failure...." Address at the 39th Annual Convention of the National Association of Broadcasters (May 8, 1961).

1558. "I feel, as a believer in freedom, ... that we want a world in which the good and the bad, successes or failures, the aspirations of people, their desires, their disagreements, their dissent, their agreements, whether they serve the interest of the state or not, should be made public, should be part of the general understanding of all people." Address at the 39th Annual Convention of the National Association of Broadcasters (May 8, 1961).

1559. "We are an open and free society. All of our strengths and all of our weaknesses are on display. They are a matter of discussion. Those of us who hold high office and high responsibilities are subject to all of the scrutiny — the careful scrutiny — which comes from a free press and a free people, operating within an open society. That is the way this country was planned...." Remarks on the White House Lawn at a Reception for Foreign Students (May 10, 1961).

1560. "We seek a free flow of information across national boundaries and oceans, across iron curtains and stone walls. We are not afraid to entrust the American people with unpleasant facts, foreign ideas, alien philosophies, and competitive values. For a nation that is afraid to let its people judge the truth and falsehood in an open market is a nation that is afraid of its people." Remarks on the 20th Anniversary of the Voice of America (February 26, 1962).

1561. "I sometimes think that we are too much impressed by the clamor of daily events. The newspaper headlines and the television screens give us a short view. They so flood us with the stop-press details of daily stories that we lose sight of ... the great movements of history. Yet it is the profound tendencies of history and not the passing excitements, that will shape our future." Address in Berkeley at the University of California (March 23, 1962).

1562. "[Editorial cartoonists] instruct us and [their] ... ability to place in one picture a story and a message and do it with impact and conviction and humor and passion, all that, I think, makes [them] really the most exceptional commentators on the American scene today." Remarks to Members of the Association of American Editorial Cartoonists (May 9, 1963).

NUCLEAR WEAPONS

General

1563. "[T]he new and terrible dangers which man has created can only be controlled by man. And if we can master this danger and meet this challenge, we will have earned the deep and lasting gratitude, not only of all men, but of all yet to be born — even to the farthest generation." Remarks of Senator John F. Kennedy, Wisconsin Association of Student Councils, Milwaukee, Wisconsin (April 2, 1960).

1564. "[T]he Russians realize, as we ourselves realize, that the spread of nuclear weapons to other nations may upset the balance power and increase the danger of accidental war — that a war of mutual destruction would benefit no one nation or ideology — that funds devoted to weapons of destruction cannot be used to raise the living standards of their own people or to help the economies of underdeveloped nations." Remarks of Senator John F. Kennedy, Earlham College, Richmond, Indiana (April 29, 1960).

1565. "As a power which will never strike first, we require a retaliatory capacity ... in such force as to deter any aggressor from threatening an attack he knows could not destroy enough of our force to prevent his own destruction." Remarks of Senator John F. Kennedy, U.S. Senate (June 14, 1960).

1566. "The world has been close to war before — but now man, who has survived all previous threats to his existence, has taken into his mortal hands the power to exterminate the entire species some seven times over." Address of Senator John F. Kennedy Accepting the Democratic Party Nomination for the Presidency of the United States — Memorial Coliseum, Los Angeles (July 15, 1960).

1567. "Because of experiments now going on ... it appears likely that almost 20 countries will have an atomic capacity by 1965 ... all possessing atomic weapons, all possessing a hydrogen capacity perhaps all possessing ballistic missiles, and the means of delivering them. When we realize that war has been the constant companion of mankind through the ages, we are about to move into a period of history when any country or combination of countries can destroy themselves, their adversaries, and perhaps the human race, all in the next 10 years." Speech by Senator John F. Kennedy, Fieldhouse, University of Wisconsin, Madison, Wisconsin (October 23, 1960).

1568. "[The] two great and powerful groups of nations [NATO and the Warsaw Pact] [cannot] take comfort from our present course — both sides overburdened by the cost of modern weapons, both rightly alarmed by the steady spread of the deadly atom, yet both racing to alter that uncertain balance of terror that stays the hand of mankind's final war." Inaugural Address (January 20, 1961).

1569. "[W]e must make certain that nuclear weapons will continue to be available for the defense of the entire [North Atlantic] Treaty area, and that these weapons are at all times under close and flexible political control that meets the needs of all the NATO countries." Address Before the Canadian Parliament in Ottawa (May 17, 1961).

1570. "[E]ach nation has the power to inflict enormous damage upon the other [and] ... such a war could and should be avoided if at all possible, since it would settle no dispute and prove no doctrine, and that care should thus be taken to prevent our conflicting interests from so directly confronting each other that war necessarily ensued." Radio and Television Report to the American People on Returning from Europe (June 6, 1961).

1571. "Three times in my life-time our country and Europe have been involved in major wars. In each case serious misjudgments were made on both sides of the intentions of others, which brought about great devastation. Now, in the thermonuclear age, any misjudgment on either side about the intentions of the other could rain more devastation in several hours than has been wrought in all the wars of human history." Radio and Television Report to the American People on the Berlin Crisis (July 25, 1961).

1572. "To recognize the possibilities of nuclear war in the missile age, without our citizens knowing what they should do and where they should go if bombs begin to fall, would be a failure of responsibility.... In the event of an attack, the lives of those families which are not hit in a nuclear blast and fire can still be saved — if they can be warned to take shelter and if that [fallout] shelter is available. We owe that kind of insurance to our families — and to our country." Radio and Television Report to the American People on the Berlin Crisis (July 25, 1961).

1573. "Today, every inhabitant of this planet must contemplate the day when this planet may no longer be habitable. Every man, woman and child lives under a nuclear sword of Damocles, hanging by the slenderest of threads, capable of being cut at any moment by accident or miscalculation or by madness. The weapons of war must be abolished before they abolish us." Address in New York City Before the General Assembly of the United Nations (September 25, 1961).

1574. "[W]ar appeals no longer as a rational alternative. Unconditional war can no longer lead to unconditional victory. It can no longer serve to settle disputes. It can no longer concern the great powers alone. For a nuclear disaster, spread by wind and water and fear, could well engulf the great and the small, the rich and the poor, the committed and the uncommitted alike. Mankind must put an end to war — or war will put an end to mankind." Address in New York City Before the General Assembly of the United Nations (September 25, 1961).

1575. "[U]ntil mankind has banished both war and its instruments of destruction, the United States must maintain an effective quantity and quality of nuclear weapons, so deployed and protected as to be capable of surviving any surprise attack and devastating the attacker. Only through such strength can we be certain of deterring a nuclear strike, or an overwhelming ground attack, upon our forces and our allies. Only through such strength can we in the free world — should that deterrent fail — face the tragedy of another war with any hope of survival." Radio and Television Address to the American People, "Nuclear Testing and Disarmament." (March 2, 1962).

1576. "[M]odern nuclear weapons and modern delivery systems ... [are] so complex that only a few scientists can understand their operation, so devastating that their inadvertent use would be of worldwide concern, but so new that their employment and their effects have never been tested in combat conditions." Remarks at West Point to the Graduating Class of the U.S. Military Academy (June 6, 1962).

1577. "There is every reason to believe that the balanced search for peace through diplomacy, military strength and economic progress will prevent nuclear war and perhaps in the years ahead reduce the risk under which we live today. We know ... how real these risks are and in the years ahead we must face the fact that they may well increase if the control of nuclear weapons spreads to more nations and possibly less responsible hands." Message to the Conference of State Civil Defense Directors (May 8, 1963).

1578. "[A] sensible and practical civil defense program has ... the potential of saving tens of millions of lives which would be exposed to lethal fallout radiation in the event of a major nuclear attack on the United States. This program does not purport to offer security under these dreadful conditions, but it does significantly improve the chances of survival of our people as individuals and as communities, and thus of national survival and recovery." Message to the Conference of State Civil Defense Directors (May 8, 1963).

1579. "The existence of mutual nuclear deterrents cannot be shrugged off as stalemate, for our national security in a period of rapid change will depend on constant reappraisal of our present doctrines, on alertness to new developments, on imagination and resourcefulness, and new ideas." Remarks at Colorado Springs to the Graduating Class of the U.S. Air Force Academy (June 5, 1963).

1580. "Since [the advent of nuclear weapons] all mankind has been struggling to escape from the darkening prospect of mass destruction on earth. In an age when both sides have come to possess enough nuclear power to destroy the human race several times over, the world of communism and the world of free choice have been caught up in a vicious circle of conflicting ideology and interest. Each increase of tension has produced an increase of arms; each increase of arms has produced an increase of tension." Radio and Television Address to the American People on the Nuclear Test Ban Treaty (July 26, 1963).

1581. "A war today or tomorrow, if it led to nuclear war, would not be like any war in history. A full-scale nuclear exchange, lasting less than 60 minutes ... could wipe out more than 300 million Americans, Europeans, and Russians, as well as untold numbers elsewhere. And the survivors, as Chairman Khrushchev warned the Communist Chinese, 'the survivors would envy the dead.' For they would inherit a world so devastated by explosions and poison and fire that today we cannot even conceive of its horrors. So let us try to turn the world away from war." Radio and Television Address to the American People on the Nuclear Test Ban Treaty (July 26, 1963).

1582. "If only one thermonuclear bomb were to be dropped on any American, Russian, or any other city, whether it was launched by accident or design, by a madman or by an enemy ... that one bomb could release more destructive power on the inhabitants of that one helpless city than all the bombs dropped in the Second World War. [No country] can look forward to that day with equanimity. We have a great obligation ... to use whatever time remains to prevent the spread of nuclear weapons, to persuade other countries not to test, transfer, acquire, possess, or produce such weapons." Radio and Television Address to the American People on the Nuclear Test Ban Treaty (July 26, 1963).

1583. "The atomic age is a dreadful age, but we must realize that when we broke the atom apart and released its energy and changed the history of the world, it was essential that the United States in this area of national strength ... should be second to none.... No one can say what the future will bring. No one can speak with certainty about whether we shall be able to control this deadly weapon, whether we shall be able to maintain our life and our peaceful relations with other countries. I can assure you we do everything we can." Remarks at the Hanford, Washington, Electric Generating Plant (September 26, 1963).

1584. "I am quite aware that if, through miscalculation or madness or design, the United States and the Soviet Union should finally clash, in what would be the last war of the human race, in a war in which in less than one day [that] over 300 million people would be killed...." Remarks at the Convention Center in Las Vegas, Nevada (September 28, 1963).

Arms Control

1585. "[O]nce the Russians learn that international control and inspection are not necessarily to be feared; once Americans learn that accommodations are not necessarily appeasement; ... [then] both sides [will] learn that agreements can be made, and kept." Remarks of Senator John F. Kennedy, South Eugene, Oregon (April 22, 1960).

1586. "I do not say that a greater national effort — or strong leadership — or an Arms Control Institute can halt the arms race. Perhaps nothing can. But we owe it to all mankind to make the effort." Remarks of Senator John F. Kennedy, Bluefield State College, Bluefield, West Virginia (April 27, 1960).

1587. "I [do not] believe that we can rely for disarmament on merely trusting the word of Soviet leaders — we must have an inspection system as reliable and as thorough as modern science can devise." Remarks of Senator John F. Kennedy, Earlham College, Richmond, Indiana (April 29, 1960).

1588. "[I]f modern science has made arms control essential — it has also made arms control more difficult. The development of underground missile launching sites — the growth of nuclear stockpiles — the evolution of new techniques for launching surprise attacks from beneath the earth, or under the seas or from the air — have all multiplied the difficulties of achieving arms control...." Remarks of Senator John F. Kennedy, Earlham College, Richmond, Indiana (April 29, 1960).

1589. "Those who talk about the risks and dangers of any arms control proposal ought to weigh ... the risks and dangers inherent in our present course. The only alternative to pursuit of an effective disarmament agreement is reckless pursuit of ... the arms race, the gap, the new weapons, the development of ever higher orders of mutual terror, all of which not only reflect tensions but obviously aggravate them." Remarks of Senator John F. Kennedy, Washington College, Chestertown, Maryland (May 11, 1960).

1590. "[I]f we can achieve a level of parity with the Communists, then we will be able to talk about disarmament.... It is impossible for us to provide for the disarmament of outer space, the disarmament of nuclear weapons, unless we are in a position of parity with the Soviet Union." Rear Platform Remarks of Senator John F. Kennedy, "Pathways to Peace," Fresno, California (September 9, 1960).

1591. "[A way must be found] ... for the United States to provide for an orderly system of disarmament ... for us to reach an agreement with the Soviet Union which will permit a cessation of nuclear tests and begin to control outer space and prevent one power or another making a decisive breakthrough in those far distant regions?" Speech by John F. Kennedy, Boys' Gymnasium, Montgomery-Blair High School, Silver Spring, Maryland (October 16, 1960).

1592. "[If] we are to ever hope to negotiate for an effective arms control agreement, we must act immediately, for as each year passes the control of increasingly complex ... [as] country after country [comes] to possess an atomic capacity.... [N]o problem is more vital, no problem is more immediate, than the problem of effective control over arms." Speech by Senator John F. Kennedy, Milwaukee, Wisconsin (October 23, 1960).

1593. "The deadly arms race, and the huge resources it absorbs, have too long overshadowed all else we must do. We must prevent that arms race from spreading to new nations, to new nuclear powers and to the reaches of outer space." Annual Message to the Congress on the State of the Union (January 30, 1961).

1594. "To destroy arms ... is not enough. We must create even as we destroy — creating worldwide law and law enforcement as we outlaw worldwide war and weapons." Annual Message to the Congress on the State of the Union (January 30, 1961).

1595. "[D]isarmament without checks is but a shadow — and a community without law is but a shell." Address in New York City Before the General Assembly of the United Nations (September 25, 1961).

1596. "Today, every inhabitant of this planet must contemplate the day when this planet may no longer be habitable. Every man, woman and child lives under a nuclear sword of Damocles, hanging by the slenderest of threads, capable of being cut at any moment by accident or miscalculation or by madness. The weapons of war must be abolished before they abolish us." Address in New York City Before the General Assembly of the United Nations (September 25, 1961).

1597. "Men no longer debate whether armaments are a symptom or a cause of tension. The mere existence of modern weapons — ten million times more powerful than any that the world has ever seen, and only minutes away from any target on earth — is a source of horror, and discord and distrust. Men no longer maintain that disarmament must await the settlement of all disputes — for disarmament must be a part of any permanent settlement. And men may no longer pretend that the quest for disarmament is a sign of weakness — for in a spiraling arms race, a nation's security may well be shrinking even as its arms increase." Address in New York City Before the General Assembly of the United Nations (September 25, 1961).

1598. "[T]he reduction and destruction of arms ... is no longer a dream — it is a practical matter of life or death. The risks inherent in disarmament pale in comparison to the risks inherent in an unlimited arms race." Address in New York City Before the General Assembly of the United Nations (September 25, 1961).

1599. "[U]nless man can match his strides in weaponry and technology with equal strides in social and political development, our great strength, like that of the dinosaur, will become incapable of proper control — and like the dinosaur vanish from the earth." Address in New York City Before the General Assembly of the United Nations (September 25, 1961).

1600. "Our ultimate goal ... is a world free from war and free from the dangers and burdens of armaments in which the use of force is subordinated to the rule of law and in which international adjustments to a changing world are achieved peacefully." Remarks in New York City Upon Signing Bill Establishing the U.S. Arms Control and Disarmament Agency (September 26, 1961).

1601. "World order will be secured only when the whole world has laid down these weapons [nuclear weapons] which seem to offer us present security but threaten the future survival of the human race. That armistice day seems very far away." Annual Message to the Congress on the State of the Union (January 11, 1962).

1602. "[T]he world was not meant to be a prison in which man awaits his execution. Nor has mankind survived the tests and trials of thousands of years to surrender everything — including its existence — now. This Nation has the will and the faith to make a supreme effort to break the log jam on disarmament and nuclear tests — and we will persist until we prevail, until the rule of law has replaced the ever dangerous use of force." Annual Message to the Congress on the State of the Union (January 11, 1962).

1603. "[O]ur commitment to national safety is not a commitment to expand our military establishment indefinitely. We do not dismiss disarmament as merely an idle dream. For we believe that, in the end, it is the only way to assure the security of all without impairing the interests of any." Annual Message to the Congress on the State of the Union (January 14, 1963).

1604. "I do not say that a world without aggression or threats of war would be an easy world. It will bring new problems, new challenges from the Communists, new dangers of relaxing our vigilance or of mistaking their intent.... But those dangers pale in comparison to those of the spiraling arms race and a collision course towards war." Radio and Television Address to the American People on the Nuclear Test Ban Treaty (July 26, 1963).

1605. "[I]n today's world, a nation's security does not always increase as its arms increase, when its adversary is doing the same, and unlimited competition in the testing and development of new types of destructive nuclear weapons will not make the world safer for either side." Radio and Television Address to the American People on the Nuclear Test Ban Treaty (July 26, 1963).

1606. "Soberly and unremittingly this Nation — but never this Nation alone — has sought the doorway to effective disarmament into a world where peace is secure." Remarks at the Signing of the Nuclear Test Ban Treaty (October 7, 1963).

1607. "[W]hen we think of peace in this country, let us think of both our capacity to deter aggression and our goal of true disarmament." Address at the University of Maine (October 19, 1963).

Nuclear Test Bans

1608. "No change in the world about us presents a greater challenge — no problem calls for greater leadership and vision — than the radioactive pollution of our atmosphere by the testing of nuclear weapons. It is not a simple problem with simple answers. The experts disagree — the evidence is in conflict — the obstacles to an international solution are large and many. But the issue of nuclear tests ... is one which should be discussed in the coming months — not as a purely partisan matter, but as one of the great issues on the American scene." Remarks of Senator John F. Kennedy, Wisconsin Association of Student Councils, Milwaukee, Wisconsin (April 2, 1960).

1609. "Radiation, in its simplest terms ... is poison. Nuclear explosions in the atmosphere are slowly but progressively poisoning our air, our earth, our water and our food. And it falls, let us remember, on both sides of the Iron Curtain, on all peoples of all lands, regardless of their political ideology, their way of life, their religion or the color of their skin. Beneath this bombardment of radiation which man has created, all men are indeed equal." Remarks of Senator John F. Kennedy, Wisconsin Association of Student Councils, Milwaukee, Wisconsin (April 2, 1960).

1610. "We cannot — we must not allow our failures of the past to recur in the future. The world's hopes for peace rest on the effort for effective arms control — we cannot disappoint those hopes. We must exert all our efforts, our will and our courage to take the first halting steps toward arms control — perhaps in the form of a ban on nuclear testing." Remarks of Senator John F. Kennedy, Washington College, Chestertown, Maryland (May 11, 1960).

1611. "[I]f ... a [nuclear test] ban is achieved, it must only be the first step toward halting the spiraling arms race that burdens the entire world with a fantastic financial drain, excessive military establishments, and the chance of an accidental or irrational triggering of a worldwide holocaust." Remarks of Senator John F. Kennedy, U.S. Senate (June 14, 1960).

1612. "[The] deterrent strength [of nuclear weapons], if it is to be effective and credible ... must embody the most modern, the most reliable and the most versatile nuclear weapons our research and development can produce. The testing of new weapons and their effects is necessarily a part of that research and development process." Radio and Television Address to the American People, "Nuclear Testing and Disarmament" (March 2, 1962).

1613. "[F]urther Soviet tests [of nuclear weapons], in the absence of further Western progress, could well provide the Soviet Union with a nuclear attack and defense capability so powerful as to encourage aggressive designs. Were we to stand still while the Soviets surpassed us ... the free World's ability to deter, to survive and to respond to an all-out attack would be seriously weakened." Radio and Television Address to the American People, "Nuclear Testing and Disarmament" (March 2, 1962).

1614. "[T]hose free peoples who value their freedom and their security, and look to our relative strength to shield them from danger — those who know of our good faith in seeking an end to testing and an end to the arms race — will, I am confident, want the United States to do whatever it must do [including nuclear testing] to deter the threat of aggression." Radio and Television Address to the American People, "Nuclear Testing and Disarmament" (March 2, 1962).

1615. "Should we fail to follow the dictates of our own security [by further nuclear testing], they [the leaders of the Soviet Union] will chalk it up, not to goodwill, but to a failure of will — not to our confidence in Western superiority, but to our fear of world opinion, the very world opinion for which they showed such contempt. They could well be encouraged by such signs of weakness.... With such a one-sided advantage, why would they change their strategy...?" Radio and Television Address to the American People, "Nuclear Testing and Disarmament" (March 2, 1962).

1616. "[O]ur ultimate objective is not to test for the sake of testing. Our real objective is to make our own tests unnecessary, to prevent others from testing, to prevent the nuclear arms race from mushrooming out of control, to take the first steps toward general and complete disarmament." Radio and Television Address to the American People, "Nuclear Testing and Disarmament" (March 2, 1962).

1617. "[A] treaty to outlaw nuclear tests ... would check the spiraling arms race in one of its most dangerous areas ... [i]t would place the nuclear powers in a position to deal more effectively with ... the further spread of nuclear arms [and] [i]t would increase our security — it would decrease the prospects of war." Commencement Address at American University in Washington (June 10, 1963).

1618. "[T]he achievement of this goal [a treaty to ban all nuclear tests in the atmosphere, in outer space, and under water] is not a victory for one side — it is a victory for mankind. It reflects no concessions either to or by the Soviet Union. It reflects simply our common recognition of the dangers in further testing. This treaty is not the millennium. It will not resolve all conflicts, or cause the Communists to forego their ambitions, or eliminate the dangers of war. It will not reduce our need for arms or allies or programs of assistance to others. But it is an important first step — a step towards peace — a step towards reason — a step away from war." Radio and Television Address to the American People on the Nuclear Test Ban Treaty (July 26, 1963).

1619. "Western policies have long been designed to persuade the Soviet Union to renounce aggression, direct or indirect, so that their people and all people may live and let live in peace. The unlimited testing of new weapons of war cannot lead towards that end...." Radio and Television Address to the American People on the Nuclear Test Ban Treaty (July 26, 1963).

1620. "No one can be certain what the future will bring.... But history and our own conscience will judge us harsher if we do not now make every effort to test our hopes by action.... According to the ancient Chinese proverb, 'A journey of a thousand miles must begin with a single step.' [L]et us take that first step. Let us, if we can, step back from the shadows of war and seek out the way of peace. And if that journey is a thousand miles, or even more, let history record that we, in this land, at this time, took the first step." Radio and Television Address to the American People on the Nuclear Test Ban Treaty (July 26, 1963).

1621. "[T]he treaty outlawing nuclear tests in the atmosphere ... affords us all a small sign of hope that war can be averted; that the terrible destructive power of nuclear weapons can be abolished before they abolish us; that our children can inhabit a world in which freedom is secure, and the air is pure." Radio and Television Address to the Nation on the Test Ban Treaty and the Tax Reduction Bill (September 18, 1963).

1622. "A test ban treaty is a milestone — but it is not the millennium. We have not been released from our obligations — we have been given an opportunity. And if we fail to make the most of this moment and this momentum ... if this pause in the cold war merely leads to its renewal and not to its end — then the indictment of posterity will rightly point its finger at us all." Address Before the 18th General Assembly of the United Nations (September 20, 1963).

1623. "I do not believe that the test ban treaty means that the competition between the Communist system and ourselves will end. What we hope is that it will not be carried into the sphere of nuclear war. But the competition will go on. Which society is the most productive ... educates its children better ... maintains a higher rate of economic growth ... [and] produces more cultural and intellectual stimulus? Which society, in other words, is the happier? Remarks of Senator John F. Kennedy, High School Memorial Stadium, Great Falls, Montana (September 26, 1963).

PEACE

1624. "[The issue we face is] whether we can achieve a world of peace and freedom in place of the fantastically dangerous and expensive arms race in which we are now falling behind." Indiana Primary Announcement of Senator John F. Kennedy, Indianapolis, Indiana (February 4, 1960).

1625. "[P]eace is man's greatest aspiration — a just peace, a secure peace, without appeasement We will not accept the peace of foreign domination — we do not seek the peace of the grave. We want more than this so-called peace that is merely an interval between wars." Remarks of Senator John F. Kennedy, Midwest Farm Conference, Des Moines, Iowa (August 21, 1960).

1626. "In a world of danger and trial, peace is our deepest aspiration, and when peace comes we will gladly convert not our swords into plowshares, but our bombs into peaceful reactors, and our planes into space vessels. 'Pursue peace,' the Bible tells us, and we shall pursue it with every effort and every energy that we possess." Speech by Senator John F. Kennedy, Civic Auditorium, Seattle, Washington (September 6, 1960).

1627. "[T]he people of the world want peace, and they sincerely wonder how much the United States wants peace.... [T]hey are discouraged by a philosophy that puts its faith in swapping insults with the Soviet Union, for they know it can lead in only one direction, and that would be toward mankind's final war." Speech by Senator John F. Kennedy, Civic Auditorium, Portland, Oregon (September 7, 1960).

1628. "I don't think that there is a war party and a peace party, a party [of] appeasement and a party that desires to be tough with the Russians. I think all Americans, whether they are Republicans or Democrats, share a common desire, to live at peace and protect the security of the United States." Rear Platform Remarks of Senator John F. Kennedy, "Pathways to Peace," Fresno, California (September 9, 1960).

1629. "Our aspiration is for peace, not merely a peace which lasts between wars, not merely a peace which hangs on the brink of war, not merely a peace of the death, but a peace enforced and controlled by the United Nations against the universal danger of common destruction. We want a peace in which the funds now poured into ... a great multinational effort to harness our rivers, eradicate disease, take care of our children, care for the aged. We want a peace in which we can truly beat our swords into plowshares, and our hydrogen bombs into atomic reactors." Speech by Senator John F. Kennedy, Democratic Women's Luncheon, Commodore Hotel, New York, New York (September 14, 1960).

1630. "I know no single issue that is of greater concern to all the American people, men or women, Republican or Democrats, than the issue of peace. No political party has a monopoly on that policy. There is no party of peace in this country, just as there is no party of war or party of appeasement. The sooner we get away from these artificial labels, the sooner we can get down to discussing the real issues and the real decisions that face us for there are real issues and there are real differences in approach." Speech by Senator John F. Kennedy, Democratic Women's Luncheon, Commodore Hotel, New York, New York (September 14, 1960).

1631. "The Communists camp divides over the best pathway to follow to world conquest. In this Nation our two parties divide over the best pathway to world peace." Speech by Senator John F. Kennedy, Mormon Tabernacle, Salt Lake City, Utah (September 23, 1960).

1632. "[P]eace takes more than talk, more than effort, more than 'experience,' particularly if that 'experience,' in Oscar Wilde's words, is 'the name that everyone gives to their mistakes.'" Speech by Senator John F. Kennedy at a Democratic Fund-Raising Dinner in Syracuse, New York (September 29, 1960).

1633. "I don't believe you can talk your way into peace. I don't believe you can gain peace by conferences merely. I believe that peace, like any other goal, requires action." Speech by Senator John F. Kennedy, Milwaukee, Wisconsin (October 23, 1960).

1634. "We can push a button to start the next war but there is no push button magic to winning a lasting and enduring peace." Speech by Senator John F. Kennedy, Cow Palace, San Francisco, California (November 2, 1960).

1635. "[T]o those nations who would make themselves our adversary, we offer not a pledge but a request: that both sides begin anew the quest for peace, before the dark powers of destruction unleashed by science engulf all humanity in planned or accidental self-destruction." Inaugural Address (January 20, 1961).

1636. "[H]owever close we sometimes seem to that dark and final abyss, let no man of peace and freedom despair. For he does not stand alone. If we all can persevere ... then surely the age will dawn in which the strong are just and the weak secure and the peace preserved." Address in New York City Before the General Assembly of the United Nations (July 25, 1961).

1637. "It is a tragic fact that these hopes [that World War I would be the war to end all wars] have not been fulfilled, that wars still more destructive and still more sanguinary followed, that man's capacity to devise new ways of killing his fellow men have far outstripped his capacity to live in peace with his fellow men." Remarks at the Veterans Day Ceremony at Arlington National Cemetery (November 11, 1961).

1638. "[W]e shall achieve that peace only with patience and perseverance and courage — the patience and perseverance necessary to work with allies of diverse interests but common goals, the courage necessary over a long period of time to overcome an adversary skilled in the arts of harassment and obstruction." Remarks at the Veterans Day Ceremony at Arlington National Cemetery (November 11, 1961).

1639. "We live in a troublesome time, but let it come in our time, so that in this country and around the world our children and their children may live in peace and security." Remarks in Seattle at the Silver Anniversary Dinner Honoring Senator Magnuson (November 16, 1961).

1640. "Those who make peaceful revolution impossible will make violent revolution inevitable." Address on the First Anniversary of the Alliance for Progress (March 13, 1962).

1641. "[W]e want peace for our people and an opportunity for them to develop, and also we wish freedom not only for our own people but for others." Remarks to the Staff at the American Embassy in Mexico City (June 30, 1962).

1642. "The mere absence of war is not peace." Annual Message to the Congress on the State of the Union (January 14, 1963).

1643. "In these past months we have reaffirmed the scientific and military superiority of freedom. But complacency or self-congratulation can imperil our security as much as the weapons of tyranny. A moment of pause is not a promise of peace." Annual Message to the Congress on the State of the Union (January 14, 1963).

1644. "[I]gnorance too often abounds and the truth is too rarely perceived — yet it is the most important topic on earth: world peace." Commencement Address at American University in Washington (June 10, 1963).

1645. "The United States ... will never start a war. We do not want a war. We do not now expect a war. This generation of Americans has already had enough — more than enough — of war and hate and oppression. We shall be prepared if others wish it. We shall be alert to try to stop it. But we shall also do our part to build a world of peace where the weak are safe and the strong are just. We are not helpless before that task or hopeless of its success. Confident and unafraid, we labor on — not toward a strategy of annihilation but toward a strategy of peace." Commencement Address at American University in Washington (June 10, 1963).

1646. "[T]he expenditure of billions of dollars every year on weapons acquired for the purpose of making sure we never need to use them is essential to keeping the peace. But surely the acquisition of such idle stockpiles — which can only destroy and never create — is not the only, much less the most efficient, means of assuring peace." Commencement Address at American University in Washington (June 10, 1963).

1647. "[Our goal is not] the absolute, infinite concept of universal peace and good will of which some fantasies and fanatics dream. I do not deny the value of hopes and dreams but we merely invite discouragement and incredulity by making that our only and immediate goal. Let us focus instead on a more practical, more attainable peace — based not on a sudden revolution in human nature but on a gradual evolution in human institutions — on a series of concrete actions and effective agreements which are in the interest of all concerned." Commencement Address at American University in Washington (June 10, 1963).

1648. "There is no single, simple key to ... peace — no grand or magic formula to be adopted by one or two powers. Genuine peace must be the product of many nations, the sum of many acts. It must be dynamic, not static, changing to meet the challenge of each new generation. For peace is a process — a way of solving problems." Commencement Address at American University in Washington (June 10, 1963).

1649. "World peace, like community peace, does not require that each man love his neighbor — it requires only that they live together in mutual tolerance, submitting their disputes to a just and peaceful settlement." Commencement Address at American University in Washington (June 10, 1963).

1650. "Too many of us think it [peace] is impossible. Too many think it unreal. But that is a dangerous, defeatist belief. It leads to the conclusion that war is inevitable — that mankind is doomed — that we are gripped by forces we cannot control. We need not accept that view. Our problems are manmade — therefore, they can be solved by man. And man can be as big as he wants. No problem of human destiny is beyond human beings. Man's reason and spirit have often solved the seemingly unsolvable — and we believe they can do it again." Commencement Address at American University in Washington (June 10, 1963).

1651. "[L]et us not be blind to our differences — but let us also direct attention to our common interests and to the means by which those differences can be resolved. And if we cannot end now our differences, at least we can help make the world safe for diversity. For, in the final analysis, our most basic common link is that we all inhabit this small planet. We all breathe the same air. We all cherish our children's future. And we are all mortal." Commencement Address at American University in Washington (June 10, 1963).

1652. "[W]e must seek a world of peace — a world in which peoples dwell together in mutual respect and work together in mutual regard — a world where peace is not a mere interlude between wars, but an incentive to the creative energies of humanity. We will not find such a peace today, or even tomorrow. The obstacles to hope are large and menacing. Yet the goal of a peaceful world — today and tomorrow — just shape our decisions and inspire our purposes." Address in the Assembly Hall at the Paulskirche in Frankfurt [Germany] (June 25, 1963).

1653. "No generation is passed — no generation is passed without a war. War has taken up most of the time of the human race, and now we have the terrible responsibility, at a time when we have weapons which will destroy the human race, of working out means of living together. That is a difficult task...." Remarks to a Group of American Field Service Students (July 18, 1963).

1654. "Peace is a daily, a weekly, a monthly process, gradually changing opinions, slowly eroding old barriers, quietly building new structures. And however undramatic the pursuit of peace, that pursuit must go on." Address Before the 18th General Assembly of the United Nations (September 20, 1963).

1655. "The task of building the peace lies with the leaders of every nation, large and small. For the great powers have no monopoly on conflict or ambition. The cold war is not the only expression of tension in this world — and the nuclear race is not the only arms race. Even little wars are dangerous in a nuclear world. The long labor of peace is an undertaking for every nation — and in this effort none of us can remain unaligned. To this goal none can be uncommitted." Address Before the 18th General Assembly of the United Nations (September 20, 1963).

1656. "[I]f either of our countries [the United States or the Soviet Union] is to be fully secure, we need a much better weapon than the H-bomb — a weapon better than ballistic missiles or nuclear submarines — and that better weapon is peaceful cooperation." Address Before the 18th General Assembly of the United Nations (September 20, 1963).

1657. "[P]eace does not rest in charters and covenants alone. It lies in the hearts and minds of all people.... So let us not rest all our hopes on parchment and on paper; let us strive to build peace, a desire for peace, a willingness to work for peace, in the hearts and minds of all of our people. I believe that we can. I believe the problems of human destiny are not beyond the reach of human beings." Address Before the 18th General Assembly of the United Nations (September 20, 1963).

1658. "It may well be that man recognizes now that war is so destructive, so annihilating, so incendiary, that it may be possible, out of that awful fact [splitting the atom] — it may be possible for us, step by step, to so adjust our relations, to so develop a rule of reason and a rule of law, that ... it may be possible for us to find a more peaceful world. That is our intention." Remarks at the Hanford, Washington, Electric Generating Plant (September 26, 1963).

1659. "It is that spirit, the spirit of both preparedness and peace, that this Nation today is stronger than ever before — strengthened by both the increased power of our defenses and our increased efforts for peace — [that] strengthen[s] ... both our resolve to resist coercion and our constant search for solutions." Address at the University of Maine (October 19, 1963).

PEACE CORPS

1660. "I ... propose that our inadequate efforts in this area [foreign relations] be supplemented by a peace corps of talented young men and women, willing and able to serve their country ... as an alternative or as a supplement to peacetime selective service, well qualified through rigorous standards, well trained in the languages, skills, and customs they will need to know.... This would be a volunteer corps ... [of] all Americans, of whatever age, who wished to serve the great Republic and serve the cause of freedom ... around the globe." Speech by Senator John F. Kennedy, Cow Palace, San Francisco, California (November 2, 1960).

1661. "I believe that as a counter to the flood of well trained ... tacticians now helping nations with their problems that the Communists are sending out ... an American Peace Corps ... of our young men could be trained to help these people live a life of freedom in agriculture, in handiwork, in road building, in government and other skills, young Americans who will represent the cause of freedom around the globe." Speech by Senator John F. Kennedy, Chicago Auditorium, Chicago, Illinois (November 4, 1960).

1662. "[A] valuable national asset is our reservoir of dedicated men and women ... who have indicated their desire to contribute their skills, their efforts, and a part of their lives to the fight for world order. We can mobilize this talent through the formation of a National Peace Corps ... to help foreign lands meet their urgent needs for trained personnel." Annual Message to the Congress on the State of the Union (January 30, 1961).

1663. "I hope that when the Peace Corps ultimately is organized, and young men and women go out around the world, that they will place their greatest emphasis on teaching; and secondly, that they will learn themselves far more than they will teach, and that we will therefore have another link which binds us to the world around us." Remarks to the Delegates to the Youth Fitness Conference (February 21, 1961).

1664. "I believe Peace Corps volunteers will give a fresh personal meaning to our diplomacy. There can be no better evidence of our good will than days of honest work in behalf of our neighbors." Remarks to the National Advisory Council for the Peace Corps (May 22, 1961).

1665. "In these days of international tension the response of these [Peace Corps] volunteers stands as a light to all who seek a peaceful world." Remarks to the National Advisory Council for the Peace Corps (May 22, 1961).

1666. "[T]he great impression of what kind of country we have and what kind of people we are will depend on their judgment, in these countries, of you [Peace Corps volunteers]. [I]f you can impress them with your commitment to freedom, to the advancement of the interests of people everywhere, to your pride in your country and its best traditions and what it stands for, the influence may be far-reaching and will go far beyond the immediate day-to-day tasks that you may do in the months that are ahead." Remarks to a Group of Peace Corps Volunteers Before Their Departure for Tanganyika and Ghana (August 28, 1961).

1667. "I feel a particular satisfaction because this is the most immediate response — the Peace Corps — that I think the country has seen to the whole spirit which I tried to suggest in my inaugural about the contribution which we could make to our country." Remarks to a Group of Peace Corps Volunteers Before Their Departure for Tanganyika and Ghana (August 28, 1961).

1668. "[The Peace Corps is] an avenue ... by which Americans can serve their country in the cause of world peace and understanding and simultaneously assist other nations toward their legitimate goals of freedom and opportunity." Remarks Upon Signing the Peace Corps Bill (September 22, 1961).

1669. "Neither money nor technical assistance ... can be our only weapon against poverty. In the end, the crucial effort is one of purpose, requiring the fuel of finance but also a torch of idealism. And nothing carries the spirit of this American idealism more effectively to the far corners of the earth than the American Peace Corps." Annual Message to the Congress on the State of the Union (January 14, 1962).

1670. "I don't think it is altogether fair to say that I handed Sarge [Robert Sargent Shriver, Jr., Director of the Peace Corps] a lemon from which he made lemonade, but I do think that he was handed and you were handed one of the most sensitive and difficult assignments which any administrative group in Washington has been given, almost, in this century." Remarks at a Meeting with the Headquarters Staff of the Peace Corps (June 14, 1962).

1671. "I can imagine if that must come [death in the field while serving as a Peace Corps volunteer], no cause — cause of peace — is more worthy of that kind of a great contribution. To be able to make a maximum effort to serve peace in a time of maximum danger, I would consider the most satisfactory of human experiences." Remarks at a Meeting with the Headquarters Staff of the Peace Corps (June 14, 1962).

1672. "Recently I heard a story of a young Peace Corpsman ... who is working in Chile ... in ... an Indian village which prides itself on being Communist. The village is up a long, winding road which young Peace Corpsman has gone on many occasions to see the chief. Each time the chief avoided seeing him. Finally he saw him and said, 'You are not going to talk us out of being Communists.' [The young man] said, 'I am not trying to do that, only to talk to you about how I can help.' The chief looked at him and replied, 'In a few weeks the snow will come. Then you will have to park your jeep 20 miles from here and come through 5 feet of snow on foot. The Communists are willing to do that. Are you?' [A] friend saw [the Peace Corpsman] recently and asked him what he was doing, he said, 'I am waiting for the snow.' Well, I hope that spirit motivates all of you." Remarks of Welcome to Participants in the Summer Intern Program for College Students (June 20, 1962).

1673. "[With the Peace Corps], [i]t seems to me we have an opportunity, particularly in the fields of education and health and related fields, to fulfill obligations which we have to the newly developing countries. And also it seems to me we serve our own citizens well by permitting an outlet of service to the world beyond our own national boundaries and we set up a pool of talent for future national service either in the Government or in teaching or public work of one kind or another...." Remarks to Officers of the International Peace Corps Secretariat (May 9, 1963).

1674. "I have always been impressed by the dedication which totalitarian societies enlist to aid rather adverse causes. I think if we enlist in a great cause like this [the Peace Corps] we will have a great deal of strength." Remarks to Officers of the International Peace Corps Secretariat (May 9, 1963).

1675. "The United States Peace Corps ... has given us an opportunity to harness the idealism which is, I think, in all free people; has given us an opportunity to be of assistance, not merely in the cold field of economic help, but in the human relations which must exist for a happy understanding between people." Remarks in Bonn at the Signing of a Charter Establishing the German Peace Corps (June 24, 1963).

PHYSICAL FITNESS

1676. "Since the time of the ancient Greeks, we have always felt that there was a close relationship between a strong, vital mind and physical fitness. It is our hope that using the influence of the National Government that we can expand this strong spirit among American men and women, that they will concern themselves with this phase of their personal development. We do not want in the United States a nation of spectators. We want a nation of participants in the vigorous life." Remarks to the Delegates to the Youth Fitness Conference (February 21, 1961).

1677. "We want to make sure that as our life becomes more sophisticated, as we become more urbanized, that we don't lose this very valuable facet of our national character: physical vitality, which is tied into qualities of character, which is tied into qualities of intellectual vigor and vitality." Remarks to the Delegates to the Youth Fitness Conference (February 21, 1961).

1678. "The strength of our democracy and our country is really no greater in the final analysis than the well-being of our citizens. The vigor of our country, its physical vigor and energy, is going to be no more advanced, no more substantial, than the vitality and will of our countrymen." Remarks on the Youth Fitness Program. (July 19, 1961).

1679. "[Every boy's and girl's] physical fitness, their willingness to participate in physical exercise, their willingness to participate in physical contests ... — all these, I think, will do a good deal to strengthen this country, and also to contribute to a greater enjoyment of life in the years to come. This is a responsibility which is upon all of us — ... who are parents — to make sure that we stress this phase of human life.... And also, of course, it is a matter of vital interest to our national Government." Remarks on the Youth Fitness Program. (July 19, 1961).

1680. "The sad fact is that ... more and more ... our national sport is not playing at all — but watching. We have become more and more not a nation of athletes but a nation of spectators.... [Most] of us — and too many of our children — get our exercise from climbing up to seats in stadiums, or from walking across the room to turn on our television sets. And this is true for one sport after another.... The result of this shift from participation to, if I may use the word 'spectation,' is all too visible in the physical condition of our population." Address in New York City at the National Football Foundation and Hall of Fame Banquet (December 5, 1961).

1681. "We are under-exercised as a nation. We look, instead of play. We ride, instead of walk. Our existence deprives us of the minimum of physical activity essential for healthy living. And the remedy, in my judgment, lies in one direction; that is, in developing programs for broad participation in exercise by all of our young men and women — all of our boys and girls." Address in New York City at the National Football Foundation and Hall of Fame Banquet (December 5, 1961).

1682. "I believe that ... we should as a country set a goal ... to emphasize this most important part of life, the opportunity to exercise, to participate in physical activity, and generally to produce a standard of excellence for our country which will enable our athletes to win the Olympics — but more importantly ... will give us a nation of vigorous men and women. There are more important goals than winning contests, and that is to improve on a broad level the health and vitality of all of our people." Address in New York City at the National Football Foundation and Hall of Fame Banquet (December 5, 1961).

1683. "There is nothing, I think, more unfortunate than to have soft, chubby, fat-looking children who go to watch their school play basketball every Saturday and regard that as their week's exercise." Remarks on the 50th Anniversary of the Children's Bureau (April 9, 1962).

POLITICAL LEADERSHIP

1684. "[When] Abraham Lincoln summon[ed] his war-time Cabinet to a meeting on the Emancipation Proclamation ... [he said] 'I have gathered you together to hear what I have written down. I do not wish your advice about the main matter — that I have determined for myself.' And later, when he went to sign it after several hours of exhausting hand-shaking that had left his arm weak, he said to those present: 'If my name goes down in history, it will be for this act.

My whole soul is in it. If my hand trembles when I sign this Proclamation, all who examine the document hereafter will say: He hesitated.' But Lincoln's hand did not tremble. He did not hesitate. He did not equivocate. For he was the President of the United States." Remarks of Senator John F. Kennedy, Phoenix, Arizona (April 9, 1960).

1685. "[Let us] avoid the confusion of political idealism with political fantasy or rigidity. We need idealism in our public life ... [b]ut let us not ... carry that idealism to the point of fantasy — to the point where any compromise or concession is regarded as immoral. For politics and legislation are not matters for inflexible principles or unattainable ideals." Remarks of Senator John F. Kennedy, Concord College, Athens, West Virginia (April 27, 1960).

1686. "There are too many crises in the future to blind our eyes weeping over the crises of the past. There are too many things that can be done to waste our efforts on events we can no longer affect." Remarks of Senator John F. Kennedy, New Mexico State Democratic Convention, New Mexico (June 4, 1960).

1687. "I would rather be accused of breaking precedents — than breaking promises." Remarks of Senator John F. Kennedy, Midwest Farm Conference, Des Moines, Iowa (August 21, 1960).

1688. "I do not consider a politician's chief duty to consider how he can gain popularity at the moment. His chief duty, his chief obligation, in fact, his only reason for service, is to tell the truth to the American people, not to serve to please them, but to serve them." Remarks of Senator John F. Kennedy, Picnic, Muskegon, Michigan (September 5, 1960).

1689. "I think that the test ... of a free society is the kind of leadership it has. The leadership and the support that that leadership can secure, really is essential to the successful working of a free system." Speech by Senator John F. Kennedy, High School Auditorium, Pocatello, Idaho (September 6, 1960).

1690. "We look to the past so we will know where we are going in the future. We look to the past because it tells us what we have been able to do. We look to the past because it gives us confidence that this country has been built by men of courage, men of character, men who are willing to risk all to develop the [the states] and the United States. We look today to the past ... because it is the past that tells us most about what the future can be." Remarks of Senator John F. Kennedy, Capitol Steps, Austin, Texas (September 13, 1960).

1691. "During the American Constitutional Convention, just before the convention, there was in Hartford, Conn., one day a storm which overcast the United States, and in that religious day men fell on their knees and begged a final blessing before the end came. The Connecticut House of Representatives was in session and many of the members clamored for immediate adjournment. The speaker of the house, one Colonel Davenport, came to his feet and he silenced the din with these words: 'The day of judgment is either approaching or it is not. If it is not, there is no cause for adjournment. If it is, I choose to be found doing my duty. I wish, therefore, that candles may be brought.' I hope in a dark and uncertain period in our own country that we, too, may bring candles to help light our country's way." Speech by Senator John F. Kennedy, Coliseum, Charlotte, North Carolina (September 17, 1960).

1692. "I don't preach the doctrine of ease. I preach the doctrine of vigor and vitality and energy and force." Remarks of Senator John F. Kennedy, City Square, Fort Dodge, Iowa (September 22, 1960).

1693. "[W]hether you may be a Republican or a Democrat — I think that you will agree that what we really need is the best talent that we can get, the most honest talent we can get, the most energetic and vital intellect that we can apply to the great problems that face the United States." Remarks of Senator John F. Kennedy, Corn Palace, Mitchell, South Dakota (September 22, 1960).

1694. "[W]ith vigorous leadership, with leadership which will realize the potential of this country, this country can maintain its own freedom and the freedom of those who look to us for help." Remarks of Senator John F. Kennedy, North Tonawanda, New York (September 28, 1960).

1695. "[T]his country ... need[s] leadership that will keep its eyes on the stars, on the fixed constellations which have guided this country in so many difficult times in the long history ... confidence in our country, a sense of the progressive, a sense of the new, a sense of willingness to break new ground, a sense of confidence in the people to meet the great problems that face them, a confidence in freedom, a confidence in a free society." Speech of Senator John F. Kennedy, Armory, Springfield, Illinois (October 3, 1960).

1696. "[W]e serve this country ... when we tell the truth, when we present the facts, honest and clearly, and give the American people an opportunity to make their judgment." Remarks of Senator John F. Kennedy, Airport, Paducah, Kentucky (October 8, 1960).

1697. "Some of you may disagree with [my] view [on civil rights], but at least I have not changed that view in an election year, or according to where I am standing." Speech by Senator John F. Kennedy, State House, Columbia, South Carolina (October 10, 1960).

1698. "Moral and persuasive leadership by the President [can] create the conditions in which compliance with the constitutional requirements of school desegregation takes place; this is the kind of leadership I intend to give, the kind of action that we shall take." Speech by Senator John F. Kennedy, National Conference on Constitutional Rights and American Freedom, Park-Sheraton Hotel, New York, New York (October 12, 1960).

1699. "I want to make it perfectly clear where I stand. I believe that this is a great country, but it must be greater. I believe this is a powerful country but it must be more powerful. I do not believe the tide of history is moving in our favor. I do not believe that we are doing enough.... I do not believe that our relative position in the world, militarily ... is as strong as it was a decade ago." Remarks of Senator John F. Kennedy, Capitol Steps, Columbus, Ohio (October 17, 1960).

1700. "[H]azard is going to be our companion, and those who can find reassurance in present events in my opinion should not hold power in the 1960s." Speech by Senator John F. Kennedy, Luncheon, Biltmore Hotel, Dayton, Ohio (October 17, 1960).

1701. "[I]t is my function and it is my duty, as the standard bearer for my own party, to tell the American people the truth as we see it, and then let you make your honest judgment." Speech by Senator John F. Kennedy, Hemming Park, Jacksonville, Florida (October 18, 1960).

1702. "This is a great country, and I have the greatest possible confidence that our generation of Americans can meet any challenge presented to us. But how can we do so when our leadership decides that rather than tell the people the truth, they will carry on this campaign of vague innuendo and suggestion, reassuring our people that everything is all right, the same thing that Stanley Baldwin and Neville Chamberlain did in the thirties to England and England's fall was all too close." Speech by Senator John F. Kennedy, Hemming Park, Jacksonville, Florida (October 18, 1960).

1703. "In my judgment the United States can meet any burden, can meet any challenge, can meet any responsibility, but it cannot possibly do so unless the President of the United States and the country moves to finish the unfinished business of our society, recognizes the perils that we are in, recognizes the challenges, determines that this country shall move again, determine that we shall work in the sixties, determine that we shall be in this country an inspiration to all those who wish to be free and to hold out a helping hand to all those who desire to follow our example." Remarks of Senator John F. Kennedy, 163d Street Shopping Center, North Miami Beach, Florida (October 18, 1960).

1704. "[W]hat this world needs and ... what our country needs, [are] not words and speeches given by candidates and others. What we need are good works and the esteem of good men, backed by good action." Speech by Senator John F. Kennedy, Auditorium, Kansas City, Missouri (October 22, 1960).

1705. "[O]ur system cannot work without leadership. Unless the President of the United States looks to the future, unless he is willing to set before our country its unfinished business ... unless he is willing to move ahead this country cannot possibly meet its responsibilities to itself and to those who look to us for assistance and help." Remarks of Senator John F. Kennedy, Chester, Pennsylvania (October 29, 1960).

1706. "[N]o free people can possibly maintain their freedom unless they and those who seek positions of responsibility are willing to face the facts of life, the facts with the bark off, the truth...." Remarks of Senator John F. Kennedy, Roosevelt Field, Norristown, Pennsylvania (October 29, 1960).

1707. "The whole history of the world, from the struggle of the Athenians against the Macedonians, to the experience of the British before World War II, in their competition with the Nazis, all show that for a free society to survive, to successfully compete, the leaders have to tell the truth. They have to be informed. They have to share their information with the people." Remarks of Senator John F. Kennedy, First-Time Voters Convocation, University of Southern California, Los Angeles, California (November 1, 1960).

1708. "This is an ancient struggle between those who look to the future, between those who share the inheritance of Jefferson [and those who do not, and] [i]t [is] a willingness to look life in the eye, to look to the future, to plan to decide what is best for our country and to move ahead, to be committed to no faction but to be committed to the truth. That is the inheritance of Thomas Jefferson. And on that inheritance I run...." Remarks of Senator John F. Kennedy, Airport Rally, Roanoke, Virginia (November 4, 1960).

1709. "It is the function of a public official and a candidate for office not merely to go to the people and give them reassurance. It is the function and responsibility of a political candidate for a national office in a free society and it has been since the time of ancient Athens, to tell the truth." Remarks of Senator John F. Kennedy, Railroad Station Plaza, Bridgeport, Connecticut (November 6, 1960).

1710. "This country cannot survive unless the political leaders, those who seek positions of responsibility, are willing to tell the people the truth...." Remarks of Senator John F. Kennedy, Teaneck Armory Teterboro, New Jersey (November 6, 1960).

1711. "For my part, I shall withhold from neither the Congress nor the people any fact or report, past, present, or future, which is necessary for an informed judgment of our conduct and hazards. I shall neither shift the burden of executive decisions to the Congress, nor avoid responsibility for the outcome of those decisions." Annual Message to the Congress on the State of the Union (January 30, 1961).

1712. "The prudent heir takes careful inventory of his legacies, and gives a faithful accounting to those whom he owes an obligation of trust." Annual Message to the Congress on the State of the Union (January 30, 1961).

1713. "No President should fear public scrutiny of his program. For from that scrutiny comes understanding; and from that understanding comes support or opposition. And both are necessary." Address "The President and the Press" Before the American Newspaper Publishers Association, New York City (April 27, 1961).

1714. "[I] bear the responsibility of the Presidency of the United States, and it is my duty to make decisions that no adviser and no ally can make for me ... and ... to see that these decisions ... are as informed as possible, that they are based on as much direct, firsthand knowledge as possible." Radio and Television Report to the American People on Returning from Europe (June 6, 1961).

1715. "The basis of self-government and freedom requires the development of character and self-restraint and perseverance and the long view. And these are qualities which require many years of training and education." Address in Seattle at the University of Washington's 100th Anniversary Program (November 16, 1961).

1716. "Men who are unwilling to face up to the danger from without are convinced that the real danger is from within. They look suspiciously at their neighbors and their leaders. They call for 'a man on horseback' because they do not trust the people. They find treason in our churches, in our highest court.... They equate the Democratic Party with the welfare state, the welfare state with socialism, socialism with communism. They object quite rightly to politics intruding on the military — but they are very anxious for the military to engage in their kind of politics. But ... most Americans, soldiers and civilians — take a different view of our peril. [They] know it comes from without, not within. It must be met by quiet preparedness, not provocative speeches." Address in Los Angeles at a Dinner of the Democratic Party of California (November 18, 1961).

1717. "As every past generation has had to disenthrall itself from an inheritance of truisms and stereotypes, so in our own time we must move on from the reassuring repetition of stale phrases to a new, difficult, but essential confrontation with reality." Commencement Address at Yale University (June 11, 1962).

1718. "[T]he great enemy of the truth is very often not the lie — deliberate, contrived, and dishonest — but the myth — persistent, persuasive, and unrealistic. Too often we hold fast to the clichés of our forebears. We subject all facts to a prefabricated set of interpretations. We enjoy the comfort of opinion without the discomfort of thought." Commencement Address at Yale University (June 11, 1962).

1719. "[L]et us not engage in the wrong argument at the wrong time between the wrong people in the wrong country — while the real problems of our own time grow and multiply, fertilized by our neglect." Commencement Address at Yale University (June 11, 1962).

1720. "Those who cannot stand the heat should get out of the kitchen.... Personally, I think the place to be is in the kitchen...." Excerpts from Address at a Meeting of the American Foreign Service Association (July 2, 1962).

1721. "[T]hose who admit [a] problem, but oppose the proposed solution ... are under some obligation to put forward some proposals of their own." Remarks and Question and Answer Period at the American Bankers Association Symposium on Economic Growth (February 25, 1963).

1722. "[R]ecognizing that the President of the United States and the Government will be responsible if we have economic difficulties, it seems to me that we have some right to present proposals which may lessen those economic difficulties. We have some right, really, to be listened to." Address Before the 19th Washington Conference of the Advertising Council (March 13, 1963).

1723. "Nothing which is important, nothing which is progressive, nothing which is new is ever accepted by those who look back to the past, who wish to stand still, who oppose every program which seeks to improve the lot of our people, but we have to go ahead...." Remarks to Members of the Amalgamated Meat Cutters and Butcher Workmen of North America (May 16, 1963).

1724. "[T]here are always those who predict everything against something new...." Remarks at Muscle Shoals, Alabama, at the 30th Anniversary Celebration of TVA (May 18, 1963).

1725. "[T]hose who live nearest the adversary, those who keep the watch at the gate, are always prouder, more courageous, more alive, than those who live far to the rear." Remarks Upon Arrival at Tegel Airport in Berlin (June 26, 1963).

1726. "George Bernard Shaw, speaking as an Irishman, summed up an approach to life: Other people, he said, 'see things and ... say: Why? ... But I dream things that never were — and I say: why not?' ... The problems of the world cannot possibly be solved by skeptics or cynics, whose horizons are limited by the obvious realities. We need men who can dream of things that never were, and ask why not." Address Before the Irish Parliament in Dublin (June 28, 1963).

1727. "The problems of the world cannot possibly be solved by skeptics or cynics, whose horizons are limited by the obvious realities. We need men who can dream of things that never were, and ask why not." Address Before the Irish Parliament in Dublin [Ireland] (June 28, 1963).

1728. "The great movements in this country's history, the great periods of intellectual and social activity, took place in those periods when we looked long range to the future...." Remarks at the Cheney Stadium in Tacoma, Washington (September 27, 1963).

1729. "These things don't just happen. They are made to happen." Remarks at the Arkansas State Fairgrounds in Little Rock (October 3, 1963).

1730. "[T]he first voyages are the hard ones and they require the perseverance and character. And I think that is a good lesson for all of us today as we attempt new things ... whether it is going into space, going to the bottom of the ocean, building a better country here, building a more prosperous country. The first voyage through our history has always been the most difficult." Remarks at the White House Columbus Day Ceremony (October 12, 1963).

1731. "I know few significant questions of public policy which can safely be confided to computers. In the end, the hard decisions inescapably involve imponderables of intuition, prudence, and judgment." Address at the Anniversary Convocation of the National Academy of Sciences (October 22, 1963).

POLITICS

General

1732. "Local victories do not make a national victory, even when added together.... [H]istory teaches us that these majorities cannot always be translated into majorities for the national ticket." Remarks of Senator John F. Kennedy, Lake County Women's Club Breakfast Gary, Indiana (February 5, 1960).

1733. "I am opening today my drive for victory in the Wisconsin Presidential Primary. This will be a positive, constructive campaign. Let me make it completely clear right now that I do not intend to attack my Democratic opponent, to review his record, or to engage in any argument or debates with him. I do intend, when his name is mentioned, to speak well of him. I request, moreover, that everyone working on my behalf in this state abide by the same principles." Opening Statement of Senator John F. Kennedy, Wisconsin Presidential Primary, Press Conference, Madison, Wisconsin (February 16, 1960).

1734. "We do not need scholars whose education has been so specialized as to exclude them from participation in current events — men like Lord John Russell, of whom Queen Victoria once remarked that he would be a better man if he knew a third subject — but he was interested in nothing but the Constitution of 1688 and himself. No, what we need are men who can ride easily over broad fields of knowledge — who have had varied experience — men like Thomas Jefferson, whom a contemporary described as 'A gentleman of 32, who could calculate an eclipse, survey an estate, tie an artery, plan an edifice, try a cause, break a horse, dance a minuet, and play the violin.'" Remarks of Senator John F. Kennedy, Convocation of Marshall County Junior and Senior High School, Plymouth, Indiana (April 8, 1960).

1735. "A good politician, I am told, should follow three basic principles: glorify the past — avoid the present — and talk endlessly about the future...." Remarks of Senator John F. Kennedy, Phoenix, Arizona (April 9, 1960).

1736. "I think the American people expect more from us [politicians] than cries of indignation and attack. The times are too grave, the challenge too urgent, and the stakes too high — to permit the customary passions of political debate. We are not here to curse the darkness, but to light the candle that can guide us through that darkness to a safe and sane future." Address of Senator John F. Kennedy Accepting the Democratic Party Nomination for the Presidency of the United States — Memorial Coliseum, Los Angeles (July 15, 1960).

1737. "The ... great trouble with American politics today, I think, is that we talk in slogans too often and symbols and we fight old battles." Remarks of Senator John F. Kennedy, Corn Palace, Mitchell, South Dakota (September 22, 1960).

1738. "I want to express my appreciation to all of you for your kindness and generosity to the Democratic Party and its candidates. I am deeply touched — not as deeply touched as you have been by coming to this dinner, but nevertheless it is a sentimental occasion. I wish there were some other way to have a party run, but there is no substitute than to call on our friends." Remarks of Senator John F. Kennedy, Hotel Utah, Salt Lake City, Utah (September 23, 1960).

1739. "I suppose campaigns are really like parades; the music and a lot of confetti and dust and then the candidates pass and move on to another State." Remarks of Senator John F. Kennedy, Hotel Utah, Salt Lake City, Utah (September 23, 1960).

1740. "It always warms the hearts of the Democrats to see contributors gathered together in one room on an occasion such as this. I wish there were some other way to run a campaign, but this is what makes the mare go...." Remarks of Senator John F. Kennedy, "Breakfast with Kennedy," Lawrence Hotel, Erie, Pennsylvania (September 28, 1960).

1741. "This week I had the opportunity to debate with Mr. Nixon. I feel that I should reveal that I had a great advantage in that debate, and I am not referring to anyone's makeup man. The advantage that I had was that Mr. Nixon had just debated with Khrushchev, and I had debated with Hubert Humphrey, and that gave me an edge. That is much tougher." Remarks of Senator John F. Kennedy, Bean Feed, Minneapolis, Minnesota (October 1, 1960).

1742. "A political campaign is an important time because it gives the American people an opportunity to make a judgment as to which course of action they want to follow, which leadership, which viewpoint, which political philosophy, and it is also an important time for political parties, because it does give the political party an opportunity not merely to live off its past successes, but also consider where it is going in the future, what contribution it can make. That responsibility falls particularly heavily on a minority party, a party out of power, because it is its function under our system to present alternatives, to suggest better ways of accomplishing the goals which all America seeks...." Remarks of Senator John F. Kennedy, Howard University, Washington, D.C. (October 7, 1960).

1743. "I believe that this race [of 1960] is between the concerned and the comfortable, between those who sit still and those who want to pick themselves up and push forward.... I believe the choice is between those who wish to stand still and those who wish to move, between those who believe in progress and those who look to the past." Remarks of Senator John F. Kennedy, ILGWU [International Ladies' Garment Workers' Union] Rally, New York, New York (October 27, 1960).

1744. "A ... dilemma, it seems to me, is posed by the occasion of a Presidential address to a business group on business conditions less than four weeks after entering the White House — for it is too early to be claiming credit for the new administration and too late to be blaming the old one. And it would be premature to seek your support in the next election, and inaccurate to express thanks for having had it in the last one." Address at a Luncheon Meeting of the National Industrial Conference Board (February 13, 1961).

1745. "I am all for debates ... because I believe that this is the way the people of this ... country can make a judgment as to the competence and knowledge of those who present themselves for office...." Remarks at a Political Rally in Trenton, New Jersey (November 2, 1961).

1746. "[T]here are not so many differences between politics and football. Some Republicans have been unkind enough to suggest that my election, which was somewhat close, was somewhat similar to the Notre Dame-Syracuse game. But I'm like Notre Dame, we just take it as it comes and we're not giving it back." Address in New York City at the National Football Foundation and Hall of Fame Banquet (December 5, 1961).

1747. "Politics is an astonishing profession — it has permitted me to go from being an obscure lieutenant ... without any technical competence whatsoever [to become President]; and it's also enabled me to go from being an obscure member of the junior varsity at Harvard to being an honorary member of the Football Hall of Fame." Address in New York City at the National Football Foundation and Hall of Fame Banquet (December 5, 1961).

1748. "Whatever other qualifications I may have had when I became President, one of them at least was that I knew Wisconsin better than any other President of the United States. That is an unchallengeable statement. My foot-tracks are in every house in this State." Address in Milwaukee, Jefferson-Jackson Dinner (May 12, 1962).

1749. "I can tell you that there is no city in the United States where a Democrat gets a warmer welcome and less votes than in Columbus, Ohio!" Remarks in Response to New York's Birthday Salute to the President (May 19, 1962).

1750. "[T]his is an off-year, and therefore you must wonder why you have been so abused and the money taken in such large quantities. Let me say it very briefly, and that is that there is no such thing as an off-year." Remarks in Response to New York's Birthday Salute to the President (May 19, 1962).

1751. "I also want to commend this idea of the $250 dinner. This is like that story of the award of prizes by the Moscow Cultural Center, the first prize being one week in Kiev and the second prize being two weeks. For $100 you get speeches; for $250 you don't get any speeches. You can't get bargains like that anymore!" Remarks at a Dinner Honoring Matthew McCloskey Upon His Appointment as Ambassador to Ireland (June 9, 1962).

1752. "I am ... the grandson of a mayor of my native city of Boston, on one side, and the grandson, on the other, of a member of the City Council; and I am quite aware, having grown up with them, that I have, in a sense, let them and my family down by not holding a similar honor in my own lifetime." Remarks at a Civic Ceremony at the Municipal Palace, Mexico City (June 29, 1962).

1753. "When I come back to West Virginia, I feel as if I was coming home. This, after all, is the State which sent me out into the world, and you are the people who made me the Democratic candidate for the President of the United States. Sometimes when Senator Humphrey and I get together to discuss the crises which pile up on the President's desk, we may wonder which of us you did the greater favor for. But nevertheless, for better or for worse, I know that if it had not been for Wheeling, and a score of other West Virginia cities and towns, 2½ years ago, I would not be here tonight." Remarks at the Wheeling Stadium, Wheeling, West Virginia (September 27, 1962).

1754. "I don't believe that citizens should pay too much attention to what candidates say in the last 4 weeks of election. I believe the old Emersonian advice that what you are speaks far louder than what you say is the best possible advice in judging a political campaign." Remarks at the State Fairgrounds, Springfield, Illinois (October 19, 1962).

1755. "[P]olitics and art, the life of action and the life of thought, the world of events, and the world of imagination, are one...." Remarks at the National Gallery of Art Upon Opening the Mona Lisa Exhibition (January 8, 1963).

1756. "After he [Abraham Lincoln] was elected President, someone said, 'What are you going to do with your enemies, Mr. President?' Lincoln said, 'I am going to destroy them. I am going to make them my friends.'" Toasts of the President and Prime Minister Fanfani [of Italy] (January 16, 1963).

1757. "[P]olitics is a most rewarding profession ... also ... for women. Except perhaps in the field of teaching, medicine, and one or two other professions, I can't think of any occupation [supporting a husband who is a member of Congress] which gives a woman a greater chance to play a more useful role in every way than in the profession of politics. To support your husbands..., to have them fulfill their lives in national service, to meet your responsibilities to them, to your children, to your country — I think this is really why there are so many happy women who living under some difficulties yet carry on their work." Remarks at a Breakfast Given by the Wives of Senators and Representatives (May 2, 1963).

1758. "I don't know whether it is regulations or not, but in any case it is going to be, because we will certainly fly this [West Virginia] flag over the White House on the June centennial [of West Virginia] day or any other day that West Virginia wants it flown. And after that we will frame this flag and put it in the White House in my office, because there is no State whose flag I would rather have." Remarks to Participants in the West Virginia Centennial Celebration (May 20, 1963).

1759. "I would not be where I now am [the President], I would not have some of the responsibilities which I now bear, if it had not been for the people of West Virginia." Remarks at the State Centennial Celebration in Charleston, West Virginia (June 20, 1963).

Political Parties

GENERAL

1760. "[N]o President, it seems to me, can escape politics. He has not only been chosen by the Nation — he has been chosen by his party. And if he insists that he is 'President of all the people' and should, therefore, offend none of them — if he blurs the issues and differences between the parties — if he neglects the party machinery and avoids his party's leadership — then he has not only weakened the political party as an instrument of the democratic process — he has dealt a blow to the democratic process itself." Address by Senator John F. Kennedy, "The Presidency in 1960," (January 14, 1960).

1761. "[N]ational conventions are not social gatherings. Political parties are not private clubs.

They are at the heart of the democratic process — they are the instrument of the popular will — they are the method, and the best method yet devised, by which the people rule." Remarks of Senator John F. Kennedy, The Dalles, Oregon (May 15, 1960).

1762. "[T]he Democratic Party and the Republican Party are means to an end, not an end in themselves. They are a means of providing gifted men and women for the service of this country in a difficult and dangerous time." Speech by Senator John F. Kennedy, Fair Grounds, Bangor, Maine (September 2, 1960).

1763. "I am not going to make a speech in this rain. The only satisfaction you get is that it is raining on the just and unjust, Republicans and Democrats." Rear Platform Remarks of Senator John F. Kennedy, Madera, California (September 9, 1960).

1764. "Our parties are like two histories, two rivers, which flow back through our history, and you can judge the force, the power, and the direction of those rivers by studying where they rose, where they flow, and the course of those rivers throughout the history of the United States." Speech by John F. Kennedy, IAM [International Association of Machinists] Convention, Kiel Auditorium, St. Louis, Missouri (September 14, 1960).

1765. "Every 4 years, ever since Alf Landon ran as a Republican and got snowed under, the Republican candidates for President run on a plank that says it really doesn't matter which party wins, what matters is which candidate wins. I think it matters which candidate wins, but I think it also matters which party wins. Because the two parties stand for different things in different times." Remarks of Senator John F. Kennedy, County Records Building, New Brunswick, New Jersey (September 15, 1960).

1766. "Of course, the goals of all Americans, since the beginning of this country, has been the same: a better life for our people. But it is a question of the means by which we achieve those goals.... What counts in a country, what counts in a system, what counts in political parties is the means by which you achieve those goals...." Remarks of Senator John F. Kennedy, Armory, Akron, Ohio (September 27, 1960).

1767. "There is some value in brand names. When you buy something at the store, you buy something you know something about.... The party labels tell a story. They tell a story of this country. They tell a story of the division between the Republicans and the Democrats on the great issues of benefit to our people." Remarks of Senator John F. Kennedy, Armory, Akron, Ohio (September 27, 1960).

1768. "I think party labels mean something. The Republicans never would have nominated me, and the Democrats never would have nominated Mr. Nixon." Remarks of Senator John F. Kennedy, Airport Rally, Erie, Pennsylvania (September 27, 1960).

1769. "I think the differences between our two parties are important. Mr. Nixon says party labels don't make any difference. It is the man. I think party labels do mean something because they tell us something about the history of this country. They tell us about where we are going and where we have been." Remarks of Senator John F. Kennedy, Bean Feed, Minneapolis, Minnesota (October 1, 1960).

1770. "Mr. Nixon said ... that parties don't make much difference, what counts is the man. I think what counts is the kind of a man a political party chooses. Mr. Nixon and I were not suddenly discovered after our two conventions. We have not been kept in ice. We are part of a long tradition, both of us, of a political service and political philosophy ... and consistently, on issue after issue, the two parties have taken different positions, because they represent different interests." Remarks of Senator John F. Kennedy, University of Minnesota, Duluth, Minnesota (October 2, 1960).

1771. "The Democratic Party is the only national party.... It is composed of miners and farmers. It is composed of potato growers in Maine. It is composed of fishermen in Washington State. It is composed of ranchers in Texas and peanut farmers in Georgia. It is composed of all the interests in the United States and, therefore, speaks for the people. The base of the Republican Party is far narrower.... If parties don't tell us something about the political philosophy of a man, then it means that our parties have outrun their usefulness.... But they do tell us something. They do give us a point of view." Remarks of Senator John

F. Kennedy, University of Minnesota, Duluth, Minnesota (October 2, 1960).

1772. "[Political] parties tell something.... What is past is prologue and the record of our two parties is written for the future as it has been for the past." Speech by Senator John F. Kennedy, Chase Hotel, St. Louis, Missouri (October 2, 1960).

1773. "[I]t is the function of the opposition, if it is going to meet its responsibility as a party, to try to suggest alternative courses of action." Remarks of Senator John F. Kennedy, Albion, Michigan (October 14, 1960).

1774. "[A]t different times in the history of our country a majority of the American people have put their confidence in one party, and then on other occasions they put their confidence in another. And I think the reason they choose one party at one time and another party at another is because history and events and the mood of history swings like a pendulum back and forth." Remarks of Senator John F. Kennedy, Kitanning, Pennsylvania (October 15, 1960).

1775. "The party is not an end in itself; it is a means to an end." Remarks at a Meeting of the Democratic National Committee (January 21, 1961).

1776. "The party is the means by which programs can be put into action — the means by which people of talent can come to the service of the country. And in this great free society of ours, both of our parties — the Republican and the Democratic Parties — serve the interests of the people." Remarks at a Meeting of the Democratic National Committee (January 21, 1961).

1777. "The President is the Commander-in-Chief and he is the head of state, and he has responsibilities as a legislative leader. But one of these responsibilities — and I think all of our Presidents ... in both of our political parties have recognized it — is also to be head of a political party, because a political party, as Woodrow Wilson so often pointed out, is the means by which the people are served, the means by which those programs of benefit to our country are written into the statutes." Remarks at a Political Rally in Trenton, New Jersey (November 2, 1961).

1778. "[A] political party is ... a means of making progress for the American people.... What use is either one of the two great political parties if they really represent, to those who are active in them, only a means of expression and exercise? They are important. They are functional. They will endure only as they contribute to the well-being of the people of this country." Remarks at the Young Democrats Convention, Miami, Florida (December 7, 1961).

1779. "A political party is like anything else in life; it is the survival of the fittest, and the fittest in American life today are those who look realistically at the challenges and attempt to move this country forward." Remarks at the Young Democrats Convention, Miami, Florida (December 7, 1961).

1780. "A party is not merely an organization or a social structure, it is a means of implementing action." Remarks to Participants in the Campaign Conference for Democratic Women (May 22, 1962).

1781. "The success of any political party is important only as it helps advance the interests of our country...." Remarks by Telephone to the Midwestern Democratic Conference at French Lick, Indiana (August 24, 1962).

1782. "I do not intend to conceal the differences between our two parties.... If the Democratic Party is charged with disturbing the status quo, with stirring up the great interests of this country, and with daring to try something new, I plead 'guilty.' And if the Republican Party is charged with wanting to return to the past, with opposing nearly every constructive measure we have put forward, then they must plead 'guilty.'" Remarks in Harrisburg at a Democratic State Finance Committee Dinner (September 20, 1962).

1783. "They [the Republicans] have made the word 'no' a political philosophy. We made the word 'yes,' since the days of Franklin Roosevelt, our political philosophy." Remarks at the Municipal Mall in Flint, Michigan (October 6, 1972).

1784. "I believe the Democratic Party, on the whole, has stood for progress, and I believe that the record indicates that the Republican Party as a whole has stood against it." Remarks at the Airport in Muskegon, Michigan (October 6, 1962).

1785. "All the political cheers, all the political speeches, don't mean anything unless in the final analysis a party functions. What use is the success of any political party, Woodrow Wilson said, unless it serves a great national purpose." Remarks in Baltimore at the Fifth Regiment Armory (October 10, 1962).

1786. "[O]ur Founding Fathers did not realize that the basic fact which has made our system work was outside the [Constitution]. And that was the development political parties in this country so that the American people would have the means of placing responsibility on one group, that group would have a chance to carry out its program, and the American people would have an opportunity to indicate their dissatisfaction by going to an alternative." Remarks to Members of National and State Democratic Committees (January 18, 1963).

1787. "[T]he purpose of any political party is to serve a great cause and I think the cause [now] ... is to see if domestically we can develop and manage our economic society so that we do not move from recession to recession with continuing and ever-increasing unemployment...." Remarks to a Group of Young Democrats (April 26, 1963).

1788. "[T]here are two parties, and ... there is some good in both of them...." Remarks to the Delegates of Girls Nation (August 2, 1963).

1789. "[I]n my experience Monsignors and Bishops are all Republicans while Sisters are all Democrats!" Remarks in New York City at the National Convention of the Catholic Youth Organization (November 15, 1963).

DEMOCRATS

1790. "We in the Democratic Party are not spenders but investors — and we are willing to show our faith in America by investing in her future." Remarks of Senator John F. Kennedy, Western Conference, Albuquerque, New Mexico (February 7, 1960).

1791. "Thomas Jefferson that there are always, in effect, 'two parties: Those who fear and distrust the people, and wish to (take) all power from them — (and) those who identify themselves with the people, have confidence in them, and consider them as the most honest and safe ... depositary of the public interest.' We Democrats have traditionally been the second party — the party which identifies itself with the people — the party which realizes that only those candidates with faith and confidence in the people and their wisdom can count on receiving that faith and confidence at the polls...." Remarks of Senator John F. Kennedy, Indiana (April 29, 1960).

1792. "[The Democrat Party] ... is neither the party of war nor the party of appeasement — [its] only war is against injustice, hunger and disease — and in that war there can be no appeasement." Remarks of Senator John F. Kennedy, Democratic National Committee Dinner, Los Angeles, California (July 10, 1960).

1793. "Eleanor Roosevelt is a true teacher. Her very life teaches a love of truth and duty and courage. The wide world is her neighborhood. All its people are her daily concern. She is frank; she is outspoken; she is forthright — and I know she always will be." Speech by Senator John F. Kennedy, Memorial Program, 25th Anniversary of Signing Social Security Act, Hyde Park, New York (August 14, 1960).

1794. "Standing on this quiet lawn [at Hyde Park] — this spacious and soothing scene — it is difficult to recall the furious battles which were fought by the man [Franklin Roosevelt] who lies here in honored glory — the conflicts which he waged; the victories which he won. Yet we who lived while he governed can, here at Hyde Park, still hear the echoes of those heroic struggles; the struggle to rescue America from poverty and economic collapse, the struggle to build a new America where all could live in dignity, the struggle to secure freedom against the ominous armed advance of tyranny and oppression, and, the last, the most arduous, the unending struggle ... to build a world of free and peaceful nations. If these battles were nobly fought, if the America of Franklin Roosevelt had a rendezvous with destiny, it met that rendezvous only because it was guided to its destination by a great leader of men." Speech by Senator John F. Kennedy, Memorial Program, 25th Anniversary of Signing Social Security Act, Hyde Park, New York (August 14, 1960).

1795. "As we enter the new decade of the sixties, America faces challenges greater than any which it has faced before. This is no time for complacency. This is no time to abandon the drive and the optimism and the imaginative creativity which has characterized this country since its birth. This is no time for timidity or doubt. This is a time for boldness and energy. This is a time for stouthearted men who can turn dreams into reality. This is a time when America once again needs the leadership of the Democratic Party, which has led this country successfully through every major challenge it has faced in this century." Remarks Via Telephone to the New York State AFL-CIO (August 30, 1960).

1796. "I regard our function as the minority party, as members of the Democratic Party, to merely offer the American people alternatives which will increase their strength, their prosperity, and their security. We do not travel in the United States and criticize present action because we feel depressed about the future of our country. We travel the United States in this campaign because it is our responsibility to present to the American people alternative courses of action which will make this a stronger and a better place in which to live." Speech by Senator John F. Kennedy, High School Auditorium, Pocatello, Idaho (September 6, 1960).

1797. "[T]he record of the Democratic Party, and its assurances for the future, is written in its record of the past: In the New Freedom of Woodrow Wilson, in the New Deal of Franklin Roosevelt, in the Fair Deal of Harry Truman." Rear Platform Remarks, Chico, California (September 8, 1960).

1798. "This country needs the Democratic Party, for so long as there is one child without a decent education, so long as there is one family without a decent home, so long as there is one able-bodied citizen who wants to work and can't find it, so long as there is one retired American who lives out his life without dignity or hope, so long will we need the Democratic Party." Speech by Senator John F. Kennedy, Civic Auditorium, Oakland, California (September 8, 1960).

1799. "I think that there is one basic issue in this [1960] campaign. We can see it in this valley, we can see it in this country, and we can see it around the world. That is the long range difference between our two political parties, between a party that believes that things are as good as they can be [the Republicans], and a party [the Democrats] that thinks we can do better." Remarks of Senator John F. Kennedy, Airport, Bakersfield, California (September 9, 1960).

1800. "The Democratic Party is not satisfied with things as they are now, not because we don't feel that this is a great country, but because we feel it can be a greater country. This is a great country." Rear Platform Remarks of Senator John F. Kennedy, Merced, California (September 9, 1960).

1801. "The Democratic Party belongs to all the people. It has spoken for the people in the great moments of crisis which our country has faced, Wilson, Roosevelt, and Truman, and spoken on behalf of the men and women ... of this country. I ask you to join us now [in the 1960 presidential election], to join in establishing once again the kind of progressive administration which has served this country so well in the past." Remarks of Senator John F. Kennedy, Cortez Hotel Plaza, El Paso, Texas (September 12, 1960).

1802. "As long as there are millions of Americans who live in substandard housing, as long as there are millions of our older citizens who wait out their lives with an income of less than $20 a week, without hope of good housing or medical care in their old age, as long as there are children in this country who go to school on a part-time basis, with teachers inadequately compensated, as long as there is unfinished business in this country, so long is their need for the Democratic Party, and there is need for the Democratic Party today." Remarks of Senator John F. Kennedy, Armory, Jersey City, New Jersey (September 15, 1960).

1803. "[W]e [Democrats] are a national party, we are not a sectional party. We have farmers from Maine and farmers from North Carolina and textile workers in Massachusetts and textile workers in North Carolina, and peach growers in California, and salmon fishermen in Washington and ranchers in Texas. We are a party of all interests, and therefore we belong to the people and our success has been in the past that we have associated ourselves with progressive programs on behalf of our country...." Speech by Senator John F. Kennedy, Coliseum, Charlotte, North Carolina (September 17, 1960).

1804. "If you are a standpatter, you don't join the Democratic Party; you go over to the Republican Party." Remarks of Senator John F. Kennedy, Sioux City, Iowa (September 22, 1960).

1805. "[A]s long as there are children denied a decent education, as long as there are old people who live out their lives without hope, as long as there are men and women who want to work and can't find a job, as long as there are 15 million American homes which ... are substandard, as long as our rivers are polluted, as long as we waste our national resources, as long as the prestige and power of the United States is not moving forward, so long is there need for the Democratic Party...." Remarks of Senator John F. Kennedy, Girard, Ohio (October 9, 1960).

1806. "We are the heirs of Jefferson. We could not conserve and look backward if we tried. We must look forward. The Democratic Party is the party of progress, and I cannot believe, in 1960, when the world is in revolution, when all is movement, that ... we are going to say it is good enough what we are doing, there are no challenges left, no unfinished business. It is merely a question of administration. I think it is a question of force and vision and foresight and vitality and energy...." Speech by Senator John F. Kennedy, Syria Mosque, Pittsburgh, Pennsylvania (October 10, 1960).

1807. "Franklin Roosevelt was the champion of little children and the champion of the aged. He understood the needs of the farmer and the worker, the big city and the small town. His heart went out to those who were handicapped as he had been, and to those who were poor as he had never been. The basic force in all this was not so much his party or his intellect — it was his spirit — a spirit he breathed into our National Government — a spirit he breathed into our party — a spirit which did not die when he died, but must be carried on by those of us who invoke his name today." Speech by Senator John F. Kennedy, the Little White House, Warm Springs, Georgia (October 10, 1960)."

1808. "I do not know whether to regard with alarm or indignation the common assumption of an inevitable conflict between the business community and the Democratic Party. That is one of the great political myths of our time, carefully fostered.... Just as the Democratic Party has benefited from the contributions of business leaders ... so has the business community benefited from the contributions of the Democratic Party." Speech by Senator John F. Kennedy, Associated Business Publications Conference, Biltmore Hotel, New York, New York (October 12, 1960).

1809. "I believe the spirit which motivates the Democratic Party is the same spirit of progress which motivated it when Thomas Jefferson made the Louisiana Purchase." Speech of John F. Kennedy, Boys' Gymnasium, Montgomery-Blair High School, Silver Spring, Maryland (October 16, 1960).

1810. "Artemus Ward from Massachusetts, my own State, 50 years ago, said, 'I am not a politician and my other habits are good, also.' This time we are politicians. We are politicians in the sense that we believe political action through one of the political parties, in our case the Democratic Party, is the best means of achieving service for our country." Remarks of Senator John F. Kennedy, Jefferson — Jackson Day Brunch, Middletown, Ohio (October 16, 1960).

1811. "[Mr. Nixon] says, 'Party does not mean anything. What counts is the man.' ... But I am a Democrat. I am a Democrat. The work of my party is not so bad that I have to deny it every 4 years." Speech by Senator John F. Kennedy, Hemming Park, Jacksonville, Florida (October 18, 1960).

1812. "I don't say that parties are an end in themselves, and I don't say that anyone should select a man merely because he has a party label. But I believe in this difficult and dangerous time that the parties do mean something." Speech by Senator John F. Kennedy, Hemming Park, Jacksonville, Florida (October 18, 1960).

1813. "On all the great issues of the last 25 years, the issues of progress, of mutual security, of national preparedness, of national strength, the development of our resources, the education of our children, jobs for men and women of working age, security for our older citizens, the Republican Party and the Democratic Party have differed, and we [the Democrats] have come down on side of progress. The Republican Party has opposed every action ... for the benefit of our people." Remarks of Senator John F. Kennedy, Penn Fruit Shopping Center, Philadelphia, Pennsylvania (October 31, 1960).

1814. "[T]he success of any President of the United States who has the distinction of being a Democrat is due to the fact that he is supported by a strong, democratic, progressive party." Remarks at the Democratic National Committee Dinner in Honor of the President's 44th Birthday (May 27, 1961).

1815. "The Democratic Party is the oldest political party in the world, and the reason it is old is because ... the Democratic Party has been realistic enough to recognize the kind of problems which are coming ... and has had programs and policies to meet them. The day that ... the Democratic Party is not prepared to come forward with those programs and policies, regardless of our old memories and our old leaders, we will fade as the Whig Party faded and made way for the Republican Party." Remarks in Miami at the Young Democrats Convention (December 7, 1961).

1816. "We cannot permit this country to stand still, and I believe it is incumbent upon all of us who participate in political activity, not as an end in itself but as a means to an end, I believe that we should associate ourselves with the great traditions of our [Democrat] party." Address in Milwaukee at the Jefferson—Jackson Dinner (May 12, 1962).

1817. "I don't think our [Democrat] party ... has ever been led by men who have promised a soft and easy existence. What they have promised, and their names and their slogans distinguish them—Wilson and Roosevelt and Truman—that the word 'American,' the title 'citizen of the United States,' will be an honorable one, and one marked by respect and dignity. And it is to that end that the New Frontier is committed." Address in Milwaukee at the Jefferson-Jackson Dinner (May 12, 1962).

1818. "[T]he Democratic Party has demonstrated ... that is a party of progress and of change, that it is the party dedicated to serve the needs of our people and to keep America forever abreast of a forever changing world." Remarks by Telephone to a Dinner Meeting of the Ohio State Democratic Convention in Columbus (September 21, 1962).

1819. "[N]ot everyone, even in America, welcomes change. Throughout our entire history there have always been people, and they are excellent people, who preferred to hold things as they were, who wanted to go back to some golden age which never was, and if change is inevitable, they want as little of it as possible. I do not agree. This has never been the view of the Democratic Party." Remarks at the Wheeling Stadium, Wheeling, West Virginia (September 27, 1962).

1820. "We [Democrats] believe that if men have the talent to invent new machines that put men out of work, they have the talent to put those men back to work...." Remarks at the Wheeling Stadium, Wheeling, West Virginia. (September 27, 1962).

1821. "[T]here is no greater responsibility in that sense [placing responsibility on one group] that a President has ... than he has as a leader of a political party, and especially this [Democrat] political party, the oldest in the world, the oldest in our country's history." Remarks to Members of National and State Democratic Committees (January 18, 1963).

1822. "A party is of no use unless it fulfills some national purpose. I said ... in the State of the Union that we were not on top of the hill, but on the side of the hill. I don't think in this administration or in our generation or time will this country be at the top of the hill, but some day it will be, and I hope when it is that they will think that we [the Democrat Party] have done our part." Remarks at the Second Inaugural Anniversary Salute (January 18, 1963).

1823. "[T]he two political parties in our history have always been divided, as Emerson said, into the party of hope and into the party of memory. From the time of Jefferson, I think we [Democrats] have been the party of hope. And therefore it is natural that artists, men and women who work in the theater and all the other related arts, should find themselves most at home in the party of hope." Remarks at the New York Birthday Salute to the President (May 23, 1963).

1824. "[I] know what the Republican Party is against and I know what the Democratic Party is for. And they [the Democrats] are for the same things that made this ... country of ours, and that means the welfare of our people, as it did in the days of Franklin Roosevelt and as it does at is to move forward and build and recognize that change means progress and progress in 1963." Remarks Upon Arrival at El Paso International Airport (June 5, 1963).

1825. "[T]he question, really, which both political parties must constantly face: what purpose do we serve, what good are we doing the Nation, of all the problems that face us at home and abroad, how is our party, whether we are Democrats or Republicans, how are we measuring up, what is our program, what are the needs of the country and what are we doing about them? [T]he Democratic Party has answered that question with remarkable success in every generation, and the result has been that what was regarded as controversial and dangerous and new from the time of Thomas Jefferson ... we now almost take for granted." Remarks in Hollywood at a Breakfast with Democratic State Committeewomen of California (June 8, 1963).

1826. "When you [party activists] work for a political party in the 1960s, and particularly when you work for the Democratic Party, you are not engaging in a social activity. This is not a means of meeting together and this is not a club. This is an organization, an institution, a system for bringing our political policy, our views on the great problems we face at home and abroad. And [after 2½ years as President] ... if I ever had any doubts about which party stands for progress ... I don't have it today. It is the party of which we are a member — the Democratic Party." Remarks in Hollywood at a Breakfast with Democratic State Committeewomen of California (June 8, 1963).

REPUBLICANS

1827. "The Republican Party is not a national party. It does not represent all sections, all interest groups, all voters. And that is why — historically and inevitably — the forces of inertia and reaction in the Republican Party oppose any powerful voice in the White House, Republican or Democratic, that tries to speak for the nation as a whole." Remarks of Senator John F. Kennedy, Spokane, Washington (May 27, 1960).

1828. "All over the world, particularly in the newer nations, young men are coming to power — men who are not bound by the traditions of the past — men who are not blinded by the old fears and hates and rivalries — young men who can cast off the old slogans and delusions and suspicions. The Republican nominee-to-be [Richard Nixon], of course, is also a young man. But his ... party is the party of the past. His speeches are generalities from Poor Richard's Almanac. Their platform, made up of left-over Democratic planks, has the courage of our old convictions. Their pledge is a pledge to the status quo — and today there can be no status quo." Address of Senator John F. Kennedy Accepting the Democratic Party Nomination for the Presidency of the United States, Memorial Coliseum, Los Angeles, California (July 15, 1960).

1829. "My chief disagreement with the Republican Party and its leadership is not because I criticize the country — it is because I think they have lost faith in the United States. They are the ones who don't think we can do better. We say we can do better because we believe that this country has unlimited resources, because we believe it has unlimited energy, and because we believe it has an unlimited potential. We don't criticize the United States because we think there is something wrong with the United States. We say we can do better. The Republicans say, 'This is as good as we can do.' That is the difference between us." Rear Platform Remarks of Senator John F. Kennedy, Marysville, California (September 8, 1960).

1830. "They [the Republicans] have opposed, they have stood against progress. I think their time is coming to an end. [T]he Republican Party that we oppose is the same old party. There is no new Republican Party. There is the same old party, stretching back into history from the days of McKinley, through Coolidge and Harding and all the rest...." Speech by Senator John F. Kennedy, Civic Auditorium, Oakland, California (September 8, 1960).

1831. "[T]he record of the Republican Party is written on the bills that never become law, on the things we failed to do." Rear Platform Remarks of Senator John F. Kennedy, Richmond, California (September 8, 1960).

1832. "Our argument with the Republicans is not because we do not know that they share a common goal for America — they do — but our argument with them is that they don't know how to do it. We do." Rear Platform Remarks of Senator John F. Kennedy, Stockton, California (September 9, 1960).

1833. "There is no new Republican Party, no old Republican Party. There is only the same Republican Party which for a half century has opposed every major piece of social legislation...." Speech by Senator John F. Kennedy, IAM [International Association of Machinists] Convention, Kiel Auditorium, St. Louis, Missouri (September 14, 1960).

1834. "I cannot think, stretching back to the end of the administration of Theodore Roosevelt, I cannot think of one single act, major act, on behalf of the people of this country that came out of the Republican Party." Remarks of Senator John F. Kennedy, Steer Roast, Euclid Beach Park, Cleveland, Ohio (September 25, 1960).

1835. "I am not impressed by this leap-year progressivism which comes upon the Republican Party every 4 years, when they support and sustain programs which they fight against year after year in the Congress." Speech by Senator John F. Kennedy, Auditorium [Coliseum], Indianapolis, Indiana (October 4, 1960).

1836. "[The 1960 election] is between those [the Republicans] whose imagination is limited, it is between those who represent a party which is circumscribed in action by its very nature, it is between those who rely for advice for cabinet appointments, for diplomatic appointments, on those who have a narrow concept of our role in the world, a limited sense of history, a limited sense of the future, of failure to recognize that we live in the most changing and turbulent times in the history of the world." Remarks of Senator John F. Kennedy, Northland Shopping Center, Jennings, Missouri (October 22, 1960).

1837. "The elephant never forgets but he never learns." Remarks of Senator John F. Kennedy, Railroad Station Plaza, Bridgeport, Connecticut (November 6, 1960).

1838. "Anyone who tries to do something new arouses opposition ... [and] the Republicans continue to regard opposition as a political philosophy ... [to] remain the 'no' party...." Remarks by Telephone to a Dinner Meeting of the Ohio State Democratic Convention in Columbus (September 21, 1962).

1839. "Now, I don't believe that any ... political party is meeting its responsibilities when it says ... in the most difficult period in our country's history ... as the opposition party, 'It is not our responsibility to propose solutions, but to oppose them.'" Remarks at the Hippodrome Arena in St. Paul, Minnesota (October 6, 1962).

1840. "They [Republicans] are against anything new because it's new, anything good because it's progressive...." Remarks on the New Haven Green (October 17, 1962).

Richard M. Nixon

1841. "The Republican Party has not asked the American people for their views on who their candidate should be. Their heir to the throne — the lone surviving heir — Mr. Nixon — has been carefully pre-selected by his party's entrenched interests — pre-digested for the American people's consumption — and pre-packaged for sale to the American voter." Remarks of Senator John F. Kennedy, Indiana (April 29, 1960).

1842. "The Republican nominee-to-be [Richard Nixon], of course, is also a young man. But his approach is as old as McKinley. His party is the party of the past. His speeches are generalities from Poor Richard's Almanac." Address of Senator John F. Kennedy Accepting the Democratic Party Nomination for the Presidency of the United States, Memorial Coliseum, Los Angeles, California (July 15, 1960).

1843. "The Republicans like to say, over and over again, that the big issue in this campaign is executive experience. Their candidate [Richard Nixon], they say, has experience in the executive branch — he has participated in its decisions — he has shared in its responsibilities — he has been educated in its programs. I will discuss Mr. Nixon's experience in other fields on other occasions. But when it comes to agriculture, I can only say that disaster has been his experience...." Remarks of Senator John F. Kennedy, Midwest farm Conference, Des Moines, Iowa (August 21, 1960).

1844. "Never before has this country experienced such arrogant treatment at the hands of its enemy. Never before have we experienced a more critical decline in our prestige ... never before has the grip of communism sunk so deeply into previously friendly countries. Mr. Nixon is experienced in policies of weakness, retreat, and defeat." Speech by Senator John F. Kennedy, Democrat Rally, George Washington High School Stadium, Alexandria, Virginia (August 24, 1960).

1845. "The Republican orators are fond of saying that experience in foreign policy is the greatest issue in this campaign. I agree. But the issue is not merely the experience of the candidates. It is the experience which the entire Nation has gone through in the last 8 years, and what an experience it has been. Never before has this country experienced such arrogant treatment at the hands of its enemy. Never before have we experienced a more critical decline in our prestige, driving our friends to neutralism, and neutrals to our right of hostility, never before has the grip of communism sunk so deeply into previously friendly countries. Mr. Nixon is experienced in policies of weakness, retreat, and defeat." Speech by Senator John F. Kennedy, Democratic Rally, George Washington High School Stadium, Alexandria, Virginia (August 24, 1960).

1846. "My argument with Mr. Nixon ... is that [he] do[es] not have sufficient vision, sufficient vigor, sufficient imagination, sufficient foresight to see that the unfinished business before us calls for us not merely to be first today, not merely to be strong enough today, but to be strong enough in 1970, in 1980." Remarks at Lorain Stadium, Lorain, Ohio (September 27, 1960).

1847. "I have the greatest confidence in the United States. Mr. Nixon says I downgrade this country. I do not downgrade it. [I] have the greatest confidence in it. What I downgrade is its leadership. I downgrade the prospect of Mr. Nixon leading the United States in the most difficult and somber time in the life of our country." Speech by Senator John F. Kennedy, Auditorium (Coliseum), Indianapolis, Indiana (October 4, 1960).

1848. "Everyone talks about civil rights now, but the Republican candidate [Richard Nixon] is the only one who talks about rights and talks about human rights in the North and States rights in the South, the only one who has a Negro traveling with him in the North but not in the South, the only one who sent Senator Scott of Pennsylvania to represent him in the North instead of Barry Goldwater who represents him in the South." Remarks of Senator John F. Kennedy, Hotel Theresa, New York, New York (October 12, 1960).

1849. "[I] must confess that I am finding greater difficulty running against Mr. Nixon than I had imagined. The reason is not because he is such a magnificent debater and it is not because he is using new lighting, but because his positions change so fast that it is very difficult to know where he stands and, therefore, it is very difficult to know what policy he is advocating for our country in the future." Remarks of Senator John F. Kennedy, New Castle County Airport, Wilmington, Delaware (October 16, 1960).

1850. "Mr. Nixon's judgment, I believe, is indicated by his willingness in this time of hazard to go to the American people with a campaign promise, the campaign statement, that our prestige has never been higher, that of the Communists has never been lower, that everything that must be done is being done, and just leave it to him, and we will be secure." Speech by Senator John F. Kennedy, Hillsborough County Courthouse, Tampa, Florida (October 18, 1960).

1851. "Mr. Nixon, like the rest of us, has had his troubles in this campaign. At one point even the Wall Street Journal was criticizing his tactics. That is like the *Observatore Romano* criticizing the Pope." Speech by Senator John F. Kennedy, Al Smith Memorial Dinner, Waldorf-Astoria Hotel, New York, New York (October 19, 1960).

1852. "One of the inspiring notes that was struck in the last debate was struck by the Vice President in his very moving warning to the children of the Nation and the candidates against the use of profanity by Presidents and ex–Presidents when they are on the stump. And I know after 14 years in the Congress with the Vice President [Richard Nixon] that he was very sincere in his views about the use of profanity. But I am told that a prominent Republican said to him yesterday in Jacksonville, Fla., 'Mr. Vice President, that was a damn fine speech.' And the Vice President said, 'I appreciate the compliment but not the language.' And the Republican went on, 'Yes, sir, I liked it so much that I contributed a thousand dollars to your campaign. And Mr. Nixon replied, 'The hell you say.'" Speech by Senator John F. Kennedy, Al Smith Memorial Dinner, Waldorf-Astoria Hotel, New York, New York (October 19, 1960).

1853. "I never know whether I am running against the Republican Mr. Nixon who goes to Arizona and who says that he stands as a Republican from top to bottom, or the Mr. Nixon who goes to Jacksonville, Fla., and says that party labels don't mean anything, what counts is the man, or the man who goes to New York it and strikes a blow for civil rights, or the man who goes to Virginia and informs them that he knows their problems as he went to school in the South once himself." Speech by Senator John F. Kennedy, Fieldhouse, University of Wisconsin, Madison, Wisconsin (October 23, 1960).

1854. "[M]r. Nixon ... continues to look behind him, he continues to look in the past, he continues to make arguments which have little relevancy with the facts. He continues to be further and further removed from reality in discussing the problems of the United States and the problems we face in the world." Speech by Senator John F. Kennedy, Scranton, Pennsylvania (October 28, 1960).

1855. "[When] Martin Luther King [was] in jail Mr. Nixon's headquarters issued a statement 'No comment.' If that is what you want, you can have him." Remarks of Senator John F. Kennedy, Rosen Apartments, Philadelphia, Pennsylvania (October 31, 1960).

1856. "A contemporary once said of Jefferson that he was a young man of 32 who could plot an eclipse, survey a field, plan an edifice, break a horse, play a violin, and dance a minuet. What on earth has he got in common with Richard Milhous Nixon?" Remarks at Granby High School Athletic Field, Norfolk, Virginia (November 4, 1960).

1857. "You have seen these elephants in the circus that go around the ring, and they grab the tail of the elephant in front, and that is what Nixon is doing. That was all right in 1952 and 1956 but there is no elephant out in front now." Remarks of Senator John F. Kennedy, Street Rally, Waterbury, Connecticut (November 6, 1960).

PRESIDENCY

1858. "[T]he White House is not only the center of political leadership. It must be the center of moral leadership — a 'bully pulpit,' as Theodore Roosevelt described it. For only the President represents the national interest. And upon him alone converge all the needs and aspirations of all parts of the country, all departments of the Government, all nations of the world." Address by Senator John F. Kennedy, "The Presidency in 1960," National Press Club, Washington, D.C. (January 14, 1960).

1859. "The modern presidential campaign covers every issue in and out of the platform from cranberries to creation. But the public is rarely alerted to a candidate's views about the central issue on which all the rest turn. That central issue ... is the presidency itself." Address by Senator John F. Kennedy, "The Presidency in 1960," National Press Club, Washington, D.C. (January 14, 1960).

1860. "The modern presidential campaign covers every issue in and out of the platform from cranberries to creation. But the public is rarely alerted to a candidate's views about the central issue on which all the rest turn.... [T]he American people ... have an imperative right to know what any man bidding for the Presidency thinks about the place he is bidding for...." Address of Senator John F. Kennedy, "The Presidency in 1960," National Press Club, Washington, D.C. (January 14, 1960).

1861. "Whatever the political affiliation of our next President, whatever his views may be on all the issues and problems that rush in upon us, he must above all be the Chief Executive in every sense of the word. He must be prepared to exercise the fullest powers of his office—all that are specified and some that are not. He must master complex problems as well as receive one-page memorandums. He must originate action as well as study groups. He must reopen channels of communication between the world of thought and the seat of power." Address of Senator John F. Kennedy, "The Presidency in 1960," National Press Club, Washington, D.C. (January 14, 1960).

1862. "However large its [Congress'] share in the formulation of domestic programs, it is the President alone who must make the major decisions of our foreign policy." Address of Senator John F. Kennedy, "The Presidency in 1960," National Press Club, Washington, D.C. (January 14, 1960).

1863. "[N]o President, it seems to me, can escape politics. He has not only been chosen by the Nation—he has been chosen by his party. And if he insists that he is 'President of all the people' and should, therefore, offend none of them—if he blurs the issues and differences between the parties—if he neglects the party machinery and avoids his party's leadership—then he has not only weakened the political party as an instrument of the democratic process—he has dealt a blow to the democratic process itself." Address of Senator John F. Kennedy, "The Presidency in 1960," National Press Club, Washington, D.C. (January 14, 1960).

1864. "[T]he executive branch—[has] the power to channel defense contracts—award patronage—purchase surplus commodities—and hold Presidential press conferences. [It] ha[s] all the vast, powerful machinery of government at [its] command." Remarks of Senator John F. Kennedy, Dover, New Hampshire (March 7, 1960).

1865. "[O]nly the President has the authority and the prestige to overcome resistance—to weld the diverse thinking of the Pentagon ... the State Department and many others into one harmonious program—one united objective—the pursuit of world peace." Remarks of Senator John F. Kennedy, South Eugene, Oregon (April 22, 1960).

1866. "[T]he next American President will not only be the symbol of hope to all Americans—he will be the central figure of the entire free world—the man who leads the destinies of a nation which alone stands between the non-communist peoples of the world, and the remorseless forces of communist despotism. Across his desk will come decisions affecting not only our welfare and our survival—but the welfare and the survival of the non-communist world. He alone will have the opportunity to make the American dream of freedom and plenty into the hope of the world—and perhaps, into a reality for millions of people in all parts of the globe. The next President must attempt to do for the world what the New Deal did for America—to protect and extend freedom and equality, and bring to every man the hope for a future of growing economic opportunity. And the price of his failure at this task may well be communist domination of much of the world." Remarks of Senator John F. Kennedy at Essex County Democratic Dinner, Spring Lake, New Jersey (June 22, 1960).

1867. "The President of the United States represents not only the Democrats of this country, he represents all of the people around the world who want to live in freedom, who look to us for hope and leadership." Speech by Senator John F. Kennedy, Fair Grounds, Bangor Maine (September 2, 1960).

1868. "I ran for the office of the Presidency after 14 years in the house of Representatives and the Senate because I have come to realize more than ever that this is the great office, that the power that the Constitution gives the President, the power and the responsibility which the force of events have thrust upon the President, makes this the center of action ... of the American system. Only the President speaks for the United States.... And he speaks not only for the United States, but he speaks for all those who desire to be free, who are willing to bear the burdens of freedom, who are willing to meet its responsibilities, who recognize that freedom is not license, but, instead, places a heavier burden upon us than any other political system." Speech by Senator John F. Kennedy, Portland Stadium, Portland, Maine (September 2, 1960).

1869. "[T]he Presidency is the wellspring of action in the American constitutional system. Only the President speaks for the United States ... and only if a President supports action can this country hope to move ahead." Speech by Senator John F. Kennedy, High School Auditorium, Pocatello, Idaho (September 6, 1960).

1870. "I think of the office of the Presidency in the same way that Franklin Roosevelt thought of it and Woodrow Wilson, in the sense that they felt the chief task of the President was to set before the American people the things that they must do, the responsibilities that they must meet." Speech by Senator John F. Kennedy, Shrine Auditorium, Los Angeles, California (September 9, 1960).

1871. "The United States is the leader of the free world, and I run for the office of the Presidency with full recognition of those responsibilities which go with that leadership." Rear Platform Remarks, Tulare, California (September 9, 1960).

1872. "I talk about a matter which is not a pleasant matter, but I think the President of the United States, who has many responsibilities, also has the responsibility of being Commander in Chief. He must under his oath of office provide for the common defense. One of the areas is in the field of national security." Remarks of Senator John F. Kennedy, U.S. Grant Hotel, San Diego, California (September 11, 1960).

1873. "[D]uring the next 4 years the task of the President, the burdens that will be placed upon him ... will be heavier than they have been any time since the administration of Abraham Lincoln. So I do not run for the Presidency feeling it is a ceremonial or caretaker's office. I run for the Presidency because I feel strongly that the United States has a great role to fulfill in the world to maintain its own freedom, and to serve as the chief defender of freedom around the world." Remarks of Senator John F. Kennedy, Towson Shopping Center, Towson, Maryland (September 16, 1960).

1874. "I think the chief task of a President of the United States is to set before the American people the unfinished business of our society, the things we have to do." Remarks of Senator John F. Kennedy, Airport Rally, Greensboro, North Carolina (September 17, 1960).

1875. "[T]he obligation of the President is not [to] please the people but to serve them." Remarks at Airport Rally, Knoxville, Tennessee (September 21, 1960).

1876. "In case any of you wanted to run for the Presidency, I would say we started this morning in Iowa, we spoke in South Dakota, we speak now in North Dakota, we speak at a dinner meeting in Montana, and end up in Wyoming tonight. I think that my election chief thinks that the election is October 8 rather than November 8." Remarks of Senator John F. Kennedy, Airport Rally, Fargo, North Dakota (September 22, 1960).

1877. "I think the Presidency is a great Office. It is enshrined in the Constitution, and it is also by the force of events and by the pressure of circumstances that it has come to have the greatest possible influence over the lives of us all." Remarks of Senator John F. Kennedy, Hotel Hollenden, Cleveland, Ohio (September 25, 1960).

1878. "The vigor and leadership of the President is an ingredient in national strength, but in the final analysis it is the sum of the total that counts. Presidents may change, but the power of the United States, in the balance of world politics, in the balance of the power struggle of the world, is the great force on the side of freedom. So in a very real sense, we are all involved. When the United States is in trouble, it isn't the President that is in trouble. It is the United States." Remarks of Senator John F. Kennedy, Lawrence Hotel, Erie, Pennsylvania (September 28, 1960).

1879. "The quality which I think the next President of the United States needs ... is the quality of judgment and the quality of foresight. The quality of judgment to be able to pick from five or six possible solutions in a crisis which affects the security of the United States, experience and judgment, but the second quality which is equally important is the quality of foresight.... Foresight, some ability to make a judgment before the event happens." Remarks of Senator John F. Kennedy, War Memorial Building, Rochester, New York (September 28, 1960).

1880. "It is the President of the United States that can set the goals for the country in housing, minimum wage, social security, unemployment compensation, and in equality of rights for all Americans, regardless of their race or color." Remarks of Senator John F. Kennedy, Auto Rally, 15th and Broadway, East St. Louis, Illinois (October 3, 1960).

1881. "[T]he President of the United States ... is not only the Commander in Chief, but he also is the center of our entire constitutional system.... [T]he Office of the President is key. We can take action to provide aid to education. We can take action to provide medical care for our older citizens. We can take action to try to stimulate the American economy. But in the final analysis whatever we may do depends on the President of the United States, depends on his vigor, depends on his concept of what needs to be done to make this a stronger and a better country. The Presidency is key." Remarks of Senator John F. Kennedy, Auto Rally, Granite City, Illinois (October 3, 1960).

1882. "In my judgment, the great questions of war and peace, of full employment, of economic growth, of a stronger society, of equal opportunity for all, will depend in the final analysis upon the President of the United States. Not upon the House and not upon the Senate." Remarks of Senator John F. Kennedy, Government Square, Cincinnati, Ohio (October 6, 1960).

1883. "[The] President, as Commander in Chief, faces no more solemn decision than whether to send American troops into battle, knowing they will not all return." Speech by Senator John F. Kennedy, Democratic National and State Committees Dinner, Waldorf-Astoria Hotel, New York, New York (October 12, 1960).

1884. "The Congress has an important function, but in a very real sense the Congress can block, but only the President of the United States can propose...." Speech by Senator John F. Kennedy, Boys' Gymnasium, Montgomery — Blair High School, Silver Spring, Maryland (October 16, 1960).

1885. "The President of the United States has the great power not only of war and peace, not only of defending our commitments abroad, but also of setting before the American people the unfinished business of our society." Remarks of Senator John F. Kennedy, London, Ohio (October 17, 1960).

1886. "[H]owever important the Senate may be, and however important the House of Representatives may be, in the final analysis our fortunes as a nation depend ... on the good judgment, the vigor, the sense of precision, the sense of foresight — the historical sense of the President of the United States." Remarks of Senator John F. Kennedy, Band Shell, Biscayne Bay, Miami, Florida (October 18, 1960).

1887. "[T]he chief responsibility of the next President of the United States is to build the strength of America, and when we build the strength of America, we build the strength of freedom." Remarks of Senator John F. Kennedy, Martin's Store, Fulton and Duffield, Brooklyn, New York (October 20, 1960)

1888. "This is a free society, and the kind of country we have, the kind of strength we have, depends in the final analysis upon the people themselves. But the function and responsibility of the President is to set before the American people the unfinished business, the things we must do if we are going to succeed as a nation." Remarks of Senator John F. Kennedy, Crestwood Shopping Center, Crestwood, Missouri (October 22, 1960).

1889. "I believe there are two basic responsibilities which the next President must meet. One is our domestic strength, the maintenance of full employment, a strong and vital society, a strong educational system, the development of our resources and a moving America. The second responsibility given to the President by the Constitution and by the force of events is the conduct of foreign affairs, and it is in this area that the great issues of war and peace, of strength and weakness, of ebb and flow will meet across the desk of the next President." Remarks of Senator John F. Kennedy, Street Rally, Elgin, Illinois (October 25, 1960).

1890. "[T]he President ... is not only the Commander in Chief, he is not only the head of his party, he is not only a legislative leader, he is not only charged with the power of appointment, he also is charged by the Constitution and by the force of events with the maintenance of our relations across the seas." Remarks of Senator John F. Kennedy, Baker Park, St. Charles, Illinois (October 25, 1960).

1891. "The function of the President of the United States ... is to build a strong society here, to maintain full employment, to educate our children, to provide security for our aged citizens, to provide justice for our people, to build an image of a society on the move, so that people around the world who wonder ... which road they should take, they decide, 'We want to go with the United States; they represent the future.'" Remarks of Senator John F. Kennedy, Keyworth Stadium, Hamtramck, Michigan (October 26, 1960).

1892. "[There are] five hats which the President of the United States wears: the legislative leader, the employment leader, the leader of the Nation, the leader of the free world, the Commander in Chief, the President of the United States." Remarks of Senator John F. Kennedy, Lawrence Park Shopping Center, Philadelphia, Pennsylvania (October 29, 1960).

1893. "[W]ithout any way downgrading the Congress, there isn't any doubt that the center of action in the American constitutional system is the President.... The Constitution places the greatest responsibility for the conduct of our foreign affairs, particularly, upon the President, and unless the President ... speaks for the Nation, unless the President ... is able to personify the force of the Nation, then the Nation does not move ahead, does not move to accomplish its unfinished business, does not give an image of vitality and strength throughout the world." Remarks of Senator John F. Kennedy, Lawrence Park Shopping Center, Philadelphia, Pennsylvania (October 29, 1960).

1894. "There is no such thing as the President being in trouble without the people being in trouble." Remarks of John F. Kennedy, Cheltenham Shopping Center, Philadelphia, Pennsylvania (October 29, 1960).

1895. "The next President's desk will not be clear, waiting for new problems and responsibilities. It will be piled high with old problems, inherited, chronic problems.... There on that one desk, on the shoulders of the next President of the United States, will converge all the hopes and fears of every American and, indeed, all the hopes and fears of every person in the world who believes in peace and freedom. Whatever the issue, however critical the problem, the President will sit alone. He will have his advisers ... [but] the final decision is the President's alone." Speech by Senator John F. Kennedy, East Los Angeles College Stadium, Los Angeles, California (November 1, 1960).

1896. "[I]t is the President's responsibility to set before the American people the unfinished business of our society, to rally them to a great cause." Remarks of Senator John F. Kennedy, Fordham Road and Grand Concourse, Bronx, New York (November 5, 1960).

1897. "[T]he Presidency is a great office. It has unparalleled influence over the lives of all of us. Every decision the President makes affects the security and well-being of every person in the United States as it never has before, as it never has before. Its possibilities, its opportunities for service are unlimited...." Remarks of Senator John F. Kennedy, Concourse Plaza Hotel, Bronx, New York (November 5, 1960).

1898. "I believe in a President who will formulate and fight for his legislative policies, and not be a casual observer of the legislative progress. A President who will not back down under pressure ... a President who does not speak from the rear of the battle but who places himself in the thick of the fight. But I also believe in a President who fights for great ideals as well as legislation — a President who cares deeply about the people he represents.... And above all I believe in a President who believes in the national interest — who serves no other master — who takes no instructions but those of his conscience — who puts no personal interest, no public pressure, no political hopes, and no private obligation of any kind ahead of his oath to promote the national interest." Remarks of Senator John F. Kennedy, New York Coliseum, New York, New York (November 5, 1960).

1899. "Sooner or later, every problem which faces us as a people comes before the President of the United States...." Remarks of Senator John F. Kennedy, Journal Square, Jersey City, New Jersey (November 6, 1960).

1900. "I believe the Presidency is the key office, not only in this country, but in the whole free world...." Remarks of Senator John F. Kennedy, Journal Square, Jersey City, New Jersey (November 6, 1960).

1901. "No man entering upon this office, regardless of his party, regardless of his previous service in Washington, could fail to be staggered upon learning ... the harsh enormity of the trials through which we must pass in the next four years. Each day the crises multiply. Each day their solution grows more difficult. Each day we draw nearer the hour of maximum danger, as weapons spread and hostile forces grow stronger." Annual Message to the Congress on the State of the Union, Washington, D.C. (January 30, 1961).

1902. "I hold an office [the Presidency] which by our very Constitution unites political and military responsibility...." Remarks at the Opening Session of the Meeting of the Military Committee of NATO (April 10, 1961).

1903. "I will say on becoming President that the only thing that really surprised us when we got into office was that things were just as bad as we had been saying they were; otherwise we have been enjoying it very much." Remarks at the Democratic National Committee Dinner in Honor of the President's 44th Birthday (May 27, 1961).

1904. "When I ran for the Presidency of the United States, I knew that this country faced serious challenges, but I could not realize — nor could any man realize who does not bear the burdens of this office — how heavy and constant would be those burdens." Radio and Television Report to the American People on the Berlin Crisis (July 25, 1961).

1905. "For of all the awesome responsibilities entrusted to this office, none is more somber to contemplate than the special statutory authority to employ nuclear arms in the defense of our people and freedom." Radio and Television Address to the American People, "Nuclear Testing and Disarmament" (March 2, 1962).

1906. "[I] do not think it wholly inaccurate to say that I was the second choice of a majority of businessmen for the office of President of the United States...." Address Before the United States Chamber of Commerce on Its 50th Anniversary (April 30, 1962).

1907. "Now I know there are some people who say that ... the President of the United States should be an honorary chairman of a great fraternal organization and confine himself to ceremonial functions. But that is not what the Constitution says. And I did not run for President of the United States to fulfill that Office in that way." Address in Atlantic City at the Convention of the United Auto Workers (May 8, 1962).

1908. "As long as the United States is the great and chief guardian of freedom, all the way ... from the Brandenburg Gate to Viet-Nam, as long as we fulfill our functions at a time of climax in the struggle for freedom, then I believe it is the business of the President of the United States to concern himself with the general welfare and the public interest. And if the people feel that it is not, then they should secure the services of a new President...." Address in Atlantic City at the Convention of the United Auto Workers (May 8, 1962).

1909. "I suppose that there is no training ground for the Presidency, but I don't think it's a bad idea for a President to have stood outside of Maier's meat factory in Madison, Wisconsin ... at 5:30 in the morning, with the temperature 10 above. When I read some of those great editorials about labor, I like to think about how it is to go to work at 6 o'clock in the morning at zero degrees. So I think it's a very valuable experience...." Address in Milwaukee at the Jefferson-Jackson Dinner (May 12, 1962).

1910. "He [Archbishop Makarios of Cyprus] has been elected by his people bishop, and also been elected by them president. We don't have that opportunity in this country — you have to choose one or the other, unfortunately." Toasts of the President and Archbishop Makarios (June 5, 1962).

1911. "I am not unmindful of the fact that two graduates of this [U.S. Military] Academy have reached the White House, and neither was a member of my party. Until I am more certain that this trend will be broken, I wish that all of you may be generals and not Commanders in Chief." Remarks at West Point to the Graduating Class of the U.S. Military Academy (June 6, 1962).

1912. "I do not think that there is any responsibility placed upon the President of the United States, even including that of Commander in Chief, which is more pressing, which is more powerful, which is more singularly held in the Executive ... than that which is involved in foreign policy." Address at a Meeting of the American Foreign Service Association (July 2, 1962).

1913. "[T]he only forces that cannot be transferred from Washington without my express permission are members of the Marine Corps Band. They are the only forces that I have." Remarks at the Evening Parade following an Inspection of the Marine Barracks (July 12, 1962).

1914. "Your President [David McDonald of the United Steelworkers] has been kind enough to invite me to your next convention in 1964, and I will be with you then." Remarks with David McDonald Recorded for the United Steelworkers Convention at Miami Beach [Florida] (September 17, 1962).

1915. "[I]t is a responsibility of the President of the United States ... to have a program and to fight for it.... I do not believe that in this most critical and dangerous period ... that Presidents, or anyone else, should confine themselves to ceremonial occasions, ornamenting an office at a time when this country and this world needs all of the energy and the action and the commitment to progress that it can possibly have...." Remarks at Fitzgerald Field House, University of Pittsburgh [Pennsylvania] (October 12, 1962).

1916. "[W]hen things go bad the chicken comes to roost on the President's house. Mr. Herbert Hoover was, we know in legend, responsible for all the difficulties of 1929. President Truman bore responsibility for the '49 recession. President Eisenhower was blamed for the recessions in '54, '58, and '60. When the stock market had its difficulties last spring, I got a good many letters. I receive no mail thanking me and expressing admiration for my economic wisdom when the market goes up, but when it goes down we all know who is wrong." Address Before the 19th Washington Conference of the Advertising Council (March 13, 1963).

1917. "All of us — those of us who are making it — would on occasion like to rewrite history. I think it very important that we are not permitted to." Remarks at a Luncheon for Sponsors and Editors of Historical Publications (June 17, 1963).

1918. "Everyone expects things of Presidents, but I am not sure that they realize how much depends upon the Members of the House and the Members of the Senate who must make the final judgment on what kind of laws a President must execute." Remarks in Philadelphia [Pennsylvania] at a Dinner Sponsored by the Democratic County Executive Committee (October 30, 1963).

1919. "The Presidency has been called a good many names, and Presidents have been also, but no President can do anything without the help of friends." Remarks at the Coliseum in Houston [Texas] at a Dinner Honoring Representative Albert Thomas (November 1, 1963).

PUBLIC SERVICE

1920. "I don't think we can capture the imagination of the world, we cannot capture the imagination of our own people, unless we have an administration manned by men and women who look to the future, who recognize that this is a changing and a revolutionary world, and that what was good enough 10 or 15 years ago is no longer good enough." Remarks of Senator John F. Kennedy, Government Square, Cincinnati, Ohio (October 6, 1960).

1921. "[We must] ask the ablest men in the country to make whatever sacrifice is required to bring to the Government a ministry of the best talents available, men with a single-minded loyalty to the national interest, men who would regard public office as a public trust. For no government is better than the men who compose it...." Speech by Senator John F. Kennedy, Wittenburg College Stadium, Springfield, Ohio (October 17, 1960).

1922. "[There is no] magic formula for achieving a government perfect in all its parts. All human weaknesses cannot be avoided. All errors of judgment can not be predicted.... The essence of any government that belongs to the people must lie in the biblical injunction, 'No man can serve two masters, for either he will hate one and love the other, or else he will hold to one and despise the other.' All America seeks a government which no man holds to his own interest, and despises the public interest, and where all men serve only the public and love that master well." Speech by Senator John F. Kennedy, Wittenburg College Stadium, Springfield, Ohio (October 17, 1960).

1923. "[H]istory teaches us that no political party has a monopoly on honesty. Both parties attract their share of crooks and weaklings. But that does not mean that these problems are incapable of solution. That does not mean that a campaign promise is enough. A new administration must screen out those who regard Government service as a door to power or wealth. Those who cannot distinguish between private gain and the public interest and those who believe that old-fashioned honesty with the public's money is both old and out of fashion. [T]he next President himself must set the moral tone ... not only to his language, but to his actions in office. For the Presidency, as Franklin Roosevelt himself has said, is preeminently a place of moral leadership." Speech by Senator John F. Kennedy, Wittenburg College Stadium, Springfield, Ohio (October 17, 1960).

1924. "[Many of the] ... problems [America faces] are new. All of them are difficult. There is no easy answer to any easy question, but because they are difficult, we need the best talent we can get. In every branch of government we need the most vigorous, foresighted, farsighted, intellectually curious, well-informed and responsible citizens we can get to serve the great Republic in the dangerous and changing years of the 1960s...." Remarks of Senator John F. Kennedy, Coronado Theater Rally, Rockford, Illinois (October 24, 1960).

1925. "[W]e need new people, new energy, new vision, new leadership. We need to attract people to our government service and the service of our country who today are in universities.... We need young men and women who will spend some of their years in Latin America, Africa, and Asia, in the service of freedom. We need others who will serve in governmental posts which lack glamour but which serve the cause of freedom." Remarks of Senator John F. Kennedy, Snellenburg's Shopping Center, Willow Grove, Pennsylvania (October 29, 1960).

1926. "Let the public service be a proud and lively career. And let every man and woman who works in any area of our national government ... be able to say with pride and with honor in future years: 'I served the United States government in that hour of our nation's need.'" Annual Message to the Congress on the State of the Union (January 30, 1961).

1927. "[O]urs is a Government of laws not of men, and it is, in the sense that we strive for equality and integrity in the administration of our Government and of justice. But this is also a Government of men, and it needs men of particular talents to make this system of ours work." Remarks at the Cornerstone — Laying Ceremonies of the Rayburn House Office Building (May 24, 1962).

1928. "Government service should be, in these days when so much depends upon the United States, the most prideful of all careers. To serve in the United States Government, to be a public employee, to be a bureaucrat in the critical sense — that should be the greatest source of satisfaction to any American." Remarks at a Meeting with the Headquarters Staff of the Peace Corps (June 14, 1962).

1929. "It is my judgment that there is no career that could possibly ... offer ... as much satisfaction, as much stimulus, as little compensation perhaps financially, as being a servant of the United States Government." Remarks of Welcome to Participants in the Summer Intern Program for College Students (June 20, 1962).

1930. "I think within all of us ... I suppose endowed almost by nature in addition to a natural desire to advance our own interests, there is also a parallel desire, and that is to be part of this great enterprise of public service." Remarks of Welcome to Participants in the Summer Intern Program for College Students (June 20, 1962).

1931. "I think that it [working in the public sector] is a more difficult and subtle problem in a democracy, with a great deal of emphasis ... on individual liberty, on the right of pursuing our private interests, and so on, so that while there is this desire, frequently it does not have a chance to [ex]press itself." Remarks of Welcome to Participants in the Summer Intern Program for College Students (June 20, 1962).

1932. "I think it is too often that the Government work has been caricatured, rather than honored as it should be." Remarks to Recipients of the Rockefeller Public Service Awards (December 6, 1962).

1933. "[T]he assignment, it seems to me ... is to produce all of the educated talent that we have, not merely to help them along, not merely to produce outstanding businessmen, though we need them, and lawyers, though we need them, and doctors, though we need them, but also to produce men and women with a sense of the public responsibility, the public duty." Remarks at the Cheney Stadium in Tacoma, Washington (September 27, 1963).

SCIENCE AND TECHNOLOGY

1934. "To use ocean depths — to find an economical way of obtaining fresh water from salt water — is a dream several centuries old that is now within our reach. If we can score this dramatic breakthrough, we shall not only immeasurably enrich our own land, make our desert bloom ... — we shall also have won the undying gratitude of every parched desert land along the Mediterranean, African, Indian and other oceans. It will do more for American prestige than Sputnik ever did for the Russians." Remarks of Senator John F. Kennedy, Phoenix, Arizona (April 9, 1960).

1935. "I don't suppose there has ever been a time, even during the days of World War II, when the relationship between science and government must be more intimate. Nearly every question which we approach — those of us who hold political office — has scientific overtones." Remarks Before the National Academy of Sciences (April 25, 1961).

1936. "[T]here is no nationality in the Nobel prize, just as there is no nationality in the acquisition of knowledge. I know that every man ... who has won the Nobel prize, not only does he build on the past ... on the efforts of other men and women, but he also builds on the efforts of those in other countries; and therefore, quite rightly, the Nobel prize has no national significance." Remarks at a Dinner Honoring Nobel Prize Winners of the Western Hemisphere (April 29, 1962).

1937. "There is no scientific breakthrough, including the trip to the moon, that will mean more to the country which first is able to bring fresh water from salt water at a competitive rate. And all those people who live in deserts around the oceans of the world will look to the nation which first makes this significant breakthrough, and I'd like to have it the United States of America." Remarks in Los Banos, California, at the Ground-Breaking Ceremonies for the San Luis Dam (August 18, 1962).

1938. "The greater our knowledge increases, the greater our ignorance unfolds. Despite the striking fact that most of the scientists that the world has ever known are alive and working today, despite the fact that this Nation's own scientific manpower is doubling every 12 years ... despite that, the vast stretches of the unknown and the unanswered and the unfinished still far outstrip our collective comprehension." Address at Rice University in Houston [Texas] on the Nation's Space Effort (September 12, 1962).

1939. "[W]e take a good deal of pride and satisfaction that our country was the magnet which attracted ... free-ranging minds who, because of their great talent and ability to concentrate that talent on new horizons, were able to make some of the most remarkable breakthroughs in scientific history." Remarks Upon Presenting the Enrico Fermi Award to Dr. Edward Teller (December 3, 1962).

1940. "Most of the scientists who've ever lived are now living. So what we have in the 20th century is this tremendous increase in knowledge which expands almost faster than the universe, and our task is to attempt to make that knowledge widely available." Remarks of Welcome to the Second International Congress on Medical Librarianship (June 19, 1963).

1941. "[I]f I were to name a single thing which points up the difference this [20th] century has made in the American attitude toward science, it would certainly be the wholehearted understanding today of the importance of pure science ... that progress in technology depends on progress in theory; that the most abstract investigations can lead to the most concrete results; and that the vitality of a scientific community springs from its passion to answer science's most fundamental questions." Address at the Anniversary Convocation of the National Academy of Sciences (October 22, 1963).

1942. "[O]urs is a century of scientific conquest and scientific triumph. If scientific discovery has not been an unalloyed blessing, if it has conferred on mankind the power not only to create, but also to annihilate, it has at the same time provided humanity with a supreme challenge and a supreme testing. If the challenge and the testing are too much for humanity, then we are all doomed. But I believe that the future can be bright.... Man is still the master of his own fate, and I believe that the power of science and the responsibility of science have offered mankind a new opportunity." Address at the Anniversary Convocation of the National Academy of Sciences (October 22, 1963).

1943. "[W]ith each door that we unlock we see perhaps 10 doors that we never dreamed existed and, therefore, we have to keep working forward." Anniversary Convocation of the National Academy of Sciences (October 22, 1963).

1944. "In the last hundred years, science has ... emerged from a peripheral concern of Government to an active partner. The instrumentalities devised in recent times have given this partnership continuity and force. The question in all our minds today is how science can best continue its service to the Nation, to the people, to the world, in the years to come." Address at the Anniversary Convocation of the National Academy of Sciences (October 22, 1963).

1945. "The great scientific challenges transcend national frontiers and national prejudices. In a sense, this has always been true, for the language of science has always been universal, and perhaps scientists have been the most international of all professions in their outlook." Address at the Anniversary Convocation of the National Academy of Sciences (October 22, 1963).

1946. "[I]n 1963 we are going to make a very important decision, to build a supersonic plane which in the 1970s will carry passengers at nearly Mach 3, three times the speed of sound, and we are also going to be ... at Cape Canaveral and in other parts of the United States ... laying the groundwork which will permit people to fly at five times the speed of sound, and before the end of the century many more times than that." Remarks in Tampa [Florida] on the 50th Anniversary of Scheduled Air Service (November 18, 1963).

SENIOR CITIZENS

1947. "At the top of the list of this nation's wasting resources is its older citizens. Too many are compelled to retire at the age of 65, regardless of their excellent health and regardless of the fact that they have skills this nation urgently needs. Too many older workers able and willing to enter a new occupation are wasting their time and talent in menial work or idleness. Too much of the contribution to our way of life which can come only from older men and women is lost...." Remarks of Senator John F. Kennedy, Kenosha, Wisconsin (February 16, 1960).

1948. "[N]o matter how they retrench — how many accustomed comforts they learn to do without the later years of many of our older citizens are attended by cruel hardships. And this hardship becomes heartbreak and despair when illness threatens. For this is the time of life when the need for medical care rises sharply. And this is also the time when income drops, and the soaring costs of medical attention become the most burdensome. Thousands of our older citizens — living on small fixed incomes — are unable to afford the medical care they desperately need. [T]he only solution is an extension of our social security system to provide hospital and medical care for our older citizens." Remarks of Senator John F. Kennedy, Androy Hotel Reception, Superior, Wisconsin (March 18, 1960).

1949. "We must immediately begin on a bold, creative program to modernize our social security program ... to ensure our older citizens a decent retirement which they can enjoy in dignity and freedom from want. [W]e must raise our scale of benefits and we must be sure that future benefits keep pace with rises in the cost of living ... [and] we must provide a sound and effective program of health insurance for those over 65 ... the time of life when the need for health care rises sharply. We must permit our older citizens to meet their basic health needs and expenses." Remarks of Senator John F. Kennedy, Williamson, West Virginia (April 25, 1960).

1950. "[O]ur older citizens should not have to ask for charity. They want more than charity — they deserve more than charity — and ... [we] must see that they get more than charity." Remarks of Senator John F. Kennedy, St. Albans, West Virginia (April 30, 1960).

1951. "We can no longer afford to have the life savings, the homes and the few possessions of our older citizens wiped out by the sudden onslaught of illness. We must provide for the health and well-being of our older citizens." Remarks of Senator John F. Kennedy, St. Albans, West Virginia (April 30, 1960).

1952. "I want to make it clear that in my judgment the only way ... to protect the interest of the country, the only way ... to provide a program which pays for itself, the only way ... to provide medical care for the aged, is through the social security system which has worked for 25 years." Remarks of Senator John F. Kennedy, Bell Aircraft Co., Niagara Falls, New York (September 28, 1960).

1953. "I believe in an America where one's latest years are the good years — years of security and dignity; where medical care for the aged is provided out of social security ... where older people can find decent housing, suitable to their needs; and where doors are not automatically shut in their face by any employer, including the Federal Government, for in those crucial years we need their wisdom and their counsel." Speech by Senator John F. Kennedy, Convention Hall, Philadelphia, Pennsylvania (October 31, 1960).

1954. "[W]e are [not] softening our society when we make it possible for older people to contribute to their own maintenance in their older age through medical care under social security. These are the things that any society must do, if it deserves its name. And I am particularly anxious that a free society of which we rightfully boast so much, that it does it better than anyone else does it." Address in Chicago at a Dinner of the Democratic Party of Cook County [Illinois] (April 28, 1961).

1955. "[N]o piece of unfinished business is more important or more urgent than the enactment under the social security system of health insurance for the aged. For our older citizens have longer and more frequent illnesses, higher hospital and medical bills and too little income to pay them. Private health insurance helps very few — for its cost is high and its coverage limited. Public welfare cannot help those too proud to seek relief but hard-pressed to pay their own bills. Nor can their children or grandchildren always sacrifice their own health budgets to meet this constant drain." Annual Message to the Congress on the State of the Union (January 11, 1962).

SOVIET UNION

1956. "How can you [Soviet Premiere Khrushchev] talk of the achievements of your system, even if you beat us again by putting a man into outer space? For we know that while you may bring a man back from outer space, you rarely bring one back alive from Siberia." Speech by Senator John F. Kennedy, Sheraton Park Hotel, Washington, D.C. (September 20, 1960).

1957. "The Soviet Union today is the greatest colonial master in the world, and until they are ready to permit the people of Eastern Europe to have free elections and a free choice, then they stand indicted before world opinion." Remarks of Senator John F. Kennedy, City Hall, Chicago, Illinois (October 1, 1960).

1958. "[The Soviets] want to know the secret of how we can produce so much food with so few people, and if they can master that secret, then they are going to use that as a great weapon in the cold war. I don't think we should use food as a weapon in the cold war. I think we should hold out the hands of friendship and I think the bread we float on the water will come back to us, many times over in the coming years." Remarks of Senator John F. Kennedy, Farmers Union Gta [Grain Terminal Association] Convention, St. Paul, Minnesota (October 2, 1960).

1959. "The Soviet Union is working night and day. They are bent on our destruction." Speech of Senator John F. Kennedy, Municipal Auditorium, Oklahoma City, Oklahoma (November 3, 1960).

1960. "We [and the Soviet Union] have wholly different views of right and wrong, of what is an internal affair and what is aggression, and, above all, we have wholly different concepts of where the world is and where it is going." Radio and Television Report to the American People on Returning From Europe (June 6, 1961).

1961. "No government or social system is so evil that its people must be considered as lacking in virtue. [W]e find communism profoundly repugnant as a negation of personal freedom and dignity. But we can still hail the Russian people for their many achievements — in science and space, in economic and industrial growth, in culture and in acts of courage." Commencement Address at American University in Washington, D.C. (June 10, 1963).

SPACE EXPLORATION

1962. [I]f the Soviet Union was first in outer space, that is the most serious defeat the United States has suffered in many, many years. The reason — not merely because outer space is important militarily, but because ... people around the world equate the mission to the moon, the mission to outer space, with productive and scientific superiority. Therefore, in spite of all our accomplishments, because we failed to recognize the impact that being first in outer space would have, the impression began to move around the world that the Soviet Union was on the march ... that it was moving and that we were standing still. That is what we have to overcome, that psychological feeling in the world that the United States has reached maturity, that maybe our high noon has passed, maybe our brightest days were earlier, and that now we are going into the long, slow afternoon." Remarks of Senator John F. Kennedy, Municipal Auditorium, Canton, Ohio (September 27, 1960).

1963. "I am not satisfied to be second in space...." Remarks of Senator John F. Kennedy, Hellriegel's Inn, Painesville, Ohio (September 27, 1960).

1964. "In 1941 Albert Einstein ... came to see Franklin Roosevelt and told him that an investment of over $2 billion would make the United States the strongest military power in the history of the world by cracking the atom. Franklin Roosevelt could have dismissed it, but the same man who saw in the Tennessee Valley an opportunity for harnessing the resources of that valley for the service of our country was the same man who said 'Yes' to that long gamble and provided security for the United States in the last 20 years. Now the same situation faced the United States in 1954 and 1955, and that was the question of how important it was to be first in outer space, and what answer did this administration give. It regarded it as a scientific experiment. Mr. Wilson, the Secretary of Defense said he was not interested to know what was on the other side of the moon. He said money spent on basic research was unimportant because he was not interested to find out why fried potatoes turned brown. The result is that the Soviet Union today is No.1 in outer space." Remarks of Senator John F. Kennedy, Fulton Lane Parking Lot, Fairborn, Ohio (October 17, 1960).

1965. "All of us in the United States and in all nations can derive many benefits from the peaceful application of space technology. The impact of this new science will be felt in our daily lives. It can bring all people closer together, improve communications; it can help control the weather and the climate around us. We can safely predict that the impact of the space age will have a far-ranging effect within industry and in our labor force, on medical research, education, and many other areas of national concern." Remarks by Telephone to the Conference on Peaceful Uses of Space Meeting in Tulsa [Oklahoma]. (May 26, 1961).

1966. "As our space program continues on even more ambitious missions, it will continue to be this Nation's policy to use space for the advancement of all mankind, and to make free release of all scientific and technological results." Remarks Upon Signing Bill Providing for an Expanded Space Program (July 21, 1961).

1967. "As we extend the rule of law on earth, so must we also extend it to man's new domain — outer space.... The new horizons of outer space must not be driven by the old bitter concepts of imperialism and sovereign claims. The cold reaches of the universe must not become the new arena of an even colder war." Address in New York City Before the General Assembly of the United Nations (September 25, 1961).

1968. "[T]here is no area where the United States received a greater setback to its prestige as the number one industrial country in the world than in being second in the field of space in the fifties. And while many may think that it is foolish to go to the moon, I do not believe that a powerful country like the United States, which wishes to demonstrate to a watching world that it is first in the field of technology and science, which represents so basic an aspiration of so many people ... that we want to permit the Soviet Union to dominate space, with all that it might mean to our peace and security...." Address in Los Angeles [California] at a Dinner of the Democratic Party of California (November 18, 1961).

1969. "We have a long way to go in the space race. We started late. But this is the new ocean, and I believe the United States must sail on it and be in a position second to none." Remarks Following the Orbital Flight of Col. John H. Glenn, Jr. (February 20, 1962).

1970. "[W]hen Colonel Glenn came by the White House, I asked him how he enjoyed the public attention, and he said that he wished that they were paying more attention to the scientific part of the voyage rather than to his wife's hair. My own feeling is that both are equally important, in the sense that we are proud of this trip because of its scientific achievement and we are also proud of it because of the men and women that are involved in it. Our boosters may not be as large as some others, but the men and women are." Remarks at the Presentation of NASA's Distinguished Service Medal to Dr. Robert R. Gilruth and Col. John H. Glenn, Jr. (February 23, 1962).

1971. "[I] believe that we are an advancing society, and I believe that we are on the rise, and

I believe that their [the Soviet] system is as old as time. As long as the decision has been made that our great system and others will be judged at least in one degree by how we do in the field of space, we might as well be first...." Remarks to the Staff at the NASA Launch Operations Center, Cape Canaveral [Florida] (September 11, 1962).

1972. "[F]rom this place in America [Houston] are going to be laid the plans and the designs which will reach out in this decade and put Americans on the moon and bring them back again." Remarks on Arrival at the International Airport in Houston [Texas] (September 11, 1962).

1973. "If ... history ... teaches us anything, it is that man, in his quest for knowledge and progress, is determined and cannot be deterred. The exploration of space will go ahead, whether we join in it or not, and it is one of the great adventures of all time, and no nation which expects to be the leader of other nations can expect to stay behind in this race for space." Address at Rice University in Houston [Texas] on the Nation's Space Effort (September 12, 1962).

1974. "[T]his generation does not intend to founder in the backwash of the coming age of space. We mean to be a part of it — we mean to lead it. For the eyes of the world now look into space, to the moon and to the planets beyond, and we have vowed that we shall not see it governed by a hostile flag of conquest, but by a banner of freedom and peace. We have vowed that we shall not see space filled with weapons of mass destruction, but with instruments of knowledge and understanding. Yet the vows of this Nation can only be fulfilled if we in this Nation are first, and, therefore, we intend to be first." Address at Rice University in Houston [Texas] on the Nation's Space Effort (September 12, 1962).

1975. "[O]ur leadership in science and in industry, our hopes for peace and security, our obligations to ourselves as well as others, all require us to ... become the world's leading space-faring nation. We set sail on this new sea because there is new knowledge to be gained, and new rights to be won, and they must be won and used for the progress of all people." Address at Rice University in Houston [Texas] on the Nation's Space Effort (September 12, 1962).

1976. "[S]pace science, like nuclear science and all technology, has no conscience of its own. Whether it will become a force for good or ill depends on man, and only if the United States occupies a position of pre-eminence can we help decide whether this new ocean will be a sea of peace or a new terrifying theater of war." Address at Rice University in Houston [Texas] on the Nation's Space Effort (September 12, 1962).

1977. "We choose to go to the moon. We choose to go to the moon in this decade and do the other things, not because they are easy, but because they are hard, because that goal will serve to organize and measure the best of our energies and skills, because that challenge is one that we are willing to accept, one we are unwilling to postpone, and one which we intend to win...." Address at Rice University in Houston [Texas] on the Nation's Space Effort (September 12, 1962).

1978. "[I]t [sending a man to the moon and back] will be done. And it will be done before the end of this decade." Address at Rice University in Houston [Texas] on the Nation's Space Effort (September 12, 1962).

1979. "In the United States every citizen of this country is involved in this effort [sending a man to the moon and back]. As I pointed out this morning, it costs every citizen, man, woman, and child, today 40 cents a week to be involved merely in the effort in space. It will shortly cost them 50 cents a week." Remarks in St. Louis [Missouri] to Employees of the McDonnell Aircraft Corporation (September 12, 1962).

1980. "[*Faith* 7, the last of the Mercury Mission flights] represents a great achievement for our society and a great achievement for free men and women." Radio and Television Remarks Following the Flight of Astronaut L. Gordon Cooper (May 16, 1963).

1981. "[H]owever extraordinary computers may be ... we are still ahead of them and ... man is still the most extraordinary computer of all. His judgment, his nerve, and the lessons he can learn from experience still make him unique and, therefore, make manned flight necessary and not merely that of satellites." Remarks Upon Presenting the NASA Distinguished Service Medal to Astronaut L. Gordon Cooper (May 21, 1963).

1982. "Why ... should man's first flight to the moon be a matter of national competition? Why should the United States and the Soviet

Union ... become involved in immense duplications of research, construction, and expenditure? Surely we should explore whether the scientists and astronauts of our two countries — indeed of all the world — cannot work together in the conquest of space, sending some day in this decade to the moon not the representatives of a single nation, but the representatives of all of our countries." Address Before the 18th General Assembly of the United Nations (September 20, 1963).

1983. "When the plane was first invented, I am sure there were a good many who wondered what possible use it could be. When the first Sputnik satellite went up, I am sure it was regarded as an extraordinary feat, but not perhaps of great international significance. I can assure you that it has ... been useful beyond measure to the United States, and I feel that way about what we are trying to do now [in the space program]. Some may only dimly perceive where we are going.... They may not feel that this is of the greatest priority to our country. [But] when this job is done ... it will then become as obvious to us, its significance as obvious to us, its uses as obvious to us, its benefit as obvious to us as a country as ... the airplane is to us." Remarks Upon Presenting the Collier Trophy to the First U.S. Astronauts (October 10, 1963).

1984. "Many Americans make the mistake of assuming that space research has no values here on earth. Nothing could be further from the truth. Just as the wartime development of radar gave us the transistor ... so research in space medicine holds the promise of substantial benefit for those of us who are earthbound. For our effort in space is not as some have suggested, a competitor for the natural resources that we need to develop the earth. It is a working partner and a co-producer of these resources." Remarks in San Antonio [Texas] at the Dedication of the Aerospace Medical Health Center (November 21, 1963).

1985. "[T]he United States should be a leader. A country as rich and powerful as this which bears so many burdens and responsibilities, which has so many opportunities, should be second to none. And ... while I do not regard our mastery of space as anywhere near complete ... this year I hope the United States will be ahead. And I am for it." Remarks in San Antonio [Texas] at the Dedication of the Aerospace Medical Health Center (November 21, 1963).

1986. "There will be setbacks and frustrations and disappointments [in the space program]. There will be, as there always are, pressures in this country to do less in this area as in so many others, and temptations to do something else that is perhaps easier. But [space] research ... must go on. This space effort must go on. The conquest of space must and will go ahead. That much we know. That much we can say with confidence and conviction." Remarks in San Antonio [Texas] at the Dedication of the Aerospace Medical Health Center (November 21, 1963).

1987. "Frank O'Connor, the Irish writer, tells ... how, as a boy, he and his friends would make their way across the countryside, and when they came to an orchard wall that seemed too high and too doubtful to try and too difficult to permit their voyage to continue, they took off their hats and tossed them over the wall — and then they had no choice but to follow them. This Nation has tossed its cap over the wall of space, and we have no choice but to follow it. Whatever the difficulties, they will be overcome." Remarks in San Antonio [Texas] at the Dedication of the Aerospace Medical Health Center (November 21, 1963).

UNITED NATIONS

1988. "[T]he great hope for peace I think in the 1960s is going to be not only our own strength but also the United Nations. This is a great forum which if given the attention and prestige and support that it needs can serve as a great clearinghouse for peace, not just summit meetings where the Soviet Union and the United States sit down, but the General Assembly of the United Nations, where all nations sit, and will all speak their will, where they share a common aspiration to be free and independent." Rear Platform Remarks of Senator John F. Kennedy, "Pathways to Peace," Fresno, California (September 9, 1960).

1989. "At its best or at its worst, the United Nations remains a symbol of all that we hope, of all that we believe, of all that we look forward to." Speech by Senator John F. Kennedy, Democratic Women's Luncheon, Commodore Hotel, New York, New York (September 14, 1960).

1990. "[P]eace requires positive American leadership in a more effective United Nations, working toward the establishment of a worldwide system of law, enforced by worldwide sanctions of justice. In this age of jets and atoms, we can no longer put our faith in war as a method of settling international disputes. We can no longer tolerate a world which is like a frontier town, without a sheriff or a magistrate." Speech by Senator John F. Kennedy, Democratic Women's Luncheon, Commodore Hotel, New York, New York (September 14, 1960).

1991. "[T]he United Nations [is] our last best hope in an age where the instruments of war have far outpaced the instruments of peace, [and] we renew our pledge of support — to prevent it from becoming merely a forum for invective — to strengthen its shield of the new and the weak — and to enlarge the area in which its writ may run." Inaugural Address (January 20, 1961).

1992. "We must increase our support of the United Nations as an instrument to end the Cold War instead of an arena in which to fight it." Annual Message to the Congress on the State of the Union (January 30, 1961).

1993. "[I]n the development of this organization [the United Nations] rests the only true alternative to war...." Address in New York City Before the General Assembly of the United Nations (September 25, 1961).

1994. "[W]e in this hall [of the General Assembly of the United Nations] shall be remembered either as part of the generation that turned this planet into a flaming funeral pyre or the generation that met its vow 'to save succeeding generations from the scourge of war.'" Address in New York City Before the General Assembly of the United Nations (September 25, 1961).

1995. "I don't think, really, in any sense, the United Nations has failed as a concept. I think occasionally we fail it. And the more that we can do to strengthen the idea of a community of the world, to seek to develop manners by which the tensions of the world and the problems of the world can be solved in an orderly and peaceful way, I think that's in the common interest of all." Remarks to a Delegation of Women Assigned to Missions of the United Nations (December 11, 1961).

1996. "[A]rms alone are not enough to keep the peace — it must be kept by men. Our instrument and our hope is the United Nations — and I see little merit in the impatience of those who would abandon this imperfect world instrument because they dislike our imperfect world. For the troubles of a world organization merely reflect the troubles of the world itself. And if the organization is weakened, these troubles can only increase." Annual Message to the Congress on the State of the Union (January 11, 1962).

1997. "For centuries, men have dreamed of a way to secure world peace. To translate these dreams into hard reality has become the great imperative of our time.... [T]he American people [are determined] to support the United Nations in this demanding task ... and to help marshal the resources needed by the United Nations in pursuit of a just and lasting peace among all nations of the world." Remarks Upon Signing the United Nations Loan Bill (October 2, 1962).

1998. "Today the United Nations is primarily the protector of the small and the weak, and a safety valve for the strong. Tomorrow it can form the framework for a world of law — a world in which no nation dictates the destiny of another, and in which the vast resources now devoted to destructive means will serve constructive ends." Annual Message to the Congress on the State of the Union (January 14, 1963).

1999. "[W]e seek to strengthen the United Nations, to help solve its financial problems, to make it a more effective instrument for peace, to develop it into a genuine world security system — a system capable of resolving disputes on the basis of law, of insuring the security of the large and the small, and of creating conditions under which arms can finally be abolished." Commencement Address at American University in Washington (June 10, 1963).

2000. "The United Nations must be fully and fairly financed. Its peace-keeping machinery must be strengthened. Its institutions must be developed until some day, and perhaps some distant day, a world of law is achieved." Address Before the Irish Parliament in Dublin (June 28, 1963).

2001. "The peace-keeping machinery of the United Nations cannot work without the help of the smaller nations, nations whose forces threaten no one and whose forces can thus help create a world in which no nation is threatened. Great powers have their responsibilities and their burdens, but the smaller nations of the world must fulfill their obligations as well." Address Before the Irish Parliament in Dublin (June 28, 1963).

2002. "The effort to improve the conditions of man ... is not a task for the few. It is the task of all nations — acting alone, acting in groups, acting in the United Nations, for plague and pestilence, and plunder and pollution, the hazards of nature, and the hunger of children are the foes of every nation. The earth, the sea, and the air are the concern of every nation." Address Before the 18th General Assembly of the United Nations (September 20, 1963).

2003. "The United Nations has been criticized, has been under attack, for a good many years, but as Mr.[Robert] Frost has said about not taking down a wall until you know why it is put up, if there wasn't a United Nations we would certainly have to invent one." Remarks in New York City to Staff Members of the U.S. Delegation to the United Nations (September 20, 1963).

VOLUNTARISM

2004. "[If] you are able by the passage of some hours of a busy life to make a significant difference in the life of one of our fellow Americans, who might, without your help slip into an experience which could prevent him from ever fulfilling his responsibilities to the maximum as a participant in our society, then I would hope you would feel that you've not only met your own obligations as an individual but also as a participating member of a great society." Remarks at a Dinner of the Big Brothers of America (June 7, 1961).

2005. "No value is more deeply ingrained in our national life than that of community responsibility. In our earliest days of the nation ... Americans helped each other build their lives, their communities, their homes. This has been a valuable part of our national experience. This country grew great by individual effort, but it was combined with a generous response to the needs of our neighbors." Remarks Recorded for the Opening of the United Community Campaigns (September 20, 1961).

2006. "[O]n more occasions perhaps than we think, acts of generosity and consideration bring back returns many times." Remarks of Welcome to the Graduating Class of the Glen Lake, Michigan, High School (June 21, 1962).

2007. "All the problems that this country has could be solved in a whole variety of ways if all of our citizens would just pick one project and give their time to it, whether it is helping those who are mentally or physically retarded ... helping young boys and girls who are in difficulty with the law ... entertaining foreign students ... [or] holding out a hand to one group or another. This can be done much better by our citizens than by the National Government." Remarks at a Meeting of the President's Committee on Employment of the Handicapped (May 9, 1963).

2008. "One of the oldest traditions in the United States has been the sense of responsibility which we have felt as a people for our less fortunate neighbors.... This country has a strong tradition of individual self-reliance, but we also recognize that there are people who, through no fault of their own, need our help — children who may be sick, who may be alone, men and women who may be ill, older people who may be deserted, all the people in our community who are our neighbors and who need our help." Message Recorded for the Opening of the United Community Campaigns of America (September 22, 1963).

WASHINGTON, D.C.

2009. "[I]t [Washington, D.C.] is a city which is somewhat artificial, unlike most capitals of the world, and therefore lacks the great asset which London and Paris and Rome ... ha[ve] in being the center not only of Government but also the center of national cultural activities." Remarks to the Trustees and Advisory Committee of the National Cultural Center (November 14, 1961).

2010. "[Washington, D.C.] is not a city belonging only to the people that live here, [it] ... is the Capital of the Nation and belongs to all the people, and was established for that reason." Remarks to the Trustees and Advisory Committee of the National Cultural Center (November 14, 1961).

2011. "Almost all of the great nations of the world have their financial and political capitals located in the same city — London, Paris, Rome, Madrid and the others. Our founding fathers chose differently, in an effort to isolate political leaders from the immediate pressures of political life and national life and national life. But this has placed a special obligation upon all of us — to speak clearly and with precision, and to attempt to understand the obligations and responsibilities which each of us face." Address Before the United States Chamber of Commerce on Its 50th Anniversary (April 30, 1962).

2012. "Our Founding Fathers, who were concerned about the difficulties which other countries had faced in maintaining their freedom, deliberately chose Washington as a city removed from the direct currents of political and social and economic life. So this is in a sense an artificial city and a Government city. This has had some advantages, but it also has disadvantages." Remarks to Members of the White House Conference on National Economic Issues (May 21, 1962).

2013. "We are particularly glad to invite those of you who come from Great Britain.... Your forebears as you know burned our White House, and it is a pleasure to welcome you here on this peaceful occasion." Remarks to a Group of American field Service Students (July 11, 1962).

2014. "This is the capital not only of the United States but the capital of the leading nation of the free world and we cannot afford to have this be anything but an ornament to our society. There is no sense in having wide boulevards and beautiful buildings if the children who live in this city do not have an opportunity to develop their talents." Remarks at the 50th Anniversary Luncheon of the Delta Sigma Theta Sorority (January 12, 1963).

2015. "Here in the District of Columbia we have great needs.... This is the capital not only of the United States but the capital of the leading nation of the free world and we cannot afford to have this be anything but an ornament to our society. There is no sense in having wide boulevards and beautiful buildings if the children who live in this city do not have an opportunity to develop their talents. They may not all have talents, but at least those who have talent should have the opportunity to develop it. That is what the essence of freedom is. We do not have that satisfactorily [answered] yet in this country." Remarks at the 50th Anniversary Luncheon of the Delta Sigma Theta Sorority (January 12, 1963).

2016. "While we are in residence temporarily, this house belongs to all of the American people, and I think it symbolizes some of the best of our history. [T]hose trees back there [near the Flower Garden at the White House] were planted by one of our most distinguished Democratic Presidents, Andrew Jackson. This house and these grounds ... are filled with recollections of great moments in American history." Remarks to Members of the Amalgamated Meat Cutters and Butcher Workmen of North America (May 16, 1963).

2017. "[T]here is nothing more encouraging than ... to leave the rather artificial city of Washington and come and travel across the United States and realize what is here, the beauty, the diversity, the wealth, and the vigor of the people." Address at the University of Wyoming (September 25, 1963).

2018. "[T]hose of us who stay only in Washington sometimes lose our comprehension of the national problems which require a national solution." Address at the University of Wyoming (September 25, 1963).

2019. "Washington was deliberately developed as a Government city in order to remove those who were making the laws from all the pressures of everyday life, and so we live far away. We talk about the United States, about its problems, its powers, its people, its opportunity, its dangers, its hazards, but we are still talking about life in a somewhat removed way." Remarks at the High School Memorial Stadium, Great Falls, Montana (September 26, 1963).

Index

References are to entry numbers

Africa 1015, 1236, 1237, 1245, 1247–1251, 1264
African Americans 775–782
agriculture 1–39, 548, 804; *see also* farmers
Alliance for Progress (Alianza para el Progreso) 948, 956–958, 964, 970, 1274
American leadership 40–160, 1990; image abroad 106–124; importance of domestic strength 125–160; *see also* prestige, America's
American Revolution 46, 107, 1011, 1015
American spirit 161–200
anti-trust laws 297, 300, 587
apartheid 770
Argentina 1238
armed forces 124, 1472–1487
arms control 1585–1607, 1610; *see also* nuclear test bans; nuclear weapons
artists 211, 219, 220, 222, 1823
arts and humanities 201–222
"ask not what your country can do for you" speech 325
Australia 1276, 1292
automation 510–518, 595, 1546

balance of trade 35, 1301, 1303, 1324–1326
Berlin 223–240, 392
Berlin Wall 236, 393, 413, 1082
bipartisanship 1389
Birmingham Agreement 793
birth control, government funding of 1215, 1409
Brazil 1239, 1265, 1277
budgetary and fiscal policies 241–296
business 297–310; relationship with government 302–304, 307, 580, 586; small business 297–300, 309

campaigns 1739, 1742, 1754, 1862
Canada 893, 909, 1254, 1255, 1283
Cape Canaveral 1946
Castro, Fidel 365, 373, 435, 437, 442, 446, 939, 942, 1250
checks and balances 1159–1166
Chile 1240
China 382, 1244
cities 522

civic duty 311–349, 1129; special burden on the educated 316, 319, 327, 342, 345; special burden on the wealthy 338, 349
civil rights *see* equal opportunity and civil rights
civil rights protests 783–788
coal *see* energy policy
cold war 146, 210, 366, 383, 386, 410, 418, 423, 454, 831, 853, 1622, 1655, 1992; *see also* communism
collective bargaining 584, 1417, 1418, 1440–1447
colonialism 405, 854, 872, 1022, 1050
Common Market *see* European Common Market
communism 360, 363, 382, 385, 389, 391, 395, 405, 416, 417, 420, 888, 938, 1081, 1844, 1961
communists 144, 169, 352, 366, 407, 408, 411, 412, 417, 852, 938, 1004, 1020, 1098, 1250, 1345, 1423, 1631, 1672; *see also* Soviet Union
Congo 109, 970
conservation *see* environmental policy
Constitution 193, 728, 787, 975, 1001, 1016, 1063, 1125, 1130, 1162, 1163, 1194
Costa Rica 959, 1282
Cousins, Norman 808
Cuba 435–448, 1456; missile crisis 449–454, 1105

Declaration of Independence 106, 135, 193, 716, 728, 846, 973, 1001, 1061, 1125
deficits 241–252
de Gaulle, Charles 209
democracy 347, 455–473, 645, 801, 952, 1040, 1067, 1082, 1678
Democrats 1790–1826
desalination 1934, 1937
desegregation 793, 1698; *see also* equal opportunity and civil rights
Dickens, Charles 55
dollar, soundness of 254, 256–259, 261, 263, 552, 559, 1323

economic policies 547–597; economic growth 277, 545, 563–576, 823, 1171; *see also* tax reform
education 143, 456, 498, 598–659, 737, 746, 1546; *see also* school dropouts; teachers
Einstein, Albert 1229, 1964
energy policy 660–667

205

Index

environmental policy 668–706
equal opportunity and civil rights 707–803, 1880; in education 718, 737, 757, 769, 778, 782; in employment 735, 744, 769; federal enforcement of 789–796; in housing 714, 727, 749, 769; in voting 707, 732, 797–803
Ethiopia 1293
Europe 919–930
European Common Market 274, 1302, 1312, 1315, 1316, 1318

Fair Deal 1167, 1539, 1797
Faith 7 (Mercury Mission) 1980
farmers 3, 4, 6, 8, 16–19, 22, 26, 27, 34, 38, 547; *see also* agriculture
Federal Reserve System 255
federalism 1189; federal role 1118, 1119, 1124, 1127, 1196; state and local role 1114, 1117; *see also* government, working together
Finland 1263
foreign assistance 804–845
foreign intelligence 1467
foreign policy 846–918; *see also* Europe; Israel and Middle East; Latin America; Southeast Asia
founding fathers 971–978, 1107, 1165, 1786, 2011, 2012
France 1256–1259, 1279
Franklin, Benjamin 971, 1161
free enterprise system 537, 575, 581, 593, 979–991, 1321
freedom and liberty 992–1090
Frost, Robert 197, 222, 2003

Glenn, Col. John 1970
God and country 74, 384, 396, 702, 766, 907, 911, 1091–1111, 1157, 1183, 1350
"good neighbor [foreign] policy" 939, 940
government 1112–1214; big 1115, 1128; building for the future 1135–1158; employees *see* public service; modern challenges 1167–1182; openness in 1123, 1551; party divide 1159–1161; working together 1122, 1183–1214
Great Britain 893, 1260, 1261, 1268, 1269, 2013
Guantanamo 439

healthcare 489, 1215–1230
Henry, Patrick 429
Hoover, Herbert 1916
housing 475, 519–523, 1802, 1880
human rights 715, 733, 738, 1231–1235, 1249
Humphrey, Hubert 1741, 1753
hunger 114, 807, 814, 942, 1248, 2002
Hyde Park 1794

India 1243, 1284
Indians, American 241, 754
international relations 1236–1296; *see also* foreign policy
international trade 1297–1326
Iran 1266, 1267; Shah of 1266, 1267
Ireland 1286, 1287, 1289, 1294, 1341, 1342
Iron Curtain 404, 440, 1456, 1560, 1609
isolationism 86, 95, 99, 925
Israel and the Middle East 1252, 931–937
Italy 1253, 1280, 1290

Jackson, Andrew 2016
Japan 1262, 1278, 1296
Jefferson, Thomas 157, 601, 610, 1008, 1026, 1236, 1708, 1734, 1806, 1823, 1856
juvenile delinquency 477, 524–527

Kennedy, Caroline 1331, 1335
Kennedy, Edward [Ted] 1337, 1338
Kennedy, Jacqueline 1334
Kennedy, John F.: age 1327–1329; Catholic faith 1399–1411; family 1330–1338; goals and aspirations 1356, 1362, 1365, 1366, 1370, 1385; heritage, Irish 1289, 1339–1342; optimism 1343–1386; political philosophy 1387–1398
Kennedy, Joseph P., Sr. 1232
Kennedy, Robert 1333
Khrushchev, Nikita 22, 351, 357, 358, 361, 362, 365, 367, 370, 371, 376, 379, 968, 991, 1345, 1504, 1581
King, Martin Luther, Jr. 1855

labor unions 1412–1439; *see also* collective bargaining
labor, unskilled 498, 544, 630
Landon, Alf 1765
Laos 966, 968, 970
Latin America 938–965
Lawford, Patricia 1330
Lincoln, Abraham 109, 173, 779, 995, 1094, 1196, 1350, 1390, 1684, 1756
lobbyists 1126

Madison, James 978, 1161
Makarios, Archbishop 1910
Marine Corps Band 1913
McDonald, David 1914
mental retardation 1223, 1226–1230
Mexico 1271, 1273–1275
military strength 1488–1518; *see also* national security
Milton, John 327
minimum wage 478, 486, 498, 528–532
monetary policy 253–264, 591, 596
Monroe, James 978
Monroe, Marilyn 1329
moon landing [Apollo Mission] 1968, 1972, 1977–1979, 1982

National Cultural Center [The John F. Kennedy for the Performing Arts] 202, 208, 216
national security 242, 924, 1325, 1448–1471, 1553, 1579, 1872; *see also* military strength
natural resources 32, 1382; *see also* environmental policy
New America 1539
New Deal 478, 590, 1167, 1530, 1548, 1797, 1866
New Freedom 1530, 1539, 1797
New Frontier 1546–1549, 1817
news media 1550–1562
Nixon, Richard M. 1505, 1741, 1769, 1828, 1841–1857
Nobel Prize 1936
North Atlantic Treaty Organization 1519–1528, 1568, 1569
Norway 1270
nuclear test bans 1591, 1608–1623; test ban treaty 1618–1623

Index

nuclear weapons 419, 451, 894, 1454, 1510, 1563–1584, 1588, 1596, 1905

O'Connor, Frank 1987
Organization of American States 947

Paine, Thomas 46, 225, 1011, 1237
Panama 1272
peace 411, 418, 423, 810, 891, 1316, 1460, 1577, 1624–1659, 1996; America's highest aspiration 48, 65, 196, 431, 856, 871, 932, 937, 1453, 1606, 1607, 1620, 1626, 1629, 1641, 1652; through American strength 40, 68, 144, 145, 232, 234, 399, 432, 434, 452, 849, 1046, 1047, 1132, 1449–1451, 1456, 1461, 1464, 1469, 1493, 1510, 1517
Peace Corps 337, 1660–1675
petition, right of 1125
physical fitness 1676–1683
Poland 1246, 1281
politicians 317, 601, 1735, 1736, 1810
politics 1732–1759, 1863; campaign contributions 860, 1332, 1740, 1750, 1751, 1852; leadership 708, 715, 721, 856, 1359, 1684–1731, 1858, 1871, 1878, 1923; parties 1760–1789; *see also* Democrats, Republicans
pollution, water 241, 480, 683, 691, 692; air 480, 683
poverty 474, 577, 1248, 1419, 1794; war on 61, 114, 441, 536, 816, 828, 957, 963, 990, 1171, 1416, 1669
prayer 1103, 1106
presidency 1858–1919
prestige, America's 117–121, 138, 147, 444, 857, 1498, 1844, 1934, 1968; *see also* American Leadership, image abroad
public service 1920–1933

Republicans 1789, 1804, 1827–1840
right-to-work laws 1412, 1415, 1439
"a rising tide lifts all boats" speech 548, 1116
Roosevelt, Eleanor 1793
Roosevelt, Franklin 50, 126, 477, 590, 1013, 1120, 1187, 1388, 1542, 1783, 1807, 1824, 1870, 1923, 1964
Roosevelt, Theodore 696, 705, 1834, 1858
rule of law 789–796, 1927

Salinger, Pierre 1258
school dropouts 498, 746
science and technology 111, 652, 673, 698, 703, 1144, 1229, 1546, 1934–1946

Selassie, Haile 1293
senior citizens 1221, 1225, 1947–1955
seniority system, Congressional 1131
Shaw, George Bernard 1726
Shriver, Robert Sargent 1670
social programs 474–509, 539
Southeast Asia 966–970; *see also* Laos; Vietnam
Soviet Union 353, 359, 380, 400, 410, 421, 433, 991, 1501, 1506, 1510, 1956–1961; negotiating with 351, 424–434; *see also* communists
space exploration 59, 1962–1987
spending, by government 249, 265–268, 299, 589, 830
Sputnik 22, 111, 1934, 1983
Stevenson, Adlai 1539

tax reform 247, 272–275, 277–282, 284, 285, 287–296
taxation 269–296
teachers 606, 613, 621, 632, 650, 658
trade unions *see* labor unions
Truman, Harry 126, 1141, 1187, 1295, 1817, 1916

unemployment 242, 533–546, 574, 981, 1416; compensation 475, 478, 502, 533, 534, 539, 541, 1880
United Nations 101, 936, 1629, 1988–2003
United States Military Academy 1911
universities 609, 615, 633, 640–643, 649, 653, 656, 657
University of Alabama 803
Uruguay 1241

veterans 314
Vietnam 966, 967, 969, 970, 1908
voluntarism 2004–2008
voting 339

Washington, George 971, 1015, 1251
Washington, D.C. 2009–2019
West Berlin *see* Berlin
West Germany *see* Berlin
West Virginia 1422, 1472, 1753, 1758, 1759
White House 265, 1285, 1744, 1858, 2013, 2016
Williams, Ted 1327
Wilson, Woodrow 50, 108, 126, 1388, 1395, 1530, 1539, 1777, 1785, 1870
women 1757

Yugoslavia 1295

www.ingramcontent.com/pod-product-compliance
Lightning Source LLC
Chambersburg PA
CBHW081557300426
44116CB00015B/2910